THE EARLY WRITINGS OF ALEX LA GUMA

Reflections on *Cultcha*, Identity and Freedom in the 1950s and 1960s

Edited by André Odendaal and Roger Field

Published by Best Red™, a registered trademark of the HSRC and an imprint of HSRC Press
Private Bag X9182, Cape Town, 8000, South Africa
www.bestred.co.za

First published in 2025
ISBN (soft cover) 978-1-928246-71-8
© 2025 Human Sciences Research Council, André Odendaal and Roger Field

The views expressed in this publication are those of the authors. They do not necessarily reflect the views or policies of the Human Sciences Research Council (the Council) or indicate that the Council endorses the views of the authors. In quoting from this publication, readers are advised to attribute the source of the information to the individual author concerned and not to the Council.

This book is number 25 in the African Lives series, an independent writing and publishing project that aims to contribute to a post-colonial intellectual history of South Africa. The series editor is Prof André Odendaal, Vice Chancellor's Writer in Residence and Honorary Professor in History and Heritage Studies at the University of the Western Cape.

The publishers have no responsibility for the continued existence or accuracy of URLs for external or third-party Internet websites referred to in this book and do not guarantee that any content on such websites is, or will remain, accurate or appropriate.

Copy edited by Alison Paulin
Proofread by Megan Hall
Typeset by Deon DP Schutte
Cover design by Shane Platt

Printed by *novus print*, a division of Novus Holdings

Every effort has been made to trace copyright holders of images and to obtain their permission for the use of copyright material. The publisher apologises for any errors or omissions and would be grateful if notified of any corrections that should be incorporated in future reprints or editions of this book.

Distributed in Africa by Blue Weaver Tel: +27 (021) 701 4477; Fax Local: (021) 701 7302; Email: info@blueweaver.co.za
www.blueweaver.co.za

Distributed worldwide (except central and southern Africa) by Lynne Rienner Publishers, Inc. Tel: +1 303-444-6684; Fax: +1 303-444-0824; Email: cservice@rienner.com
www.rienner.com

No part of this publication may be reproduced, stored in a retrieval system, or transmitted by any form or by any means, electronic, mechanical, photocopying, recording or otherwise, without prior permission from the copyright owner.

To copy any part of this publication, you may contact DALRO for information and copyright clearance.
Tel: 010 822 7469 (from within South Africa); +27 (0)10 822 7469
Fax: +27 (86) 648 1136
Email: dalro@dalro.co.za
Postal address: PostNet Suite #018, PO Box 9951, Sandton, 2146, South Africa
www.dalro.co.za

Any unauthorised copying could lead to civil liability and/or criminal sanctions.

Suggested citation: Odendaal A & Field R (eds) (2025) *The Early Writings of Alex La Guma: Reflections on Cultcha, Identity and Freedom in the 1950s and 1960s*. Cape Town: Best Red

Contents

Prologue..V
Foreword...IX
Cape Town's Urban Griot: A Tribute to Alex La Guma........................XVIII
Photo gallery...XXVI

Introduction..1

Part 1 Theatre of life
1. Identical books...30
2. A day at court 33
3. The dead-end kids of Hanover Street..36
4. In the shadow of the kwela-kwela...38
5. Ten days in Roeland Street jail...41
6. Law of the jungle..44
7. Out of the darkness (short story)...47
8. Battle for honour (short story) 51

Part 2 Treason trial
9. 156 families to feed...55
10. Court cameos...62
11. Ncincilili! In praise of Wilton Mkwayi..66
12. Time to think...67

Part 3 Jo'burg
13. The city of gold...72
14. Doing the town...74
15. Fietas...81
16. Muddy pools which could be tears...82
17. Little Libby: The adventures of Liberation Chabalala (cartoon strip) 84

Part 4 Cape Town
18. Back up my alley...94
19. Me and 'cultcha'..104
20. 'Why must we move?'...110
21. Christian National Education..113
22. Elections for the 'coloured representatives'....................................116
23. Ah, dis die economic boycott...122
24. 'Coloured Affairs' and Uncle Toms...124
25. Langa 1960...133
26. State of Emergency..137
27. No to the white republic! 144

Part 5 Cold wars

28. The picture in the parlour 154
29. Uncle Sam 157
30. Sputnik 163
31. The hot, grey streets, the blistering tenements, the foul alleyways
    (Why I became a communist?) 166

Part 6 The ordinary or garden Nat (ruling-class politics)

32. Herr Doktor Verwoerd and Nationalist small-fry talk 171
33. 'Immorality': Says who? 187
34. Fishy business 193
35. Pampoen-onder-die-Bos 201

Part 7 Into exile

36. Love song 212
37. The note in the roast potato 214
38. From canary cage to albatross wings 219
39. Vietnam 1973: A repetition of the pictures of Hiroshima and Nagasaki 223
40. Visit to Vilnius 228
41. 'I came here to sing': A tribute to Pablo Neruda 232
42. Israel and South Africa: Where the vultures perch 235
43. Alex La Guma's full body of work and his final assignment 239
44. Never mind, you will see Table Mountain again 246

Acknowledgements 250
Alex La Guma's writings: A select bibliography 253
Index 257

Prologue

Alex La Guma's first novel, *A Walk in the Night*, published by Mbari in Nigeria in 1962, brought him instant recognition as a pioneering writer on the African continent. Appearing as the tide of decolonisation gathered momentum, the book's 'startling realism and accurate imagery' drew high praise from contemporaries then also entering the literary firmament of African writing.[1]

Wole Soyinka, later awarded the Nobel Prize for Literature, wrote the first review. He observed that La Guma, with 'a painter's brush' or rather a detailed 'ink sketch' that 'does not obtrude', had achieved in 90 pages 'what several novels by Africans, three or four times its length are still merely groping towards'. Quoting Langston Hughes, who asked 'what is the lavender word for lynch?', Soyinka said the way Alex La Guma grappled with racialised violence 'deals also in hatred but declines to work within its constriction'. 'Uncompromising truth governs his observation, a total lack of hysteria and a terse economic prose controls his theme'.[2]

Ngũgĩ wa Thiong'o labelled La Guma 'a central figure alongside Chinua Achebe, Wole Soyinka and others in the making and consolidation of modern African literature' (Wa Thiong'o 2016 quoted in Lee 2024: xii). In the same vein, the accomplished South African critic and writer Lewis Nkosi compared La Guma's intense and sombre vision of the individual in society to that of Dostoevsky (Nkosi 1978, chapter 5).

This book celebrates the centenary of Alex La Guma's birth on 20 February 1925 and gives us insight into the making of La Guma the novelist. It consists of his early journalism and short stories between the mid-1950s and 1962, when he was banned, his work was declared illegal and the government henceforth prohibited him from being quoted in any way in South Africa. His banning happened a week before the publication of *A Walk in the Night* was announced, neatly delineating these two phases in the writer's life.[3] For the next four years, he would be either under house arrest for 24 hours a day or in detention and solitary confinement – at one stage he did not leave his post-box size home for 16 months.[4]

Like many of South Africa's best black writers of fiction, Alex made the journey to the novel via journalism and short stories. The early writings included in this volume provide unique cameos of South African life and politics during the turbulent years around Sharpeville. They also reveal the 'hidden' world of La Guma – material, social, emotional, political and intellectual – at a time when when his literary reputation was expanding internationally. Many of the themes in his fiction are first encountered and developed in these early newspaper articles, providing useful material for literary scholars seeking to understand the progression of his writing. At the core of these early writings are his nearly 250 'Up my alley' columns which appeared in the *New Age* newspaper between September 1957 and his banning in November 1962.[5] These contributions were delivered dutifully week after week over a five-year period, bar one long detention and security police disruptions of his routines.

In 1959, while well into his series of columns, La Guma also started on his novel, meaning that these two projects were inevitably feeding off and reinforcing each other. The timing of this increase in his writing ambitions and output also helps us to understand how years of state repression slowly but surely squeezed La Guma out of public life to the enforced privacy of typewriter and desk until he became engrossed in a structured way in the inner sanctum of his home with novels and 'the life of the mind'.[6] By the time he was pushed into exile in September 1966, La Guma had endured three years as one of the accused in the long-running treason trial, five months of State of Emergency detention after Sharpeville, then several years of 24-hour-a-day house arrest interspersed with two other stints of detention under new laws which empowered the state to hold him in solitary confinement for 90 days, later extended to 180 days (La Guma B 2010: 111).

While writing his fifth novel, *Time of the Butcherbird*, Alex La Guma showed his writer friend Vernon February the manuscript. Asked what it was about he replied, 'Ag, just about the folks back home' (February 1991: 48).

Alex, his wife Blanche, and their sons Eugene and Barto flew into exile in a DC10 aircraft, sitting in the back seats reserved for 'non-Europeans', and spent the next twenty years looking forward to the day they could come home and see Table Mountain again. They fought tirelessly to make that possible (La Guma B 2010: 131). Friends recall how, with an electric dialogue learned on the streets of District Six, he loved mimicking the mannerisms and distinct language of the people among whom he had grown up. At New Year's parties for the scattered 'family' of South African comrades, Alex would stay till the early hours, strumming away at a guitar and singing the carnivalesque songs so typical of the Cape. 'Staan op, julle bruinmense [kinders] van slawe' ('Stand up, you brown people, children of slaves') he would sing to the tune of the Internationale as he walked home with a friend through the streets of London after a night out.[7] And Sundays at the La Gumas were always a bit 'Kaaps', Vernon February recalled – roast potatoes, vegetables and meat, 'just like at home' (February 1991: 48). With the longing, the warmth and the humour went the commitment.

The novelist André Brink wrote of District Six:

> This ... is what truly spells Cape Town for me: its indomitable, raucous, rebellious way of confirming a heretic otherness, of saying no – not only to apartheid, but to everything that tried to domesticate and inhibit the human spirit and its wild, affirmative freedom, its laughter, its compassion. And also its outrageous and jubilant way of saying yes to life itself. (Brink 2009: 183)

Alex La Guma grew up at 2 Roger Street, District Six and became one of its griots, as Michael Weeder puts it in the accompanying tribute. His words still resonate across the decades, archives for a space whose spirit still survives, although it was infamously bulldozed into dust under the Group Areas Act.

Home in Roger Street was also the cradle where Alex La Guma learned his politics. His father, schooled in trade unionism and struggle, was one of the originators of the Native Republic thesis within the Communist Party of South Africa (CPSA) in the 1920s. Its Marxist-derived departure point was that in the particular conditions that existed in South Africa, the class struggles of workers and the national struggles of oppressed Africans for freedom from colonial domination should be merged into one struggle to directly confront interlinked colonialism, racial discrimination and economic exploitation, rather than continue on separate tracks. This Colonialism of a Special Type analysis emerging in the 1920s was to profoundly influence the direction of South Africa's liberation movement in the decades that followed. The portrait of the 'Uncle' that hung in the living-room in Roger Street during Alex's youth happened to be, not of family, but of Lenin (see chapter 28). He contributed significantly to the struggle for freedom in South Africa. Influenced by communism from a young age (see chapter 31), La Guma became a leader of the South African Coloured People's Organisation (aligned to the African National Congress), a Treason Trialist, and later the long-serving chair of the ANC branch in London and its chief representative in the Caribbean – based in Cuba, where he supervised the education and training of hundreds of young South Africans. With his talent for writing, he also frequently used his pen to help keep alive the conscience of the world about the situation in his country (see for example, La Guma 1972). He emerged from the budgie cage of detention and trial at home to fly to every corner of the globe with albatross wings – almost uninterrupted for nearly 20 years – becoming internationalist in practice as much as through the writings we are introduced to in this book.

Sadly, Alex La Guma was one of those exiles who never made it back home. He was 60 years old when he died of a heart attack in Havana on 11 October 1985. It was a typically balmy Cuban afternoon. Blanche, his wife, rushed to get him into the back of their car, then to hospital several miles away. Driven by adrenalin and anxiety, she sped through the peak-hour traffic, here mounting a pavement to take a shortcut and there hooting and weaving through knots of traffic and red lights without regard for rules. But it was too late. Slumped in the middle of the back seat, Alex called his wife's name twice and breathed his last breath just before Blanche, watching helplessly in the rear-view mirror, reached the hospital.

Alex La Guma was buried in the Cementerio de Cristóbal de Colón, a quiet colonial-style resting place thousands of miles from home, named, ironically, after Christopher Columbus. It was no ordinary funeral, though. Many ambassadors and government dignitaries came to pay their respects and Fidel Castro sent 'a huge wreath which reached the ceiling of the [funeral] parlour'.[8] In keeping with a quaintly Catholic tradition that survives comfortably with post-revolutionary socialist practices, people are often buried in family pantheons (or mausoleums) in Cuba. There are over 500 of these in Cristóbal de Colón, and as a sign of respect for the man and the movement he represented, La Guma was laid to rest in the Panteón de los Emigrados Revolucionarios, the Pantheon of Revolutionary Emigrants, where the remains of the parents of José Martí, popularly known as the founder of the Cuban nation, also lie.[9] On the centenary of his birth, we offer this book as a kind of homecoming for that tall, gangly man from District Six who rests far away in Havana, a place that somehow 'showed me mirror images of my own folk, and … made the exile easier' (Carew 1986).

André Odendaal
Vice Chancellor's writer in residence and Honorary Professor in History and Heritage Studies,
University of the Western Cape
23 September 2024

Notes

1. Alex La Guma personal scrapbook, La Guma A, South Africa, Lotus Afro-Asian Writings, October 1978: 133, UWC-RIM Mayibuye Archives, Alex La Guma Collection, MCH 118-2-1.
2. Alex La Guma personal scrapbook, Wole Soyinka, The fight for human existence, *Post*, 3 June 1962, UWC-RIM Mayibuye Archives, Alex La Guma Collection, MCH 118-2-1.
3. Alex La Guma's first novel – banned by the Sabotage Act, *New Age,* 9 August 1962, MCH 118-2-2-9.
4. Alex La Guma personal scrapbook, He hasn't left home for 16 months, *Post*, 10 May 1964, UWC-RIM Mayibuye Archives, Alex La Guma Collection, MCH 118-2-1.
5. Alex La Guma personal scrapbook, Names and details of listed people, *Cape Times,* 17 November 1962, UWC-RIM Mayibuye Archives, Alex La Guma Collection, MCH 118-2-1.
6. Phrase borrowed from Memela S, Pallo Jordan is no fraud, *Mail & Guardian,* 8 August 2014.
7. ANC Veteran, Hamba kahle Comrade Alex La Guma, *Sechaba,* January 1986: 30.
8. Blanche La Guma to Wolfie Kodesh, personal communication, 19 November 1985.
9. Hein Willemse, personal communication, 20 August 2024.

References

Brink A (2009) *A fork in the road: A memoir*. London: Harvill Secker

Carew J (1986) Tribute. *Rixaka* 3: 16–18

February V (1991) Skrywer en vryheidsstryder, *Die Suid-Afrikaan* February/March 1991

La Guma A (ed.) (1972) *Apartheid: A collection of writings on South African racism by South Africans*. New York: International Publishers

La Guma B with M Klammer (2010) *In the dark with my dress on fire: My life in Cape Town, London, Havana and home again*. Johannesburg: Jacana Media

Lee CJ (ed.) (2024) *Alex La Guma: The exile years, 1966–1985*. Voices of Liberation series. Cape Town: HSRC Press

Ngũgĩ wa Thiong'o (2016) [or it might be 2016, depending on the author's response to the query in this regard in this chapter. Author must supply rest of reference per style]

Nkosi L (1978) *Tasks and masks: Themes and styles of African literature*. Harlow: Longman

Foreword

Nine days after Alex La Guma died of a heart attack in Havana, he was buried in Cementerio de Cristóbal de Colón, the burial place of the ordinary and the extraordinary: the country's political figures; musicians such as Ibrahim Ferrer of Buena Vista Social Club; writers such as Lola Rodríguez de Tió and Alejo Carpentier; the national poet, Nicolás Guillén; and Alberto Korda, the photographer of the ubiquitous image of Che Guevara.

As described in the prologue, it was an ambassador-level funeral with many dignitaries present, and La Guma was interred opposite the cemetery's ornate main entrance in the Pantheon of Revolutionary Emigrants, an imposing brown marble art deco mausoleum that also contains the remains of Leonor and Mariano, the parents of the venerated 19th century revolutionary, José Martí. La Guma's final resting place is a tribute to the man, a committed internationalist; to his life of service and sacrifice; and to the struggle for political liberation in his country of origin.

At the beginning of October 1985, I was preparing a visit to Havana with the purpose of interviewing La Guma. The interview was meant to serve as the reintroduction of a silenced writer to a younger generation of South African readers and writers. I was even thinking of novel ways of presenting his views in a local publication, for his words – written or spoken – were prohibited from publication. Publishing them would have been a crime. Such were the times. His death meant that the interview never materialised.

It is evident that many of the dissident South African writers whose books were banned in the 1950s and 1960s were classified African or coloured, including La Guma, Bloke Modisane, Es'kia Mphahlele, James Matthews, Lewis Nkosi, Mazisi Kunene, Gladys Thomas, Miriam Tlali, Mongane Wally Serote, Richard Rive, Sipho Sepamla and Todd Matshikiza. The voices of almost an entire mid-century generation of black writers were silenced. In consequence, the links of the emerging 1980s generation of South African writers to this earlier tradition were at best tenuous.

La Guma's novels and all his other writings were banned from distribution or citation under the terms of the Publications and Entertainments Act No. 26 of 1963. The Act brought into being an extensive centralised censorship system. Publications could be deemed undesirable for a variety of reasons, including indecency, obscenity, and for being 'blasphemous or offensive to the religious convictions or feelings of any section of the inhabitants of the Republic' (Section 5(2)b). In apartheid South Africa the regulations stipulating prohibition on account of being 'harmful to the relations between any section of the inhabitants' or being 'prejudicial to the safety of the State, the general welfare or the peace and good order' (Section 5(2)d, e) were often used to prevent books of dissident writers from dissemination following publication.

Prior to his exile, La Guma carried a burden additional to those of his fellow writer compatriots. As a communist he could not be quoted under the provisions of the Suppression of Communism Act No. 44 of 1950, and he was banned and placed under house arrest. Since the mid-1950s he had endured several spells of detention and sustained periods of banishment, and in 1966 he eventually went into exile.

Readers, aspirant writers, literary critics and the like could not legally possess La Guma's *A Walk in the Night and Other Stories* (1962), *And a Threefold Cord* (1964), *The Stone Country* (1967), *In the Fog of the Seasons' End* (1972), or *Time of the Butcherbird* (1979). Possession of these novels, his travel journal, *A Soviet Journey* (1978), or *Apartheid* (1972), a collection of 'writings on South African racism' he edited, constituted a crime. The same was true for *Quartet* (1963), a short story collection to which he contributed and that Richard Rive edited.

Literary censorship had an enduring impact. Except for pockets of interested individuals, La Guma's novels and the man himself were largely unremembered in the repressive age of high apartheid. Apart from a brief note, less than one hundred words, in a Cape Town daily, a week after his death,[1] and a small exhibition of his books in an enclosed glass case at the African Studies library at the University of Cape Town,[2] the literary community and the public in general in South Africa hardly registered his passing. In exile, the ANC's journals *Sechaba*[3] and *Rixaka*[4] published extensive obituaries which, fortunately, through underground channels eventually found their way into the hands of internal activists, cultural workers and literary critics.

* * * * *

La Guma published *A Walk in the Night* with Mbari Publications in Nigeria while he was still living in South Africa, and his next three novels *And a Threefold Cord*, *The Stone Country*, and *In the Fog of the Seasons' End* followed in quick succession after his exile in 1966, which meant that these novels were probably conceived and prepared during his banishment in Cape Town. As the editors show in this volume, many of the themes and events detailed in his novels had their roots in his early journalism. Even though the banning orders 'isolated him politically and socially from his colleagues and friends and colleagues', the anonymous *Sechaba* obituary writer observes perceptively the 'irony [that] these restrictions may very well have provided him with the time to exploit his undoubted skill at writing, which was in fact his greatest contribution towards exposing the wickedness of the apartheid regime'.[5]

From his earliest writings La Guma positioned himself as a committed novelist depicting conditions of life under apartheid, particularly in the coloured working-class districts of Cape Town. Ever present in his writing is the revolutionary's penchant for raising awareness towards political and even armed resistance. In *A Walk in the Night*, descriptions of squalor and poverty predominate, while political awareness among the main characters is limited and they have little sense of organised political resistance.

The main character in *And a Threefold Cord* does develop a greater sense of political solidarity, while an imprisoned political prisoner in *A Stone Country* exhibits a more defined political consciousness in his interaction with other inmates and wardens. Whereas the individual consciousness took preference in the earlier novels, La Guma broadens his scope of political commitment in *In the Fog of the Seasons' End* to that of action within a resistance organisation. His fifth and last published novel, *Time of the Butcherbird*, deals with the forced removal of a rural African community from their ancestral land in the Karoo, and the impact a murder has on the broader community.

La Guma, like his contemporaries James Matthews, Richard Rive and Adam Small, is quintessentially a Capetonian writer. He 'loved the Cape, and especially Cape Town, with a deep, patriotic emotion'.⁶ Early on in *A Walk in the Night*, the following description of the setting captures some of the essence of La Guma's Cape Town.

> Up ahead the music shops were still going full blast, the blare of the records all mixed up so you could not tell one tune from another. Shopkeepers, Jewish, Indian, and Greek, stood in the doorways along the arcade of stores ... and the vegetable and fruit barrows were still out too, the hawkers in white coats yelling their wares ... Around the bus-stop a crowd pushed and jostled to clamber onto the trackless trams, struggling against the passengers fighting to alight ... A half-mile of sound and movement and signs, signs, signs: Coca Cola, Salt Now On, Jewellers, The Modern Outfitters, If You Don't Eat Here We'll Both Starve, Grand Picnic to Paradise Valley Luxury Buses, Teas, Coffee, Smoke, Have You Tried Our Milk Shakes, Billiard Club, The Rockingham Arms, Chine ...nce, in Korea, Your Recommendation Is Our Advert, Dress Salon. (La Guma 1967: 7)

The passage encapsulates human and cultural variety, contemporary in its presentation as a modern city with the billboard signs of a consumer society, and providing evidence of the expectations, pursuits and desires of its inhabitants. The phrase 'all mixed up so you could not tell one tune from another' may very well refer to more than musical tunes, indicating La Guma's own recollection of the Cape Town of his youth and the 1950s and 1960s. See, for example, how chapters 1 and 13 in this volume, written a decade earlier than *A Walk in the Night*, exude similar images of colourful cosmopolitanism in Cape Town and Johannesburg respectively. It is this image of diversity, melange and acculturation that apartheid ideologues sought to disentangle through increasingly brutal means.

La Guma mostly concerns himself with the plight of characters on the fringes of apartheid society, where 'people [were] plodding and stumbling through the stickiness', living in desperate living conditions:

> His weight sinking into the mud, and he left behind him a soggy trail, quickly filled by brown water, around the wet, leaning, tin-and-lath side of the house, to where it faced the straggling, swampy lane between the ragged rows of tatterdemalion shacks, some of them crowded together as if to suck warmth from each other's dugs, others standing aloof with a sort of decrepit pride in their individual bogs. (La Guma 1988: 19)

In particular, La Guma is telling the story of the people of Cape Town in a language variety characteristic of the environment, one that reaches beyond its surface appearance.

In these surroundings, La Guma's characters are marked through the distinctiveness of their speech. In his fourth novella, *In the Fog of the Seasons' End*, the narrator relates the complexity of language use:

> [The Sergeant] looked up irritably: 'I say, what is this about words written up on walls?'
> He spoke in Afrikaans which was the language of all white police.
> 'Well, they have been writing on the walls, again, *meneer*,' one of the black policemen said.
> 'The same things? Those damn agitators, *bliksems*.'(La Guma 1972: 99)

Interestingly, this novella is dedicated to Basil February, one of the first (coloured) ANC cadres to be killed in action in 1967, someone 'whose home language was Afrikaans and who used [it] more easily than he used English' (Marius Schoon quoted in Coetzee & Polley 1990). Furthermore, La Guma adroitly uses Cape working-class speech as a feature of characterisation of poor and marginalised coloured people. This heteroglossia signifies a great deal more than mere linguistic expression. It bears at once the imprint of the merging of languages and cultures, the histories of colonial rule and subjugation, and social marginalisation and poverty.

The lexifier of contemporary Cape working-class speech is Afrikaans (and earlier, Cape Dutch) which La Guma translates and adapts into English. He captures to various degrees of success the rhythm and musicality of the vernacular, while retaining some of the versatility of everyday speech. For instance, in his rendition of dialogue, the characteristic, but untranslatable word *mos* serves several linguistic functions, besides signalling the utterance's original Afrikaans provenance.[7] In the following excerpt from *And a Threefold Cord, mos* acts as confirmation, in the same manner as the common expression 'is it', and as adverb in the intensifying adjectival adjunct in the second sentence.

> 'Is not nice to fight in the street, *mos*.'
> He looked at her and said, with a little pride: 'They was interfering with my brother. A man must *mos* fight for his brother, don't I say?' (La Guma 1988: 31)

In the next snippet of dialogue from *In the Fog of the Seasons' End, mos* acts as an interjection in an implied tag question, and in the second sentence again as an intensifying adjectival adjunct but also as a modal adjunct, indicating certainty in the utterance.

> 'Then you are just jealous, *mos*. I reckon you would enjoy being on the field, whether they are weak teams or no.'
> 'Man, I can *mos* go the following week.' (La Guma 1972: 31)

These excerpts reveal the cadences of Afrikaans speech. For example, the latter sentence is a literal translation of the Afrikaans: '*Man, ek kan mos gaan volgende week*' or '*Man, ek kan mos volgende week gaan*'. Overall, *mos* points to a world of Cape working-class expression and experience beyond the rendered text. The origin of this narrative style is well exemplified in chapter 2 in this volume, where La Guma skilfully relates the interactions between the magistrate, Percy Dreyer, and Florence in his column on 'A Day at Court' published in *New Age* in 1956, a full sixteen years before the *And a Threefold Cord* passages:

> The dispenser of justice eased his collar away from his throat, gulped and fiddled with his papers. Percy was called to give evidence from the witness-box.
> 'Agbaar [your honour], on the twenty-ninth of the eighth month I was coming from Mowberry [Mowbray]. I came up Primrose Street and in Caledon Street I heard somebody call my name. It was Florence. She says to me, Hoe gaan 'it. I says, Not so bed. And she says, You feel like a liddle dring? And I says, Ek sal nie mind nie. So we go into a smokkel-huis in Caledon Street and she buys me a borreltjie ...'
> His Agbaar mopped his brow feverishly. The cops grinned behind their hands. The public tittered.

Cape working-class speech, designated Kaaps, is a manifestation of the syncretism that became the hallmark of the Cape of Good Hope settlement in the 17th and 18th centuries. Slave capitalism spawned creolisation and acculturation. This language variety, the lingua franca of La Guma's mid-century Cape Town, went beyond the sound or the idiomatic creativity of Capetonians to the place's demographic diversity. The language, as are its speakers, is instilled with disparate histories, developed through the interaction of people from various parts of Africa, Asia and Europe (Davids 2023).

The anonymous obituary writer of *Sechaba* describes their comrade as being fond of 'mimicking the mannerisms and jargon of the Cape coloured working class. This he did out of sheer love and togetherness with them', and states that over the New Year and *Tweede Nuwejaar* (second new year), a peculiarly Cape Town custom commemorating the slaves' rare days off, 'Alex loved nothing better than to relax and get geared up for his favourite Cape songs and ditties … The "skollie" slang and jokes would keep us in fits of laughter – and more than a little nostalgia.'[8]

Cape vernacular is a feature of La Guma's social realism in his creative writing, and he generally treats it with circumspection in his portrayal of working-class life. The *Sechaba* obituary writer's reference to 'mimicking the mannerisms' and 'skollie slang' unfortunately suggests that in private the speakers of the variety were the objects of ridicule or patronisation, which certainly would not have been La Guma's intention. The Afrikaans poet-dramatist Adam Small in a consequential defence of the vernacular dubbed it 'Kaaps', criticising the sneering haughtiness of 'some English-speaking people in South Africa who call it *Capey* [or] what some [white] Afrikaans people call *Gamat* language'. He writes,

> Kaaps is a *language*, a language in the sense that it carries the full lot and destiny of the people who speak it: the full lot, their full life 'with all that is in it'; a language in the sense that the people who speak it give their first scream of life in this language, settle all the transactions of their lives in this language, and they die with the language on their lips. Kaaps is not a joke or comical, but a language. (Adam Small 1973: 11)

Presently, a generation of Cape Afrikaans writers from working-class backgrounds, the literary heirs of La Guma and Small, is reclaiming Afrikaans and valorising Kaaps in ways that were previously unimaginable, putting paid to upper class and outsider derision.

Cape Town, like Cuba, has a long and deep history of acculturation, a reality that apartheid ideologues found threatening and therefore imposed stringent policies of social and political separation preventing it by force from happening throughout South Africa. At the very basis of the ANC's resistance, as well as La Guma's personal commitment, was the creation of a society where racial and social differences were deemed negligible. During his posting in Cuba, La Guma saw his envisaged 'new society' realised.

On the island a pronounced awareness of syncretism had developed, often referred to as *ajiaco* or melting pot, meaning the bringing together of different traditions, backgrounds and perspectives that created the Cuban identity that La Guma so admired. After many years in Cuba, he writes appreciatively of this sense of creolised identity:

> Many of us, when we arrive in Cuba, we think that we have returned to our fatherland: to the fatherland as it will be some day. Here there are peoples of various races: blacks,

coloureds, chinese; people who have created a new society, and we say: 'Ah, in South Africa we will see these same scenes'. There might be different experiences, different particularities, but, in general, we see the image of our future. (La Guma quoted in Gonzalez 2005)

La Guma's commitment to social justice and his political beliefs reflected in these pages of *Early Writings* also inform the central themes and ideas of his novellas, set mostly in urban landscapes. These depict the brutality of systemic apartheid repression, and the economic hardship and exploitation of the working class. At the core of many of his thematic concerns is the resilience of individuals and communities amidst dehumanisation, violence and brutality. As a revolutionary he primarily references resistance and liberation to oppression, while forging a greater sense of solidarity among its victims.

His oeuvre explores the development of political consciousness from acquiescence to expressed militancy. As a political writer he persistently appeals to the coloured people to raise their political consciousness, free themselves of apathy, and commit themselves to the struggle for liberation. By the time of his death, the rise of consciousness and activism among the coloured people had come to fruition. The involvement of the coloured youth had been most prominent during the 1970s and 1980s with the establishment of the UDF, the African National Congress's associate organisation, and of underground structures in the Cape, and with the emergence of urban guerilla insurrection. In the same issue of *Sechaba* in which the tribute to La Guma is published, an unnamed ANC analyst reports on the 'massive involvement of the "Coloured" people' where the brutality of 'the fascist police ... [welded] the "Coloured" people even more firmly to the mass forces of our revolution.'[9] In hindsight, La Guma's novellas are harbingers of an evolving political identity and practice moving towards an 'image of our future'.

The themes prevalent in La Guma's novels are also present in his journalistic writing, cartoons and short stories. In the introduction to this book, Odendaal and Field state that their aim is to 'help recover and make accessible the work and views of one of the "lost" writers and political figures from the sixties'. They offer this collection 'as a kind of homecoming for that tall, gangly man from District Six', bringing together short stories, a cartoon strip series and his long-running weekly *New Age* column, 'Up my alley'.

Odendaal and Field's wide-ranging Introduction is a well-documented contribution on the life and times of La Guma. It covers a range of topics from his *New Age* and *Fighting Talk* writing and his spells of detention in prison to a skilful analysis of the influence these experiences had on his creative writing. It is also a well-edited study. The editors took much trouble in editing this book, regrouping material to create a coherent narrative. They literally had to 'snip the columns and rearrange them thematically so that readers could get an overall picture of La Guma's views on various issues of his day'. Even though the perceptive reader may at times detect differences in intention and tone of these reorganised snippets, my general impression is that this collection has gained much from the editors' considered and clearly documented editorial interventions, creating a valuable resource.

The collection is vintage La Guma. The style, the vernacular and the concerns are those of the Cape Town writer we have encountered in his novellas. La Guma, the journalist, becomes more than a reporter of events. He evokes the nature and quality of social, economic and political relationships, recreating the places, feelings and the linguistic attributes of his real-life subjects. La Guma often goes beyond strict reportage to a more passionate treatment of topical events where his sensibilities as a writer shine through, for instance in the newspaper article 'Law of the Jungle' (chapter 6 this volume) which opens with 'Crime has no colour-bar, but evidently punishment in South African has', and ends with a memorable paragraph: 'Men leave [prison], but not as new men. They step through the gates broken in health, cowed by brutality, or hardened with bitterness'.

La Guma's descriptions of the 1956 Treason Trial go beyond the well-known facts or historical figures. As a writer he is a keen observer, often creating appealing diarised accounts of the trialists, their detentions and lodgings, the judicial officers and the humdrum happenings during the trial. The treatment of these events provides the contemporary reader with insight into the emotions, feelings and aspirations of the individuals on trial much more than any professional historical account could have done.

Particularly pertinent are La Guma's reflections on the politics of identity. He shows himself as a steadfast Freedom Charter supporter in constant polemical opposition. These exhortations are very much part of La Guma's mission as a political leader. Throughout the collection, but especially in Part 4, entitled 'Cape Town', his concerns with the social and political identity of those around him clearly shine through.

La Guma's insight into life in Johannesburg is never jaundiced, always intriguing, and observant of the frailties and exigencies of human existence. In 'The City of Gold' (chapter 13 this volume) he writes, 'Beneath the stony façade of the City of Gold there is a song which singing cannot express. There is a cheerfulness that laughter cannot satisfy, a tragedy which tears cannot obliterate.' Ever the revolutionary, he concludes, 'There is a vision that freedom will make as real as the sweat and the agony and the gold which is its heart'.

Most surprising is the cartoon strip collection (chapter 17 this volume), showing off the versatility of La Guma. Again, he explores creative, non-traditional ways of communicating his political message with Libby Chabalala, the itinerant youngster, experiencing South African life in its variety: being kidnapped, forced into farm labour, rescuing a damsel in distress, falling in with criminals and eventually distributing political pamphlets. More than 60 years after its first appearance, La Guma's use of a popular cultural mode is as innovative as contemporary graphic novels.

Although not completely liberated from elitist notions of culture, La Guma's views on Cape Town popular culture are nevertheless refreshing. Ever the Marxist ideologue, he often swims against the stream of the Cape's then contemporaneous opinion makers. He argues, for instance, that one should understand the social fabric that gives rise to cultural expressions like the Minstrel Carnival, rather than sneering at it. Among the decidedly middle-class political leadership in Cape Town, such views were regarded with a little suspicion.

This collection is a record of the polemical views on politics, culture and identity La Guma held during the 1950s and early 1960s. Since his death, local academics have researched his oeuvre, and recently several runs of a play based on *In the Dark with My Dress on Fire* (2010), the autobiography of his wife Blanche (née Herman), have been produced. Today, there is a greater awareness of La Guma's contribution and that of his generation of Cape activists to our political freedom, although a great deal more still needs to be done.

La Guma's literary and journalistic writings are noteworthy documents providing insight into South Africa during the apartheid period. The new edition of this book, more than 30 years after its initial publication, will underscore the enduring need to recognise a key figure in our political and cultural history. Odendaal and Field have brought together an important volume that benefits us all.

Hein Willemse
Emeritus Professor, Department of Afrikaans, University of Pretoria and former President of the International Society for the Oral Literatures of Africa
September 2024

Professor Hein Willemse completed his undergraduate and postgraduate studies at the University of the Western Cape, where he also taught for several years. He has published widely on South African literature and taught for extended periods as visiting professor at several local and overseas universities, in Central and North America, Europe and in the rest of Africa.

Notes

1. Own Correspondent, Death of La Guma, *Cape Times,* 17 October 1985.
2. ANC Veteran, Hamba kahle Comrade Alex La Guma, *Sechaba*, January 1986: 28–31.
3. ANC Veteran, Hamba kahle Comrade Alex La Guma, *Sechaba*, January 1986: 28–31.
4. Obituary, 1986, *Rixaka* 3: 16–18.
5. ANC Veteran, Hamba kahle Comrade Alex La Guma, *Sechaba*, January 1986: 29.
6. ANC Veteran, Hamba kahle Comrade Alex La Guma, *Sechaba*, January 1986: 31.
7. My thanks to Suléne Pilon for clarifying the syntactical intricacies.
8. ANC Veteran, Hamba kahle Comrade Alex La Guma, *Sechaba*, January 1986: 30, 31.
9. The eyes of our people are focused on this conference, *Sechaba*, January 1986: 5.

References

Coetzee A & Polley J (eds) (1990) *Crossing borders: Writers meet the ANC.* Johannesburg: Taurus

Davids A (2023) *The Arabic Afrikaans writing tradition 1815–1915.* Edited by H Willemse and SE Dangor. Johannesburg: Jacana

Gonzalez D (2005) Alex La Guma: Twenty years in Cuban memories. *Review of African Political Economy* 32(106): 646–651

La Guma A (1967) *A walk in the night and other stories.* Evanston: Northwestern University Press

La Guma A (1972) *In the fog of the seasons' end.* London: Heinemann

La Guma A (1979) *Time of the butcherbird.* London: Heinemann

La Guma A (1988) *And a threefold cord.* London: Kliptown Books

La Guma B with M Klammer (2010) *In the dark with my dress on fire: My life in Cape Town, London, Havana and home again.* Johannesburg: Jacana Media

Small A (1973) *Kitaar my kruis.* Cape Town: Hollandsch Afrikaansche Uitgevers Maatschappij

Cape Town's urban griot: A tribute to Alex La Guma

> Societies never know it, but the war of an artist with his society is a lover's war, and he does, at his best, what lovers do, which is to reveal the beloved to himself and, with that revelation, to make freedom real.
> — James Baldwin 1985: 670

Alex La Guma was born in 1925 at a time when the vote of the coloured community was much sought after. A feature of Sunday afternoon tea in the family home on Roger Street in District Six[1] would have been the ubiquitous koesista[2] and Baumann's lemon creams from the factory on Sir Lowry Road in Woodstock. But a later addition to the Sunday tea table, the Hertzoggie, was inspired by the politics of the day in a season of political courting and the promises of an election campaign that resulted in the Pact government, a coalition between General JBM Hertzog's National Party of Afrikaner Nationalism and Colonel FHP Cresswell's Labour Party in June 1924. Their rule and that of successive governments provided a socioeconomic infrastructure for whites at the expense of a diminished quality of black life.

The coloured vote, as qualified a franchise as it was, was influential in determining who governed the Cape. Hertzog assiduously courted the coloured electorate, promising exemption from the restrictions applied to Africans. They would benefit from the privileges legislated for white workers – but as a separate 'racial' group who shared the values and culture of whites.

The Hertzoggie, named in honour of Hertzog, emerged from Bo-Kaap kitchens. Baking skills nurtured in the kitchens of slave-holding estates of the past conjured this tasty offering of a baked pastry tart filled with a dollop of apricot jam and topped by a coconut and egg white mixture.

Yet despite the Pact victory in the 1924 elections, the promises of the New Deal for coloured people never materialised to the extent that had been anticipated. And the jilted ones expressed their dissatisfaction in a unique, culinary manner: The Hertzoggie was coated with proportional halves of brown and pink icing and renamed *twee-gevrietjie*.

La Guma reflects the psyche of the community that birthed him by what James Baldwin identified as the commitment of the artist to self-knowledge:

> We become social creatures because we cannot live any other way. But in order to become social, there are a great many other things that we must not become, and we are frightened, all of us, of these forces within us that perpetually menace our precarious security. Yet the forces are there: we cannot will them away. All we can do is learn to live with them. And we cannot learn this unless we are willing to tell the truth about ourselves, and the truth about us is always at variance with what we wish to be. The human effort is to bring these two realities into a relationship resembling reconciliation. (Baldwin 1985: 317)

In the epigraph at the beginning of this tribute, Baldwin, a 38-year-old queer black man writes in 1962 of the consequential impact of this approach both on the artist and society. From the first paragraph of *Early Writings*, Alex La Guma reflects the consciousness of an urban griot[3] when he tells a story sourced from the oral traditions of South Africa's coloured people:

> There is a story told among the old people which says that one day, many years ago, God summoned White Man and Coloured Man and placed two boxes before them. One box was very big and the other very small. God then turned to Coloured Man and told him to choose one of the boxes. Coloured Man immediately chose the bigger and left the other to the White Man. When he opened his box, Coloured man found a pick and a shovel inside it; White Man found gold in his box. (chapter 1 this volume)

This parable, notes La Guma, speaks to a self-awareness informed by a 'common consciousness that oppression, suffering and hardship is a fact of life. And they have learned to temper hardship with humour and to sweeten the bitter pill of their drab lives with the honey of a satirical philosophy. But always they have been aware of pain' (chapter 1 this volume).

Other Africans in other parts of the country organised around issues pertinent to their particular experience of oppression as well. As early as the mid-1920s Alex's father, James La Guma, and like-minded activists started the short-lived League of African Rights (LAR) with JT Gumede (ANC) as its president, SP Bunting (Communist Party of South Africa) chairperson and Nimrod B Tantsi (ANC), vice-chairperson. Edward le Roux (CPSA) and Albert Nzula (ANC) were joint secretaries.

The LAR launched a One Million Signature Campaign, whose petition of rights called for, inter alia, the removal of the pass laws, free speech, the securement of the vote for Cape-based Africans and its extension to black South Africans in the three northern provinces. The intention was to present the signatures to parliament after a conference scheduled for Dingaan's Day, 16 December 1929.

A telegram from Moscow demanding the disbanding of the League put an end to all that. The reasons: the reformist demands of the LAR were bolstering up reformist leaders such as Gumede (Simons & Simons 1983: 439).

But the song derived from the slogan of this fledgling organisation, 'Mayibuye iAfrika' (Let Africa return), proved popular beyond expectation. The words were written by Tantsi and Roux and sung to the tune of 'Clementine'. It was published in *Umsebenzi*, the Communist Party's journal, on 26 June 1931.

Mayibuye!	Let it come back!
Tina Sizwe esi ntsundu	We the people who are brown
sikalel' iAfrika	bless Africa,
eyahlatw' obawo betu	which was taken from our fathers
besese bu' mnyameni.	when they were in darkness.
Mayibuye, Mayibuye	Let it return, let it return,
Mayibuye! iAfrika!	let Africa return to us!
Makapele namapasi.	Down with passes.
Sitoli nkululeko.	We demand freedom.

Roux wrote an Afrikaans version of Mayibuye which was soon sung enthusiastically by coloured farm workers and their fellow African compatriots.

Gee ons land terug!	Return our land!
Ons bruinmense, seuns van slawe,	We brown people, sons of slaves,
Vra ons eie land terug,	Demand the return of our land
Wat gesteel is van ons vaders,	Stolen from our forebears,
Toe hul in die donker sug,	While they sighed in darkness,
Gee dit t'rug nou! Gee dit t'rug nou!	Give it back now! Give it back now!
Weg met al die slawerny!	Away with all slavery!
Pirow kans ons nie ophou nie:	Pirow can't restrain us:
Afrika sal Vryheid kry.	Afrika shall be free.

The first version of this freedom song emphasises 'makapele namapasi' (down with passes), while the Afrikaans version refers to a slave past, illustrating the perennial challenge of regional differences, the uneven pace of resistance, and how these inform the strategy and tactics of mobilising different sectors of the oppressed.

James La Guma, who had been orphaned at a young age, was of French-Malagasy descent and had started working at the age of eight in a Parow bakery. He had identified very early in his life with the struggles of the labouring poor. He was enamoured of Robert Tressell's *The Ragged Trousered Philanthropists*, which gave a prosaic account of the struggles of the English working class. Jimmy, as he was popularly known, is numbered among the pioneers of the struggle against colonialism and the progeny it spawned, apartheid. He suffered the consequences, which included being twice expelled from the Communist Party of South Africa, of compelling the left of his day to engage – whether they agreed with his thesis or not – in a contextualised reading of the lived reality of the oppressed.

Wilhelmina, the matriarch of the La Guma family, worked in the garment industry adjacent to District Six and often augmented the family's income with the earnings from her knitting and crocheting, especially when her husband was either unemployed or working as an organiser for little or no pay.

After their marriage they moved in with Wilhelmina's widowed mother Lena in her terraced cottage on 1 Roger Street in District Six. And by the time Alex was born, and later his sister Joan, the La Gumas had moved next door into rented accommodation.

These were Alex La Guma's formative years in the mid-1920s to 1930s, when Cape Town was a republic of ideas, still to be tested in the rigours of political struggle.

The African People's Organisation (APO), by then in its waning years, existed almost aloof from the nascent challenges to the status quo. Since its inception in 1902 the APO, inspired by British Liberal principles, had walked the constitutional path measured by protests and delegations to London. It espoused the accommodationist philosophy of Booker T Washington that if your head is in the jaws of a lion, then it is best to reach over and tap it on the shoulder.

Dr Abdullah Abdurahman, a pragmatic, astute politician, stood at its helm. A portion of Abdurahman's closing remarks at the APO's 1935 conference was directed at the young people of his immediate constituency. These included his daughter Cissie Gool. They were keen to take the fight hitherto determined by their biological and political elders from protest to challenge. The ailing statesman, four years before his death, in his closing speech at the APO's 1935 conference asked of the youth 'to come along and help to solve one of the most difficult and perplexing problems that confront the world, namely, how to adjust ourselves to the changing world – how black and white can live together in peace and amity, each contributing his share to make this country truly great' (Abdurahman 1935).

Abdurahman cited lines from an anti-slavery poem 'Charity', written by an Anglican cleric, William Cowper. The poet, a close friend of the anti-slavery campaigner John Newton, was an active abolitionist. The poem underscored Abdurahman's political convictions, which were premised on a strategic patience and decisive action at the opportune time:

> Bid suffer it a while, and kiss the rod,
> Wait for the dawning of a brighter day,
> And snap the chain the moment when you may.
> (William Cowper 1731–1800, poem 'Charity')

Numbered among Abdurahman's political adversaries were those who sought to expedite the long-delayed dawn of a new day for the oppressed. They would seek to achieve this through extra-parliamentary actions, chief among which would be the mobilising on all levels of society against the emerging apartheid state. And they were willing to prise open the jaws of the lion and face the consequences of harsh terms of imprisonment, torture and death.

A young Alex La Guma took his first tentative steps on this road through *The Liberator*, a magazine published by the National Liberation League (NLL).

A George Hallet photograph, most likely taken in the 1960s, features the late nineteenth century Victorian Hanover Building in District Six. A group of young people, a Battalion of the Anglican Church Lads' and Girls' Brigade, are marching along Hanover Street from the nearby St Mark's Church. They are turning left into Tennant Street, and the front section of the brigade is directly in line with the Hanover Building.

It was outside this building that Reg September, Alex's senior by a few years and fellow traveller in the congress movement, had stood in 1936. He was waiting for a fellow matriculant, Peter Meisenheimer, who had entered the building on an errand. Reg was unaware that he was standing outside the offices of the NLL. It was there that James La Guma, the controversial proponent of 'The Black Republic', approached the young September, who was dressed in the Trafalgar High school uniform. He asked why Reg was standing here. After hearing the reason, La Guma invited the youngster to accompany him into the building. There, in one of the offices, he found his friend Peter chatting to none other than Moses Kotane. The latter was busy setting type for the Communist Party newspaper.

Jimmy was probably coming back from a lunch break at his home in nearby Roger Street. Since 1934, a group of friends and struggle stalwarts had organised themselves into the Fifteen Circle. This informal study group met at the Hyman Liberman Institute in District Six for a while and also participated in the Cape Literary and Debating Society. But divisions arose among them because of the tendency of some members to render a communist analysis of society.

The ideological offenders formed the Fifteen Circle consisting of individuals such as Johnny Gomas, a member of the Communist Party, Chris Ziervogel, librarian at the Hyman Liberman Institute, and James La Guma. They shifted their meeting place to the wooden shed in the La Guma family's backyard. It was here that they developed the idea of forming an organisation for organising the oppressed by linking local needs with national issues such as the abolition of the colour bar and the pass laws.

These were the founding members of the National Liberation League of South Africa in December 1935. Cissie Gool was invited to be its first president and Jimmy La Guma its general secretary. Johnny Gomas and James La Guma co-wrote the league's anthem, 'Dark Folks Arise', which was sung at NLL meetings (Musson 1989: 90). The League located itself within the South African slave story. Its emblem was that of a slave who had broken free of his chains, holding a flaming torch aloft with the chains still manacled to his wrist.

Many of the children of League members were co-opted into assisting with tasks useful for the completion of *The Liberator*, and Alex, at a young age, displayed a talent for drawing cartoons for the organisation's magazine. Later, he completed a course in life drawing at the Cape Technical College in District Six. This practice in the visual arts would serve him as a writer in ways of seeing beyond that which is obvious, as demonstrated in his prison sketches and the inclusion in this volume of his cartoon series 'Little Libby: The adventures of Liberation Chabalala' – originally published in *New Age* – demonstrates. (See chapter 17.)

James Baldwin remembers standing on a street corner in Greenwich Village with the painter Beauford Delaney, who pointed to the ground and told him to look:

> I looked and all I saw was the water. And he said, 'Look again,' which I did, and I saw oil on the water and the city reflected in the puddle. It was a great revelation to me. I can't explain it. He taught me how to see, and how to trust what I saw. Painters have often taught writers how to see. And once you've had that experience, you see differently. (Plimpton 1989)

Just as readers will see that references to newspaper reports featured regularly in La Guma's newspaper writings that form the core of this book, his first novel, *A Walk in the Night*, was born of the curiosity that arose due to a short mention in a newspaper about what La Guma describes as 'a so-called hooligan had died in the police van after having been shot in District Six' (La Guma 1967). He sets out to excavate what the possible circumstances could have been.

As the main character, Mikey Adonis, moves about the district in this novel, his entrance into a pub becomes the door that La Guma opens onto the city that he loved and brought to life through the characters of his stories: 'It was a forum, a parliament, a fountain of wisdom and a cesspool of nonsense, it was a centre for the loss and the despairing, where cowards absorbed Dutch courage out of small glasses' (La Guma 1967: 13).

The writings of Alex Guma memorialise a forgotten time in the history of his home town, Cape Town. His canon of work is characterised by a perceptive reading of the underexplored nature of the commonwealth of South African communities of whom he writes:

If you identify a people, not by names and the colour of their skin, but by the hardship and joy, pleasure and suffering, cherished hopes and broken dreams, the grinding monotony of toil without gain, despair and starvation, illiteracy, tuberculosis and malnutrition, laughter and vice, ignorance, genius, superstition, ageless wisdom and undying confidence, love and hatred, then you will have to give up counting. People are like identical books with only different dustjackets. The title and the text are the same. (chapter 1 this volume)

In the statement 'people are like identical books with only different dustjackets' and with the same title and text, La Guma is prescient in pointing to the perennial challenge of building a society. It is there in Abdurahman's dream of the need to change the world in response to the question of 'how black and white can live together in peace and amity'.

* * * * *

The Cuban soldiers who fell on the battlefields of Angola were reinterred in the cemeteries of their island home in the Caribbean. These included the Cementerio de Cristóbal de Colón in Havana where another African of slave descent, Alex La Guma, also lies buried. He had been the ANC's chief representative in Cuba and the Caribbean.

In her autobiography, *In the Dark with My Dress on Fire*, Blanche La Guma, Alex's wife and comrade, recalls their courting days: 'Alex was debonair. He'd sing a song or recite a poem. I was struck deeply when he recited Cyrano de Bergerac, "Your name hangs like a bell around my heart. When it rings it says, 'Blanche, Blanche, I love you'"' (La Guma B 2010: 42). After Alex's deployment to Cuba, Blanche joined him a few months later after settling their affairs in London where they had lived since leaving South Africa in the 1960s. A beaming Alex greeted his beloved with the words, 'Companera! Companera! My comrade has come to see me' (La Guma B 2010: 164). Appointed ANC Deputy Chief Representative for the Caribbean, she joined him at the office as well. Their love, undimmed over the years of house arrest, death threats and detention, was premised on mutual respect and imbued with the values of the struggle for liberation, at home and abroad.

As we learn in the prologue to this book, La Guma, our African Dostoevsky, died of a heart attack in Havana. Her name, the bell around his heart, was the last word she heard him say.

If I was in Cuba today
If I was in Cuba today
I would be at the grave of Alex La Guma
in the *Cementerio de Cristóbal de Colón*.

Our District Six Dostoevsky.
I will sing: '*da ga'rie padtjie narie kramat toe.*'
A coconut shell slanging a goema riddim.

You, my love, will catch the tune and sing with me,
as I libate the ground with a tot of buchu-brandy.

Cigar smoke, infused with a sniff of Jamaican sunshine,
will incense the air with the forgotten familiar of home.

If I was in Cuba today
we will slow salsa under a Carib moon,
keening low, like old lovers do.

We will sing about '*jou matras en my kombers*'
like Blanche and Alex would once have sung:
their eyes on the waters of the *Playas del Este*.

Their hearts blissed by the breeze slinking
down the moonlit lanes beyond Roger Street, across
The Parade to the bay of their sighed longing.

I will stand in gratitude at your grave, Uncle Alex,
in Havana today, and to say that we
have not forgotten you and your words

that led us through the fog and beyond
the night of draconian ghosts
to where we walk the days of freedom. (Weeder 2021: 39)

Reverend Michael Weeder
Poet, community activist and Dean of the Anglican Cathedral of St George the Martyr,
Cape Town, 2011–2024
August 2024

Michael Weeder was raised in the Cape Flats and qualified as a priest in 1985. He has also received a BA (Hons) and an MA in History (cum laude) from the University of the Western Cape. He was a founder member of December 1st, a social movement formed to work around the memory and legacy of slavery, and Archbishop Desmond Tutu appointed him as his representative on the PEACE and Dialogue Platform, an international peace-making initiative of some Nobel Peace-prize laureates.

Notes

1. District Six was an inner-city neighbourhood in Cape Town that was declared a 'whites only' area in 1966. Black people's homes were destroyed to make way for a white neighbourhood, and families were forcibly removed. The removal was implemented by invoking apartheid discriminatory laws: the Group Areas Act and the Population Registration Act, which were both passed in 1950.
2. 'Koesista' (also spelled 'koesister or koe'sister) is a teatime delicacy closely associated with Cape Town, particularly District Six and the Bo-Kaap (Upper Cape). There are various versions of this creolised recipe, but in its basic form it consists of a spiced, leavened dough deep-fried in oil and then immersed in sugar syrup and coated with coconut.
3. 'Griot' is derived from a French word *guiriot* and is associated with West African story-tellers, musicians and historians. Over time, it came to be used commonly in the African diaspora to refer to a sage or keeper of the community's history.

References

Abdurahman A (1935) Closing remarks at African People's Organisation conference 1935. Abdullah Abdurahman Family Papers, University of Cape Town Libraries Special Collection

Baldwin J (1985) *The price of the ticket: Collected nonfiction, 1948–1985*. New York: St Martin's Press

La Guma A (1967) *A walk in the night*. London: Heinemann

La Guma B with M Klammer (2010) *In the dark with my dress on fire: My life in Cape Town, London, Havana and home again*. Johannesburg: Jacana Media

Musson D (1989) *Johnny Gomas, voice of the working class: A political biography*. Cape Town: Buchu Books

Plimpton G (1989) *The writer's chapbook: A compendium of fact, opinion, wit, and advice from the 20th century's preeminent writers*. New York: Viking Penguin

Simons J & Simons R (1983). *Class and colour in South Africa 1850-1950*. London: International Defence and Aid Fund for Southern Africa

Weeder M (2021) If I was in Cuba today. In Weeder M, *The promise of memory*. Johannesburg: African Perspectives Publishing

Photo gallery

The photographs in this gallery are all from the La Guma family collection or the Alex La Guma Collection at the UWC-RIM Mayibuye Archives ('Mayibuye'), unless otherwise indicated. We thank Blanche and Barto La Guma for permission to use them. Babalwa Solwandle and Andre Mahommed at Mayibuye were as usual very helpful. Lucas Rosenfield helped with digitisation.

Figure 1   Alex La Guma's marriage to Blanche Herman in Cape Town in November 1954 marked the beginning of 12 years of regular security police harassment followed by a long exile for them both.

Source: La Guma family

Figure 2   Alex La Guma pictured during a climb on Table Mountain with Irwin Combrinck late 1940s.

Source: Dr I Combrinck

Figure 3 District Six and a deep-rooted family tradition of working-class struggle were the nurseries for Alex La Guma's writing and activism. Alex together with his father, Jimmy La Guma, (well-known for being one of the South African architects of the Native Republic thesis in the 1920s, a leader of the National Liberation League in the 1930s and of SACPO in the 1950s) shared an unbroken record of 65 years in the frontlines of the liberation struggle from the 1920s to the 1980s.

Source: La Guma family

Figure 4 Roger Street in District Six, where the family home was located amidst, 'The hot, grey streets, the blistering tenements, the foul alleyways', he wrote about.

Source: Gawie Fagan in Field (2010), Alex La Guma: A literary and political biography. Johannesburg: Jacana Media

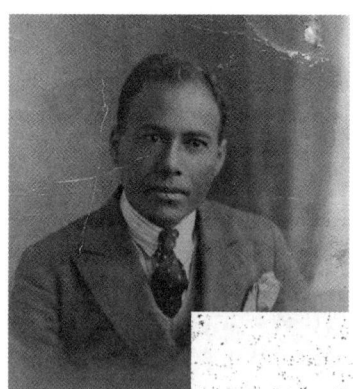

Figure 5 Jimmy La Guma

Source: La Guma family

SOUTH-AFRICAN-PUBLIC-LIBRARY
5 MAR 1937

The Liberator

A NON-EUROPEAN ANTI-IMPERIALIST MAGAZINE

EDITORIAL & PUBLISHING OFFICE
1 LONGMARKET STREET
CAPE TOWN

The Editors of the LIBERATOR invite contributions. They cannot however be held responsible for M.S.S. sent to them or undertake to enter into correspondence regarding rejected contributions. Same will be returned if stamped and addressed envelope for the purpose is enclosed

Subscription Rates (Paid in Advance)

One year 3/6
six months 2/-

Advertisement Rates
Inside Cover Page £2-10-0 p.a
Outside " " 3-0-0 "
Pro-rata for smaller space

Official Organ of the National Liberation League of S.A.
Edited by J. A. La Guma. Sub-editor S. Sisam
Business Manager L. Morley-Turner.
Designs & Reproductions by J. M. Brown Jun: & J. A. La Guma Jun:
Roneod by N.L.L. of S.A. at above address.

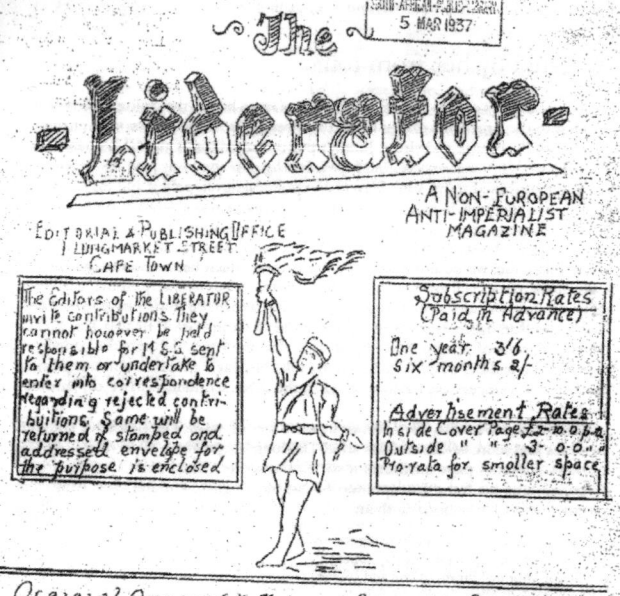

Figure 6 Extract from *The Liberator,* showing Jimmy La Guma and his 12 year-old son's roles

Source: Field (2010)

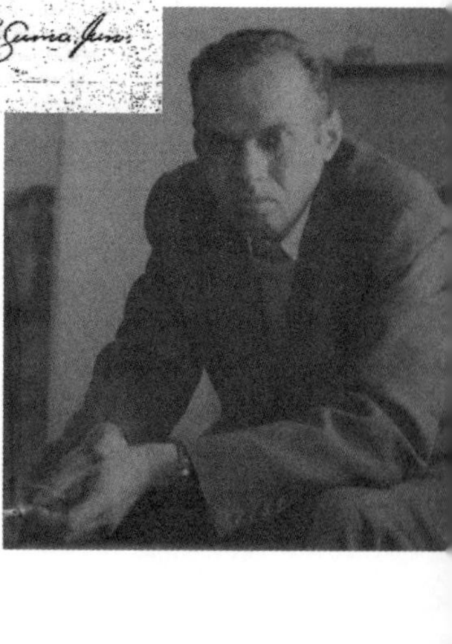

Figure 7 Alex La Guma

Source: La Guma family

Figure 8 The 156 leaders of the Congress Alliance arrested for treason in December 1956 spent several years together, plotting a future course for the struggle and countering the state's apartheid narrative in what become known as 'The People's Parliament'. La Guma is third from right in the seventh row.

Source: Eli Weinberg, UWC-RIM, Mayibuye Archives

In the 1960s, as state repression grew, both Alex and Blanche La Guma were banned, harassed and arrested, with Alex spending several years under 24-hour house arrest and in detention. In 1962, his first book was banned. It became illegal to quote him in South Africa.

Figure 9   Blanche struggled on as an activist, attending the banned Coloured National Convention in Malmesbury (seated second left in the right hand-side block). Dennis Brutus representing the South African Convention Movement provided support.

Source: André Odendaal Collection

ALEX LA GUMA'S FIRST NOVEL— BANNED BY THE SABOTAGE ACT

Figure 10   Alex La Guma was banned soon after his first novel was published.

Source: New Age, 9 August 1962

Figure 11   How *New Age* announced the banning in 1962 of La Guma's long running *Up my alley* column, which forms the core of his writings in this book

Source: La Guma family

Figure 12   Blanche battled to put food on the table and provide for her two young children, Barto left, and Eugene, right. In September 1966, the La Gumas were finally forced into exile, setting up their base in London.

Source: La Guma family

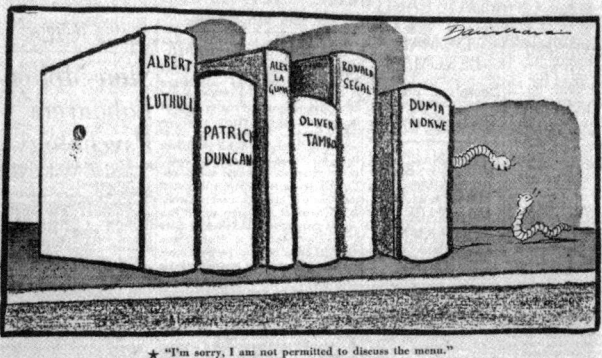

Figure 14 A *Cape Times* cartoon depicting the banning and silencing of Alex La Guma and other prominent South Africans

Source: La Guma family

Figure 13 Prohibited from being published in South Africa, but his colleagues predicted that 'The fate of Alex La Guma's book will prove once again the dictum that the pen is mightier than the sword'

Source: La Guma family

Figure 15   One of La Guma's sketches of prison life at 'The Fort' Prison, Johannesburg in 1956, where the Constitutional Court of democratic South Africa now stands

Source: Field (2010)

Figure 16   One of La Guma's sketches of a political education class in prison. His sketches and reports provide intimate insider accounts of the Congress Movement leadership at this time.

Source: Field (2010)

Figure 17   The Treason Trial and La Guma's writing made him a figure of national prominence. Both Alex and his father James became leaders of the South African Coloured People's Organisation (later Congress). James is pictured here at a meeting in Cape Town in 1958 with ANC President Chief, Albert Luthuli, and ANC Western Cape leader, Oscar Mpetha.

Source: Eli Weinberg, UWC-RIM Mayibuye Archives

Figures 18 and 19 Alex, Barto and Eugene at their new home in London.

Source: La Guma family

Figure 20 Southern African writers in conversation in London, 1971. From left to right: Albie Sachs, Doris Lessing, James Curry, Alex La Guma and Richard Rive

Source: Rive (2013), Writing Black

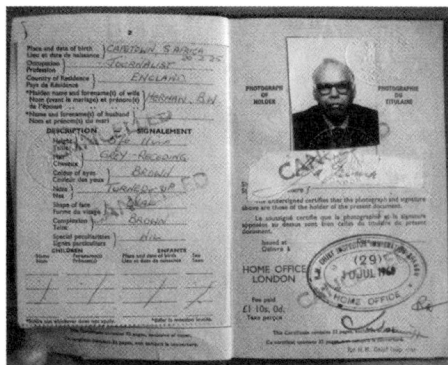

Figure 21　Alex La Guma's British passport, 1960s
Source: La Guma family

Figure 22　La Guma published his second novel, *And a Threefold Cord*, in 1964.
Source: André Odendaal Collection

Figure 23　A book-signing by La Guma in London
Source: La Guma family

Figure 25　London-based exiles Alex La Guma and Mazisi Kunene at a writer's event in Tashkent, USSR, 1968
Source: La Guma family

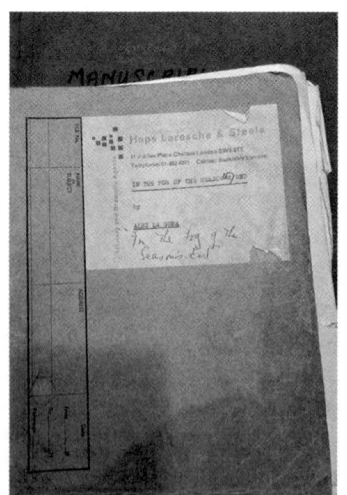

Figure 24　The manuscript for *In the Fog of the Seasons' End*, dedicated to his Cape Town comrade, Basil February
Source: La Guma family

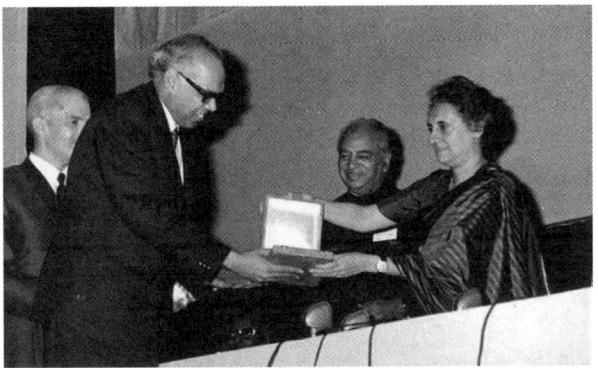

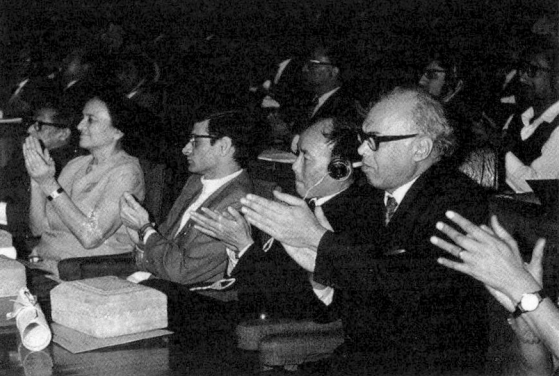

Figure 26 India's Prime Minister, Indira Gandhi, awarding the Afro-Asian Writer's Association's Lotus Prize for Literature to La Guma in 1970

Source: La Guma family

THE TIMES OF INDIA

P.M.'s call for literary exchanges among Afro-Asian countries

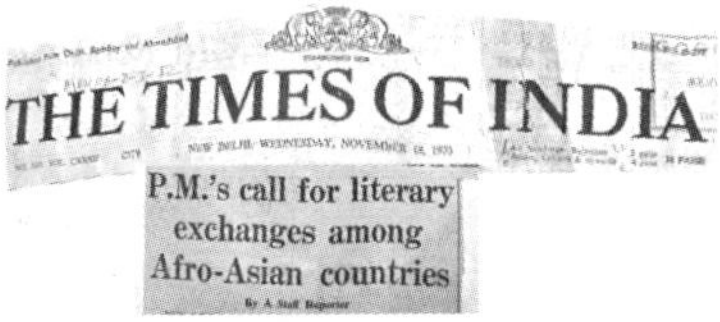

Figure 27 Extract from *The Times of India* announcing La Guma's award

Source: La Guma family

Figure 28 The Lotus Prize

Source: La Guma family

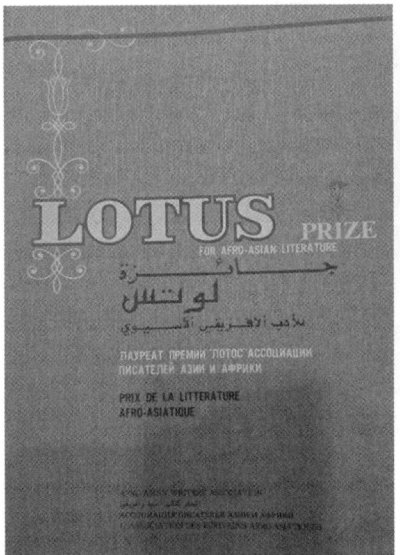

Figure 29 Alex and Blanche La Guma at the Lotus Prize awards ceremony

Source: La Guma family

Alex La Guma received the Lotus Prize of the Afro-Asian Writer's Association from Prime Minister Indira Gandhi in New Delhi, India in November 1970, eight years after he had been listed, banned and silenced in South Africa. Some renowned literary figures followed La Guma as Lotus prize-winners, including the poet and president-to-be Agostinho Neto, Ousmane Sembène, Marcelino dos Santos, Ngũgĩ wa Thiong'o, Chinua Achebe and Mahmoud Darwish.

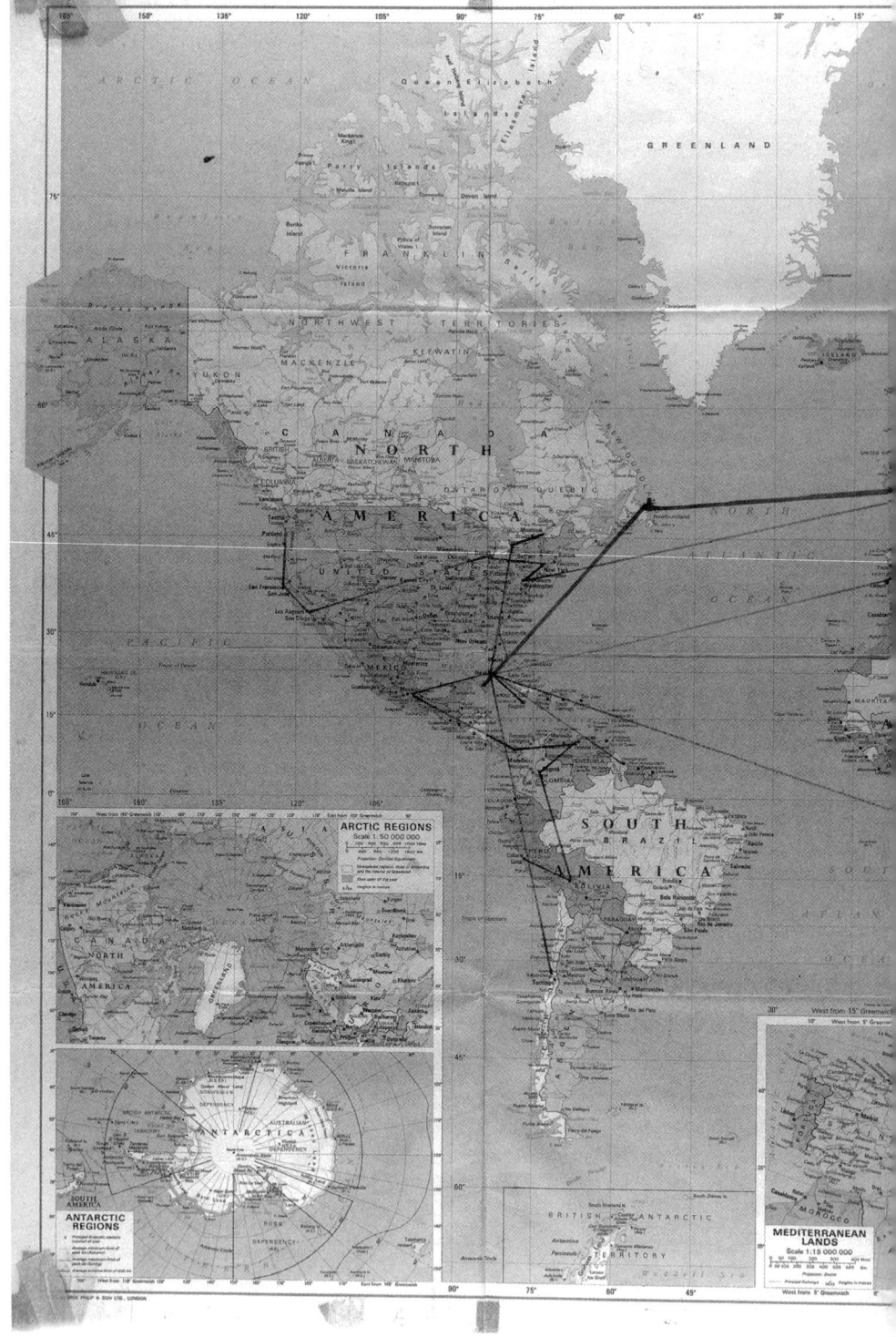

Figure 30 As Alex La Guma traversed the world, he started drawing the routes he was taking, by hand with ink and ruler on maps, pencilling in the outlines of the history he was part of making and the identity he was building for himself as a global traveller and revolutionary internationalist.

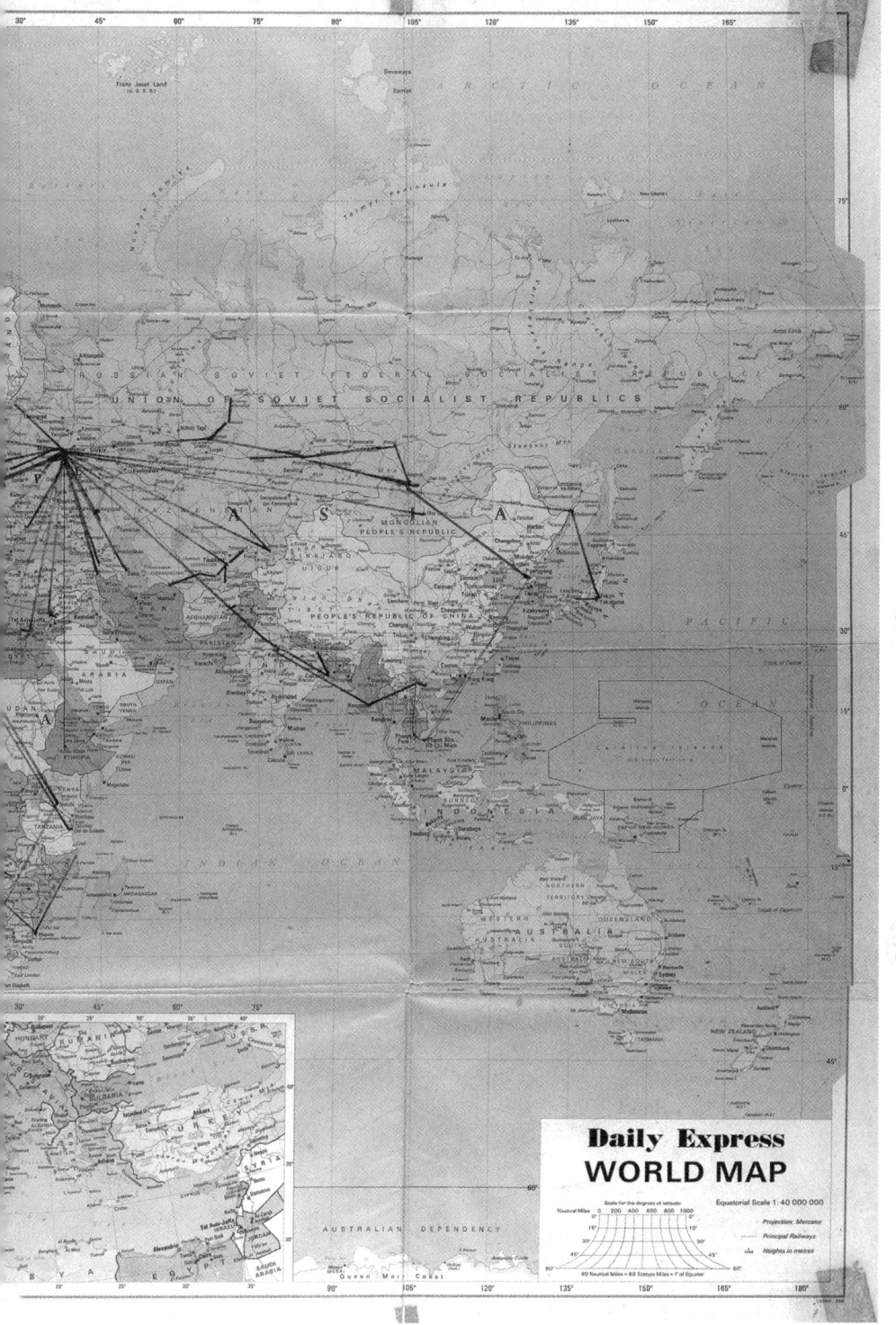

These annotated maps convey in an intimate way the appreciation the once-caged writer had for the intellectual, writing and political opportunities his second life outside South Africa had brought him.

Source: Photographed by Steve Gordon for UWC-RIM Mayibuye Archives

Figure 31 An ANC writers' delegation arriving in Alma-Ata, Kazakhstan, for the Afro-Asian Writers Conference, 1973. From left to right: Barry Higgs, Larissa Saratovskaya (interpreter), Barry Feinberg and Alex La Guma.

Source: La Guma family

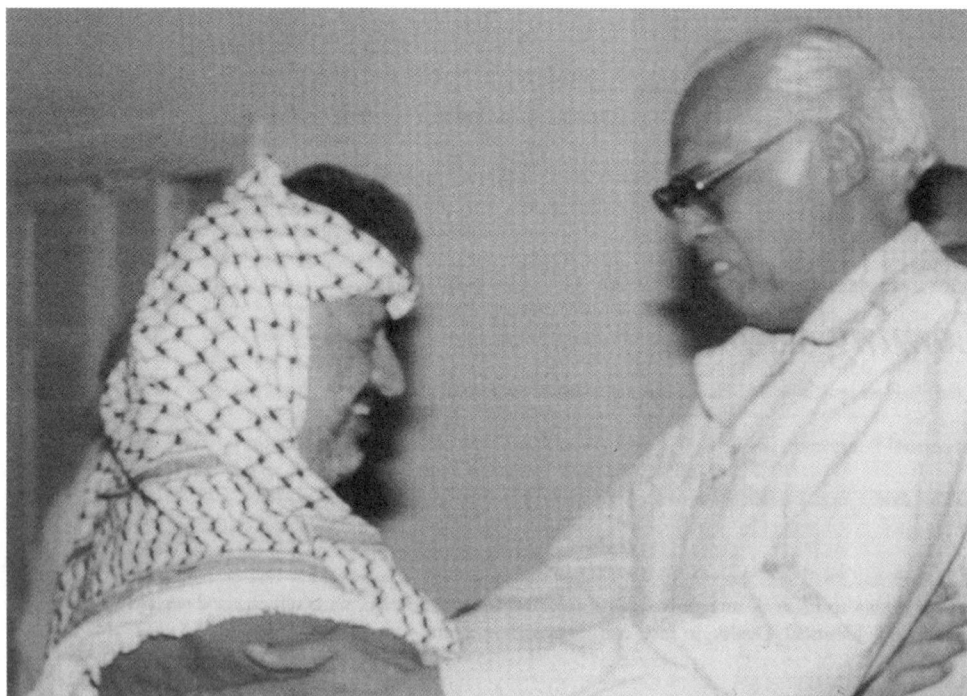

Figure 32 Alex La Guma meeting Yasser Arafat, leader of the Palestine Liberation Organisation, in Tunis where the PLO had its headquarters between 1982 and 1984

Source: La Guma family

Figure 33 'For Alex and me, going to Moscow was like Muslims going to Mecca', Blanche noted.
Source: La Guma family

Figure 34 Award ceremony, Moscow, May 1985
Source: La Guma family

Figure 35 Alex, Eugene and Blanche La Guma in Moscow
Source: La Guma family

Figures 34 and 35 In May 1985, after turning 60 and shortly before his death, Alex La Guma (as the general secretary of the Afro-Asian Writer's Association and an ANC chief representative) was awarded the Soviet Union's highest honour, the Order of Friendship of the People, at the Kremlin in Moscow. The citation noted it was 'in tribute to the literary, social and political work done by him in the promotion of friendship among the peoples of Africa and Asia and other countries, and in the cause of world peace'. Blanche and his son Eugene were present to celebrate with him.

Source: La Guma family

Figure 36 For Alex and Blanche, the ANC's ambassador to the Caribbean and Latin America and his assistant who 'held the fort' in the office when he was away travelling, the seven years in Cuba were the 'happiest times' of their life. On one day every year, Alex and Blanche and colleagues in the diplomatic corps helped harvest fruit as volunteers. They are pictured here in Domingo Rojo.

Source: La Guma family

Figure 37 Alex La Guma died of a heart attack in Havana on 11 October 1985, where he was buried in a hero's acre in the Cementerio de Cristóbal de Colón. Jesus Montane Oropesa of the Communist Party of Cuba's Central Committee signs the condolences book while an ANC comrade stands by.

Source: La Guma family

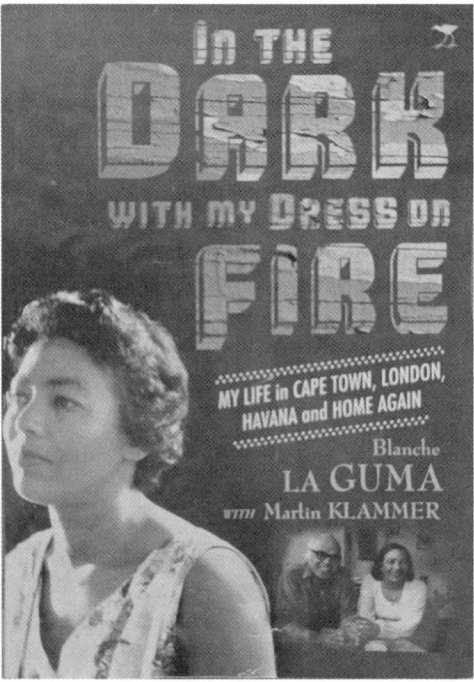

Figure 38 The legacy lives on. The 2022 musical *Dance of the La Gumas* celebrated their lives of 'Revolution, Rumba and Romance'.

Source: André Odendaal Collection

Figure 39 Blanche's story as a woman who stood firm on the frontlines of struggle in the 1950s and harsh 1960s – and in exile – as a strong member of the La Guma 'team' has been told in her autobiography published in 2010.

Source: André Odendaal Collection

Introduction

Standing next to Alex La Guma's grave a few years after his death, one of the editors felt anew the destructiveness and wastefulness of apartheid. Here was one of South Africa's major twentieth-century writers and a native of District Six lying in far-away Havana, while his wife was in London, and his sons Eugene and Bartholomew in the then-Soviet Union and German Democratic Republic, respectively. Like so many other South Africans, the La Guma family were dispersed in one generation to far-flung corners of the world. Charged with treason, shot at, detained for months without trial, held in solitary confinement, banned, prohibited from circulating any of his writing, placed under house arrest for 24 hours a day and finally forced into exile, Alex La Guma was officially airbrushed out of South African public life for nearly thirty years. His writing and views could not be circulated in his own country, except illegally, and his books were among the 38 813 banned by the state censors between 1962 and 1990.[1]

Yet, when La Guma was prohibited from writing in 1962, his colleague Brian Bunting predicted that, 'The fate of Alex La Guma's [work] will prove once again the truth of the dictum that the pen is mightier than the sword'.[2] The prophecy began to be fulfilled almost immediately. One week after his writings were banned and he was forced to give up journalism, *New Age*, the newspaper he had been writing for up to that time, announced that the African writers' and artists' club, Mbari, based in Ibadan, had published La Guma's first book, *A Walk in the Night*.[3] The work brought him instant recognition. It was a major talking point at the first African Writers Conference held in Kampala in the same year. Its 'startling realism and accurate imagery … evoked many bravos from writers, especially those from West Africa'.[4]

Zeke Mphahlele, then teaching at Makerere University College in Kampala, wrote saying 'What a story and what beautiful writing … it's so crisp, cool and reads like a poem'. He said it would be one of the texts 'we shall examine at Makerere'.[5] The list of participants on the conference programme discussing his work included the likes of Langston Hughes, Ralph Ellison, Chinua Achebe, VS Naipaul, Ngũgĩ wa Thiong'o and Wole Soyinka, as well as a host of South African writers such as Alfred Hutchinson, Bloke Modisane, Arthur Maimane, Richard Rive, Peter Clarke, Lewis Nkosi, Randolph Vigne and Mphahlele himself. The confined La Guma was soon being contacted by publishers and writers from Brazil, Britain and Germany and his work started being translated into other languages. By 1964, his second novel, *And a Threefold Cord,* had been published in London to acclaim from *The Times Literary Supplement* and the *New Statesman*, which described it as 'brilliantly done'.[6] La Guma's third book *The Stone Country* was completed the next year, though publication would be delayed until 1967. By 1965, under the headline 'Another triumph for gagged Alex', it was reported that noted London-based jazz pianist Dollar Brand (later better known as Abdullah Ibrahim) was planning to adapt *A Walk in the Night* for a musical, working with the banned Cosmo Pieterse, Maud Damons who had fled South Africa after being charged under the Immorality Act, Mazisi Kunene who would be responsible for the lyrics and – Dollar Brand hoped – Duke Ellington. It would be a musical play in three-parts called 'Shush'. The career of the griot from District Six was on course, though he remained confined under 24-hour house arrest to the 50 square feet of land upon which stood his small home in Garlandale in Athlone, which Blanche had bought for them during the Treason Trial.[7]

La Guma's novels *In the Fog of the Seasons' End* (1972) and *Time of the Butcherbird* (1979) were written later, after his flight into exile. Though some critics argue that none of his subsequent fiction reached the heights of his first book, he became firmly established as a writer of international repute, his work being translated into many languages. He would be the recipient of important international awards, including the Lotus Prize for Literature presented by the Afro-Asian Writers Association, which he received from Prime Minister Indira Gandhi in New Delhi in 1969, and the Ordre des Arts et des Lettres, conferred by French Culture Secretary Jack Lang.[8]

After democracy La Guma's novels became freely available for the first time in South Africa. Prescribed in many university courses, they are also now the subject of a number of critical literary studies and have acquired canonical status within the field of African literature (see, for example, Field 2010).

The first 1993 edition of this book aimed to recover and make accessible the work and views of one of the 'lost', long-banned writers and political figures from the fifties and sixties, and to contextualise his South African 'world' before he was forced into a long exile. It consists of a selection of Alex La Guma's early writings before he became a published novelist. For six years, from 1956 to July 1962, when he was banned and officially silenced, La Guma worked as a journalist on the *New Age* newspaper, the unofficial mouthpiece of the Congress movement and the illegal Communist Party. Besides his news reports, he also wrote a long-running weekly column, 'Up my alley', crammed with provocative wit and irony, and he even created a cartoon strip. The *New Age* material forms the basis of this book.

The Early Writings of Alex La Guma provides unique cameos of South African life and politics during a turbulent time in the country's history – the late 1950s and early 1960s, the years just before and after Sharpeville. If the fact has not yet been fully appreciated, the following chapters will also show that La Guma was very much part of the explosion of new writing identified with the '*Drum* generation' of the fifties. These new writers were distinctly urban, confident in the language of the ghettos, and loud about exclusion and denial. They were the conductors of a new South African voice emerging at the time from the increasingly cosmopolitan and sprawling black townships being thrown up by an expanding industrial economy.

Richard Rive explained that being a *Drum* writer meant two different things 'according to whether one was in Cape Town or Johannesburg' (Rive 1989: 45). In Johannesburg there were writers like Henry Nxumalo, Todd Matshikiza, Casey Motsisi, Zeke Mphahlele and Bloke Modisane, 'essentially the Sophiatown people', while in Cape Town there was a much smaller group consisting of James Matthews, Alf Wannenburgh, Rive and La Guma, who used to meet regularly and read their stories to each other (Rive 1989; see also Kirkwood 1986: 104). While most of the *Drum* generation tended to shy away from active politics, La Guma, throughout his career, was a writer of commitment, virtually born into politics, and concerned always to balance the tension between creativity and struggle in his writings (see, for example, Asein 1986). He was to write:

> If life is a source of artistic inspiration, we will never be able to avoid social, political and economic problems. Of course, we do not limit ourselves to spouting slogans. We are creative artists, we have talent and we apply this talent in modern life to touch and excite the hearts of our readers. The literature that touches the human heart is a literature which reflects their best hopes and dreams, their human essence.[9]

* * * * *

Alex La Guma was born in Cape Town on 20 February 1925. He was the first child of Wilhelmina and James La Guma of No. 2 Roger Street, District Six. His father was a pioneering figure in the history of the South African liberation movement. After undergoing his political initiation while leading a diamond miners' strike in Lüderitz Bay in 1918, James (or Jimmy as he was commonly known) was soon at the forefront of national politics. By 1926, when his son was a year old, he was on both the national executive of the Industrial and Commercial Workers' Union of Africa (ICU) and the central committee of the Communist Party of South Africa (CPSA), playing a prominent and often controversial role in both organisations.

The ICU was the first black mass movement in South African politics. Led by Clements Kadalie, it spread like wildfire through the country in the 1920s, reaching a membership of 100 000 before disintegrating rapidly again at the end of the decade (see Bradford 1988 and Wickens 1978). James La Guma was at one stage assistant general secretary and 'one of Kadalie's most important lieutenants' (Gerhardt 1977: 18).

However, he was expelled when he refused to distance himself from the Communist Party at the insistence of Kadalie. Formed in 1921, the party initially focused primarily on the concerns of the more organised and skilled white workers. La Guma was a forceful early advocate of the Africanisation of the party, as well as the Native Republic thesis adopted in 1928, which emphasised the importance of a broad anti-imperialist struggle against colonialism and racism in South Africa rather than a narrow, class-based approach focusing only on the working class and trade unions. The programme was adopted at the insistence of the Communist International (Comintern) – and, in particular, of Nikolai Bukharin, an influential member of its executive, causing considerable tension within the South African party. La Guma, who travelled to Brussels for the 1927 League Against Imperialism Conference and twice to Russia in 1927 and met Bukharin, was thought to have played a part with his comrade Josiah T Gumede in the drafting of the Native Republic thesis. Its adoption was to have far-reaching political and theoretical consequences, eventually paving the way for the current alliance between the ANC and the Communist Party and the adoption by the party of an analysis which typified the South African situation as 'colonialism of a special type'.[10]

During a chequered career, James La Guma also held various other important positions. For a short while in the late 1920s, he was secretary of both the Western Cape ANC and the Federation of Non-European Trade Unions. In 1935 he became a founding member of the Cape Town-based National Liberation League (NLL). Formed in opposition to the moderate African Political Organisation of Dr Abdullah Abdurahman, and led by his daughter Cissie Gool, the

NLL adopted a radical programme calling for universal franchise, militant action and working-class unity across racial lines. However, it did not make much headway and disintegrated in 1939. After enlisting in the South African army at the outbreak of World War II, James spent seven years in uniform, reaching the rank of staff sergeant in the 'Indian-Malay' corps. After the war he continued to be active in politics. When the Communist Party dissolved itself in anticipation of the passing of the Suppression of Communism Act in 1950, he had again become a member of the central committee (following two expulsions). From 1957 to 1961, after Alex and other SACPO leaders had been charged with treason, James re-emerged from retirement to head the South African Coloured People's Organisation (later Coloured People's Congress). He was detained for four months during the 1960 State of Emergency following Sharpeville, and died in the following year, partly as a result of the effects of his detention.[11]

Alex La Guma, therefore, grew up in a political household, and was intimately connected through his father to the left-wing movement in Cape Town from its infancy in the 1920s through to the 1950s when he himself reached political maturity. He learned on his father's knee about Marxism and the key left issues of those decades, for instance, about the divisions internationally between orthodox communists and followers of 'permanent revolution' after the split between Stalin and Trotsky; how these translated into different analyses and strategic approaches with regard to the national and class struggles in South Africa; what programmes the early left groups in Cape Town such as the CPSA, NLL, Lenin Club, Workers' Party, Fourth International of South Africa, Non-European United Front, New Era Fellowship and All-African Convention followed; why they were often at odds with each other, and which personalities were involved; the wars against fascism in Europe; the institutionalisation of racism at home; the rise of a strong tradition of 'non-collaboration' at the Cape from the early 1940s onwards, which was given form by the Anti-CAD (Coloured Affairs Department) movement; and the Non-European Unity Movement and the Teachers' League of South Africa, whose Ten Point Programme differed fiercely from the approach of the Communist Party.[12] At an early age, Alex also whiffed the sweat and excitement of meetings, marches and clashes with authority. It is recorded that at the age of four his father carried him 'shoulder-high, waving the black, green and gold colours of the ANC, down Adderley St, in Cape Town during a demonstration against the Riotous Assemblies Act organised by the ANC, ICU and CPSA' (La Guma n.d.: 67–68). Aware that his father 'was always away at what were called meetings', his grandmother told him that this was because James was trying to help free workers and their children from poverty. She said he was following the example of the 'Uncle' in a picture that always hung on the wall of the family home: the Uncle's name was Lenin (La Guma 1975: 372–374). Alex remembered as a child seeing James under a red flag with a hammer and sickle on it. 'Once he went to prison and when I met him again at the prison gate, coming home, I remember I did not recognise him because he was wearing a thick beard. Only when he'd shaven, was he my father again'. And, 'all the time, one heard discussions of the teachings of Lenin' in the La Guma household, Alex later recalled (La Guma 1975: 372–374).

He acknowledged the influence of his father in those early years:

> My father had a great deal to do with moulding my philosophical and political outlook and guiding me towards the reading of serious works, both political and literary. He himself was an avid reader, and I suppose this had something to do with my development one way or the other ...
>
> I loved reading books. Since early childhood I was always looking for books. I read at first the books that children loved: Robert Louis Stevenson, Dumas, Victor Hugo, and so on. Then I read adventure stories, westerns, detective stories, and gradually began to turn towards the more serious classics such as Shakespeare, the Russian authors, Tolstoy, Gorky, and then the American writers, James T Farrell, Steinbeck and Hemingway. Whenever I could lay my hands on a book I took the opportunity. In fact, I used to use my meagre pocket money to buy books at second-hand bookstores and sometimes I had saved enough to enjoy the luxury of buying a book at an expensive bookstore. (Abrahams 1985: 3, 5–6)

By the time Alex was 12, he was being introduced to journalism by James, who was editing the monthly journal of the National Liberation League, *The Liberator*. Alex and the children of other editorial members assisted as 'artists' (La Guma n.d.: 86). This was an early indication of his creativity, artistic inclination and love for writing and story-telling. He recalled that he was popular among his peers at school because of an ability 'to spin yarns almost at will and to command their attention'. Also, that he 'always put pen to paper':

> On a couple of occasions, I produced essays in school which were read out to the class. It didn't strike me as being the genius of authorship, but the teachers said that I had a certain talent for writing. I used to concoct stories which were ... schoolboy adventures, and filling exercise books which mounted up at home. And I remember in the springtime when my mother cleaned out the house, then all my valuable manuscripts went into the garbage. (Abrahams 1985: 13)

Alex also attended art classes at the Hyman Liberman Institute in District Six. The institute was one of the few places of 'high' culture in District Six. Besides serving as a reading room for the 'poorer' people of Cape Town, it was used as a community centre. Its library was run by Christian Ziervogel, a bibliophile and member of the Fifteen Group political discussion circle of which James was a member (see Edgar 1992: 78–79, 332–333; Jeppie 1991: 73; La Guma n.d.: 80). Moreover, like many other families in District Six in the days before radio and the cinema provided relatively cheap mass entertainment, the La Gumas of Roger Street enjoyed family sing-songs. James La Guma could sing well and he composed lyrics on political issues which were set to popular tunes of the time, including 'Dark Folks Arise', the song of the National Liberation League which has been attributed to a collaboration between himself and Johnny Gomas. He played the piano, violin, guitar and mandolin, and while in the army during World War II, he organised a string band (La Guma n.d.: 10).[13] The mix of popular and 'high' culture that Alex imbibed as a child in District Six created a distinct style which fundamentally shaped his later writing and political activism.

Influenced by this patrilineal brand of Marxism, Alex La Guma volunteered in the fight against fascism at an early age. In 1938, as a 13-year-old schoolboy in his first year at Trafalgar High School, he tried to join the International Brigade supporting the Republican cause in Spain. Then in 1940, he tried to enlist for service in World War II. Both offers were promptly refused owing to a combination of his age and physical build.

In 1942 he left school and worked in a variety of jobs while completing his matriculation through night school at the Cape Town Technical College. Alex's first formal trade union involvement was in 1947 during the economic slump after the war, when he participated in a strike over low wages and poor working conditions at Metal Box Company, where he had been working for two years. After he was sacked he worked as a bookkeeper and as a clerk for Caltex, an American petroleum company. In 1947 – when he is thought to have written his first letter to the newspapers, a piece in the *Cape Standard*, celebrating the 26th anniversary of the CPSA[14] – he joined the Young Communist League, and the following year he became a member of District 20 of the Communist Party (Abrahams 1985: 6–7).

In 1950 the central committee of the CPSA voted to disband the party in the face of imminent banning by the Nationalist government. Although James was a member of the central committee at the time, he ruled that Alex – who was then still living at home – should distance himself from party activities and associations. No doubt James did not want his son to suffer restrictions and harassment, but the injunction, which Alex apparently obeyed, did not go down well with some of their comrades (Lerumo 1971: 82; Bunting and Kodesh interviews 25 July 1993).[15]

For the next few years Alex kept a relatively low political profile, although there was considerable political activity at the time in Cape Town aimed at new apartheid legislation and the government's attempts to remove coloured voters from the voters' roll. The Franchise Action Committee (FRAC) and the Non-European Unity Movement were at the centre of these protests. However, FRAC was unable to sustain itself beyond the 1952 Defiance Campaign and the activities against the tercentenary celebrations of Van Riebeeck's arrival at the Cape. In September 1953, remnants of FRAC formed the South African Coloured People's Organisation (SACPO), a national political organisation for coloured people that soon became part of the Congress Alliance. At this stage La Guma was still working in the 'art section' at Caltex, but in 1954 he became a full-time organiser for SACPO and an executive committee member. He was married in the same year to Blanche Herman, a nurse and midwife (Blanche La Guma interview 4 April 1989).

In the two years after Alex became organiser, the SACPO organised bus boycotts against segregation on the buses and local amenities in Cape Town; attempted to mobilise coloured people against the imposition of the Group Areas Act in the Cape Peninsula; protested against the Separate Representation of Voters Bill, which became law in 1956; and tried generally to promote the Congress Alliance (Lewis 1987: 269).

Alex was now moving towards political centre stage. In June 1955 he was elected an SACPO delegate to the Congress of the People. Among the other Western Cape delegates were George Peake, chair of SACPO, John Mtini, chair of the Western Cape ANC, Eveline Nqose of the Women's Anti-Pass Committee, and Albie Sachs, a 20-year-old law student from the University of Cape Town 'active in the Modern Youth Society'.[16] La Guma wrote:

> The Congress of the People is an historical occasion in the history of the struggle for liberation ... There the non-European and democratic forces will take stock of their forces and plan the final stages of the struggle. I look forward to attending it and hope that the example set by many other coloured people who are attending will be an inspiration to their people to come closer to the struggle for democracy in South Africa.[17]

But La Guma was one of the 60 Western Cape delegates who never reached Kliptown. They were detained en route at Beaufort West for the duration of the event.[18]

A few months after the Freedom Charter was adopted at the Congress of the People, La Guma became SACPO's national chairperson. The following year he became its more hands-on general secretary, with his long-time comrade Reg September replacing him in his old position. Freedom would only come through struggle, he said, and the coloured community must be prepared to 'stand shoulder to shoulder' with Africans in the process. He said for those in SACPO, 'it is better to fight like a lion than to be led to the slaughter like a sheep' (Field 2010: 60–61).[19] Field notes that in his political speeches at this time, La Guma displayed the same aggressive humour that 'usurps the power of the oppressors and uses it against them' that would become a feature of his later writing, including his Pampoen-onder-die-Bos stories in chapter 35 of this volume (Field 2010: 61).

Supporters of the Congress Alliance were exhorted to carry the Freedom Charter to every corner of the land, to acquaint all those who were outside the liberatory struggle with the ideas embodied in it.[20] But SACPO was an under-resourced organisation, and it battled to make headway.

For Alex, three big personal milestones loomed. In 1956, Blanche became pregnant with their first child, Eugene. This prevented her from working and the La Gumas had no income. Alex gave up his position as SACPO organiser – although he remained an executive committee member of SACPO and its successor, the Coloured People's Congress – and started work at *New Age*, the unofficial mouthpiece of the ANC and its allies. A few months later, in December 1956, La Guma and eleven other staff members of *New Age* were among the 156 members of the Congress Alliance who were arrested in dawn raids throughout the country and charged with treason.

*****

Alex La Guma's new job at *New Age* and his involvement in the long-running Treason Trial as 'Accused Number 85' dominated his life for the next few years, and set him firmly on the path to becoming both a writer and politician of national stature. The Treason Trial was a direct consequence of the adoption of the Freedom Charter 18 months earlier. Having resorted to mass action for the first time in the early fifties, the burgeoning African nationalist movement in the form of the ANC was now elaborating by means of the Charter a vision for a non-racial, democratic South Africa which was diametrically opposed to the policy of apartheid. The state clamped down, charging that the Charter was part of a communist-inspired conspiracy to foment revolution in South Africa. Pointing out parallels with the Nazi-inspired Reichstag fire trial in the 1930s, the Congress Alliance in turn used the trial to explain its democratic aspirations and to attack apartheid. The trial became another playing field in the contest for ideological hegemony between African and Afrikaner nationalism. It dragged on for five years, during which time the leadership of the Congress Alliance was largely incapacitated, and many of the accused lost their livelihoods before the state's case collapsed and all charges were withdrawn (see Forman & Sachs 1957; Pinnock 1993).

From the time of his arrest in December 1956 to October 1958, La Guma spent most of his time in Johannesburg. The trial gave him his first chance to visit there since 1928, when his father had briefly been general secretary of the Federation of Non-European Trade Unions (La Guma n.d.: 61–64). According to Blanche, 'Johannesburg was a new experience for him … and he was able to learn quite a few new things' (Blanche La Guma interview 4 April 1989). He made full use of the opportunity to acquaint himself with *eGoli*, writing on a variety of topics ranging from shebeens and illegal gambling to pass law arrests and the destruction of Sophiatown. Here he also confronted an apparently new phenomenon that precipitated further ironic observations about racial superiority, and about which Ruth First would later write about in her experiences of jail: 'white hobos littering the parks and the library gardens in dirty, dishevelled, diseased and wretched groups' (First 1972: 33). La Guma's dispatches from Johannesburg on the trial stressed a common experience and attitude among the defendants: despite the strength of the state, the threat of execution and the tedium of the proceedings, those brought together involuntarily in this 'people's parliament' developed a strong personal camaraderie and a deepening political commitment. There were also the lighter moments, for example: 'I'm objecting. My pal Barney Desai charged with incitement had his bail fixed at 100 quid. That's twice as much as my bail for treason. What do they think I am? A cheapskate'?[21]

Having recently started working as a journalist and with time on his hands during the trial, Alex now 'really started to write seriously'. In May 1957, the first of his nearly 250 weekly 'Up my alley' columns appeared in *New Age*. Following the publication of his first short story, 'Etude', submitted for the *New Age* short story competition and published in January 1957, he also started concentrating on writing short stories (Abrahams 1985).[22] With a large proportion of its staff on trial, and facing an unusually grave financial crisis in mid-1957, *New Age* was cut to four pages, and the staff received reduced salaries (Abrahams 1985: 9; Pinnock 1991: 1). To compound matters for the La Gumas, Blanche, who had been prominent in protests against the extension of apartheid practices in nursing, left the hospital at which she had been working and started a private practice.[23]

The problems faced by *New Age* and staff members on trial, such as Lionel Forman, Ruth First, Govan Mbeki, MP Naicker, Fred Carneson and Sonia Bunting, were not new ones. The newspaper has a unique place in the history of the South African press. Started in 1937 as *The*

Guardian, it appeared weekly for 25 years, becoming the longest-running left-wing newspaper in the country. Its survival has been described as something of a political and financial miracle:

> From week to week, it teetered on the brink of closure, with pennies in the bank and policemen at the door. It was banned outright five times, sued, fire-bombed, spied on and had its presses sealed. It was banned from news-stands and constantly raided by the police. Several Commissions of Enquiry investigated its activities. Its editors received personal banning orders, most of the staff were arrested and charged at one time or another, its street sellers were harassed and beaten up, and … staff members went on trial for high treason. (Pinnock 1991: 1)

When it was banned for the first time, it became only the second paper to be closed for political reasons since Lord Charles Somerset halted the *Commercial Advertiser* in 1824. It kept bouncing back, changing its name after every banning: from *The Guardian* to the *Clarion*, the *People's World*, *Advance*, *New Age* and finally *Spark*.[24]

The paper was important for a number of reasons. Firstly, it provided the Communist Party with an effective mouthpiece. Party members denied that it was an official organ, but this public stance was tactical. It was controlled and run by party members, it consistently reflected party policy and its position on international matters was virtually indistinguishable from the foreign policy of the Soviet Union. Secondly, the newspaper played an important role in building the Congress movement in the 1950s, laying the basis for the formal ANC–SACP alliance which was cemented in the 1960s. The dissolution of the CPSA in 1950, and the rapid growth of the ANC into a mass movement at the same time, encouraged communists to work much more closely with the national movement than they had in earlier decades. They started to give priority to the national struggle and threw their energies into it. This position was reflected in the pages of *Advance* and *New Age*. By the mid-1950s it had become the semi-official mouthpiece of the ANC, the 'weekly heartbeat' of the liberation movement. According to Don Pinnock, the ANC relied heavily on the skills, finances and media of the party and its members as it transformed itself from a 'disparate organisation (geographically compartmentalised and without funds or a newspaper)' into the 'single fighting force' it had become by the end of the 1950s (Pinnock 1991). The newspaper served as a key mobilising and organisational tool for the ANC and it was generally accepted that it was an important factor in consolidating the alliance between the ANC and the Communist Party in the face of growing state repression.

Though they continued to be active behind the scenes, the Treason Trialists were restricted from taking part openly in politics and this led to severe organisational problems within the Congress Alliance, including SACPO. With the president, George Peake, as well as La Guma (secretary general) and Reggie September (national chair) on trial, the organisation was faced with a leadership vacuum. James La Guma was persuaded to come out of retirement and take over as president at the 1957 conference (La Guma n.d.: 111). At the conference, SACPO once again rejected the Separate Representations of Voters Act and demanded voting rights for all South Africans. It also resolved to call for a boycott of the forthcoming elections in which coloureds would elect white representatives. But as the election drew closer, SACPO's position changed on the advice of the ANC. At a second conference later that year, it agreed to support white candidates whom SACPO had 'selected from persons who have already suffered and sacrificed on behalf of the liberatory movement'.[25]

As a result, coloured voters faced a choice between boycott tactics advocated by the Non-European Unity Movement, voting for the white opposition United Party, or supporting SACPO's belated entry with Congress of Democrats candidates. Piet Beyleveld, president of the Congress of Democrats and one of the Treason Trialists, contested the Cape Peninsula constituency, supported vocally by Alex La Guma in *New Age*. Much of his writing on this election alternated between support for Beyleveld and criticism of the Unity Movement, ridiculing its intellectualism and what he said was a contradiction between its name and its activities. 'The "Unity Movement" mob, looking at the parish through rose-coloured glasses, are inundating voters with lengthy screeds which, after close study (use a microscope), tell them not to vote for "dummy representatives".'[26] He also found space for bitter words about Cissie Gool, 'one-time styled as the Joan of Arc of the coloured people',[27] who was now backing Abe Bloomberg, the United Party candidate opposing Beyleveld. However, Beyleveld was heavily defeated and his performance reflected what, it was accepted later, was a generally confused approach by the Congress Alliance to the whites-only elections that year (Lodge 1985: 194–196).

An assassination attempt on Alex while he was working in his study at home one night in May 1958 came as further proof that his political profile was growing rather than decreasing. Two shots were fired at him through the window, one 'grazing his neck slightly'. La Guma received a threatening letter a few days later: 'Sorry we missed you. Will call again. The patriots' – but the attackers were never traced.[28] The following year he was again arrested for entering Nyanga township without a permit, after the car in which he was travelling with Ronald Segal and Joseph Morolong was stopped and found to have pamphlets calling for an economic boycott of Afrikaner nationalist-supporting firms in the boot.[29]

By then South Africa was on the slippery slope leading to Sharpeville, the banning of the ANC and the newly formed Pan Africanist Congress (PAC), the imposition of a state of emergency, and draconian security legislation which provided for detention without trial for extended periods. After Sharpeville, 20 000 people were arrested in countrywide swoops. La Guma was among them. Initially Blanche La Guma did not know where he was being held. 'We went from police station to police station, Wynberg and others, then we heard they were being held at Roeland Street' (Blanche La Guma interview 4 April 1989). The appearance of the detainees shocked her. 'They looked terrible, they looked wild', she recalled. She, Sadie Forman and Hettie September went to see Margaret Ballinger, one of the so-called 'Native Representatives' in parliament, after which she was allowed two half-hour visits per week. Then the visits were suddenly stopped. 'I nearly went mad ... banged on that bloody door ... because I demanded a visit' (Blanche La Guma interview 4 April 1989). She suspected, correctly, that Alex would be moved to Worcester. On the day of the move, she organised a lift to Worcester, where the prison authorities were very surprised to see her for the afternoon visiting times.

Despite his age and the fact that he was no longer politically involved, James La Guma was arrested together with his old comrade John Gomas and held for several months. The Black

Sash was able to arrange transport to Worcester on a regular basis. Sometimes Blanche and her mother-in-law Wilhelmina would be ready at 5 a.m. in order to arrive at the prison by 9 a.m.

The five months in prison during the emergency were not wasted for Alex. He was able to finish the manuscript of *A Walk in the Night*, which he had started in 1959 (Blanche La Guma interview 4 April 1989). And he came out armed with new material for his writing. When *New Age* started up again after being banned for five months during the post-Sharpeville clampdown, La Guma was 'once more in circulation and being nasty to the Nats'.[30] Concerned about the implications of the divided political response by coloured people to the State of Emergency and the liberation struggle, he also urged the coloured community 'to seriously assess their relationship with the struggle to liberate South Africa and the rest of the continent. Our place is with the active forces of progress so that we can honestly claim that we deserve our place in the sun.' Characteristically, he ended with a pun on the recent unsuccessful assassination attempt by David Pratt on Dr Verwoerd: 'Now I must stop Pratt-ling and get down to work'.[31]

In March 1961 Nelson Mandela organised the All-in Conference in Pietermaritzburg, which decided on a campaign that would lead to a national convention. The first phase would be a three-day national strike, to be followed by a campaign of 'mass non-cooperation' if the demand of the liberation movement for a convention was ignored. With the SACP, ANC and PAC banned, the surviving Alliance organisations carried an extra responsibility. During the next few months La Guma was hard at work preparing for the national stayaway timed to coincide with South Africa's inauguration as a Republic on 31 May, staying on the move and spending each night at a different address (Blanche La Guma interview 4 April 1989). Several large meetings were held in Cape Town, giving him hope that the stayaway would be successful. Describing this as the coloured community's biggest political undertaking, he predicted that the response would exceed the campaign by the Franchise Action Council exactly ten years before.[32] But the government took drastic measures against the stayaway. For the second time the La Gumas' house was attacked, as were the homes of other stayaway organisers. The army and police conducted nightly township searches and set up roadblocks. La Guma and four other Coloured People's Congress members were among the approximately ten thousand detained under a special 12-day detention law (Lodge 1985: 196).[33] *Fighting Talk* commented that this was a South Africa 'where martial law had been declared in all but name … and a "Republic" from which every vestige of the noble principles of republicanism had been deleted by the Verwoerdites'.[34]

Charged under the Suppression of Communism Act, La Guma was released in mid-June 1961. Although conditions were getting more and more difficult, he continued with his articles and his weekly column. He reported on the South African Coloured National Convention, which he had helped organise, though he was not able to attend the event. The convention was a continuation of the political agenda adopted by the All-in Conference, but it also reflected the limits of coloured commitment to the Freedom Charter, despite the fact that SACPO had committed itself to its principles. The Convention supported the idea of a non-racial national conference, rejected any 'special status' for coloureds, and demanded universal adult suffrage and an end to all forms of racial discrimination, but it also rejected the Charter's proposals for the nationalisation of private sector monopolies.[35]

In July 1961 the state imposed a five-year banning order on La Guma and the SACPO general secretary, Reg September, under the Suppression of Communism Act. In Cape Town an open air-meeting to protest against their banning drew 2 000 people.[36] Sadly, that month La Guma's father died of a heart attack in Groote Schuur hospital. Detention during the State of Emergency had badly affected his health.[37] The terms of his banning order prohibited Alex from attending gatherings in any capacity. Although this did not prevent him from writing, there were now very few articles on which his name appeared, though reports datelined Cape Town were attributed to 'A Reporter'. 'Up my alley' was the exception. The column became his only form of non-fictional, public expression. But as open expression was becoming increasingly difficult, he resorted more and more to allusory stories in his column, creating the rural backwater of Pampoen-onder-die-Bos as the setting. Reminiscent of Herman Charles Bosman's situations and characters, the stories provided a vehicle for his angry satirical wit, highlighting the horror, absurdity and hypocrisy of apartheid and white ruling-class politics, and enabled him to comment on current developments. His piece on Radio Pampoen-onder-die-Bos, whose 'call sign … can only be described as sounds made by an announcer trying to read through a gag'[38], ridiculed the National Party's rigid control of the South African Broadcasting Corporation and the xenophobic ignorance in which it left white South Africans, while the 'Christmas cracker which some skulker had put into Oom Van der Mielieblaar's festive pudding' deals with the first action of uMkhonto we Sizwe on 16 December 1961: 'But the last word was had by the Foreign Minister who sent out a special message from his ostrich farm: These things never happened at all, so there's no cause for alarm, man'.[39] Soon this avenue was cut off as well. 'Up my alley' appeared for the last time on 21 June 1962. By the following week, La Guma had been prohibited from publishing anything. *New Age* reproduced the column's usual heading with a blank space below and the word 'PROHIBITED' stamped across it.

* * * * *

As noted earlier, the bulk of the material in this book is drawn from Alex La Guma's writings in *New Age* between 1956, when he started working as a journalist, and 1962, when he had his first book of fiction published (and was prohibited from writing further). His 250-odd 'Up my alley' columns form the core of the *New Age* material used. These presented a big challenge to the editors: though crammed with rich material, 'Up my alley' generally consisted of fragments – particular subjects or events were often dealt with in only one or two paragraphs or a few lines at a time. A typical column in October 1958, for example, covered in less than 400 words the Treason Trial, the French referendum, the death of a miner, South Africa's 'bad press' overseas, an agricultural union congress and a tale about Jo'burg cinema-goers.[40] And in a piece of the same length a few weeks later, La Guma wrote about the Coloured Affairs Department, a religious tract, a municipal congress in Bloemfontein, an MP's visit to Scandinavia, an Indian South African's meeting with Pandit Nehru and statistics about 'European' women.[41] The challenge for La Guma every week was to be provocative, entertaining and illuminating on a range of issues in the pithiest way possible. That he generally succeeded in this attests to his writing skills, analytical clarity and his 'feel' for popular culture and opinion.

However, the fragmented, often disconnected and multitopical nature of the 'Up my alley' columns made the task of editing the material a difficult one. They could not simply be arranged chronologically to form a ready-made book. The only way to ensure coherence was literally to snip the columns and rearrange them thematically so that readers can get an overall picture of La Guma's views on the various issues of his day. Therefore, for the sake of readability, the material is not always arranged chronologically, even within chapters. To give one example: chapter 18 on Cape Town starts with two pieces written three months apart describing La Guma's return to the city after periods away from home. The piece written later, starting with 'It certainly is good to be back in my own stamping ground after many months', provides a ready introduction to the topic, and sits better placed before the earlier one, which starts with 'Hanover Street is still the place it was when I was removed to the Fort in Johannesburg last December'. And because the value of these two sketches lies mainly in their style and generalised description of Cape Town life (and historical accuracy is not being compromised) they have been put in reverse chronological order. While this approach by the editors creates a form of narrative in certain chapters that exists in tension with historical chronology, the net result is to give *The Early Writings of Alex La Guma* a coherence and flow it would not otherwise have had – indeed, it is doubtful whether the book would have been possible if this path had not been followed. Serious scholars wishing to approach La Guma from different angles can go back to the original columns, copies of which are available via the author and the UWC-RIM Mayibuye Archives.

To ensure that the reader is able to keep track of the editorial arrangements, the exact source for each of the pieces that make up the book is indicated at the end of each text. Square brackets and ellipses indicate editorial interventions and comments. These have been limited in order not to interrupt the flow of La Guma's writing. The editors also decided against the use of detailed footnotes to explain and contextualise pieces in the text. La Guma's subtle and punchy style when dealing with contemporary events would have required virtually hundreds of notes if every piece were to be contextualised fully. While many allusions may be too topical to be grasped readily by current readers, 'Dr EG the GG' (Dr EG Jansen, the Governor General) and 'Now I must stop Pratt-ling' (in the aftermath of Pratt's attempted assassination of Dr Verwoerd) can be enjoyed both in a superficial reading and on a more in-depth level by those with a historical knowledge of the period. 'Kerkbode Kudu', a character in a piece on the so-called Immorality Act and the attendant religious hypocrisy that went with it, works whether or not the reader knows that the *Kerkbode* was the monthly journal of the Dutch Reformed Church (see chapter 32 this volume). And the regular caricatures about the 'Enlarged Senators' do not require a knowledge of the National Party's misuse of constitutional devices in the 1950s to artificially change the constitution and enlarge the Senate to deprive the coloured voters of the franchise to have effect. Deconstructing the many sketches of this type for the reader would have turned this into an over-segmented work which only the most pedantic and intrepid would have been able to wade through.

Similarly, with La Guma's use of language: given his frequent resort to slang and the patois of the Cape – as when he urges readers to 'vote vir ou Piet' and when he refers to the coloured 'juniversity' (UWC), the 'Portagees' café, the 'genuwine Wild West show' and 'Herr Doktor' Verwoerd – the editors have decided it would serve little purpose to explain every deviation from standard English. One of Alex La Guma's strengths as a writer was that he could bring alive the popular culture of the Cape in which he was rooted. Reading him, one can almost hear the repartee of working-class Cape Town. He could write like that because 'he breathed the air of District Six', a friend recalled (Sarah Carneson interview 30 July 1993).

The Early Writings of Alex La Guma is divided into seven parts, each dealing with a theme from La Guma's writings. Part 1 focuses on everyday life in Cape Town, providing a background to South African life in general, the context for the unfolding story. Poverty, hardship, the shack-dweller, the unemployed, the skollie, the prostitute, the shebeener and the gangster – the underclasses form the basis of much of La Guma's writing. In assessments of his first two novels, Brian Bunting wrote:

> Nobody who has ever passed through District Six can ever forget its winding crowded streets, its jostling humanity, its smells, its poverty and wretchedness, its vivacity and infinite variety … [La Guma] knows the people and their problems … their hopes and fears. He knows the desperation and humiliation of poverty, the defiance which grows from despair, the hatred of 'the law' … Here are no cardboard characters strutting lifelessly through his pages, but real, live flesh and blood men and women who, though weighed down by the neglect and insult of the world, yet proclaim insistently their determination to survive, to eat, drink and make love, to endure the night.[42]

Bunting states: 'It could have been depressing, this picture of South Africa's lower depths, with its incidents of sordid brutality and infinite desolation. But Alex La Guma's compassion and fidelity to life infuse it with a basic optimism' (Bunting 1988: viii). These words apply aptly here.

Part 2 makes the link between the conditions and experiences of those living at the bottom of the pile and formal politics. In the heyday of apartheid, if you opposed oppression, it was called treason. La Guma's impressions from the Treason Trial of the 1950s provide a first-hand introduction to his own political activities and an insider's perspective on that historic event. Part 3 contains his reports from the 'City of Gold', and includes the cartoon strip of 'The Adventures of Liberation Chabalala', which was inspired by his sojourn in Johannesburg. Some of his prison sketches are provided in the photo inserts. In Part 4, La Guma is back 'Up my alley' in Cape Town. His cameos of everyday life there are supplemented by contemporary reports of a number of important (and still largely unchronicled) political events in the Cape between 1958 and 1962. Though not as comprehensive as they might have been, because many of his news articles were not directly credited to him, they nevertheless paint a fascinating picture of local politics. Part 5 on 'Cold Wars' highlights La Guma's international and ideological perspectives. A life-long socialist and anti-imperialist, he commented regularly on world events, usually making the link with what was happening in South Africa. A new chapter 31 (written in a later period) is included here describing how growing up in District 6 impelled him to join the Communist Party. Part 6 deals with La Guma's biting comments, both serious and satirical, on ruling-class politics. Never at a loss for words, he was merciless in showing up the absurdities of apartheid. In the Pampoen-onder-die-Bos stories referred to earlier, he mocks Afrikaner and colonial English-speaker holy cows, showing them up to be petty, small-minded and bigoted, inverting on behalf of the oppressed the superiority a racist apartheid establishment liked to assume for itself.

This book has a new Part 7, which describes the departure of the La Guma family from South Africa and how Alex quickly established himself in exile as an internationally recognised writer and high-level cultural and political ambassador for the Congress Movement and the SACP. It shows how, from being confined to home and detention for his last four years in South Africa, he grew wings, visiting dozens of countries and growing in his status as a writer in his exile years. A small sample of La Guma's non-fiction articles in exile is included to indicate how his departure from a censored South Africa and engagement with the world led him to new places, new themes and new ways of narrating his stories. He became a true internationalist, not only through his writings, but now also through extensive engagements in every continent in the world. Finally, Part 7 recognises the importance of Blanche La Guma in the life and work of Alex, and we see that though he did not live long enough to return home with Blanche, there was a homecoming of sorts for him in the way that his writing became recognised and canonised in democratic South Africa.

*****

What does Alex La Guma's early journalism tell us about his fiction? There are several connections worth pursuing. Firstly, many of the themes in his short stories and novels are first encountered and developed in the early newspaper articles found here. His second published story, 'Out of the Darkness', for example, appeared in *Africa South* shortly after two articles on prison conditions in Roeland Street jail, 'Ten Days in Roeland Street Jail' and 'Law of the Jungle Rules in Jail', and draws on them extensively.[43]

A brief comparative analysis of the articles and the story provides an opportunity to explore the process through which a political short story can emerge from contemporary or historical information – and continue to articulate the fear and hostility with which perceived deviations from a (hetero-)sexual norm, even if caused by the apartheid system, were received (on this, see Jeppie 1991: 63).

'Law of the Jungle' contains descriptions of a 'husky lifer' who 'prowled like a savage gorilla in captivity, giving vent to all the primeval brutalities forced upon him by frustration' (chapter 6 this volume), while in 'Out of the Darkness', one of the protagonists refers to a fellow inmate as an 'ape-man roaming a jungle … In a cave the cave-man is king' (chapter 7 this volume). In 'Out of the Darkness', La Guma replaces the earlier articles' stress on harsh prison conditions and homosexual rape with politically and sexually less threatening and more acceptable issues: the tale of a man whom the other inmates call 'Ou Kakkelak' (Old Cockroach), who had been imprisoned for killing a friend as a result of racial classification laws that alienated him from the woman he loved. In a feature common to his other stories from this period, such as 'A Matter of Honour', the participant narrator is more literate than most of the other characters. This difference enables the participant narrator to surmise that Ou Kakkelak may have been a teacher, which in turn enables him to use the latter's observation that the 'whole of mankind's history consists of a series of struggles' (chapter 7 this volume) as a device for suggesting why the narrator is in jail.

In 'Ten Days in Roeland Street Jail', Willie Frazer, a first offender on remand, describes how cockroaches prevent him from enjoying the food his wife had smuggled into the jail with the connivance of the most powerful convict in the cell, significantly known as the 'huis-baas', and thus ironically symbolic of the home's idealised nurturing organisation of pleasure and authority. 'The basin of food was there, but crawling with cockroaches. There were really thousands of them, rustling and clicking all over the food, gorging themselves' (chapter 5 this volume). By contrast, in 'Law of the Jungle', the cell's dominant inmate is presented as a physically powerful and sexually predatory figure who completely lacks the organisational skills and influence of the 'huis-baas', and who represents a desire that is legally and morally forbidden inside and outside the prison. As a precedent for the later portrait of Butcherboy Williams in *The Stone Country*, which has been described as 'fascinated, obsessive', La Guma has reverted to a 'nineteenth-century anthropology in which biological and cultural evolution are indistinguishable' (Carpenter 1991: 88).[44] These character traits may have contributed to this character's death in this novel, which was the last of his texts concerned primarily with prison life.

In the transition from the articles to the short story 'Out of the Darkness', the cockroach, which had previously denied the organised pleasure derived from the consumption of smuggled food, becomes Ou Kakkelak. This is a safe, non-threatening figure, 'like a snail withdrawn into its shell' (chapter 7 this volume), who pre-empts, mediates and diverts threatening and disorganised desire into socially acceptable and politically necessary resistance. As the jailer, a figure of power and organised oppression, approaches the cell, 'each man retreated quickly within himself' before he orders them to 'Shut [their] filthy mouths', but after his departure the ape-man 'hawked and spat straight onto the [cell] door' (chapter 7 this volume). Significantly it is the voice of organised political repression that precipitates the gesture of defiance which affirms the character's physicality and suggests that for La Guma, effective political resistance requires the denial of disorganised and threatening desire. Indeed, his third prison article, 'Sodomy and Assault in Roeland Street Jail', which appeared after the publication of 'Out of the Darkness', and which deals with prison justice, sodomy and the resistance of an imprisoned ANC member to prison conditions, suggests that what La Guma perceived as the law of the jungle could only be articulated, but never totally controlled and denied, after organised political resistance had been named and established.[45]

The prison articles and stories published before *A Walk in the Night* also provide us with insights into strengths and weaknesses of La Guma's narrative strategies. In 'Ten Days in Roeland Street Jail', La Guma's squeamish source loses his appetite when he sees cockroaches on the food. 'But not so with his fellow prisoners. What? This was real rice, roast meat and vegetables. Huis kos [home food]. To hell with the cockroaches. They brushed off the vermin quickly, and got stuck in' (chapter 5 this volume). While the report is clearly a comment on prison conditions, La Guma also extracts some humour out of the situation through rapid discursive shifts. From Willie Frazer's direct quotation consisting of fully formed sentences, the report changes to a combination of narration and reported speech articulated in phrases and sentences. After La Guma's intervention as narrator, 'But not so with his fellow prisoners', the narrative style shifts to the linguistic and physical responses of the long-term prisoners in the form of reported speech that mixes standard English with prison slang, before finally returning to the main narrative.

Reported speech and rapid, subtle discursive shifts enable La Guma to distinguish different groups, such as remand and serving prisoners, without interrupting the narrative flow. This is a practice common to oral literature and the novel, and since La Guma enjoyed telling stories to his friends as a child and read a great deal, we do not know if he applied it consciously or unconsciously. Its effect, however, is to blend the perspectives of author and characters into the text so that we understand each character from their own position while remaining receptive to the commentary that the writer communicates through the language, tone and actions he associates with each character.[46] Thus this story, which enacts a subversion of the fixed relations in language upon which cultural and political power depend, expresses the resistance to apartheid and authority that District Six and the culture of many of its inhabitants represented (see Fabian 1986).

But his writing did not always display this polyphonic quality, and a brief comparison with a clumsier manipulation of language and subjectivity will help to highlight a number of issues implicit in his movement between journalism, fiction and political work: the significance of the control of language in defining social groups and their access to power and authority in the conflict between oppressor and oppressed, and between sections within the oppressed – the difference between the existing consciousness of a class in itself and the liberatory potential of a class aware of its historically determined role (see Uspensky 1973).

La Guma's article on the contradiction between the image of Hollywood-style tough and independent cowboys and the struggle against segregated education in America's southern states, which is based on a conversation with unemployed youth in Hanover Street, avoids the reported speech forms which might have given individual characters greater specificity. Instead, it favours the imposed abstraction implicit in the phrase 'The general consensus of opinion turned out to be' with which he sums up their response to his contradiction.[47] Its message to the oppressors and to self-styled arbiters of left-wing political correctness is clearer – do not be fooled by appearances – but La Guma's use of language obstructs our participation in the event and distances us from the speakers as active subjects, thereby undermining the article's political intention.

The annual 'Coon Carnival', and the regular political and cultural debate it generated articulated an equally ambiguous response to the dominant white culture. 'Are the coons degrading, or not? Should they be abolished, boycotted, ignored, etc. etc.?', was a question asked every year.[48] Writing in *New Age* shortly before the Carnival in the new year of 1958, he enters the debate on an apparently dour and economistic note which simultaneously undermines and reinforces politically and culturally elitist arguments against the carnival:

> A people's cultural level can't be divorced from their economic level … and folks who are poor don't get a chance to develop, so they are only able to appreciate culture of

a lower type. The characters who are yelling about getting rid of the coons because it reveals a very low standard of culture and so on, have got the wrong end of the stick, I think. The big job is to raise the economic level of the people, with it their cultural level will go up, and the coons will die out.[49]

But his ending subverts the apparent seriousness of his own argument and asserts anti-authoritarian aspects of the popular culture of Cape Town's working-class coloured population with the high profile which Carnival troupes gave to the 'moffie' – a stereotypically gendered inner-city working-class male transvestite (see Jeppie 1991: 62). 'Last New Year's day I saw a coon with a picture of Herr Strijdom sewed to the seat of his pants. That's one coon whose side I'm on, anyway.'[50]

'A Matter of Honour', the other La Guma short story in this publication (chapter 8), first appeared in *Drum* in November 1958. Here La Guma does not use the historical present tense characteristic of the Americanised 'tough tale', but the story shares other features such as a background of petty crime, a close connection between local environment and character, and the bar-room world of Damon Runyon to which many *Drum* writers and contributors turned for stylistic and atmospheric inspiration (Chapman 1989: 201–217).

While 'Out of the Darkness' is set in a prison, the action in 'A Matter of Honour' occurs in a bar. Both stories take place in predominantly male worlds in which the women referred to have no physical presence, yet are seen as the precipitators of conflict between men, and both stories have a narrator who is literate and more literary than most of the people around him.

Two petty criminals, ex-husband and ex-lover of the same woman, end up in a fight after the handsome ex-lover has unwittingly gloated about his sexual conquest in the presence of the woman's ex-husband. The ex-lover, who was a boxer and 'backdoor man', expresses his amusement at the fact that after he left her, she became a prostitute. The ex-husband beats up and disfigures the ex-lover. The 'denouement' is achieved when the victor reveals his identity as the ex-husband, and informs the narrator and his companion that he was compelled to beat up the ex-lover because 'it was a matter of honour' (chapter 8 this volume). In this short story, La Guma established his characters deftly. He provides a plausible context for their interaction, shows that District Six was a socially and racially mixed area, and indicates upward and downward social mobility between District Six and the more affluent Walmer Estate higher up the slopes of Table Mountain. If the action ends unexpectedly, its moral conforms to the characters' assumptions about the power relations between men and men and between men and women.

But contemporary readers may regard the story's sexual politics as extremely problematic. Clearly, sexist references to women were not confined to *Drum* and other sensationalist magazines. Though politically progressive, in 1958 *New Age* decided to organise 'a gigantic beauty contest' and Miss New Age was crowned in August that year (Zug 1991: 69). La Guma drew the body of Rhumba, one of the female characters in Little Libby, with exaggerated curves, and while in Chinatown during the Treason Trial he meets 'a lady who was by no means Chinese, but who looked like Marilyn Monroe, Jayne Mansfield, La Lollo and Dorothy Radebe all rolled into one'.[51] (See also La Guma's 1970s description in chapter 31 of this volume of Habiba, who he remembered as being beautiful in her youth but who – because of

District Six's slum life – had become 'something which had been a woman' and now was 'just a hag', which underlines how his social concerns and the sexism of his age went together.) Nor was *Die Banier*, the conservative Cape Town coloured newspaper any different – it was quite prepared to illustrate 'vital statistics' of the coloured population with a woman in a bathing costume.

This and the unexpected conclusion to the action would confirm for Njabulo Ndebele that 'A Matter of Honour' displays the typical characteristics of *Drum* fiction – glitzy, violent and stereotyped. At the same time, Ndebele criticises the 'lack of specificity of place and character' and the absence of causality in 'protest literature' (Ndebele 1986: 147). Does this mean that the short stories La Guma wrote during this period fluctuate between political tableaux and that 'penchant for the spectacular' that Ndebele claims is characteristic of *Drum*'s apolitical fiction? At best, from Ndebele's perspective, La Guma's stories display bad politics and have improbable endings or play out good politics in a perfunctorily constructed context (Ndebele 1986).

Certainly, La Guma was not consistently adept at combining a well-told story with a political message. But where there were contradictions and inconsistencies in his work, we should consider the cultural and political context in which he became a journalist and writer. Many black writers of the time moved between and borrowed freely from the styles of fiction writing and journalism when reporting or producing short stories, and American gangster B-movies and pulp fiction contributed to this blurring of the boundaries between fact and fiction writing. One-time *Drum* boxing correspondent Arthur Maimane, who was educated at St Peter's College in Rosettenville and wrote detective stories under the name of Arthur Mogale, drew heavily on Peter Cheyney and Damon Runyon. American films played a large part in shaping his ideas about journalism. 'I never had any journalistic training … Everything I learnt about journalism, I learned from Hollywood', he later acknowledged (Arthur Maimane interviewed by I Manoim, quoted in Choonoo 1991: 12).

La Guma's fiction and journalism also show the impact of American popular culture. From 1966 to 1968, during his early years in exile, he wrote a series of detective stories based on the character of a fictitious African detective called Captain Zondie (Abrahams 1985: 17). But there were also significant political differences between him and the *Drum* generation, particularly the pro-Soviet and anti-imperialist culture of his family life, and left-wing culture from the Spanish Civil War to the Cold War, of which he was both product and producer. The result was an often ironic, sarcastic and satirical use of American popular cultural symbols.

During the Treason Trial, he mentions the regular presence of 'Special Branch dicks',[52] while the trialists voted Sergeant Sharp, Sgt Shark in 'Little Libby', 'matinee idol of the treason trial'.[53] At a press conference organised by the US embassy, a black American journalist, accompanied by an 'eagle-eyed hombre from the State Department', warned against the dangers of African nationalism. Even the music at this event, which should have been 'jazz as played in SA … sounded like jazz as it is played "back home" in the USA'. Having established the music's lack of authenticity, La Guma uses it to criticise one of his chief antagonists at the time, 'Dr Van der Ross (rhymes with brass)'.[54]

A later piece, written after South Africa had left the Commonwealth, on 'the ole Lone Rider Republic' run by 'Hank Verwoerd' and his 'ole buddy Six-gun Vorster of the sheriff's office', shows that La Guma could transform symbols of the Hollywood cowboy into effective political satire. This 'genuwine Wild West Show', with its 'Population Registration branding irons all nicely warmed up and ready to sizzle', had the 'only real, live and kickingest Westerners' with 'their own stamping grounds'.[55]

While the Cold War mediated his perceptions of American popular culture, it also produced its own symbols, the most popular being the space race of the late fifties and early sixties. Sputnik confirmed the Soviet Union's superiority over the United States: 'Big politicians in the States might try to make excuses for not being able to beat the Russians to the draw when it comes to launching satellites, but the little people will remain convinced that the Russians have got what it takes'.[56] He was amused at the fear and envy the Soviet Union generated among proponents of *die rooigevaar*, as well as by their inability to think beyond a limited frame of reference:

> So you want to be a spaceman, huh? … Well, boetie, you'll have to become a Springbok first … According to 'an Afrikaner's' description of Yuri Gagarin reported in *Die Burger* he looked as handsome as a Springbok centre! That's about the highest you can rise in the estimation of Afrikanerdom!'[57]

As he acknowledged, Sputnik also provided 'the most effective sales-talk for socialism'.[58]

Assessments of *Drum* as an articulation of urban African culture have tended to concentrate on two areas: firstly, the apparent contradiction of a commercially successful magazine that carried pin-ups and salacious articles alongside serious exposés and short stories of literary merit, and secondly, analyses of the class and ideological position of its writers as an African 'petty bourgeoisie', the so-called '*Drum* generation', in relation to the development of the ANC into a mass-based organisation. As a journalist and writer, La Guma's class position was 'petty bourgeois', but while Bloke Modisane might burn his ANC Youth League membership card (Chapman 1989: 203), and Can Themba might express ambivalent support for the ANC in 'The Bottom of the Bottle' (Themba 1961), La Guma's commitment to mass politics and active involvement in the Congress Alliance deepened. La Guma's rejection of 'art for art's sake' provides obvious support for critics who see only a committed communist writer and lament the increasing mechanisation of his literary plots. Ironically, without assuming that the social pressures and political constraints he experienced were automatically and comprehensively restrictive, we should look to his journalism and politics, the practices out of which his fictional writing emerged, for evidence that his celebration of the anti-authoritarian and his sense of irony, characteristics of the early and non-literary La Guma, never disappeared.

Politics separated La Guma from the 'Drum generation' and may even have saved him from its members early deaths. Johannesburg writers generally set many of their stories in areas where they were familiar figures and which they knew well. La Guma never experienced the 'swarming, cacophonous, strutting, brawling, vibrating life' that Can Themba described in 'Requiem for Sophiatown', for by the time he arrived in Johannesburg to attend the Treason

Trial, the area was a ruin – its community scattered and emotionally broken. But Cape Town, with its vibrant District Six, cold wet winters and callous government attitudes towards African family life, provided its own ready-made material for the socially committed writer. This was the wellspring of La Guma's creative energy and the source of his narratives.

The relationship between La Guma's work in the later 1950s and early 1960s – particularly the acclaimed *A Walk in the Night* published in 1962 – and his subsequent texts poses numerous questions for La Guma criticism and scholarship. Was *A Walk in the Night* his most coherent and original text? Did extended house arrest and banning from 1962 onwards set in motion an artistic decline that exile in 1966 and separation from his subject matter exacerbated, or did these experiences act as aesthetic and political catalysts? Can La Guma's work from *A Walk in the Night* onwards be characterised as a drive to repeat a limited number of memories in a variety of combinations precipitated by the subsequent experiences in exile? Which memories was he driven to repeat?

Alternatively, were his works driven by a dialectic in which each successive major literary text transcends, internalises and preserves its predecessor in a process marked by an increasingly sophisticated historical consciousness accompanied by ever greater political and compositional sophistication? While the scope of such an analysis requires a more comprehensive assessment, a brief examination of some aspects of *A Walk in the Night* may be useful.

The book is prefaced with a quotation from *Hamlet*, which provides the novel's title, indicates its subject matter and introduces Uncle Doughty, whose accidental death precipitates Michael Adonis's descent into crime and Willieboy's death. A brief examination of the character of Willieboy in relation to the plot of *A Walk in the Night* suggests that a process of repetition may already be at work in La Guma's writing. Willieboy is one of the 'Dead-End Kids of Hanover Street' (Abrahams 1985: 4), whose dreams of personal power and grandeur were based on Hollywood B-movies. La Guma would have had contact with many possible subjects as a child, an adolescent and a politically active journalist. As an adult he recalled meeting Daniel, an old boyhood friend with whom he had lost contact as a result of the Group Areas Act: 'He was not the same Daniel I had known before. He had become a gangster, been to prison, and his whole life before him didn't hold any sort of rosy prospects. It was quite a moving, touching experience for me to meet a victim of the circumstances which he couldn't cope with' (Abrahams 1985: 4).

But the character also draws heavily on the style and content of *Drum* magazine writing, particularly a three-hander entitled 'Willie-Boy' written by Cape Town contemporaries James Matthews, Richard Rive and Peter Clarke. There are similarities between Matthews' and Clarke's contributions and *A Walk in the Night* in the death of Mr Doughty and the scolding calls of his mother as Willieboy dies in the back of the police van, while Rive's sketch articulates Willieboy's desire for violent revenge and his response of automatic guilt at the sight of two policemen. He also presents the cinema as a source of refuge from the world through fantasy (Rive 1963). But La Guma's collaboration with Matthews, Rive and Wannenburgh in the anthology *Quartet* precludes any accusation of bad faith, and from a post-modernist perspective the presence of a sketch in *New Age* entitled 'Willie' and the Willie Frazer referred to earlier suggests that for the *New Age* audience the character was already established, thus making irrelevant narrow questions about origin.[59] Indeed, chapter 5 in this volume, 'Ten days in Roeland Street jail', shows La Guma had already framed the Willie Frazer character back in 1956.

However, the corollary attached to rejection of questions of literary origin is the acceptance that we can read the text in a variety of ways. An overtly and politically self-conscious reading might establish one of La Guma's most pressing political concerns – the need for united action among the coloured population against oppression and exploitation. The lack of organised resistance to forced removals and the threatened destruction of District Six itself provided a powerful reminder of the gap between political consciousness and the need for political action and organisation.

Alternatively, behind and beneath this concern was the figure of his father, who continued to make his presence felt. From this perspective, the novel's underlying concern is not with James La Guma's recent death, since his father was alive when he finished the novel, but with the effect of a father who was both influential and absent, and whose political conflicts and expulsions presented him as both powerful and vulnerable. Though influential, his father's extensive political activity meant that there were times during his infancy and childhood when Alex saw little of him. As he later recalled, 'I seldom saw my father … He was always away at what were called meetings' (La Guma 1975). The information provided by Alex's biography of James suggests that the latter's politics determined and mediated much of the son's relationship with his father.

Alex La Guma drew on and was influenced by contemporary popular culture and accessible sources of classical culture. These ranged from the Coon Carnival, *Drum* and American B-movies and pulp fiction to events at the Hyman Liberman Institute and symphony concerts at the Cape Town City Hall, established literary classics such as *And Quiet Flows the Don* and *Candide*, Robert Tressell's *The Ragged Trousered Philanthropists* and other working-class literature his father had collected. Family life was a significant aspect of District Six culture, but cramped living conditions made life on the streets equally important and interesting for a young boy. He later maintained contact with the gangsters of the area, informing them of recent developments and incorporating their thoughts and feelings into his work (Blanche La Guma interview 4 April 1989). This provided him with a rich source of experience and information for his journalism and fiction. It also contributed to the powerful sense of place which *A Walk in the Night* communicates. But he was also aware of the differences between these gangsters and himself, and this finds expression where he speaks for rather than with people about whom he is writing.

As a child, Alex La Guma was exposed to a broad spectrum of approaches to nationalist and class struggles in South Africa. His father's visits to the Soviet Union, and his work in the CPSA and other left groups, underpinned Alex's own support for the Soviet Union throughout the Cold War until his death in 1985 in Havana. These factors contributed to the strong political and class consciousness evident in his early political work, journalism and fiction. Though this consciousness marked him as a serious and politically committed writer, and was probably the cause of a materialist determinism in his fiction, it was often balanced and undermined by an irreverence that articulated his identification with the individualistic anti-authoritarian and subversive tendencies in coloured urban working-class and lumpenproletarian culture.

His political work and writing during this period largely focused on issues of concern to coloured people in the Western Cape, and the depth of his involvement can be judged by the fact that only *Time of the Butcherbird*, his last published novel, does not have a majority of coloured protagonists. While he assumed a coloured social and political identity, he clearly rejected definitions of coloured identity based on fatalism, cynicism and escapism – corollaries of the carnivalesque. Change could be brought about through struggle. And as a member of the Communist Party and the Congress Alliance, he made it clear in his work and writing that coloured people had no future outside the liberation struggle led by the African majority.[60]

Alex would have approved when Blanche wrote at the time of his death: 'Well, life goes on and the struggle continues until final victory'.[61] Only the bravest or most foolish would answer with an unqualified 'yes' – but there is no denying that the liberation struggle and democracy have profoundly changed South Africa for the better in many ways.

In 1991 Blanche was able to return to the country again after a quarter of a century. Attending the musical *Fairyland*, which deals with the exuberance of working-class life in the old District Six, she was 'really gripped', crying with laughter at the sharp humour and expressions. Afterwards she said, 'How Alex would have enjoyed seeing it'.[62] After all, this was a validation of his own struggles over decades to gain recognition and respect for ordinary working people, their culture, idioms and aspirations. But the words of his characters from Hanover Street in 1956 still cast a haunting question mark over the future: 'Die country het white supremacy, maar ... nie jobs nie'.[63]

André Odendaal and Roger Field, 1993 and 2024

Roger Field is the author of Alex La Guma: A Literary & Political Biography *(2010, Jacana). After returning from exile, he joined the Department of English at the University of the Western Cape. He is retired and currently immersed in the study of classical Greek poets.*

Notes

1. Silber G, Censorship, *Sunday Times Magazine*, 25 July 1993: 21.
2. Bunting B, Alex La Guma's first novel – banned by the Sabotage Act, *New Age*, 9 August 1962.
3. See Alex La Guma personal scrapbook, Hendrickse B [secretary to Alex La Guma], 3 July 1962, UWC-RIM Mayibuye Archives, Alex La Guma Collection, MCH 118-2-1.
4. Writer's conference at Kampala: What *is* African literature, *New Age*, 28 June 1962.
5. Alex La Guma personal scrapbook, Zeke Mphahlele to Alex La Guma, 28 May 1962, UWC-RIM Mayibuye Archives, Alex La Guma Collection, MCH 118-2-1.
6. Alex La Guma personal scrapbook, Mbari Writer's Conference programme and various other items, UWC-RIM Mayibuye Archives, Alex La Guma Collection, MCH 118-2-1.
7. Alex La Guma personal scrapbook: 'Dollar turns La Guma novel into musical', *Post*, [date unclear] and 'Cape exiles to star in London', *Post*, 27 May 1965, UWC-RIM Mayibuye Archives, Alex La Guma Collection, MCH 118-2-1.
8. Obituary Alex La Guma, *The Times* (London), 23 November 1985.
9. Alex La Guma personal scrapbook, Moscow News, Information, 24/78, UWC-RIM Mayibuye Archives, Alex La Guma Collection, MCH 118-2-1.
10. For details of La Guma's role in the CPSA in the 1920s and the proposal in Brussels, see James La Guma Obituary, *New Age*, 3 August 1961; La Guma (n.d.): 19–39; and Simons & Simons 1983: chapter 17.
11. Biographical details taken from Gerhardt (1977); La Guma A (n.d.); and Simons & Simons 1983.
12. The different left strategies and organisations in the Cape over the years are discussed in Rassool C (1987).
13. This is probably the original source of the song referred to in the first page of this Introduction.
14. See *Cape Standard*, 5 August 1947.
15. Ray Simons (interview with Roger Field, 23 June 1993) claims that James took this step because politically he felt it was important that as many party members as possible were not restricted.
16. *New Age*, 23 June 1955.
17. *New Age*, 23 June 1955.
18. Police throughout Union alerted to hinder congress, *New Age*, 30 June 1955.
19. See chapter 3 of Field's work (2010) for more on La Guma's political activism from 1947 to 1956.
20. Resolution adopted by the Congress of the People, *New Age*, 30 June 1955.
21. Up my alley, *New Age*, 21 November 1957.
22. *New Age* organised three short story competitions, held in 1956, 1957 and 1958. By contrast with *Drum*, which began its competition in 1951 with a first prize of £50 and £4 for every story published, the *New Age* competitions were small-scale and financially unrewarding. But, when *Drum* later started to cut its fiction content in favour of feature articles, *New Age* and the other political journals supporting the Congress movement, *Africa South* and *Fighting Talk*, became the most sympathetic outlets for socially committed writers.
23. See also Nursing apartheid will ruin a noble profession, *New Age*, 20 June 1957, and A child is born, *New Age*, 2 August 1956.
24. The discussion on *New Age* is taken from Forman and Odendaal 1992: xxi–xxii.
25. SACPO to fight elections, *New Age*, 26 December 1957.
26. Up my alley, *New Age*, 3 April 1958.
27. Up my alley, *New Age*, 27 March 1958.
28. Shots fired at New Age reporter, *New Age*, 15 May 1958.

29 Africa South editor arrested, lists seized, *New Age*, 18 June 1959.
30 Up my alley, *New Age*, 8 September 1960.
31 Up my alley, *New Age*, 8 September 1960.
32 Coloured support for mass demonstrations, *New Age*, 4 May 1961.
33 Another wave of raids and arrests, *New Age*, 4 May 1961.
34 Doyle A, Striking out under the Republic, *Fighting Talk*, July 1961.
35 Coloured Convention outwits the government, *New Age*, 13 July 1961.
36 2 000 protest at banning of CPC leaders, *New Age*, 27 July 1961.
37 Death of Mr Jimmy La Guma, *New Age*, 3 August 1961.
38 Up my alley, *New Age*, 9 November 1961.
39 Up my alley, *New Age*, 28 December 1961.
40 Up my alley, *New Age*, 23 October 1958.
41 Up my alley, *New Age*, 20 November 1958.
42 See Bunting B, 'Alex La Guma's first novel – Banned by the Sabotage Act', *New Age*, 9 August 1962: 6; Bunting B (1988/1964) Preface. In A La Guma *And a threefold cord*, London: Kliptown Books.
43 La Guma A, Ten days in Roeland Street jail, *New Age*, 27 September 1956; La Guma A, Law of the jungle rules in jail, *New Age*, 4 October 1954; La Guma A, Out of the darkness, *Africa South*, October–December 1957.
44 William Carpenter (1991), JM Coetzee (1971), Gareth Cornwell (2002) and Adrian Roscoe (1977) have noted the frequency with which cockroaches are referred to in La Guma's work.
45 La Guma A, Ten days in Roeland Street jail, *New Age*, 27 September 1956; Sodomy and assault in Roeland Street jail, *New Age*, 22 May 1958.
46 Analysis based on Voloshinov (1971).
47 Up my alley, *New Age*, 3 October 1957.
48 Up my alley, *New Age*, 5 December 1957.
49 Up my alley, *New Age*, 5 December 1957.
50 Up my alley, *New Age*, 5 December 1957.
51 Up my alley, *New Age*, 18 July 1957.
52 Up my alley, *New Age*, 5 September 1957.
53 Up my alley, *New Age*, 23 January 1958.
54 Up my alley, *New Age*, 29 January 1959.
55 Up my alley, *New Age*, 7 September 1961.
56 Up my alley, *New Age*, 14 November 1957.
57 Up my alley, *New Age*, 20 April 1961.
58 Up my alley, *New Age*, 19 December 1957.
59 See Rive 1963; La Guma A, Ten days in Roeland Street jail, *New Age*, 29 September 1956.
60 For some of La Guma's later writing on the subject, see La Guma 1972; Dear comrade editor [letter to the editor], *Sechaba*, June 1984; and Dear comrade editor [letter to the editor], *Sechaba*, November 1984.
61 La Guma B, personal communication to W Kodesh, 19 November 1985.
62 La Guma B, personal communication to A Odendaal, 5 April 1991.
63 La Guma A, The dead-end kids of Hanover Street, *New Age*, 20 September 1956.

References

Abrahams CA (1985) *Alex La Guma*. Boston: Twayne Publishers

Asein SO (1986) Alex La Guma's short fiction. *Tricontinental.* 5(March): 5–10

Bradford H (1988) *A taste of freedom: The ICU in rural South Africa, 1924–1930.* Johannesburg: Ravan Press

Bunting B (1988) Preface. In A La Guma *And a threefold cord*. London: Kliptown Books

Carpenter W (1991) Ovals, ellipses and sundry bulges: Alex La Guma imagines the human body. *Research in African Literatures* 4(22): 79–98

Chapman M (ed.) (1989) *The 'Drum' decade*. Pietermaritzburg: University of Natal Press

Choonoo N (1991) Exposing the system: The protest tradition in African literary journalism during the apartheid era. Paper presented at the conference A Century of the Resistance Press in South Africa, UWC Historical and Cultural Centre, Cape Town (June)

Coetzee JM (1971) Alex La Guma and the responsibilities of the South African writer. In J Okpaku (ed.) *New African literature and the arts, Vol. 3*. New York: Third World

Cornwell G (2002) *And a threefold cord*: La Guma's neglected masterpiece? *Literator* 23(3): a343

Edgar RR (ed.) (1992) *An African American in South Africa: The travel notes of Ralph J Bunche, 28 September 1937 – 1 January 1938*. Johannesburg: Wits University Press

Fabian J (1986) *Language and colonial power*. Berkeley: University of California Press

Field R (2010) *Alex La Guma: A literary and political biography*. Johannesburg: Jacana

First R (1972) *117 days*. London: Penguin

Forman L & Sachs ES (1957) *The South African Treason Trial*. London: John Calder

Forman S & Odendaal (eds) (1992) *A trumpet from the housetops: The selected writings of Lionel Forman*. London: Zed Books

Gerhardt GM (1977) Political profiles, 1882–1964. In T Karis & GM Carter (eds.) *From protest to challenge: A documentary history of African politics in South Africa, 1882–1964, Volume 4*. Stanford: Hoover Institution Press

Jeppie S (1991) Aspects of popular culture and class expression in inner city Cape Town, circa 1939–1959. MA thesis, University of Cape Town

Kirkwood M (1986) Fifties people. *Leadership South Africa* 5(6): 100–104

La Guma A (n.d.) *A biography of James La Guma* (unpublished manuscript commissioned by the James La Guma Memorial Committee)

La Guma A (1972) *Apartheid and the coloured people of South Africa*, United Nations Unit on Apartheid, Department of Political and Security Council Affairs, Notes and Documents, No. 18/72

La Guma A (1975) The picture in the parlour. In *Lenin in profile: World writers and artists on Lenin*. Moscow: Progress Publishers

Lerumo A (1971) *Fifty fighting years: The Communist Party of South Africa 1921–1971*. London: Inkuleko Publications

Lewis G (1987) *Between the wire and the wall: A history of South African 'coloured' politics*. Cape Town: David Philip

Lodge T (1985) *Black politics since 1945*. Johannesburg: Ravan Press

Moore G (1980) *Twelve African writers*. London: Hutchinson University Library for Africa

Ndebele N (1986) The rediscovery of the ordinary: Some new writings in South Africa. *Journal of Southern African Studies* 12(2): 143–157

Pinnock D (1991) Keep the red flag flying. Paper presented at the conference A Century of the Resistance Press in South Africa, UWC Historical and Cultural Centre (June)

Pinnock D (1993) Writing left: Ruth First and radical South African journalism in the 1950s. PhD thesis, Rhodes University

Rassool C (1987) Going back to our roots: Aspects of Marxist and radical thought and politics in South Africa 1930–1960. MA thesis, Northwestern University

Rive R (ed.) (1963) *Quartet: New voices from South Africa*. New York: Crown Publishers

Rive R (1989) An interview with Richard Rive. Interviewed by Abraham de Vries. *Current Writing: Text and Reception in Southern Africa* 1(1): 45–55

Roscoe A (1977) *Uhuru's fire: African literature east to south*. Cambridge: Cambridge University Press

Simons J & Simons R (1983) *Class and colour in South Africa 1850–1950*. London: Penguin

Themba C (1961) The bottom of the bottle. *Africa South in Exile* 5(3): 49–55

Uspensky B (1973) *A poetics of composition*. Berkeley: University of California Press

Voloshinov VN (1971) Reported speech. In L Matejka and K Pomorska (eds). *Readings in Russian poetics: Formalist and structuralist views*. Cambridge MA: MIT Press

Wickens PL (1978) *The Industrial and Commercial Workers' Union of Africa*. Cape Town: Oxford University Press

Zug J (1991) Mouthpiece of the revolution: The history of a progressive South African newspaper. Hons thesis, Dartmouth College

Interviews

Brian Bunting, Alex La Guma's long-standing SACP/ANC comrade, Cape Town, 25 July 1993

Sarah Carneson, Alex La Guma's long-standing SACP/ANC comrade, Cape Town, 30 July 1993

Wolfie Kodesh, Alex La Guma's long-standing SACP/ANC comrade, Cape Town, 25 July 1993

Blanche La Guma, Alex La Guma's wife and comrade, London, 4 April 1989

Ray Simons, Alex La Guma's long-standing SACP/ANC comrade, Cape Town, 23 June 1993

Part 1
Theatre of life

1

Identical books

There is a story told among the old people which says that one day, many years ago, God summoned White Man and Coloured Man and placed two boxes before them. One box was very big and the other small. God then turned to Coloured Man and told him to choose one of the boxes. Coloured Man immediately chose the bigger and left the other to White Man. When he opened his box, Coloured Man found a pick and a shovel inside it; White Man found gold in his box.

The people have many explanations for their lot. Some of these take the form of folk-tales, superstitions and myths; others are downright logical. But in all there is a common consciousness that oppression, suffering and hardship are facts of life. And they have learned to temper hardship with humour, and to sweeten the bitter pill of their drab lives with the honey of a satirical philosophy. But always they have been aware of pain.

According to the census there are 1 170 000 coloured people in South Africa. Herded into slums, shivering in shanties, scattered along the hillsides, rocking in buses to housing schemes, living comfortably in bright homes: Frigidaire, His Master's Voice, Edblo. They toil in thousands in big factories and push vegetable barrows, dig up roads and teach in schools, grow flowers and run shops. They steal and sometimes murder, they beg or carry loads from the markets. They drink, curse, make love and beat their wives or cheat their husbands. Heroes and cowards, villains and gentlemen, saints and sinners, people.

They went through wars and marched through the muck of France and Belgium. They sweated in Abyssinia, Egypt and Libya, and stole the company beer, laughed at the German army and cracked jokes as the dive-bombers hurled steel death at them. Some of them died and the rest came home and shook their heads and wondered what they had fought for. They voted at the polls and shook their heads some more. They clashed with the police when they became a little tired of voting, and held their bloody heads. The law, harness-bulls, carried its guns openly afterwards, to honour them.

I passed a tiny mission church one night and stopped at the door to listen. The flock was gathered under the pale light of a single bulb, and on the whitewashed wall at one end Christ looked down in his agony. The old preacher spoke and said: 'Thus saith the Lord God: Let it suffice you, O princes of Israel; remove violence and spoil, and execute judgement and justice, take away your exactions from my people …' He was an old man whose face had known pain and whose hands had grown hard with toil in the country. His collar was frayed and his shoulders stooped. His voice was warm as a mother's touch. His people listened and murmured their Amens when he had finished. They sang and the air was full of their happiness and their agony was lifted from them for that brief time.

Saturday night is dance-night. The hall is crowded by nine o'clock and the band has got into its stride. The drummer has taken his coat off and the saxophonist is tireless. The bassman's head wags with each slap of the strings. 'Mister Sandman, Give Me a Dream …' Kwela. Commercial quadrilles: Arm in arm, corner swing, halfway, home James. Sambas all the way from Brazil. The girls are gay, wild, ecstatic. Their brilliant skirts whirl and their hairdos are awry; red lips parted, panting; eyes bright as jewels. The boys are sharp in their zoot-suits, yellow socks and Tony Curtis haircuts. They swagger between the dances, showing off their patterned neck-ties and jingling their silver wrist chains. When it is over and the band plays the Queen they scatter reluctantly, perspiring. 'See you next week.' 'Drill Hall.' 'Philadelphia rhythms.'

In the slums the people huddle, sleeping on staircases and in packed rooms. Everywhere is the smell of stale cooking, sweat and stagnant water. On the corners groups gather in the lamplight and the dice come out and the pennies and tickeys clink on the asphalt. Somewhere a guitar twangs quietly and then ripples as skilful self-taught fingers fly along the frets. The music throbs and an artificially hardened voice rises:

> Onder deze piesang boom,
> Al op 'n eilandtjie,
> Daar staan ons twee te vry,
> Sy rol haar ogies vir my …

When the pubs close the shebeens are open for business. The mailers work all day buying in stocks and are paid a commission on each bottle they obtain. Coloureds are only allowed two bottles of wine per day, or one brandy, so the mailers move from store to store, giving false names and addresses. You can drink in elegant parlours where liquor is served discreetly in teapots, or in sordid little dens where children watch wide-eyed as the bootleg bottles are pulled from hiding places in backyard drains and from under the floorboards. Anywhere you pay through your neck: the cheapest wine costs three-and-six-pence a bottle, and brandy ranges from fifteen to twenty-five shillings. It is whispered that the big houses pay protection to keep the police away.

Yankee ship just come in, and the taxis ply their trade between the docks and the bawdy houses. 'Know a place we can meet some gals, buster?' There are places. A house can be pointed out where the girls are beautiful as fashion models, and others where bitter, ground-under, young-old professionals smile blearily and flash their gold fillings.

* * * * *

There was a man I heard of who possessed a plot of ground but had no money to buy building materials. So for a whole year he scavenged amongst the rubble of demolished blocks and in other odd places. He carried bricks and timber and sheet-iron to his site in small loads. He carted sand from the beach and scrounged cement and built a house.

* * * * *

In the third-class carriage they were packed tight. I sat opposite a big tough-looking docker and talked to him. His face was streaked with coal-dust and dried sweat and he wore a loading hook in his belt.

'The government?—'

'What are we going to do about it?'

He spat through the window. 'Don't worry, chummy. We'll give them a go some day. Same as Hitler got.'

When the pegamoid covers have been placed over the office machinery and the massive ledgers have been stored in the vaults, the cleaners take over. Stout, middle-aged ladies armed with dusters and brooms. Cooking has to be done early so that supper will be ready when the old man comes home. Nelly or Rachel or Tiema can dish up. High above the lighted city, in chrome, plush and marble offices they work and exchange gossip through the buzz of vacuum cleaners.

'The ou was full of nonsense again last night. Wish he'd stop his blerry drinking.'

'Did you hear about Mrs Meyer's daughter? Going to have a baby and won't say who the father is. The children of today …'

'What did the Chinaman pull today?'

On the Grand Parade the unemployed sit, chatting idly, around the base of a statue. 'Never king had more loyal subjects.'

The census declares that we are almost one and a quarter million. But if you identify a people, not by names and the colour of their skin, but by hardship and joy, pleasure and suffering, cherished hopes and broken dreams, the grinding monotony of toil without gain, despair and starvation, illiteracy, tuberculosis and malnutrition, laughter and vice, ignorance, genius, superstition, ageless wisdom and undying confidence, love and hatred, then you will have to give up counting. People are like identical books with only different dustjackets. The title and the text are the same.

And since man is only human, he must rise in the morning, throw off the blanket of night and look at the sun.

A pick and a shovel, *New Age*, 30 August 1956

2

A day at court

To many of the people in the crowds that gather in the long hallway inside the building, the magistrate's court in Cape Town is just another centre of attraction.

The idle gather there, unemployed workers, messengers and chauffeurs, passing their time listening to judgment being passed on their unfortunate fellows who have overstepped the law, sitting through the long rigmarole of the administration of justice, following each case with a mixed air of sadistic humour and well-intended pity.

To others, the groups of whispering people gathered nervously around the doorways marked 'Witnesses', the red-brick building in Buitenkant Street is a place abhorred, a place where no 'respectable person' should be seen.

But to all it is a great theatre of human drama, of tragedy and comedy, where lives can be broken or repaired, marred or made clean.

The car thieves

In the Regional Court two young, well-dressed European youths faced the magistrate. They had just been found guilty of car theft. The administrator of justice shook his head and clucked. What had got into two nice young men like them to have done such a thing? They could spoil their lives. They must try to turn over a new leaf in future. They could apply for positions in the Civil Service, even if they had a criminal record. Would they promise to turn over a new leaf in future? Four strokes. And six months' imprisonment suspended for three years. They needn't be removed back to jail for the lashes. The sergeant would see to them downstairs.

The clerk of the court rustled his papers, cops standing around eased their gun harnesses.

Man from Glasgow?

'Percy Dreyer!'

The accused shuffled up into the box from underground: a lank figure with a shaven head, long beaked nose and bug-eyes. The prisoner was accused of stealing an overcoat out of a car. The owner of the coat gave testimony that he had left his car parked with one door unlocked, and upon returning to it fifteen minutes later had found the coat (Exhibit A) missing.

Preston, an African, was called next. He had been at his home in Caledon Street one night when the prisoner had arrived with a woman. He, the prisoner, had said he was from Glasgow and had offered to sell the coat. Preston had accepted and paid two pounds two shillings and sixpence to Dreyer. He had not recognised the prisoner at the identification parade, but later when he had seen the woman with him in court he was positive that this was the man from Glasgow.

'Have you understood everything the witness has said?' asked the magistrate.

The prisoner cupped a hand to an ear and leaned forward looking puzzled.

'He's deaf, Your Worship,' somebody said.

His Worship stared, then gazed ceilingward with a sigh. Would the clerk please repeat everything to the accused?

The clerk began to bellow into the ear of the accused, who nodded sagely, glancing at the witness now and then. When the clerk had exhausted himself, His Worship asked whether the accused had any questions to put to the witness.

Percy put on his best legalistic air. He had the confidence of one who had gone through this kind of thing before. He coughed into his fist, glared at the witness.

'Agbaar, how is it that the witness recognises me now after thirty-five days, with my head shaven, if he couldn't identify me a day after the alleged crime with all my hair on?'

The witness was certain that this was the man from Glasgow.

How did the witness know? Was the house dark or lighted up?

A wrangle started. 'You cannot argue with the witness!' roared His Worship. The witness was finally not sure whether this was the man who sold him the coat.

Florence was called. Scarred and battered but firm as a rock. She was the wife of the accused. She had accompanied him to a house where they had met Preston. Percy had sold him the coat (Exhibit A) for the sum previously mentioned.

The magistrate looked half-amused, half-bewildered. Florence was Percy's wife, wasn't she? Yes, they had been living together for the last six years. To Percy, 'You hear? She says you had the coat and you sold it to that other man.'

It wasn't true. He knew nothing about the coat. She was lying to get him into trouble. She was jealous because he had had another woman. He wasn't living with Florence any longer. Florence maintained firmly that she was still his wife.

The dispenser of justice eased his collar away from his throat, gulped and fiddled with his papers. Percy was called to give evidence from the witness-box.

'Agbaar, on the twenty-ninth of the eighth month I was coming from Mowberry. I came up Primrose Street and in Caledon Street I heard somebody call my name. It was Florence. She says to me, Hoe gaan 'it. I says, Not so bed. And she says, You feel like a liddle dring? And I says, Ek sal nie mind nie. So we go into a smokkel-huis in Caledon Street and she buys me a borreltjie.'

His Agbaar mopped his brow feverishly. The cops grinned behind their hands. The public tittered.

Percy returned to the dock later, pleased with his display of forensic oratory.

The court recovered itself. Justice scowled across at the prisoner.

'Are you really a Scotchman? Well, Scotchmen are supposed to be lucky. You are lucky. I am going to give you the benefit of the doubt. Case dismissed.' Sighs of relief.

From the doorway Florence called gaily: 'Percy, I'm waiting outside.'

The oldster

In another court-room an elderly European stood in the box. He was one of society's derelicts, disowned, cast aside like chaff by the great thresher of life. Stoop-shouldered, wrinkled, with hair uncut in his neck, he stood in the dock, bewildered, broken and scared.

A magistrate with a hatchet face and a dry voice spoke unemotionally. The detective in the stand had said that he had found the old man wandering about in Buitenkant Street in the early hours of the morning. 'He has known you over the past four months as one who does not want to work. You sleep in empty houses on the foreshore. You have a long record. Have you anything to say before I pass sentence?'

The old man looked frightened, mumbled meaninglessly, and shook his head. A flat-nosed harness-bull grinned at his mate.

'Three months' imprisonment with compulsory labour. Next case.'

And so the show goes on. Before the cynical eye of the armed police, the interested gaze of the public, the blindfolded eyes of justice, the play passes with its varied scenes of despair, love, hatred, violence and lust. Day by day, new faces, new actors, but one old story which started with the beginning of the human race which will go on unending: Life.

Alex La Guma spends a day at court, *New Age*, 1 November 1956

3

The dead-end kids of Hanover Street

From Castle Bridge to Sheppard Street, Hanover Street runs through the heart of District Six, and along it one can feel the pulse-beats of society. It is the main artery of the local world of haves and have-nots, the prosperous and the poor, the struggling and the idle, the weak and the strong. Its colour is in the bright enamel signs, the neon lights, the shop-fronts, the littered gutters and draped washing. Pepsi Cola. Commando Cigarettes. Sale Now On. Its life blood is the hawkers bawling their wares above the jazz from the music shops: 'Aartappels, ja. Uiwe, ja'; ragged youngsters leaping on and off the speeding trackless trams with the agility of monkeys; harassed mothers getting in the groceries; shop assistants; the Durango Kids of 1956; and the knots of loungers under the balconies and in the doorways leading up to the dim and mysterious rooms above the rows of shops and cafés.

People have come to regard these youngsters with suspicion, and many make a detour when coming within sight of them. The brass-buttoned caps, the studded belts and the dangling shirt-tails are often identified with battle, murder and sudden death.

But often they have been judged without being tried.

We want to work

In the shadow of a veranda a group of young men kicked their heels and watched life pass by. 'People will see our picture in the paper and say, "There are some more skollies,"' one of them told me. 'They say that we don't want to work. Everybody wants to work. Everybody wants to earn a living. We want to work, too.'

Gasant Fredericks, 22, said: 'I've got a wife and child. They've got to eat, and I've been unemployed for nine months already. I'm tired of hanging around the Labour Department. I might as well hang around here.'

On another part of the street a bunch of hard-faced youths, dressed in new sweat-shirts and wide-brimmed hats, broke up as I approached. 'O's is camera shy, pal,' one of them grinned as they drifted into a nearby 'Social Club'.

Up and down the street there are little knots of them, chatting idly, chaffing the girls walking by. 'Ek sê, bokkie, hoe is't dan?' They play cards on the pavement or debate the merits of a popular movie star, usually one of the screen toughs. Humphrey Bogart, Burt Lancaster.

In the opinion of a doctor who practises in Hanover Street: 'The parents, in order to try to live at a decent level, inevitably get into debt. As a result the mother has to go out to work, the child is left with another woman who probably has problems of her own, or a number of other children to care for, so that she is unable to handle them all properly. They get no proper care. There is no control. The first words the children learn are curses. They are allowed to wander around in surroundings of vice, squalor and crime. Parental affection and care is virtually non-existent. The children drift into a world that holds no future except degradation.'

A struggle to survive

Most of the boys have little or no education. From childhood they must augment the family income as newsboys and hawkers. The whole of life becomes a struggle to survive, by any means whatsoever. But they are nevertheless aware of some of the causes of their plight.

The police are Number One Enemies to them. Many of them have undergone the beatings in the cells. They have a bitter disregard for anybody with a white skin, the badge of privilege and good jobs, lots of money and leisure. They dislike the 'Stiffies' among their own people who condemn them and look upon them as the dregs of society.

Many of them have talent. On the balcony of a tenement a group of boys went through an impromptu jam session with guitar, bass and maracas that would make any jazz expert wonder. 'Lady Be Good.' 'The Sheik of Araby.' But the only outlet for their talent is through the coon carnival at the beginning of each year, or at contests held at local cinemas.

Waiting

They hang around all day, waiting for something to turn up. Hanging around and waiting. Perhaps the police will pick up some of them for gambling on the pavement or for vagrancy, and they will go to jail. After that comes the swift ride down the dark tunnel to the underworld, the gangs, the sharpened kitchen knives, the bicycle chains. Perhaps some of them will get work, but it will be just another dead-end job. The swift ride may be delayed.

Hanging around and waiting. Slums, disease, unemployment, lack of education, the terrible weight of the colour-bar which withholds the finer things of life – all help to grind them down until many of them become beasts of prey roaming an unfriendly jungle.

As one of them put it to me: 'Die country het white supremacy, maar hulle het nie jobs nie.'

The dead-end kids of Hanover Street, *New Age*, 20 September 1956

4

In the shadow of the kwela-kwela

The old story of clearing up the so-called 'black spots', turning people out of their homes and not providing alternative accommodation, is being repeated in Windermere, one of Cape Town's oldest slums.

And this time the municipal Native administration officials are swooping at 4 a.m. to start pulling down pondokkies with crowbars, ropes and jeeps.

Dwellings have been pulled down over the heads of old women, men and children, and many families have moved into the bush for want of anywhere else to go.

The underlying motive for the actions of the authorities is preparation for the removal of African families to the dreaded Nyanga Location and 'bachelors' to the barracks at Langa.

An example of this action is the case of Mr Johnstone Tsebu. Mr Tsebu is a pensioner, over 60 years old, and had lived in Windermere so long he cannot remember. His house had cost £63 to build and had been standing for years.

Yet he received notice from the Cape Town City Council, stating that he was 'in the course of erecting a pondokkie' and that it was to be demolished 'by noon on the 19 November 1957', and, although a widower with a daughter, he was to move to the bachelor's quarters at Langa.

At 4 a.m. last Wednesday, officials and workmen from the Native Administration Department arrived and ordered out Mr Tsebu, his daughter and other occupants of the house, and removed them to the municipal offices nearby.

The passes of Mr Tsebu's visitor and another man were taken by the officials and they were told to remain at the offices until they had been examined. The daughter's papers were found to be 'out of order' and she was removed to Langa where the court later sentenced her to 10 days or £2.

Johnstone Tsebu was then told to return to the site of his dwelling and had to stand by, watching, while municipal workmen attacked it with crowbars, levers and other tools and tore it down.

They took three hours to break down the structure.

The houses of neighbours who had been rounded up at the same time were dealt with in the same way. One house was torn down with a rope attached to a jeep.

But although the demolition of shacks is supposed, at this stage, to apply to those owned by bachelors, whole African families have been turned out and their homes destroyed.

Officials have said cynically that the heads of these families are in fact bachelors, with reputed wives who should return to the reserves.

At a loss as to what to do, and in fear of municipal officials, a number of residents wrote a letter to the *Cape Times* drawing the attention of the public to their plight and pointing out that although they were willing to move out of slum conditions, no alternative housing was being provided for them. The letter, at the time of going to press, was not published.

The African people in Windermere are now living with a sword of Damocles over their heads, expecting the authorities to issue notices to quit and to arrive to tear down their homes at any minute. At the same time the arrogance of officials, particularly a Mr Terblanche who is about 22 years old and recently transferred from Langa to Windermere, has aggravated the feeling of resentment, hopelessness and frustration.

Houses pulled down over heads of women and children, *New Age*, 28 November 1957

[In New Nyanga too] the African shack-dwellers know that as soon as they've found a place to settle and build their homes, the authorities will be there moving them on again. And that when they've moved on and settled and built again, the authorities will be back, telling them to get away.

It's like some terrible nightmare, without meaning, filled with terror.

…

An atmosphere of fear pervades the sandy wastes of the African site-and-service camp there. Hundreds of women have been refused renewal of their permits to remain in the proclaimed area, and have been ordered to leave almost immediately.

'New Nyanga' was established as a screening camp for Africans, but it has become a home for hundreds of families who were removed from other parts of the Peninsula. Money and toil went into the erection of dwellings which in the majority of cases have taken on a permanent aspect.

But now, suddenly like a bolt from the blue, the meagre world which these families were forced to build in the packing-case and iron-sheet desert is crumbling under the rubber stamp of the Native Administration authorities at Langa.

Women who have gone to the registration offices at Langa to have their permits to remain in the area renewed have been told that they must leave the proclaimed area. In most cases two or three weeks' notice has been given, and many consider themselves 'lucky' to get four to six weeks.

Already many have packed up and left their homes for the place of their birth.

And a large number of women have been arrested in police raids on those whose notice period has expired.

Women who have left their place of birth in childhood and no longer have homes or relations there asked the officials where they were expected to go.

'Go to the river, or to the sea, anywhere,' was the reply. 'But we don't want you in Cape Town.'

'And what about our children and husbands?'

'Take them with you.'

One woman said, 'The permits seem to be more important than our families. The people must get the government's permission to live with their families. And if you do not have a permit they can divorce you forcibly from your husband.'

Another woman is being treated by a doctor for an ailment and a medical certificate states that if this treatment is not successful she will have to be admitted to Groote Schuur Hospital, but the officials at Langa simply ignored her certificate and extended her permit only long enough to 'pack her belongings'.

Many other women have lived in the Cape since the days when the African location was at Ndabeni, twenty years ago, long before Langa was established, and have no place outside the Peninsula to which to move. Many more are those who were moved from the Elsies River area where they had been living for years until the removals to Nyanga started.

Mrs Hilda Dlamini came to the Cape when she was two years old and is now 20 and has no relations in the Transkei, but she has been told that her permit will not be renewed when she applies again.

Another who has been in the Peninsula since 1938 and at Nyanga since 1955 lost her permit, and when she approached the authorities for another, was turned away.

When she protested that she would be arrested for being in the area without a permit, she was told, 'That is a matter for you and the police. It is not our business.'

There is also the case of a woman who paid over £30 to certain people in order to obtain a permit to remain in the area with her husband. All that money has gone down the drain because she has been told to get out.

And those husbands who do not accompany their wives and families will have to go to the 'bachelor's quarters' at Langa.

Daily, women who have stood for hours in long queues at Langa are turned away with orders to leave the proclaimed area, and the Nyanga camp is now standing in the shadow of the kwela-kwela.

Ordered out of their homes, *New Age*, 12 December 1957

5

Ten days in Roeland Street jail

In Roeland Street, Cape Town, with the blue bulk of Table Mountain in the background, stands the mass of brick and stone which is the city jail. In spite of the carefully tended lawns and flowers which front it, this place has never been able to disguise the cold atmosphere about it, and none of the periodic statements of prison authorities have succeeded in glorifying its grim record. It is a place where criminals are always punished, but seldom reformed. Hardened old-timers refer to it with macabre humour as 'Oubaas', and behind its walls exists a world ruled by stony-eyed guards who have become as cold as the iron bars over the windows, and long-term convicts as calloused and hard as the stones which enclose them.

Justice is replaced by fear, and fear is not an efficient reformer.

Willie Frazer [not his real name] spent ten days in the remand yard where prisoners awaiting trial are held, and as far as he is concerned it was enough. There first offenders, juveniles and petty criminals mingled and rubbed shoulders with the old graduates of the underworld: gangsters, thugs, thieves, torpedoes (hired bullies) and killers; and what he saw and lived there is his own story and a memory that will be with him always.

Willie Frazer was picked up by the police for carrying an unlicensed firearm. It was his first offence.

After spending five days in the Wynberg Police Station he was transferred along with a group of other criminals to Roeland Street. Upon arrival inside the jail, everybody was lined up. A long-term convict took the height of each newcomer, calling out the measurements to a warder: 'Six-foot-one, baas. Five-foot-ten, baas.' Another convict took thumb-prints on small blue cards and snarled at anybody who moved too slowly.

While they waited, Willie Frazer says, a young man who had just been sentenced to death arrived from the Supreme Court. A guard snapped:

'Who did you kill? A white man or a hotnot or a kaffir?' The murderer hesitated and an attendant convict growled at him to answer the baas promptly, and correctly. 'A hotnot,' the condemned man mumbled. He was then issued with a new uniform, red jersey and shorts, and removed to the section where the condemned awaiting transfer to Pretoria for execution are kept.

The file moved on. The snarling trusties went on taking measurements and prints. Each man was issued with an identification card. With Willie Frazer were four charged with murder, several with housebreaking, and a deaf-mute for robbery. After that they were ordered to strip naked and were led to the showers. Those who wished to dry themselves had to use their shirts as towels. The toughs merely pulled their clothes on over their wet bodies. More orders were yelled and the prisoners lined up and were marched into the remand yard, a long rectangular space surrounded by the walls of cell blocks, to join others awaiting trial.

The first night Willie Frazer together with others spent in a big cell casually referred to as 'Opstairs'. It was lighted by a single dim electric bulb and had the luxury of a wooden floor. A bucket served as a latrine. Opposite this cell are the single 'boxes' where juveniles are held.

The following night the prisoners were divided into squads of twelves and allocated cells on the ground floor. Each cell was in charge of a 'huis-baas' who kept order and cleaned the cell every day. He was usually one who had served imprisonment before, and who knew the ropes. The man in charge of Willie Frazer's squad was an old lag awaiting trial for murder. The prisoners slept in rows on threadbare blankets, called 'gonnies' in prison slang. There were two latrine buckets and a bigger bucket of drinking water.

'Before turning in for the night we were marched upstairs where we had to strip down to our shirts and pack the rest of our clothes away. We were then taken in single file to our cells. At the cell door we lined up. A guard looked into our mouths in case anything was hidden there. The rest of our bodies were searched and then we were let into the cell one at a time. Nothing can be taken in at night. On one occasion a prisoner attempted to smuggle in a cigarette hidden under a bandage on his hand. He was beaten up on the spot and removed to one of the "boxes".'

There are no watches among the prisoners, but the 'old cons' can judge the time of day pretty closely. It is between five and six o'clock in the morning when the cells are opened and their inmates hustled into the cold dawn to the showers. Everybody lines up in their shirts and a superintendent checks the number of people present. Then, after dressing, breakfast is served: pap without salt or sugar. After breakfast they are crowded into cells near the showers, about fifty to a cell, packed in so tight that it is impossible to sit. The single wire-meshed and barbed window provides poor ventilation and the smell is awful. Cigarettes appear, but there are no 'hond' (matches). Somebody had invented a primitive but ingenious device consisting of a tiny container stuffed with charred flannel, a sliver of steel from a razor blade and a point of flint stuck in the stub of pencil. Flint and steel are struck and the flannel smoulders. Cigarettes are lighted.

For hours the prisoners remain in their uncomfortable position, just standing with nothing to do, until lunch-time when they are let out again: beans, mealie-rice, a tiny chunk of sweet-potato or turnip. Back to the cell, cramped, sweating, waiting for supper-time. The day ends at four o'clock and supper is two slices of bread, about two or three inches thick, smeared with a dab of what appears to be margarine. Then back to the cell blocks in twelves. Strip, search, the doors clang and another day is gone.

Once a week is washing day. A scrap of hard blue soap and a scrubbing brush are issued, and everybody gets down at the ditch across the middle of the yard to do their clothes. When the washing is hung up all laid out to dry, each man watches his property with hawk eyes. But the old-timers rule with unchallenged authority. A new shirt, a smart jacket and they claim them, looking about, hard-faced, for the owners to object. Nobody dares protest or complain to the guards. In the yard the strong and the violent are kings. The law of the jungle has returned.

The guards watch, but the 'agterryers' keep a harder discipline, see that the yard is clean, give orders. Gangleaders, they assume authority according to the positions they held in the underworld outside. To question or to challenge them is to provoke a wrath more terrible than that of the official guards.

Those in the remand yard are entitled to more privileges than serving convicts. Their families can bring them food at meal-times, and see them twice a week. But the food delivered at the gates passes through the hands of trusties who help themselves to the choicest morsels. Food from outside is transferred to tin 'bakkies', often rusty. Packets of cigarettes are opened and examined, but never reach their owners full. Those who have money on their Property Sheets are able to buy sugar, coffee or soap, and the cost is deducted when they leave.

Willie Frazer says: 'One Sunday our "huis-baas" agreed to smuggle the dinner my wife had brought me into our cell that night. By some unknown means he was able to do that, and that evening we filed in, looking forward to sharing a decent bit of grub. The basin of food was there, but crawling with cockroaches. There were really thousands of them, rustling and clicking over the food, gorging themselves. My stomach turned, and all my appetite for Sunday dinner left me.'

But not so with his fellow prisoners. What? This was real rice, roast meat and vegetables. Huis kos. To hell with the cockroaches. They brushed off the vermin quickly, and got stuck in. When he came up for trial Willie Frazer was found guilty. He paid his fine. Ten days in Roeland Street's remand yard had shaken him, and he wanted to get away from it. 'He looked like a ghost when he came out,' his wife said.

But what happens to those who are sentenced without the option of a fine? What happens beyond the remand yard? Willie Frazer is unemployed now. What does the future hold for him?

Ten days in Roeland Street jail, *New Age*, 27 September 1956

6

Law of the jungle

Crime has no colour-bar, but evidently punishment in South Africa has. In Cape Town's Roeland Street jail, white hard-labour criminals work sitting on benches made comfortable with cushions, and protected from the weather under long sheds. Stones are transported from Bellville quarries for them to break up inside jail. The vast majority of non-white prisoners work outside, on farms and public buildings in the city. Non-European prisoners are issued with shorts and red flannel shirts, and although those serving more than one year are entitled to long trousers and shoes, these luxuries are only acquired after considerable effort on the part of the convicts. Europeans wear shoes and socks, long trousers, khaki shirts, and in winter receive long-sleeved jerseys.

These are some of the revelations made by one hard-labour prisoner, relating his experiences behind the high walls of Cape Town's notorious 'Big House'.

The sight of white men being given comparatively easy treatment for crimes similar to those for which they are being punished serves to deepen the hatred of non-European convicts for a system which discriminates on the grounds of colour and has little intention of reform.

Food is bad all round in jail, but, come mealtimes, Europeans are better off than non-Europeans. The European's breakfast: pap with sugar, coffee and bread; lunch: soup and bread; supper: beans, soup, bread and coffee. A non-white convict's diet consists of pap with salt for breakfast, cooked mealies at midday, and bread and fat with coffee for supper.

Day begins at 5 o'clock in the morning. All over the jail bells ring, the convicts rise from their huddled sleep to fold the vermin-infested blankets, unwashed for years, in fact never to be washed, but to be used until they simply wear away into nothing. Again the bells ring and they line up in twos, in the half light of dawn coming in through the barred windows. The heavy doors grind open and the human cattle are counted under the watchful eyes of armed guards.

Orders are snapped and the long rows march into the wide yard, surrounded by the grim walls. At the gates leading from the cells the stern faced 'corpies' (guards) watch with guns ready for any sign of resistance or rebellion. Those who cannot follow the orders are sometimes savagely beaten. Once in the open the men squat in rows along white lines painted on the floor of the yard, eating their pap served in rusty, metal bowls.

'You eat from the middle of the mess, working your way down to the bottom and towards the sides of the bowl, until you get near the rust,' my informant says. 'Then you have to stop, unless you are very hungry and don't mind the rust.'

The work-gangs of 10 to 15 men are assembled. Those allocated to work on farms in the country are transported by lorries. Convicts detailed for labour at nearby police stations and

European schools are marched through the streets, carrying the four-gallon bucket containing cooked mealies which will be their midday meal.

Treatment in the work-gangs is hard. Handling is rough, and the convicts are not allowed to stop for a drink of water when they become thirsty. They are often beaten when they slacken through tiredness. At 4.30 p.m. they are marched back to the prison house to a nightmare.

In the cells packed tight with forty or fifty convicts – men who have graduated from the violent college of the underworld, murderers, gangsters, vicious desperadoes – the weak are doomed to an existence of terror and depravity.

Shut off for years from normal life men become slavering beasts preying upon their own sex. The young and defenceless men are forced to submit to abnormal relations and are threatened with death or torture if they refuse. The meek are easily conquered and the tougher elements escape only after desperate and savage fights.

One husky lifer used to strike terror into his cell-mates. Doomed to spend all his days in jail, he prowled like a savage gorilla in captivity, giving vent to all the primeval brutalities forced upon him by frustration.

Only the strong dared challenge him. The weak cowered, whimpering, before him and surrendered. Discovered with a young convict one night, he was taken away, found guilty of this misconduct and flogged. But it is not through strokes with a cane that these men will be cured of the animalism which overcomes them.

In the hard-labour yard the convicts squat during mealtimes and Saturday afternoons, under the cold eyes of the 'corpies'. They have learned to talk without moving their lips in the manner of prisoners all over the world. Smuggled 'foo' (tobacco) is passed around furtively, and quick pulls of smoke are taken when the gaze of the nearest guard shifts. Ingenious methods have been discovered to secrete tiny things which make life a little more tolerable. Even dagga, known as 'majat' in prison slang, finds its way into the cells.

Medical treatment is scanty. Minor ailments are completely ignored. Roeland Street has a hospital for 12 to 15 patients only, attended by a warder with First Aid qualifications. A doctor from outside is in attendance on Wednesdays and Saturdays only, and until he calls on these days, castor oil or epsom salts are the standard medicines for all sicknesses. Most convicts suffer from stomach complaints because of the poor food received.

Some of the long-term prisoners are put to work as yard-boys, office-boys and cooks, positions of comparative ease and coveted by their less fortunate fellows. There is George M—, a lifer who is doing his thirteenth year in jail. Barefooted and grey-haired, a broken man with a friendly air, he cooks the prison meals. Now about fifty years old, he has forgotten the outside world and has adapted himself to his caged existence with calm resignation.

Sunday is the day for spiritual comfort. Ministers of various denominations arrive to preach the ways of righteousness and repentance. To the callous and hardened the services are merely a break in the monotony of prison life; to the soft and the hopeful it is a chance to seek atonement. But everybody joins in with gusto. Everybody seems to know the hymns, at least the tunes. O God, Our Help in Ages Past. Murderers, thieves and gangsters, the vicious and depraved, the first-timers and the long-term prisoners, all sing lustily, while the grim guards watch, the guns ever present.

Somebody's time is up. Tomorrow he steps out into another world, away from the stone walls, the iron bars, the bestiality. Parting is always a sentimental business, and that night there is singing in the cells as the fortunate man is given a 'farewell party'. Sometimes by a sheer miracle liquor appears, and the singing reaches ecstatic proportions.

Men leave, but not as new men. They step through the gates broken in health, cowed by brutality, or hardened with bitterness. Many will stalk the world as new Public Enemies. Many may return to Roeland Street, back to the admission office within the gates where the 'reception boys', convict monitors, shout questions on behalf of the officials: name, age, married or single, religion. Back to the blows when you are too slow, to the cold showers, and the convict barbers who shave skulls bare with a razor blade wielded with rough fingers, to the savagery of beast-men, the depravity, and the ever-vigilant eyes of the stony-faced men who guard the high walls.

Law of the jungle rules in jail, *New Age*, 4 October 1956

7

Out of the darkness (short story)

The smell of unwashed bodies and sweaty blankets was sharp, and the heat in the cell hung as thick as cotton wool.

The man on the rope mat beside me turned, grunted and flung a long arm across my face.

'How do you do?' he said, waking up and giggling.

'Very well,' I replied soothingly, for he was a little mad.

In the dark other bodies turned, cursed and tried to settle back into perspiring sleep.

'Did Joey bring the eggs?'

I could make out the dim shapeless bulge of his body curled up on the mat. He had entered the seventh of his ten-year sentence for culpable homicide, and being shut up for so long had unhinged him somewhat. He was neither staring mad nor violent. His insanity was of a gentle quality which came in spells. It was then that he would talk. Otherwise he was clamped up and retired, like a snail withdrawn into its shell. He was friendly enough, but it was the friendliness of a man on the other side of a peep-hole.

To the rest of the inmates he was known as Ou Kakkelak, Old Cockroach, and was either the butt of their depraved humour or completely ignored. He took everything with a gentle smile. From parts of his conversations during his spells I gained the impression that he was an educated man and might have been a schoolmaster before he had committed his crime.

'Cora,' he went on in the dark. 'You know, I like that part where Juliet dies over Romeo's body.'

From somewhere beyond the high barred window came the steady crunch of boots as a guard passed in the night.

'Is the heat troubling you?' I asked as kindly as I could make it. 'It is damn hot, isn't it?' He did not reply. I decided to do a little probing. 'You speak of Cora now and then. Who is she?' But he had turned on his side and was asleep again.

In the morning there was the usual shouting and clanging of doors. Blankets were folded; the long lines of convicts streamed down to the yards. The guards stood by, lashing out with leather belts.

'Spring, bliksems! Come on, you black bastards!'

We squatted, packed into the cement yard, and breakfasted on mealie meal and black bitter coffee. Old Cockroach sat near me, smiling his gentle, vacant smile and wolfing his food.

I saw him again when we were locked up after supper. He sank down in his place beside me. Around us secret cigarettes were emerging, the primitive flint and steel contraptions were struck, and smoke drifted up from behind cupped fingers. Figures in washed-out red shirts and canvas shorts packed the floor of the cell.

'Here we are,' Old Cockroach said and giggled at me. 'The wreckage which mankind, on its onward march, left behind.'

'Well,' I answered, smiling at him. 'Perhaps it's better to say that we are the results of mankind's imperfections.'

'Perhaps. Perhaps. I wonder where Joey is tonight.' He sat with his knees drawn up and his long arms clasped about his shins, gazing vacantly about at the faces around him. 'Ah, there he is now.'

I looked and said, 'That's Smiley Abrahams. Remember? That's not Joey. That's Smiley Abrahams.'

'Oh, ja. He's here for murder. I believe he's killed three people in his lifetime. They got him for the last one. An ape-man roaming a jungle. Here he is king. In a cave the cave-man is king.'

He fell silent again. Around us conversation took the form of a low muttering that formed a ragged buzzing. I sat with my back against the concrete wall and looked at Old Cockroach. He was tall and thin and bony, folded up now like a carpenter's ruler. His skin was as dark as burnt leather, and he had slightly negroid features and kinky hair going grey, close to his skull, like a tight-fitting cap.

'This place is like an oven,' I said, trying to build up another conversation.

'Cora,' he rambled. 'I think—'

'She'll turn up on visiting day,' I told him, although I knew she would not, whoever she was, because nobody had ever visited him for as long as I had been in. I began to wish I could learn more about him.

From outside came the scrape and thump of boots on the stone staircase. Steel gratings clanged like boilers being opened and closed. Silence fell in the stone caserne with the finality of sound on a radio being switched off. Cigarettes were killed and carefully concealed, and each man retreated quickly within himself and looked dumb.

Through the peep-hole in the heavy, studded door a voice trumpeted angrily. 'Hou julle bekke! Shut your filthy mouths, you bastards.'

The silence remained inside; a cautious, discreet silence which hung like a veil while the gratings clanged and the footsteps receded. When they had faded completely, the veil was lifted slowly and carefully as the broken murmurs came out of hiding.

Smiley Abrahams climbed to his feet, kicked a pathway through the sprawling humanity around him and plodded deliberately towards the door. His great shoulders hunched under the torn red shirt. He hawked and spat straight onto the door and wiped his mouth on the back of his hand. Then he turned and stalked back along the pathway to his place.

'Just a warning,' Old Cockroach smiled. 'No, not meant for those "corpies". He can't afford to be hard-case with them. That was really meant for us all. The ape must make it known that he is still king of the jungle, even if the elephant is bigger than he is.'

The sun faded behind the barred windows like lights being dimmed in a theatre. It had become hot again in the caserne, and from the bucket latrine came the sharp, acid smell of ammonia. Old Cockroach lay on his mat and pulled the thin blanket up to his waist. He did not seem to feel the heat, but just lay there, calmly gazing at the dim bulb in the white-washed stone ceiling. It was as if he had drawn an invisible armour around himself.

'Have you any family, old man?' I asked, gently attacking the armour.

'Huh?' He looked blank and then smiled softly at me.

'A man's got to have somebody. People.' But the armour was tightly strapped and riveted.

The next night started much the same. The heat was overpowering, and the stench of bodies increased quickly. Men fought and clawed around the water buckets, snarling like jackals around their carrion. The cave-man, Smiley Abrahams, hurled men from the centre of the turmoil, growling and snapping at his cringing subjects. A man rose to challenge him. A great, clubbed fist drew back and then struck him with the sound of a pick-handle against a pumpkin. The rebel went down like a stricken ox and lay still, to be trampled by the others.

'A slave has revolted,' Old Cockroach observed in a voice as gentle as the fall of dust. 'Do you know that the whole of mankind's history consists of a series of revolutions?'

'You're an educated man, Old Cockroach,' I said. 'You don't belong here. How did you come to kill anybody? If you don't mind me asking.'

'I used to be a schoolmaster,' he replied, confirming my old suspicion. Then his mind wandered again, and he murmured, 'I hope Joey brings that book he borrowed last week. *Treasure Island*. Have you ever read *Treasure Island*?'

'Yes. Long ago, when I was a pikkie.'

The brawl around the water buckets had subsided since they had both been emptied. There would be no water for the rest of the night. Men sat around, hunched stark naked under the light, exploring their clothes and blankets for lice. The cracking of the vermin between thumbnails sounded like snapping twigs. My own body was slippery with sweat.

It was no better when the light was turned off. The cloying heat and the stench of the latrine seemed to take advantage of the darkness. Old Cockroach had settled down on his blankets and I could hear him scratching himself. I was doing the same, and sleep became impossible. From all around us grunts, curses and tiny cries came like suppressed voices out of hell.

'… Cora,' Old Cockroach's voice came out of the dark, quiet as a trickle of sweat. 'Cora.'

'Take it easy, old man,' I murmured.

'Oh, you're not Cora …'

'Nay, man. Sorry, though.'

Silence.

I decided to probe a little more. 'By the way, who is Cora?'

Silence. Then he said, 'Hullo, Joey. I'm glad you've come. I'll tell you a story. Would you like to listen to a story?'

'Okay. That would be fine.'

'Alright, then. It was a long time ago. A very long time ago, I think. I was in love with her. You don't think this is going to be a silly story, do you?'

'Certainly not.'

'I was a teacher at a junior school and was doing a varsity course in my spare time. And I was in love with Cora. She was beautiful. Really beautiful. Her skin was soft and smooth and the colour of rich cream. She was almost white, you see. I was in love with her. We had grown up together in Dublin Street in Woodstock, and I think I must have been in love with her as long as I can remember.

'I became a schoolmaster. We were going to be married, and I worked hard because I wanted her to have everything that would make her happy once we were married.'

He was silent again while the sounds of sleep went on around us. When he went on his voice had taken on a dullness. 'Then she began to find that she could pass as white. She could pass as white, and I was black. She began to go out to white places, bioscopes, cafés. Places where I couldn't take her. She met white people who thought she was really white, and they invited her out to their homes. She went to parties and dances. She drifted away from me, but I kept on loving her.

'I talked to her, pleaded with her. But she wouldn't take any notice of what I said. I became angry. I wept. I raved. Can you imagine how much I loved her? I grovelled. I was prepared to lose my entire self-respect just to keep her. But it wasn't of any use. She said I was selfish and trying to deny her the good things of life. The good things of life. I would have given anything I could. And she said I was denying her the good things of life.

'In the end she turned on me. She told me to go to hell. She slapped my face and called me a black nigger. A black nigger.'

'Then you lost your head and killed her,' I said quietly. 'That's why you're here now.'

'Oh, no,' Old Cockroach answered. 'I could never have done that to Cora. I did lose my head, but it was Joey whom I killed. He said I was a damn fool for going off over a damn, play-white bitch. So I hit him, and he cracked his skull on something. Ah, here's Joey now. Hullo, Joey. I hope you've brought my book …'

Out of the darkness. *Africa South* 2(1): 118–122, October–December 1957

8

Battle for honour (short story)

We parked the transport lorry on one side of the little square and climbed down from the driving cabin.

Arthur peeled off his driving gloves. We strolled over towards the Buckingham on the other side of the square. A bunch of sharks hung around the non-European entrance, and watched as we went in.

We moved up to the bar and stood there, elbows on the smooth, grained teak, until Bruisky, the barman, came in from the European side. He was short and stout and clay-faced.

'Vell! Vell! You boys just get in?'

'South West,' Arthur told him. 'Dry as hell.'

'South Vest Africa? But it's nice ven you've got company.' He smiled at me, 'How you keeping, sonny boy?'

'I'm fine. How you, Mister Bruisky?'

'Company,' Arthur said and grinned sourly. 'You call this sonofabitch company? Him and his books.'

I winked at Bruisky. 'This ignorant joker. Got no culture. Even if I got to talking to him, all he wants to talk about is women, women, women.'

Arthur said: 'Gimme a double and a ginger ale.'

I asked for a lager beer and we stood there.

The swing-doors opened and a young man came in. We knew him a little from coming to this pub now and then. He was tall and good-looking, except for the battered nose. He had been a welter some time back and there had been pictures of him in the papers. Right then, I didn't know how he earned a living, but he always had money. He wore flashy suits. I guess that was why everybody called him Fancy.

He said, 'Hoit, boys,' and came around, bellying up next to Arthur.

'Howzit,' Arthur returned.

'You johns going to have a drink?'

Bruisky filled up for us and went away. Arthur asked, 'What you doing these days, Fancy?'

'I don't have to do nothing,' Fancy answered, smiling. 'I don't have to work. Horses work, mos.'

'You're a lucky rooker.'

'Got me a goose up in Walmer. Nice piece. Her old man don't know about it either.'

The swing-doors opened again and it was one of the sharks. He was wide and flabby, with his belly hanging over his belt, and he had a soft, shiny, booze-bloated face covered with greyish stubble. He slouched up beside me and leaned on the bar.

Then Bruisky moved up from the other end of the bar, looking first at the shark and then at me. 'This bloody rubbish bothering you?'

'No, he's okay,' I said, feeling a little awkward.

'Vat d'you vant?' Bruisky asked the shark.

'Hell, give him a drink,' I suddenly found myself saying.

'You sure?'

'Go on! Give him a drink,' I didn't look at the shark, not wanting him to find any sympathy. Bruisky glared at him and reached for a wine bottle.

On the other side of me Arthur said, 'What the hell you messing your chink on a blerry shark for?'

'Never mind,' I told him. 'Take it easy. It's my money, isn't it?'

He glowered at the shark for a moment, and then turned back to his conversation with Fancy. In the mirror I saw the shark look at me and grin crookedly, his eyes screwing up inside the folds of greyish flesh.

Fancy was saying, '… should have seen the goose I had before this one. Left her man for me.'

'Had me a goose on the Port Elizabeth run,' Arthur said, trying to hold his own. 'Knobs like pineapples.'

'Man,' Fancy said. 'That one was really awake. But I got tired of her and so I took a stroll. She walked out on her old man for me and I walked out on her. He was a no-good barstid, anyway, accor'ing her. She told old Fancy he was always on the bottle. Have another roun?'

He signalled to Bruisky and waited while the drinks were poured.

'She go back to her ou?' Arthur asked.

'Hell, no. Scared, I reckon. Maybe too much pride, too. Last time I heard she was in one of those houses. Those goosies can make money easy.' He chuckled. 'Real nice goose. Name of Lilly McDaniels.'

'You're a real lucky juba,' Arthur said grinning.

Then from beside me the shark said suddenly and thickly: 'Fancy, you're a …'

I looked at the shark. He had his thick hands on the top of the bar, and had turned, looking past me at Fancy. Arthur put his glass down and looked at him. Fancy was looking at him too, a pink flush rising under the tan of his face. 'Talking with me, pal?' he asked, a hard look in his eyes.

'Who then?' the shark said. 'You're a …,' he repeated. 'And you can go to hell on a broomstick, you dirty, little wise barstid.'

Fancy reached out, taking the front of his greasy shirt in a fist, and said: 'You old …! You want to get flogged?'

'Leave him alone, Fancy,' I said.

'Listen,' Fancy said. 'This old barstid insulted me. It's a matter of honour.'

Then the shark seemed to lose his temper and took a wild swing at Fancy's face. Fancy danced away, pulling the flabby man with him so that he stumbled awkwardly towards the door, releasing him at the same time so that he staggered out, scattering the men gathered on the pavement at the entrance.

We all went outside after Fancy. I said to Arthur: 'You better stop him. He'll murder that old boy.'

'Hell,' said Arthur. 'He asked for it didn't he?'

Fancy stepped off the pavement towards the shark, squaring off as if he was in the ring. He danced in feinting and laughing softly, and the old boy watched him come, backing away. The crowd jeered and yelled at him to go in and fight, but he kept on retreating further into the square. Then somebody got behind him and gave him a push that sent him right into Fancy.

Fancy hit him low. The flabby man was down on his knees. The crowd hooted.

He climbed back to his feet, shaking his head to get his long, matted hair out of his face. Fancy grinned and said: 'Come on, Oupa!'

The shark stood there. Then he charged.

Fancy swung again and again, catching the thick, wine-ruined body in the midriff and face, but the sheer weight of the onrush drove him back. He broke the wide, drooling mouth before the big arms encircled him in a clumsy bear-hug and tightened.

I could see the savage look in the shark's face, and the look of pain and terror coming into Fancy's eyes. The crowd was on the shark's side now, yelling, eager to see somebody get hurt. Then the shark gave a sudden wrench sideways and Fancy staggered away crazily making muling sounds with his pain-twisted mouth.

The shark went after him. He had his hands clasped together into one big double fist, and raised above his head as if he was lifting a sledge-hammer. He reached Fancy and brought the joined hands down in a clubbing swing. There was a sound of snapping bone and tearing cartilage as Fancy's nose went.

Fancy sat down on the kerbside holding his face, and the shark came after him again, saying, 'You barstid! You barstid!' lifting him by the front of his coat and clubbing him, until the rage was out of him. Then he let Fancy drop back onto the pavement.

'Come on, let's blow,' I said.

'I don't get it,' Arthur said as we walked towards the lorry. 'How come did that old man want to start the fight. Fancy wasn't bothering him. We was just standing there talking about some goosies. I don't get it.'

We climbed up into the driving cabin and Arthur started her up. The diesel hummed and thundered, then settled down into its steady roar. The shark came around the back of the truck and past the cabin, still breathing hard.

Arthur stuck his head out of the window and called down: 'Hey, old dad, how come did you do that to that john?'

The shark looked up, grinning, a little painfully with his split lips. He said above the sound of the diesel: 'Well, it was a matter of honour. You see, pally, my name is Joseph Henry McDaniels.'

A matter of honour, *Drum*, November 1958

Part 2
Treason trial

9

156 families to feed

The cop at the door looks bored. He tilts his chair back and eases his gun harness, stares at the hessian ceiling as if he sees something hypnotic up there. In front of me a ladybird crawls carefully up the back of Achie Patel's chair, hesitates about six inches from the top and decides to turn back. You can cut the heat with a knife. A hundred and fifty-six bodies stir uncomfortably in the diamond-wire dock. Somewhere voices clack metallically.

Duplicated copy of a speech by Lilian Ngoyi.

Yes, Your Worship, I hand in this document.

… Peace Council …

Do you know a man named Stanley Lollan?

I am surrounded by South Africa. Damons, Nthite, Hoogendyk, Horvitch, Moonsamy, Shanley. Workers, housewives, clerks, lawyers, journalists, doctors, priests, trade unionists.

Pamphlet called *New Life in China*, by Ruth First.

I hand in this document, Your Worship.

There is Dr Motala who cannot find somebody to replace him, so many of the sick in Maritzburg must go unattended. And the Lion of the East [Gert Sibanda] whose home has been the country roads ever since he was deported from the area where he had lived and his house sold for £10 at a public auction.

The ladybird has reached a paling across the back of the chair and advances cautiously along it, waving its tiny antennae.

The court orderly is a youth in a khaki uniform, with a gun as big as a plough-handle at his waist. He carries the exhibits from the prosecutor across about twenty yards of floor to the witness in the wooden frame box. Two and a half miles a day. Thirteen miles a week.

Is this an invitation to a dinner …?

Yes, Your Worship. I hand it in.

In the wire dock the accused spend five and a quarter hours each day.

Five and a quarter hours taken from one-hundred-and-fifty-six lives every day. Five and a quarter hours wondering whether the folks at home are all right. Whether the baby will recognise his daddy when he gets back home. Whether the Defence Fund had collected enough money to support one-hundred-and-fifty-six families.

One-hundred-and-fifty-six families to feed.

The ladybird has encountered an obstacle in a projecting fold in Achie Patel's coat. The antennae feel forward cautiously. The tiny oval body goes into reverse for a few minute paces.

Did you, on the 26th September, search …

That's correct, Your Worship. The heat beats down in waves. Heads nod. Eyelids struggle to keep open. Ears strain to listen. In Nazi Germany the Gestapo used a deadly vicious and ridiculously simple method of torture in order to force confessions. They didn't allow the prisoner to fall asleep. Night and day. Day and night.

Twelve million people to liberate, and one-hundred-and-fifty-six families to feed. What is the price of freedom? The thunder on the door in the early dawn? A ride in an aeroplane? The roaring, swaying drive in a steel truck? The roar of the crowds? Afrika Mayibuye! All these small instalments.

And one-hundred-and-fifty-six families to feed.

The ladybird advances again, carefully, heaves itself on to the crest of the fold in Achie Patel's coat, crosses gently, and descends the far slope.

A pamphlet called 'Educating for Ignorance' …

I hand in this document.

In ordinary everyday life there is a variety of things which make life interesting. Here life has become a fixed pattern; a routine, a monotonous repetition like a machine turning out bottletops. The ladybird finds interest in its journey.

A copy of *New Youth*.

Correct, Your Worship. I hand in this document.

Overhead the skies protest. Thunder mutters menacingly. The heat is thick as cotton wool. The thunder grows louder, then rolls out with the sound of an artillery barrage. The ladybird has disappeared now, as if it had been frightened by the enormous sound and has hidden itself.

One-hundred-and-fifty-six people half-listening, wondering about homes and children and wives and hoping that they will be looked after. The price of freedom is great. Now it is the price of food for our families, and the rent, and the instalments on the furniture, electricity and food for the baby.

One-hundred-and-fifty-six families to feed.

Do you hand in this document?

Across the skies the thunder rolls as the angry gods engage in mighty battle.

One hundred and fifty-six families to feed, *Fighting Talk*, February 1957

Whodunit?

The Treason Trial seems to have turned out to be a whodunit.

Somebody set fire to Letty's house way down in the Eastern Cape and the Special Branch, hot on the trail as usual, decided that maybe the job can be blamed on the 156 accused.

'Do I understand', asked Joe Slovo, 'that I am here because somebody in Port Elizabeth burned down Letty's house?'

Drawled Accused Number Eleven, Alfred Hutchinson: 'I'm not interested in Letty's house. What I want to know is, who is Letty?'

Up my alley, *New Age*, 25 July 1957

I was on my way for the usual 11 o'clock cup of coffee during the court recess one morning when I came across what appeared to look like three 'ducktail boys'. They wore peg-bottomed trousers, flashy jackets and windbreakers.

But upon further investigation I discovered that the three musketeers were none other than a trio of real, genuine, dyed-in-the-wool, so-called 'Freedom Fighters' all the way from Hungary [having fled the 1956 Soviet invasion of that country].

They didn't like South Africa, they said in broken English. 'No work.' They had been here since January and hadn't found a job yet. They didn't want to go back to Budapest. They didn't even want to go to America.

Up my alley, *New Age,* 9 May 1957

We can go on about that Hungarian business forever. We've had a bellyful of 'Freedom Fighters', and atrocities and slave camps and long lines of other goings-on about what is supposed to be going on 'behind the iron curtain'. All this we got from the local press.

And this weekend we got a bit more. Writes a Dirk De Villiers in the local blab: 'To a Hungarian freedom means that when there's a knock there is no need to whisper in fear – who's at the door?' PHOOEY!

I'm not going to argue with the subject of the article, a Mr Hargitai from Hungary, about the tough time he and his family might have had over there. But, Mr Hargitai, you don't know from nothing.

No knocks on the door in free South Africa? You know what kinds of knocks I mean.

Ask me, Mr Hargitai, and Mr De Villiers.

I've had knocks on my door, right here up my alley, in free South Africa.

And every time those knocks came, my house was ransacked by nice cheerful Special Branch dicks. The last time that knock came it was at 4 a.m. and they hauled me off without even giving me a chance to wait for my wife to come home from delivering a baby. They wouldn't let me eat breakfast, and didn't allow me to take a change of clothes. They just hauled me out and shipped me to the Fort.

Uh-uh, Mr Hargitai. You just become a Freedom Fighter in South Africa, and you'll get knocks on your door. But puh-plenty.

Up my alley, *New Age,* 19 December 1957

Apparently Swart [the Minister of Justice] does not believe that prevention is better than cure. His enquiry into the typhoid outbreak [at the Johannesburg Fort] comes somewhat late, but we hope it will open his eyes to the horrid life prisoners live in the Fort, and for that matter any jail.

One of the greatest reasons for any disease is found in his jails. Filth.

The mats are filthy, the blankets are filthy, the latrines are filthy, the food is filthy, the utensils are filthy, the convicts' clothes are filthy.

My own experience at the Fort was confined to the awaiting trial section. It was only protests that brought improvements for those of us who were waiting to go on trial for 'treason'. The experience was bad enough.

The latrines overflowed and made a stench. When we sunned our clothes those crawly things, cynically dubbed 'the prisoner's friends', crept out of every seam and paraded in columns. When the food came it looked as if the vegetables had been dumped into the pot straight out of the soil. The tin plates in which other prisoners received them were unwashed and encrusted with layers of dried food accumulated over months, well mixed with rust.

These conditions make for disease, Mr Swart, so get rid of them quickly.

On one occasion when we had a surplus of sandwiches from outside we asked a warder to distribute them among other prisoners. He just tossed them about in handfuls and the prisoners stampeded for the bread.

And when you go to bed at night, Mr Swart, just think of that unfortunate prisoner who gets a sleeping place in his cell – right in front of the overflowing latrine.

… Don't tell us prisoners shouldn't be molly-coddled. In civilised countries prisoners are reformed, not turned into diseased beasts.

Up my alley, *New Age,* 21 May 1959

People's politics

May Day is upon us again and all over the world the workers are celebrating their victories and pledging their solidarity one with the other. In our own country we are passing through critical times, what with the Nats pushing through Parliament new laws against the people, and the Treason Trial entering its sixth month.

The ordinary men and women of South Africa are being called on to make new efforts for freedom, peace and harmony, and I can think of nothing more fitting for the occasion than the words of a great American, Tom Paine: 'These are the times that try men's souls. The summer soldier and the sunshine patriot will, in this crisis, shrink from the service of their country; but he that stands it now, deserves the thanks of man and woman. Tyranny, like hell, is not easily conquered. Yet we have this consolation with us, that the harder the conflict, the more glorious the triumph … Heaven knows how to put a price upon its goods; and it would be strange indeed if so celestial an article as FREEDOM should not be highly rated.'

Up my alley, *New Age,* 2 May 1957

May Day has come and gone and at the Drill Hall, Johannesburg, it went off with a bang. The women, accused and visitors, were gay in their Congress colours and red ties, and carnation buttonholes were favoured by the men. The handshakes and back-slapping and cheerful greetings all added to the atmosphere of solid friendship and confidence which exists among the Treason Trial accused. Since December 1956 a great love has grown up among the 156; a great family of brothers and sisters, a marvellous picture of a New South Africa.

At lunchtime everybody gathered in the area-way next to the Drill Hall and the air shook with freedom songs while the cops stood looking on, apparently awestruck at the spectacle of white and non-white hugging each other, laughing and singing. Or were they waiting hopefully to be invited to join in the fun?

To add to the festivities we were put into the right mood with a scrumptious lunch of hot-dogs, fresh doughnuts, avocado pears and bananas. Thank you, catering committee. I am sure none of us will object to May Day coming more often.

And some of the Special Branch dicks spent May Day hanging around the pavement opposite the Congress offices in West Street. They looked pretty tired and bored by 6 p.m. The department ought to hire a stack of deck chairs for their weary warriors.

Up my alley, *New Age,* 9 May 1957

On 26 June the Golden City went pale. The usual dark faces thronging the streets, the bustling streams of workers on their way every morning, were absent. And on corners and along the pavements, shivering cops huddled in the drizzle, waiting for 'incidents' which would give them a chance to warm up. There were none.

There was no tea for many office workers that day, and in Industria a line of loaded lorries stood in the rain with nobody to unload them.

The Evaton bus, usually packed in the mornings, carried only three passengers into the city, and two of them were treason suspects. Other of the treason accused coming through the 'stay-at-home' areas sported large signs, TREASON SUSPECTS, as passports.

And in Sophiatown a crowd watched the cops patrolling the deserted bus-ranks.

'Hey, baas,' somebody shouted. 'When are you going to shoot? We want to go home.'

Up my alley, *New Age,* 4 July 1957

Another boycott has broken out in Johannesburg. I should say, rather, in Fordsburg. This time it's the boycott of a fish-and-chip shop, and apparently it is being organised entirely by school-children.

I was ambling along Bree Street when a leaflet was thrust into my hand. I like fish-and-chips, and it's a long time since I was a schoolboy, but the leaflet called on me to boycott this particular shop. In stirring words it said: 'Let our boycott be a lesson to others who shamelessly ignore the will of the people!'

All this arose out of the events of June 26. Indian businesses, the leaflet continued, closed down for that day. 'Only a few blacklegs were to be found.' Well, it appears that the owner of this fish-and-chip emporium had black legs and stayed open. What was more, the school kids say, not only did he refuse to close his shop, but he actually called in the cops to arrest those who tried to convince him. Hence the wrath of the junior set is descending on him like a ton of bricks – I mean, chips.

Well, Mister Shopkeeper, there you have it. The will of the people. It's my guess that every one of those youngsters will be going around for a long time with a chip on his shoulder.

Up my alley, *New Age,* 23 May 1957

Cops

We had a brush with Col. Olivier's 'Ghost Squad' last Friday. My colleague Tennyson Makiwane and I were strolling down Commissioner Street when an oaf in plain clothes elbowed Mr TM and snarled: 'Pass, man. Pass.'

We may be on trial for treason but I'm sure we don't look like suspicious characters. Tennyson grinned and hummed 'All day, all night, Marianne', and showed the cop the Certificate of Merit with which all treason accused have been issued by the Clerk of the Court. The 'ghost' glared at the paper, glared at us and handed it back.

This round-up of 'loiterers and suspicious characters' has turned out to be nothing else but another series of pass-raids – in fancy dress.

And sticking to the cops. Said General Rademeyer, Commissioner of Police of this Security Branch: 'We have better techniques now. We do not have to rely on stories. We can do better than that.'

The General ought to pop in at the treason enquiry and hear some of his boys giving evidence.

Up my alley, *New Age,* 23 May 1957

In ancient Rome and all other slave empires it was part of the technique of oppression to allow some slaves a certain amount of authority over their fellows. This helped to relieve the duties of the official whip-wielders, and the slave police became the most hated and abhorred by the unfortunates of their own class who suffered under their brutal treatment.

Among the last Crown witnesses called at the treason enquiry, before the prosecution decided to abandon the procedure of having each document identified by the detective who seized it, were members of South Africa's own slave police. And many of the accused found it difficult to conceal their feelings as African members of the Special Branch appeared in the witness box to give evidence against their own people. Blank-faced and cynical, these men moved among the suspects in the wire dock, searching and pointing out people whom they had helped to arrest. They answered flatly, acting like robots, yet perhaps a little aware of the atmosphere of distaste created by their presence.

Treason court cameos, *New Age,* 21 February 1957

The offices of the Congresses in West Street, Johannesburg, like the offices of liberation movements in many parts, are not big, flashy places. The building is drab and dusty, the upper floors deserted and gloomy. However, it is dear to the hearts of all Congressites. And the presence of Special Branch dicks Douglas Ndaba and Gladwell Ngcai do not help brighten the front of our premises in any way. These two gents spend a lot of their time holding up the wall around the entrance, and they are beginning to look like permanent fixtures.

They look as though they could do with a coat of paint too.

Up my alley, *New Age,* 5 September 1957

Funny feeling around my neck

Okay, I'm on trial for treason. The cops hauled me out at four in the morning, put me on a plane and dropped me in the Fort. I have to sit on a hard chair from nine-thirty a.m. to four every day, trying not to scream with boredom. I can take all this.

But I don't like the prosecutor referring to me as EXHIBIT NUMBER 85.

Up my alley, New Age, 5 September 1957

I'm objecting. My pal Barney Desai charged with incitement, had his bail fixed at 100 quid. That's twice as much as my bail for treason. What do they think I am? A cheapskate?

Up my alley, New Age, 21 November 1957

Two big celebrations are coming off this week. I shall have to buy a packet of starlights for the little man at home for the night of the Fifth [of November], and a large ... er ... cake for myself for the Seventh. It's not funny that on the Fifth all the kids will be celebrating because a character named Guy Fawkes committed Treason and got skewered. And if anybody does too much celebrating on the Seventh, that might be construed as treason, and they might get skewered.

I've got a funny feeling around my neck, but it's only because my tie's too tight.

Up my alley, New Age, 7 November 1957

Look at my face. Do I look as if I've done anything awful? Yet the Attorney-General refused to let me go. Sixty-one of my pals have been let off and not even with a finger-wagging.

Joe Slovo is sending to Pretoria for a re-mark of his papers.

Anyway, good luck, boys and girls, and no thanks to Minister Swart.

I can hardly imagine him playing Father Christmas.

Up my alley, New Age, 26 December 1957

When you reach the alley this week, yours truly will be packing his bags and preparing ... for the ... the Treason Trial [again].

I have been saying goodbye to people, and have heard a lot of encouragement which I can't write about because it amounts to contempt of court.

But one kind person presented me with a book with a quotation from John Donne on the flyleaf, which says: 'No man is an island entire of himself; he is part of the continent, a piece of the main ...'

I like the sentiments.

Another friend, well-intentioned, I'm sure, gave me a copy of Julius Fučík's *Notes from the Gallows*!!!

But the present I really do like is the easy folding chair. It will replace the hard-backed Seat Number 85 in the Drill Hall next week.

Up my alley, New Age, 9 January 1958

10

Court cameos

The 'treason' enquiry continues, but the monotonous pace at which it is proceeding has not hampered the speed of Dan Cupid. For this weekend has seen a triple wedding festival.

The accused extend their heartfelt good wishes to three of their comrades who, undaunted by the gloomy shadow cast over their careers by the Minister of Justice, have decided to face the future with steadfast confidence and a courageous determination to build their new life, come what may.

We wish Oliver Tambo and Adelaide Tshukudu, Syd Shall and Joan Anderson, Ronny Press and Miss JB Sack, all the happiness in the world.

And they might find examples of fortitude and courage in the lives of all their comrades in the treason 'line-up'.

* * * * *

I spoke to some of the younger married. Peter Nthite is about to become a father for the second time. 'I hope it will turn out to be triplets,' he told me, smiling impishly. 'We need more recruits for the struggle.'

Peter was the Good-humour Man of the Fort. His impersonations of well-known characters split the sides of his cell-mates, and his convening of the 'United Nations' is still being talked about.

* * * * *

Henry Tshabalala, 'Chubby' to his comrades, is a young man with an elfish face and an indomitable spirit. Both he and his wife have lost their jobs as a result of the treason arrests, but nothing can get them down.

'We have two children,' Henry told me, 'And no income. We have to depend on the Defence Fund now. But we're happy, that's what matters.'

'Chubby' is a bus-boycotter and walks the long miles from Sophiatown to the Drill Hall every day. 'We must set an example for the masses – besides, exercise is good for young people.'

* * * * *

Banished from Durban where he lived with his family, Mr [MB] Yengwa earns his living doing books for small storekeepers and traders in the district where he was forced to live. His arrest has cut him off from his four children, who are cared for by his aunt, and his source of income. Again the Defence Fund must become the fountain of life.

'I miss my home and my children, but politically, this is the best place to be.' Everywhere there is hardship and longing for home, but nowhere are there any regrets for what they have done and what has happened to them in the cause of liberation. Worry about the home, worry about money, but always a rugged determination to see this through.

*****

Little Lungile Kepe longs for his family in Port Elizabeth. He has not heard from home and is a little worried about what is happening down there. His family's financial position is precarious. But he strokes his long moustache and always smiles. There are many of the accused who are waiting anxiously to hear that the Defence Fund has moved into action as far as the welfare of their families is concerned. Perhaps there is a little impatience for hunger and starvation, and ejectment orders do not wait upon the deliberations of finance committees.

But everybody has confidence it will come right in the end. Patience, courage and goodwill are the order of the day.

Treason court cameos, *New Age*, 7 February 1957

My comrade in the treason trial, Lawrence Nkosi, has to report to the cops weekly, too, even though he is in hospital. They visit him regularly on Thursday mornings and make him sign in, bed number and all.

Up my alley, *New Age*, 31 October 1957

Perhaps the busiest and the most popular man in court is Sobantu Makazana. He is our postmaster. A tall impressive gentleman with his furled umbrella over one arm and a pile of telegram forms, stamps and envelopes clasped against his chest, his 'Any letters to post? Stamps and telegrams?' is a welcome sound to the accused. He buys the stamps and sends off the messages, and has become as well known at the Johannesburg Post Office as he is at court.

One-time clerk at the NAD [Native Affairs Department], he was fired 'because I was always obstinate'. He became a soft-goods salesman, and when the arrests took place he gave up selling shirts and underwear to become the Pony Express of the 156 accused. His slogan is: The Mail Must Get Through.

'This is my contribution,' he told me. 'I wish I could do more for the accused. My wife is a nurse and I and our children now depend on her income for a living.'

All of the accused appreciate this noble gesture. It can be seen in the way Sobantu Makazana is swamped with letters and orders for stamps whenever he appears.

Treason court cameos, *New Age*, 21 February 1957

Seated between Annie Silinga and Len Lee-Warden in the Drill Hall in Johannesburg is short, bespectacled, cheery Benny Turok, Accused Number 97 of the Treason Trial, who is due to be declared African Representative for Cape Western in the Cape Provincial Council this week.

Born of Russian parents in Libau, Latvia, in 1927, Benny has come to be one of the most popular of the 156, and with everybody who has associated with him in Congress circles. This is because of a genial disposition, an easy jocularity and the fact that he has succeeded in adopting the world outlook of the working man.

…

At varsity he played an active part in student political life, and then and afterwards participated in the work of the Modern Youth Society in Cape Town.

In 1953 he was in London where he served on the London Festival Committee of the World Youth Festival. Later he attended the Third World Festival of Youth and Students in Bucharest, as a representative of the Modern Youth Society, also visiting Budapest and Warsaw.

Back in South Africa he became an organiser for the Congress of Democrats and, when the campaign for the Congress of the People was launched, organiser for the Cape Western COP Committee.

In September 1955 he entered the trade union field to organise the bag workers, metal and timber workers. The workers took to him immediately and on the occasions when I had the opportunity of accompanying him to factories, I discovered that 'Comrade Benny' had gained the faith and confidence of all the workers, coloured and African, with whom he was associated.

He helped to organise three strikes for better wages and working conditions. The union office was always swarming with workers eager to gain his help and advice. He is a fearless and efficient organiser. I have heard him talking to factory bosses over the telephone on behalf of his unions and verbally rapping them over the knuckles for any injustice to their employees.

At the Congress of the People he introduced the clause of the Freedom Charter: 'The People Shall Share the Country's Wealth.'

Later in 1955 he was banned under the Suppression of Communism Act from attending all gatherings for a period of five years. But he continued his trade union work because the workers wanted him.

He is married to Mary Butcher, one of the first women to be banned under the Suppression Act and one of the first women defiers to take part in the 1952 Defiance Campaign. They have two sons.

Benny is entering the Cape Provincial Council, unopposed, to represent the African people. He is not in agreement with the undemocratic nature of this sort of representation, but the Africans nominated him and he will go to the Council to champion the Freedom Charter and the cause of liberation and equality for all – Europeans, coloureds, Africans and Indians.

Perhaps the Opposition realised that they could not find a better man than Benny. They are right.

I know him and I'm sure he'll stick to his guns.

Profile of a people's MPC, New Age, 23 May 1957

The man with the biggest smile in the Treason Trial is Accused Number Fifteen, Fish Keitseng. And of all the 156, Fish probably has the least to smile about, for while having to appear in the Drill Hall on a charge of treason every day, he has to serve a year in the Fort at the same time. He is brought to the Drill Hall under escort every day and taken away in the afternoon. But in spite of all that, the big smile is always there, together with a cheery 'Hullo, comrade' for everybody who approaches him.

It seems that one day Fish and some of his followers came upon a group of Africans who had been arrested for pass offences by a brace of gendarmes. According to the evidence Fish and company advanced on the cops and demanded the release of the prisoners.

'Your Worship,' said the cop in the dock, 'he said if we did not let the prisoners go they would shoot us. We were afraid and so we released the prisoners.' Looking at him, one wonders whether this cheerful young man in the black leather coat would hurt a fly, let alone threaten to shoot anybody.

One-time Volunteer-in-Chief in Newclare, Fish possesses the ability to make everybody like him. Even his escort seems to have become attached to him.

With about six months more to go, Fish Keitseng seems unaffected by the rigours of the Fort, and watching him leave with his guard every afternoon I have the feeling that his cheerful disposition, his refusal to be forced under, his confidence in the future of his cause, will see him through.

He is somebody from whom many can take an example.

Up my alley, *New Age,* 15 August 1957

Some of the accused have their own explanation for the Crown's decision to tender documents in bulk instead of continuing to call detective-witnesses to identify each one separately. They say it is all due to the powers of the Reverend DC Thompson. The prosecution was dealing with the last of the Transvaal accused and the Reverend's documents were being handed in.

'Can you identify the Reverend Thompson?'

'Yes, Your Worship.'

'Please do so.'

The Reverend was pointed out. He rose in his seat, a tall, big, imposing figure with a genial, kindly face. Unlike the radio-Christians whose grandiose sermons about peace on earth are broadcast every Sunday morning, he is a Christian who lives Christianity. Chairman of the South African Peace Council, a true man of peace, and a mighty hunter before the Lord.

'Number seventy-eight,' his voice rang out. And the heavens cracked. Overhead the lightning split the sky, and the thunder rolled suddenly with the sound of a mighty avalanche, drowning the voices in the court-room. It was as if the sky wept and the angels had been angered. They hurled their thunderbolts across the sky and the court was forced to adjourn. After that the new procedure was adopted by the Crown. Some say the Reverend Thompson started it all. Who knows?

Treason court cameos, *New Age,* 21 February 1957

11

Ncincilili! In praise of Wilton Mkwayi

When the summer of 1923 had come to the village of Cwaru, a son was born to Nowest and Henry Velele Mkwayi, and he was named Wilton Zimasile. This village, Cwaru, was the village of Velile Sandile, the chief, the son of Faku Sandile who had inherited it from Gonya.

Now it came about that Velile sold all his lands and the village without speaking to the people and they were angry and came in numbers from all over to talk together with the chief.

To this assembly came the Native Commissioner, saying: Sandile has sold the land and all living on it must go.

And the people wept and could not rest at night and left the land which had belonged to Velile, the son of Faku, the son of Gonya.

This was in the year 1940.

So Wilton Zimasile who attended school at Debe found a home for his parents and brothers and sisters at Zihlahleni, and when he had passed the fourth standard he left school to work in order to buy bread for his family.

For six months he pushed wheelbarrows of concrete and thereafter worked in a dynamite factory in Somerset West as a clerk for £7 a month, until Nowest Mkwayi was called to her ancestors and Wilton Zimasile returned to his home. In East London influx control made it hard to find work and he went to Port Elizabeth. Then it came about that Henry Velele, his father, also died, and Wilton Zimasile became the father of his sisters and brothers.

For a long time he worked in a factory which manufactured things of tin. Then it came about that the workers in this place went on strike, and Wilton Zimasile, being one of them and a leader, was told to go. And thereafter he was a leader among the workers in many places and led two strikes and became an organiser of the African Textile Workers, Volunteer-in-Chief of the New Brighton and Eastern Cape African National Congress, Treasurer of the SA Congress of Trade Unions.

Now in the year 1956 there was a great gathering at Cholomnqa near Kingwilliamstown at the headquarters of the chief, AV Sandile. This was a gathering of the Iinkosi Zama Ngqika (Ngqika chiefs) and many of their people attended. Here Wilton Zimasile spoke to the people about the Bantu Education Act and the Bantu Authorities Act and the people cried for him to become Sihlalo Wethu Wakomkulu, chairman of the Gaika Tribal Council, but the chiefs said this must not be.

On their way home Wilton Zimasile was cheered by the people: Mayibuye iAfrika! That meeting was held in August and September 1956. On 5 December 1956, he was arrested on a charge of 'High Treason'.

This is the story of Wilton Zimasile Mkwayi, a son of the people. Ncincilili.

Treason trial profile: Wilton Zimasile Mkwayi: A son of the people, *Fighting Talk*, March 1957

12

Time to think

All future despatches will be coming via Pretoria, which they tell me is a suburb of the Voortrekker Monument.

When I first saw that block of stone I was told that it had been put there to commemorate the historic achievements of Afrikaner chauvinism. One of the things the plasterer who designed it left out was the notches on the guns of the Voortrekkers, used as a record of the Africans they shot en route.

But then the Voortrekkers couldn't be shown off in too bloodthirsty a light … after all, the descendants of the 'Kaffirs' they robbed of land are also allowed to come along and see the Monument … on washing days!!!

Up my alley, New Age, 31 July 1958

Friday, 1 August 1958: Dreamed I was back home eating a bathful of periwinkles. The Lord only knows why it should have been periwinkles. Why not bean stew or peaches and cream? But it was periwinkles and halfway through the banquet, shhhush, boom, the lift in the block of flats wakes me up and there's the dirty grey sunlight coming through the chinks in the curtain like a bum sneaking into a parish tea. D-day, comrade. Rise and shine. T-day, you mean. It's as chilly as an ice-cube's belly outside. Give me the sunny south. Orders of the day: All accused to assemble outside the Congress office and therefrom to march in open order to the point of embarkation, namely Leyds Street. Spit and polish to be applied to all shoes, and hair combed according to regulations. There's a breeze up that cuts like a razor. They should've held this trial in Durban, somebody grumbles. All aboard! Hey, why's that bus got a hump on its back? Special with soft seats, with the compliments of the Minister of Justice, in case any of the fair white accused want to avail themselves of apartheid as prescribed in the million-and-one regulations, legislation and proclamations that make this sunny land of ours such a nice place to live in. Everybody's got cigarettes. Miraculous! The famous Putco buses. Guaranteed to take you where you want to go, provided you don't mind arriving with addled brains and your ribs around your neck. Pretoria. Everybody's singing in the buses. Pretoria stares. The peace and quiet of this centre of reaction has been drastically impaired.

Is this the synagogue? With its domes and cupolas it has been given a new name. The accused now call it the Little Kremlin. Nah, wait until you see a lot of cops standing around and that's it. Here we are. Afrika! Mayibuye!

How long do you think this will last? Guess we'll sit right through now, month, two months, year.

All seats please! For goodness sake, it's Sergeant Davidson of the Drill Hall. Handshakes, grins, laughs. Will you all please be seated? Well, this place looks like something. Nice white paint on the ceiling with the sun coming through a skylight of stained glass. Polished woodwork. Balconies of the public overhead, black on the right, white on the left. We're all here. PWD brown and cream. Hey, look at all those law books. Words, your fate depends on words. How many million words in the English language? The *Concise Oxford Dictionary* has 1498 pages of words, excluding the addenda and abbreviations, beginning with the letter A, and ending with zymotic. The tables around the defence counsel look like the gathered loot from several libraries. I suppose there'll be a lot of talking. A trial in Japan, it was estimated, would last fourteen years. Fourteen years of words. How many words can be spoken in a court case lasting fourteen years? Listen, this treason trial right here has gone on long enough for me. Say, when I got home nobody recognised me. And another five years to come? Well, you ought to worry. All your creditors might be dead and under by the end of it.

Silence in court. Here come the judges. All red and grey, bowing formally. That's Rumpff in the middle. On the other side is Justice Ludorf. Seems a friendly-looking chap. Smiling. The defence team are lined up, their sights whetted. That's Pirow himself over there. Heard he's not going to talk much. Got a cold or something. So his voice is like breaking bottles. The registrar of the court is reading the official appointment of the court. A hush falls. It's on. A million words of copy for umpteen newspapers. Overhead, behind us the pressmen are ready, working out the headlines. The Accused Henry Makgothi has been hospitalised for six months. The Crown withdraws the charges against him. Somebody cracks: Lemme out of here. I've got a stomach-ache. The spectators hang over the crowded galleries. Maisels, number one defence counsel, is on his feet, big, easy, an old hand. Bombshell. The accused have reason to believe that they will not have a fair trial. The judges Ludorf and Rumpff are asked to recuse themselves. Argument continues. The law books are unlimbered, quotations, quotations, judgment in this trial and that trial. Maisels goes on, pulling everything out of the bag. Steady and controlled as an axe cutting into a tree. The Crown looks blank. Beyond them the 'experts' Father Bochenski and Professor Murray, probably waiting for the cue, sit patiently. It never comes. Justice Rumpff: Have you anything to say, Mr Pirow? Milord (like a creaking door), I am precluded from saying anything. I wish I were not! The court adjourns until Monday to consider the defence application. Everybody troops out amid a hubbub of comments. The reporters flee for the telephones. Outside the court the accused are assailed by photographers. No pictures can be taken in the limits of the court so the cameramen hang over the green railing after they've been put out by the cops. Will you hold it please? I'd like to have a picture of the Professor talking to Chief. Thanks awfully. Do you think they'll recuse themselves? I don't think Ludorf has any alternative … I don't know about Rumpff … I don't think Rumpff will recuse himself … Ludorf, sure. Well, we'll see. I've been speculating about this case for nearly two years now, and it's never turned out the way I thought it would. All the way back to Johannesburg. Headlines: Treason Trial's Dramatic Start.

Saturday and Sunday: Do you think they'll recuse themselves? Do you think Rumpff will step down? Do you think Ludorf will? What happens when a judge recuses himself? Do you think …? Do you think …? Do you think …? Celebration. Get out that old guitar boy. What'll I sing? If I had the wings of an angel. Sunday papers, Treason Trial, Treason Trial, Buck Rogers, Mapula Roodt.

August 4: Back to Pretoria. How'd the weekend go? So-so. Did some reading. Finished *Candide* and *Quiet Flows the Don*. Some reading, that. Jokes on the bus and roars of laughter … Outside the court the photographers are waiting like hawks. The spectators are queuing. It doesn't look as if they'll all get in. Got a cigarette? Oh, oh, it's starting. Damn this cold. All seats please. Sergeant Davidson is no longer with us. The new officials stagger through the business of checking everybody in. Somebody missed the bus because the trains from Orlando went the wrong way or something. Please refer the matter to Minister Schoeman. Tension. The red-gowned judges. The tree falls. Mr Justice Ludorf reads carefully from his script and ends: I recuse myself. Mr Justice Rumpff: I was not consulted by the Minister regarding the appointment of my brothers, neither did I recommend their appointment … The suspicions of the accused are without foundation, and I can only obey the dictates of my conscience. I cannot recuse myself. Mr Maisels replies politely for the defence that the accused greatly appreciate the explanation given. There is a slight argument about the position of the court now that one of the judges had recused himself. Court adjourns until next Monday when it is hoped the Minister will have appointed another judge.

August 5 to 10: Time to think. Ninety-one of us. Single, married, divorced, black, white, brown, male, female, mothers, fathers, democrats, Ghandi-ists (sic), Christians, communists, socialists, all the ists and isms to which the liberatory movement gives rise. To the interests of the nation as a whole, all lesser interests are subordinate, whether of Right or Left, whether they be an employers' federation, trade union, banking or professional interests … All those who pursue a sectional and anti-national policy will be opposed by the might of the organised State. Who said that? Strijdom? No. That was the other Oswald. Moseley. They haven't established the true fascist state. I don't think they can do that. But they're on the right track, brother. They've got the idea. All this concerning us, and the other whites, those Union Jack, flag-waving chaps, and the kids shunted out of schools, Afrikaans only. Since to each man has been given but one life … There are some hard boys in this trial. Tough organisers from the slums and the townships, and the mob who went through the Defiance Campaign, and who can go through this, too, I'm sure. Comrades. The spirit of the struggle.

August 11 to 22: The weather's getting warmer. The Durban boys haven't shed their overcoats yet, but they don't keep their hands in their pockets so much. The European gallery has thinned out, but the non-Europeans are steady. House full every day. Leaning over and listening intently. This case has certainly produced some sea lawyers. Somebody jokes: When I'm through here I'm going to apply for my QC.

Everybody's got an explanation, a way out. A new judge. Mr Justice Becker. Mr Maisels is on his feet again. His gown's going to fall off. Oops, just in time, and it's back on his shoulders. Bombshell. The defence will apply for the quashing of the indictment. A war of attrition. The marathon speech begins. Twelve hours of words spread over two days. A giant saw cutting into an old redwood tree. Milords … this mass of rot and rubbish … the defence is expected to read through the entire record of the preparatory examination … twenty-six volumes of the selected works of Lenin … this trial can go on for years … further particulars … exhibits, a Russian recipe book (recipes for what, Mr Maisels?) for poisoning wells, I suppose, m'lud … a school magazine … take the case of Heyne (or did he say Heimie?) … *SA Law Reports*, 19 … at page … further particulars. The voice of Maisels goes on, relentlessly, the saw sinks deep. Lunch in the grounds of the rectory with Father Nye as host, tall, lean, smiling, passing around the cigarettes. Would you like some more bread and butter? Orange squash? The committee has done sterling work. The stew and the curries, not too hot, to suit everybody's taste. Somebody even donated ice-cream. Like a garden party. Should've worn my morning pants and top-hat. Maisels continues. Thousands of words are reduced to inches in the columns of newspapers. Mr Kentridge. Smooth, precise and devastating as a scalpel … this indictment should be quietly buried. Do you find no movement in it at all, Mr Kentridge? If there is, m'lud, I suggest that it should be quickly put out of its misery. Advocate Fischer, quiet, confident, exact. Advocate Nicholas, shatteringly expert, arguing with experienced ease, answering each question without hesitation. The saw cuts into the tree, deeper, deeper. The Crown replies. The indictment shows with absolute clarity the charge against each of the accused. What is the position of each accused? Each person wants to know the details of the conspiracy and his part in it. Why can't you give them those facts? … Any manifestation of a hostile state of mind renders a person guilty of treason. Trengrove and Hoexter wade on. Surprise. Pirow wishes to hold discussions with the defence about the possibility of limiting the scope of the trial. The loudspeaker has broken down, anyway. Court adjourns until Monday. More time to think. Reflections upon the political situation in the country and the financial position of the accused. Got a cigarette? Here we go again. No agreement between the defence and the Crown, but we assure your lordships that no time was wasted. The Crown struggles on. Take the case of Heyne. Who is this Heimie, anyway? It's Hymie Barsel and the case he's always carrying around with him, somebody jokes. It's hot. Some of the accused are nodding. The fans whirr ineffectively. Somebody has received a Darling Dear and reads it surreptitiously, smiling. The Crown grinds to a finish. Reply by the defence. Mr Justice Rumpff would like Mr Trengrove to answer questions with reference to misjoinder. These law books are like the Bible, says accused Mgugunyeka, anybody can quote from them and each gives his own interpretation. The last stages of the replies grind to a stop. We hope to give our decision on Wednesday. Not our reasons, however. Those we will only be able to give at a later date. Court adjourns.

August 27: This is it. Twelve talking days, twelve days of law books and marathon argument, listening and waiting to hear. On the bus to Pretoria it is the morning again of the sea lawyers. When Wilson Conco dishes out the pocket-money there is a rush for the café opposite the court. Stilte in die hof. All eyes on Mr Justice Rumpff. The first part of the alternative charge quashed. The rest stays but Mr Pirow and his team are ordered to supply umpteen further particulars – many of them asked for by the defence in the first place. That was one month ago. Now the court adjourns for a month. The whole business to start all over again on September 29 – Heyne's case, misjoinder, prejudice to the accused? Time to think. The months go by.

Treason trial diary: 'A time to think', *Fighting Talk*, September 1958

Part 3
Jo'burg

13

The city of gold

Long ago it was all rolling land which grim, stern, bearded men guarded with long guns and narrow-minded bigotry. They guarded the land from the people from whom they had taken it. They lived in isolation, one from the other, and their minds grew stunted and warped and murky with the disease of racial prejudice, until mental anaemia saw only white and the black was to be feared as a little child fears the dark.

Then one day a man walking in the long fields came across a stone. It was soft as lead and dull yellow. This stone could be smelted, refined, processed and turned into the shiny metal which crowns were made of. And then the people knew that wealth lay beneath the brown earth.

And then men came with spades and pans and tools to tear up the land and wrench the richness from its bowels. They fought and cursed and killed for wealth below the green grass. They built shanties and sunk shafts. They poured in from all horizons. They built a roaring, roistering town, and called it Johannesburg.

But greed is a disease that gnaws at the vitals and eats at the soul. It spreads like mould and its remedy is its satisfaction. Foreign men coveted the richness of the Transvaal and the stern, bearded men took their rifles down from the walls and their long columns rode out to fight the invaders. They lost because they were overpowered by superior numbers and their own bigotry. And thereafter the gold was owned by strange men who sat in clamouring offices and watched long ribbons of paper winding out of their clicking machines. Far across the seas, the gold became tiny numbers which increased or diminished. The owners of the gold did not dig it from the ground, they did not hear the sharp sound of a pick striking rock or hear the clatter of pneumatic drills. They did not feel the sweat dripping from the brow or the hurt of strained muscles, the hard horniness of calloused palms.

Chinese were brought to dig the gold, and when they could not do it, the black men were torn from families, wives, children and the ripe land to dig down into the darkness to find the yellow metal. They sweated and died and created mountains where once the land had been green and virgin. And around the man-made mountains the shanties dropped away, and in their place grew a jungle of granite and steel and chromium. The mud paths became boulevards and macadam roads. The swaggering miners of old were replaced by new swarms of harassed, worried people, fenced in by stone and concrete and all forms of oppression. Alongside the mines new industries grew up and the army of workers grew in numbers and absorbed the atmosphere of strength. And the workers were dark-skinned in the main, and the rulers of them feared them, and made laws to bind and pinion their strength.

Today the mark of racialism, oppression and brutality lies like a hideous birthmark on the face of Johannesburg. It is seen in the slums and locations, the bulldozed stretches of the Western Areas, the jam-packed gaols and the police with pistols and Sten guns.

It is seen in hunger and rags, site and service, gangsterism and rioting. You can tramp the miles of streets and see no place to quench your thirst or appease your hunger. The bright signs reflect the rule of white supremacy. Bar-B-que, 20th Century Fox, Giacomino, Palace Beer Hall, Woodpecker Inn.

The Flying Squad hurtles past, dodging the all-white buses. At the railway stations the cops stand by to demand passes. Black men walk in fear.

But every coin has its reverse. Beauty is found even in a swamp. And the beauty is in the determination of the people. Beauty is in the long line of bus-boycotters, the roar at a meeting of a people who no longer wish to be slaves. There is beauty in the coffee stalls where you can buy a cup of steaming hot brew and two delicious fat-cakes for a sixpence, and chat idly with the friendly man behind the counter.

There is a richness greater than gold in the penny-whistle man walking easily along Pritchard Street, playing his lively tunes. There is a wealth untold in the welcome given by a working family in Vrededorp, the cups of tea and the factory-made biscuits; the at-home in the location where the can of beer is passed from hand to hand, mouth to mouth. There is beauty, too, in the welcoming smile of the shebeen queen, for the shebeen has become a place of relaxation, the local pub where pleasantries are exchanged and the chatter is quiet and meaningless.

Beneath the stony facade of the City of Gold there is a song which singing cannot express. There is a cheerfulness that laughter cannot satisfy, a tragedy that tears cannot obliterate. There is a vision that freedom will make as real as the sweat and the agony and the gold which is its heart.

The real wealth of the golden city, *New Age*, 25 April 1957

14

Doing the town

Life, and the Golden City, is full of contrasts.

I was walking down one of the streets the other afternoon. The air was nippy and the sky as grey as last year's underwear. Fortunately I was well wrapped up in overcoat, muffler and gloves. Well, there I was, just strolling along and thinking of Cape Town in summer when a voice at my elbow said: 'Excuse me, sir.'

I looked around and there was this man. He was stoop-shouldered and his threadbare jacket and ancient flannels were of an undefinable colour. They were ragged at the elbows and the knees. The only other garment seemed to look like the last vestiges of a shirt. He shivered, his face pinched under the layer of grime and stubble, and he smelled of a mixture of sleep, sweat and stale vomit. His grey hair hung like coarse, dirty hemp into his neck.

'Excuse me, mate.'

'Hullo,' says I.

'If you don't mind, mate, how about sparing a sixpence for a coffee? Haven't had nothin' to eat since yesterday mornin'.'

I dug down, thinking, here goes tomorrow morning's bus-fare, and handed over. A hand lined with tiny dirt-filled wrinkles clutched eagerly at the coin and smoke-stained, carious teeth grinned back at me.

'Thanks a lot, mate. Gawd bless yer.'

He tugged at a ragged forelock and shuffled away. I watched him go, and then noticed the name of the street and the building around.

We were on Hollard Street, the shortest and the richest street in Johannesburg. Around us the vast bulk of the Anglo American company headquarters, the grey cubes of other mining houses and insurance companies cast their chill shadows.

Up my alley, *New Age*, 6 June 1957

Crime

Of late the headlines of Johannesburg's dailies have been reading like those of Chicago in the heyday of Al Capone, John Dillinger and the hectic days of illegal booze.

Businessmen and messengers walk in fear of their lives and their cash since armed mobsters, prowling the granite canyons of the Golden City, have launched what verged almost on a gangster reign of terror over the last few weeks. Messengers on their way to the banks have been held up and robbed; the look-out at a drive-in restaurant was 'coshed' and all the cash taken; a merchant tailor was knocked out, losing £800 to armed thugs; an Indian lawyer was held up; houses have been broken into; £2 000 worth of Scotch whisky was the haul of another gang after beating up and stabbing an African watchman. 'Another Armed Robbery – and Vicious Assault,' shouted *The Star* last Wednesday evening.

To counter the wave of crime the top-brass of the cop department have sent into action a special mobile police squadron, plus a 'Ghost Squad' of plain-clothes men mingling with the public in Johannesburg's crowded thoroughfares.

'We have decided on this move to provide increased protection to the public,' trumpeted Colonel J Olivier, chief of the Rand CID in the best imitation of J Edgar Hoover himself. 'With immediate effect and working around the clock the squadron will round up loiterers and suspected criminals in every part of the city.' But like everybody in authority in this fair land of ours, his story doesn't ring true.

A society based on suppression, violence, armed force, poverty and unemployment creates violence, bloodshed, gangsterism and murder. Bad schools produce bad pupils.

America's worst gangsters were bred in the slum-ridden districts of the East Sides, Harlems and Little Italies of every city. Crime and vice breeds where there is poverty and filth, where proper home life and education are non-existent and unemployment is rife. Add to all these conditions the frustration and misery caused by pass laws, permit systems, the colour-bar that denies the non-European people advancement and a proper place in society, and you will see the breeding grounds of South Africa's underworld. A gangster is not born, he is created by a reactionary social system.

Up my alley, *New Age*, 23 May 1957

Chinatown

We had a week off from the Treason Trial, so yours truly decided to do the town. You can't see enough of this burg. By the time I was through, my legs felt worn down to the knees.

I hit Chinatown. Most of the Chinese community have moved, but there are a few clubs and a grocery here and there, and little restaurants. I remember the time I staggered through a nine-course meal that ranged from chicken soup á la Chinois, duck, sweet and sour pork, and a line of various other dishes that left me in a state of collapse at the end of the three hours it took to get through the lot. I didn't want to try it again this time, so I fought shy of the restaurants and the clubs and took a walk down a tunnel between two wretched-looking buildings in search of a Cantonese bird by the name of Charley.

A lady who was by no means Chinese, but who looked like Marilyn Monroe, Jayne Mansfield, La Lollo and Dorothy Radebe all rolled into one, grinned at me from the foot of a sagging staircase at the end of the tunnel. I grinned back and edged around her into the smelly courtyard beyond. A drunk lay on a pile of wet rags, sleeping it off. You could have bitten the smell of blocked plumbing if your teeth were strong enough. Something that was neither man nor woman came out of a doorway on the courtyard. I decided to enquire from the lady at the staircase.

She said, upstairs, so I clawed my way up. I had a glimpse of people, men, women and children, cats, dogs, packed into tiny rotten cells hired out as rooms. I found Charley in one of them, with a crowd of others, gathered around a fan-tan game.

It goes something like this. A lot of beans or buttons are dumped on a table and the banker covers some of them with a cup. Then he pushes the rest away in fours with a stick, and you have to bet on how many of the beans or buttons are left under the cup. The pile of notes scattered about the numbered cloth on the table was big enough to choke a horse, so the game looked serious.

Charley grinned at me across the crowd, showing his gold teeth. He said, 'You write?'
'I write,' I said.
The mob looked at me. I decided to mention no names.
'You drink?' Charley asked blandly.
The mob looked at me again.
'I drink,' I replied, putting on my best smile.
The remains of a bottle of Korea were conjured up.
After the first slug I said goodbye and retired to the solitude of a Chinese gift shop.

Up my alley, *New Age*, 18 July 1957

The 'Ghost Squad'

I pounded on the heels of a quartet of the 'Ghost Squad' one afternoon. Dressed in shabby raincoats, they ambled up Market Street. They gazed into shop windows, lounged at the kerbside, chatted idly. I poked a hole through a newspaper and watched them through it, leaning against sundry lamp-posts on the way. They were just four boys taking a stroll.

Then suddenly they pounced.

An African was jostled, hemmed in, pinned up against a wall. He didn't have a pass, or maybe it wasn't in order. The handcuffs were snapped on. He was hustled around a corner and guarded by one of the foursome. The other cops hung around, like wolves in sheep's clothing, waiting for their prey. Unsuspecting Africans, bicycle messengers, shoppers, to them everything was grist to the mill. Human cargo. Beasts of burden for the farms.

The cargo around the corner increased gradually. Only Mr Swart knows where the quantity of handcuffs came from. Pretty soon the pick-up van rolled up to load its human freight.

Earlier, I was told, the four bright boys had held two men who appeared to be coloured, and had kept them handcuffed in the street for almost a half-hour before releasing them.

Me, I'm not encouraging gangsterism, nor discouraging the cops from pursuing the normal course of their duties, but I must say that the two of the 'Ghost Squad' who shot it out with a gunman the other night and received holes in their intestines have got a lot to think about. They've got a lifetime to think about it.

And in spite of the police terror, the pass-raids, the grinding poverty, there is still time to be happy, to make music. On President Street I found a quartet of African musicians consisting of three men and a younker who was knee-high to nothing making with some real solid stuff, on what do you think? Three penny-whistles and a guitar. They had a repertoire that ranged from rock 'n roll right down to that Old Black Magic. At the corner of Eloff and President a crippled African played a weird instrument that looked like a xylophone, constructed of a row of planks built up over another row of tin cans of various sizes. He was playing 'Suikerbossie', which made me quite homesick.

Up my alley, New Age, 18 July 1957

Night classes
The other night I decided to clear the post box in the hope of mail from home and so found myself ambling in the direction of Johannesburg's General Post Office. On a corner in the centre of the city a couple was trying to stand. At least, she was trying to stand and he was trying to help her remain in that position. Her legs refused to cooperate. They appeared to be made of several hinges, well-oiled, that kept folding up. I stopped and watched with curiosity. She became double-jointed second by second, until accompanied by several hics and awks she finally decided it was time for bed and promptly went to sleep on the pavement. He became exasperated and decided that the only remedy was brute force. So he immediately began to belabour her oompterara. More hics and awks of protest. A crowd gathered.

Up stepped an indignant gallant, his physiognomy contorted with ire, and straightway set out to belabour the belabourer of the fair white and drunk damsel with the flat of his hand.

'Pig!' quoth the gallant in die Taal. 'How dare you hit a woman while she's down. AND IN FRONT OF ALL THESE KAFFIRS! JUST THINK! HOW DO YOU THINK SHE FEELS BEING SLAPPED IN FRONT OF ALL THESE KAFFIRS! YOU ARE A DISGRACE TO THE WHITE RACE!'

'Hic,' said the fair white damsel from the pavement, disentangling her skirt from her hair. 'ASK HIM. THASH RIGHT, ASK HIM HOW I FEEL. AWK.'

* * * * *

I returned from the GPO with the letters and ran into some of the boys. They suggested an ice-cream orgy. I am very partial towards ice-cream and agreed to join their expedition. We piled into a car and proceeded in the general direction of Doornfontein, where there is a place noted for its ice-cream. The frau who was serving looked harassed.

Said she: 'The natives of today simply don't want to work. You ask them to work nine hours a day and they want to revolt. I asked my boy to stay on and he refused.'

'Well,' said one of the boys. 'What's wrong with six hours a day?' Said she, indignantly: 'My man, in order that I should live comfortably, he should work nine hours a day.'

Up my alley, New Age, 21 August 1958

Around and about
Vacancy advertised in a Johannesburg newspaper:

'Cook, houseboy, highly experienced. Elderly boy preferred, refs essential, good wages and home for suitable boy.'

Dear advertiser, how old is an elderly boy, and when are us blacks going to grow up?

Up my alley, New Age, 15 August 1957

Up in Jo'burg a miner is appearing in court for causing the death of an African mineworker by directing a hose carrying compressed air with a pressure of 84 lbs a square inch on to his body. He died in agony.

'I was only playing with him,' the miner said.

Up my alley, *New Age*, 23 October 1958

Up here three fourteen-year-old boys were sentenced to four cuts each for damaging tombstones and vases in the Brixton Cemetery. Asked for an explanation, they replied that they had been playing at 'hitting kaffirs'.

A nice game, they must have thought it was. When I was fourteen my favourite game was 'cops and robbers'. These youngsters were no doubt living up to the times. A nice example of 'training them young'.

Up my alley, *New Age*, 15 August 1957

I was browsing in a local bookshop the other day when by chance I overheard a conversation between the shopkeeper and a customer.

It appeared that the customer was from Linksfield, near Johannesburg, where attempts had been made to organise a civic fire brigade. The idea was to get the Fire Department to train the residents in fire-fighting and organise them into units. The customer was in charge of the matter and consequently canvassed the neighbourhood for recruits.

'It's a good idea,' said one who was contacted. 'But what's going to happen if a fire breaks out during the day when we're all at work?'

'Well,' replied the gentleman doing the organising, 'We'll train our domestic servants too and they'll be able to handle fires when we're away.'

The other stared in amazement. 'What? Impossible! It'll mean that if a fire broke out and a white woman was trapped she would have to be rescued by a black man! That would be terrible … I want nothing to do with this thing.'

Up my alley, *New Age*, 4 July 1957

Les miserables

Above the front entrance of the Johannesburg Public Library (Europeans Only) is a carved slogan which says, if I still remember my Latin, 'Books are the storehouses of the mind.' At the back of the library, painted in black, which nobody up to now has been able to wipe out, is another slogan. This one says: 'Us blacks ain't reading yet.' In front of the library there is also a little park with flowers and trees and benches (also Europeans Only) where the lunch-hour crowd hang out to devour their hamburgers and milk, and where ragged, greasy, stubbly-chinned derelicts lounge, waiting for a handout or ready to sell you anything from a pair of shoelaces to a seventeen-jewel gold wrist-watch. Once one of them tried to sell me a trick alarm-clock that played 'I can't give you anything but love, baby' every hour after midnight.

Well, I was on my way to my digs from the cinema the other night and making a short-cut through this park when out of the shadow of a tree sailed one of these pieces of flotsam and jetsam. He was like all the rest of them floating around the Golden City: unshaven, uncombed, smelly and tattered. This one was also a family man, for beyond him, under the tree, the street light revealed a young-old woman with dishevelled hair and a bony, once-pretty face, carrying in her arms what appeared to be a baby wrapped in an old coat.

The man said: 'Boss, spare something for the wife an' kid. They haven't ate all day, and we've gotter sleep right here in this park. Please, mister.'

This didn't sound like the old line so I forked out something. This cinema's shows are free, anyway.

'Thanks a lot, boss,' he whispered. Then added, 'Boss, my woman … if you like. For a favour.'

'Take care of her, old man,' I told him and pushed past.

This was the other side of the much-boasted-of white South Africa. The ripe and juicy fruit of Western civilisation. It reminded me, somehow, of the film I'd just seen: *Les Miserables*.

Up my alley, *New Age*, 8 August 1957

Fatal statistics

Wow! I've heard of guinea pigs being cut up to advance science, and Laikas being shot way up yonder in Sputniks to advance the knowledge of man, but now I see that the crime rate in the Golden City is helping the progress of surgery.

The 7 000 casualties a year resulting from gangsterism and violence in the townships around the Golden City provide doctors at Baragwanath with so much experience that it has led to the development of new methods of surgery,

The vital, or fatal, statistics read like this: 3 000 head injuries, 1 468 penetrating wounds of the chest, more than 2 000 wounds of the stomach and 495 combined chest and stomach wounds, per year.

It would appear as if we're faced with grim alternatives. Let the crime wave continue and advance surgery, or stop it and our doctors will suffer from lack of experience on the operating table.

What we really need is a nice civilised society where people don't chop each other up, and the doctors can concentrate on keeping us healthy citizens instead of having to sew us up all the time.

Up my alley, *New Age*, 18 September 1958

One of those things

With a few days off … I made one of the usual excursions round and about my temporary home town … to see what I could see. I couldn't find anything new. On the corner of Diagonal and Market streets the cops were lining up a group of bewildered Africans, all strung together with handcuffs, while others ganged up on further victims passing by. The usual pass arrests. It's become so usual in the lives of Johannesburgers that nobody pays any attention to a scene like this, except for maybe a passing glance.

Johannesburg has come to accept African arrests in public with the same indifference they have for the municipal waste baskets.

Just another one of those things.

In Eloff Street a ragged quartet was performing on penny-whistles and guitars, and just around the corner a cripple was banging out 'You are my sunshine' on a home-made xylophone. A spiv slunk up to me and tried to sell me a watch. In the park in front of the all-white 'public' library the bums were still sitting under the trees.

Just some more of those things.

Up my alley, *New Age*, 14 August 1958

15

Fietas

Dusk covers Vrededorp. The streets are narrow and cramped, and at one end of the district the teeming houses overflow into the streets. Homes have been set up on the pavements, and over braziers made of empty petrol drums the evening cooking goes on in the open, sending up dense clouds of smoke which seem to bring the dark on sooner.

Everywhere people are gathered around the fires. Women in headcloths attend to the bubbling pots. The chatter is endless. On one corner an open-air butchery has set up its stalls and workers on their way to the gloomy hovels examine the chunks of mysterious-looking meat on sale.

A man with a guitar slung from one shoulder fingers a greyish-yellow joint and shakes his head. The stout woman behind the displaying dish frowns. Everywhere the black smoke rises. A customer selects a cutlet and it is wrapped in a fragment of old newspaper. The damp parcel disappears into a ragged pocket.

Up the narrow streets the lights from oil lamps are dim and smelly in the packed houses. Battered furniture is piled on verandahs. The fires on the pavements flicker and jump and the smoke keeps on rising, while the ragged children gambol among the blackened drums and drunken men curse impatiently. Across the way a line of men clap and chant in rhythm as an African with trousers rolled up whirls and kicks in a tribal dance. Everywhere the smoke rises as if from sacrificial altars.

The Chinese and Indian shopkeepers are putting up their shutters for the night as the darkness falls. Out of the dip the overloaded Putco buses strain and jangle on their swaying, rickety way west. Sleek new cars swing up the narrow streets to park incongruously before the rows of grimy houses. Here and there a few blocks of flats stand among the squalor like the castles of feudal barons surrounded by the hovels of their serfs.

The smoke rises and the darkness comes and on the corners the groups gather.

'Fietas', Vrededorp, the Village of Peace, awaiting the Group Areas axe that will turn it into another ruin-scattered area which has become a feature of this great city.

Up my alley, *New Age*, 16 May 1957

16

Muddy pools which could be tears

'As regards the carrying out of this Bill, I just want to say that it must be based on justice.'
— Dr Dönges speaking on the Group Areas Bill in Parliament, 1952

Throughout Sophiatown, and the other western areas of Johannesburg, the jagged skeletons of ruined buildings and piles of brick and debris, scattered among homes still standing, give one the impression of the aftermath of an aerial bombardment. But no bombers passed this way. The ruins of the Western Areas are wounds made on this country by the prowling monster of Apartheid.

Once these ruins were houses, homes – and people lived in them. True, many of them were poor homes, for the people were poor. The houses were old, but the people had, by the sweat of their brows, turned them into something a man could come home to every evening and sit down in with his family or gather in with his friends.

He sacrificed to fix the leaks and to paper the walls. He did what he could to buy the things that go to make life a little better. Maybe he was too poor to own everything, but he made a home. His children were born and raised and he settled down and longed for the days when there would be more money, electricity, refrigeration, radios, playgrounds.

But the Group Areas Act says that South Africa must be divided like a vast chequerboard. African, Indian, coloured, Malay, Chinese, white. The iron curtain of racial hatred must be lowered between people of different colours.

Speaking at the hearing of the Group Areas Board in Cape Town on proposals to split up the Southern Suburbs of the Peninsula, Advocate Broeksma pointed out:

> 'You will kill all human endeavour as far as the non-Europeans are concerned. The feeling of resentment will develop into a feeling of hatred. The writing is on the wall.'

And the people are forced out. At bayonet-point Africans were herded from their homes and transported out of the City.

The benefits of new locations have been eulogised, but nothing is said of the passes and permits which made every location a concentration camp. Nothing about raising wages to cover transport. Nothing about the fundamental human right of every human being to live where he chooses.

Site and service is glorified. But there can be no better description than the one given by a witness at the Treason enquiry:

> Magistrate: 'What is this site and service?'
> Witness: 'Your Worship, the authorities build the lavatories and the people must do the rest.'

And all over South Africa, from the Cape Peninsula to the Reef, the non-white people live under the shadow of removal and 'resettlement'. It doesn't matter how long your church or school or mosque has been standing. If the area is declared or required for another group – down comes everything, out you go!

> At a hearing of the Group Areas Board:
> Lowen: And would they have to build a new religious school, new teachers' quarters?
> Joubert: Ja, dit sal natuurlik alles moet aangebring word.
> Lowen: Your Council doesn't consider to pay anything for that, to help them, give them money?
> Joubert: Nee.

A group of men climb a barren hill and view the vast stretch of wasteland around it. That stretch is all right for Indians. I think coloureds will be OK in that part.

In a big room maps are spread out on tables. The City Council, the So-and-so Ratepayers' Association, think this section should be declared white. Red pencils, blue pencils, green pencils, all mark off the map. Every line demolishes the work of a lifetime.

Sixty thousand Africans must be moved from the Western Areas. To the movers they are not people. To the movers they are statistics. Their homes, their lives are a coloured mark on a map. Indians, coloureds, Chinese.

'We are engaged on a clear and purposeful plan, and we are making progress with it,' said Dr Verwoerd at Ficksburg in 1952.

Five thousand Indians and Chinese, 3 000 coloureds must be moved from Pageview, where they lived for 50 years. Four thousand coloured people, an entire community, must be uprooted from Albertsville.

On the big maps the lines move like guillotine blades.

Where should the Ventersdorp Indians go?

Where in the Cape? In the middle of the Kalahari, or the bottom of Table Bay?

And people in the vain hope of escaping the inexorable clutch at straws. My great-grandfather was Scotch. Or Irish. Or, I was baptised in St Mary's Cathedral. I attend European cinemas.

You consider yourself a European? – Yes.

Tell me if I'm right or wrong, the average European looks down on the coloured? – Yes.

Actually, at the Test match you were admitted at gate 5 which is the gate that admits coloured and Indian people? – That is not true.

There are shadows falling over the land. Black, white, brown, yellow. And the shadows creep like ghosts among the strips called buffer zones, the bulldozed ruins of one-time homes, the muddy pools which could be tears.

On Group Areas, of human bondage, Fighting Talk, June 1957

17

Little Libby: The adventures of Liberation Chabalala (cartoon strip)

From March to November 1959, Alex La Guma contributed a weekly 37-part cartoon series in *New Age* called 'Little Libby: The Adventures of Liberation Chabalala'. His fellow Treason Trialist, M 'Chubby' Tshabalala, was the inspiration for the Little Libby character, and the other main characters were Mustafa Moonsamy, Kasper Katchum, Frikadel and Sergeant Shark (based on one of the least-liked Treason Trial witness). The series touched on political campaigns of the Congress movement at the time and drew on La Guma's observations of life in Johannesburg during the trial. After being kidnapped and forced to work on a potato farm, Little Libby undergoes numerous adventures (including a visit to the *New Age* offices), falls in with criminals and eventually joins the struggle, distributing pamphlets calling for a stayaway. The potato boycott theme followed a number of exposés on forced child and convict labour on Transvaal potato farms in *Drum* and *New Age* which led to a boycott campaign by the ANC.

Roger Field (2010: 84) has observed: 'Nothing suggests La Guma set out to produce a "graphic novel", but as his first published work of extended fiction and his only one in a popular genre in which very few South African writers have worked, *Little Libby*, occupies an important place in the history of South African popular culture and the study of his work'.

As Field (2010: 84–94) explains, we see in his cartoon strip and in his 'Up my alley' columns from 1957 onwards the sign of the more subversive, anarchic and anti-establishment La Guma that existed alongside his serious and politically correct, often dourly orthodox, Communist Party political persona. This was Alex the working-class youngster who was a great story-teller and who, Richard Rive in *Writing Black* (1981: 31) tells us, 'maintained an excellent sense of humour and was the life and soul of any party' despite his firmly-held radical political views and many brushes with the security police.

Little Libby came later than *Drum* magazine's 'Goombi The Great Goom!', but it was a radical departure for serious liberation struggle newspapers. While the figures in 'Little Libby' are reminiscent of Popeye and of the Katzenjammer Kids, the series is interesting for its explicitly political context. Seven *New Age* journalists had been arrested during the police Treason Trial raids and this led to considerable financial and logistical problems for the newspaper. It survived by using volunteers, cutting the number of pages and reducing salaries. La Guma and his colleagues had to find material that could travel well between Cape Town, Johannesburg and Pretoria and adapt to unpredictable interruptions.

As a child La Guma had attended art classes at the Hyman Liberman Institute in District Six and in 1947 he enrolled for life drawing classes at what was called the Contemporary Art

School in Roger Street, District Six, which later became part of the coloured section of the racially segregated Cape Technical College. His fellow students included the artist, illustrator and poet Peter Clarke, the sculptor Louis Maurice and the poet SV Petersen. Roped in to assist his father at the National Liberation League offices, by, for example, painting posters, decorating banners and illustrating leaflets, Alex had his first, child-like sketches published in the first issue of *The Liberator: A Non-European Anti-Imperialist Magazine*, edited by his father, in 1937 at the age of 12. During the Treason Trial he produced a portfolio of ink sketches in his Croxley drawing book, to be found in his papers in the UWC-RIM Archives. He gave it the title '"The Fort" Prison, Johannesburg, 1956'. La Guma sketched his fellow prisoners while they read newspapers, held political education classes, played cards or chess, or endured haircuts. Some are poor likenesses, but he had to use a blue ballpoint pen – a medium that left little room for error. Not for nothing did the great novelist Wole Soyinka observe in the first review of La Guma's first novel that 'Alex La Guma writes with a painter's brush, no it is more accurate to call it an ink sketch'.[1] In his obituary, more than a half a century later, one of La Guma's comrades remembered that he was forever sketching in meetings and when sitting around. La Guma saw little difference between popular and high culture, and in his cartoons, 'Up my alley' columns and his writing lampooning ruling class politics – see, for example, his Pampoen-onder-die-Bos stories in chapter 35 – he used an aggressive humour that usurped the power of the oppressors and used it against them.

Notes

1   Soyinka, W, The fight for human existence, *Post*, 3 June 1962.

References

Field, R (2010) *Alex La Guma: A literary and political biography*. Auckland Park: Jacana Media

Rive, R (1981) *Writing black*. Cape Town: David Philip

LITTLE LIBBY: THE ADVENTURES OF LIBERATION CHABALALA (CARTOON STRIP)

LITTLE LIBBY: THE ADVENTURES OF LIBERATION CHABALALA (CARTOON STRIP)

Part 4
Cape Town

18

Back up my alley

Here we are, back in the old home town down South. It's a quiet town. When I walked out of Cape Town station I automatically looked for the 'Ghost Squad' hanging around to stop Africans for their passes. They weren't around. We haven't those kinds of weeds in our garden yet. We haven't any mine dumps – only dear old Table Mountain. Of course we do have the Houses of Parliament. They're still on the same old spot, waiting for the next round of legislation.

Well, there are a lot of things I'm going to miss for the next four months. The Treason Trial, of course (praise be to Allah), seat number 85 (a thousand curses), Vrededorp, Sophiatown, a certain Chinese gentleman by the name of Johnny, rock 'n roll, and two characters of the Special Branch, Messrs Douglas Ndaba and Gladwell Ngcai. (May their feet hurt.)

Most of all, I'll miss everybody who made my stay in Johannesburg a happy one. Practically a home from home.

Up my alley, New Age, 26 September 1957

It certainly is good to be back in my own stamping ground after many months in the Golden City. Hanover Street is still the place it was when I was removed to the Fort in Johannesburg last December. The hawkers are still there, crying their wares; the boys are still lounging idly under the balconies; the housewives still getting in the groceries.

There are a few more empty shops, however. Some of the old businesses have gone bang. The manager of a shoe store stood in the doorway of his shop waiting for a customer. I remarked that business seemed quiet.

'You can say that again,' he said. 'People just don't seem to have any money to spend these days. A few years ago I used to take in about thirty pounds on a Friday. It's four-thirty now and I've only sold three pairs of shoes. Two of them children's.'

'Do you think business would be better all round if the workers were paid higher wages?'

'Definitely. Pay the people more and they'll spend more. People have got to buy things.'

I told him about the campaign for £1 a day minimum wage for all workers.

'That's the stuff. More wages and we'll all be happy.'

* * * * *

A man selling fruit shook hands with me. 'Long time no see, ou man. Have an apple.'

We talked about this and that and he remarked that he had read that Great Britain was going to explode another hydrogen bomb.

'Daai mense is mal,' he said. 'They are making the bombs bigger and bigger. One day they'll blow us all sky-high. We'se poor people. We just want to make a living. I want to sell my fruit.' He described his attitude towards nuclear weapons with a string of colourful phrases.

All over the world there are millions of Talip Arendses, who want to live in peace, earn a living, sell their fruit.

Up my alley, *New Age*, 13 June 1957

Trying time

Winter is a trying time for the poor. The rains are awaited with dread, and in the pondokkies scattered throughout the Cape Flats, the families eye their flimsy ceilings with doubt and hope that they will prove strong enough to keep the rain out.

Every year it's the same story. Families are washed out, people live shivering for weeks on end. And charity must come to the rescue. Well-meaning citizens come running with blankets and old clothes, soup kitchens are set up, mutterings of 'Shame' are heard all round. When the spring breaks, the freezing poor are forgotten until the next winter. In the meantime, large sums of money are voted for the development of lidos and plans are suggested to turn Cape Town into the 'Mecca' of tourists. The seas of mud in the distressed areas appear as regularly as the blooms along the beachfront at Sea Point.

* * * * *

In Rylands Estate, Athlone, a pondokkie burnt down the other night. The ever-present brazier in the refrigerator-cold shanty was the cause of the fire. In the morning the family was wandering among the debris of their former home, salvaging what could be used again, blackened sheets of tin, pieces of wire, here and there a pole that had survived the fire. By nightfall another pondokkie had been erected in its place. A bizarre structure consisting of cardboard, rotting planks, galvanised iron, rusty Coca Cola signs; all propped up with crooked pine poles, lengths of discarded timber; held together with bits of wire, pieces of rope, rusty nails; the roof held down by a collection of bricks and stones.

One night another fire may start, or perhaps a storm will come up, and the rickety 'building' will be destroyed once more. The salvaging will start all over again, the collecting of materials to rebuild once more. The life of the pondokkie-dweller is a permanent 'period of reconstruction'.

Up my alley, *New Age*, 27 June 1957

Don't sneeze

Residents of the municipal housing schemes have many complaints about the new houses being built by the Cape Town City Council in Bridgetown and Silvertown, Athlone.

'The municipality is cashing in on the acute housing shortage by erecting cheap and inferior dwellings and letting them at unreasonably high rents,' they say.

These new structures, plain, ugly rectangular blocks which look like miniature barracks in contrast with the older, neat and more comfortable cottages and flats built when the schemes were first opened, are being erected at the rate of twenty per week at the cost of £400 for each block of two semi-detached, according to a builder working for the City Council. 'On many occasions we have to use mortar which has been left standing over the weekend,' the builder said. 'By Monday it has hardened and as a result bricks cannot be laid evenly.'

The houses have three-inch walls, unplastered cement floors and, except for the bathroom, have no doors inside. The bathrooms have no baths or showers, and all electric light switches are placed together in one part of the house.

Tenants complain strongly of the lack of privacy due to the thinness of the walls and the absence of doors to the rooms. Rents charged for these uncomfortable and unattractive dwellings range from 26/– to £2 per week.

'I realise that under the present circumstances one cannot pick and choose when it comes to getting a house,' one of the tenants told *New Age*. 'The shortage is critical. But these new places are definitely not worth the rent we are paying. Since we are compelled to pay high rents, why can't the council build better places instead of these "glorified pondokkies"?'

'It looks as if one sneezed too hard the walls will fall in,' said another disgruntled tenant. 'I think I can describe every brick in my bedroom.'

...

The City Council is collecting thousands of pounds a year in rents, and the flats and houses built in the past have been paid for over and over again, the residents say. Vast sums have been spent on beautifying the beachfront at Sea Point, so there can be no excuse that better housing cannot be provided.

The housing schemes in Athlone were originally established for the coloured people of the lower income group, and let at sub-economic rentals. Now many of the dwellings are being let to people earning economic wages, and rentals charged on a differential basis, according to the incomes of all members of the family over 16 years of age.

Yet these people are still excluded from the municipal voters' roll. The time has come, they say, that the present qualification for the municipal franchise should be revised. Municipal tenants, who pour so much into the coffers of the City Council are entitled to have a say in its affairs.

Don't sneeze – the walls may fall down, *New Age*, 8 November 1956

'Beter dan daai ou'

District Six is still ecstatic about the fact that it will appear on the TV screens in Great Britain. Many people are even under the impression that the BBC team that toured 'Die Ses' was a movie outfit, and are making enquiries as to when they will be starred at the local cinemas.

But what impresses many is the fact that the teeming alleys and backstreets, the horrors of Windermere and the general poverty of these parts of South Africa will be revealed to the overseas public 'straight from the shoulder'. No doubt the State Information Bureau will have some explaining to do, but no amount of glossy magazines like *South African Panorama* will help to counteract the impression made by the actual scenes depicted on the BBC's own 'Panorama' programme.

Mr Strijdom was interviewed by the same television team and I suppose that he will appear on the same programme along with the people of District Six and Windermere. On Hanover Street a scarred and battered-looking gentleman claimed that he had been picked up by the camera lens too.

'But I bet you ek lyk beter dan daai ou,' he remarked enthusiastically.

Up my alley, *New Age*, 20 June 1957

My favourite barber

As usual my favourite barber had lots to say. Most of it was contempt of court, but a lot was a general political review and long philosophical dissertations. His big complaint (not restricted to barbers only) is the treatment under the lousy colour-bar system.

He was on his way to church with his family one Sunday morning when his little son wanted a cold drink. Pa gave him permission to pop into a nearby café. The place had once welcomed all comers, but had recently been taken over by a gentleman of the apartheid breed. He mistook the little boy for one of the chosen race and invited him to sit down at one of the tables. But when father turned up to see why junior was taking so long over his cold drink, the café owner saw red (I mean black) and manhandled the youngster out of the shop. Of course, the father objected. The cops showed up and reviewed the situation. They decided that if the youngster had been asked by the café proprietor to sit down and have his drink he ought to be allowed to finish it, irrespective of whether it had been a 'mistake'.

Jo'burg, Cape Town, anywhere in the country, it's the same old story. But it's a good sign that many people refuse to get used to the colour-bar, and are prepared to put their backs up.

Up my alley, *New Age*, 26 September 1957

First-class

The passengers in the mixed first-class on the train to Cape Town were packed as tight as beans in a tin of pork. By the time we reached Observatory I was systematically being strangled by a little boy who had hold of my camera strap, and at the same time slowly being anaesthetised by [someone] who had apparently had her morning bath in something probably called Evening in Paris, but which smelled like On the Waterfront.

The ordeal proved too much for several passengers.

Said a stout woman who appeared to be on the verge of apoplexy: 'This is awful, why – take your elbow out of my back – don't they put on more coaches?'

'We are dogs,' muttered an old grey-head. 'We are dogs to be beaten and chased from pillar to post.'

'I've had enough,' snapped another man. 'There are three coaches for Europeans, all half empty, on this train. I'm not going to take this another yard.' We pulled into Salt River and he was out and heading for the European coaches. He climbed into the first one he reached with everybody craning their necks to see what was going to happen. Nothing did.

Apartheid on the trains makes its effects felt particularly at peak hours, and that's when it often falls apart. But peak hour or no peak hour, resentment smoulders all the time, and we're all heading for the stage when everybody is going to say of the entire apartheid system:

'I'm not going to take this another yard.'

Up my alley, *New Age*, 10 October 1957

I once thought that the SAR [South African Railways] did not allow political propaganda of any nature being displayed on stations. But now I see that some mysterious committee called 'Anticom' are sharing the billboards along with the evils of drink.

'Liberty dies where Communism thrives', 'Communism makes a beast of you', are two of the howlers that caught my eye.

If all this is true, then it appears that we are really living in a communist state and not in an Apartheid one.

Up my alley, *New Age*, 27 March 1958

I would have liked to send a large, economy-size bottle of kidney pills to Dr de Wet of Vanderbijlpark as a present from the 'disloyal press' but thought better of it, since he is probably suffering from a bad liver.

He would no doubt consider me a very disloyal character indeed if I were to report to you that subways may be built under Adderley Street and Heerengracht, here in Cape Town, to enable WHITE passengers to leave the new apartheid railway station in safety.

Or that the sun did turn BLACK the other day, when the moon passed in front of it – without permission of the Group Areas Board, too.

Up my alley, *New Age*, 17 August 1961

The weather, the bomb and the bible puncher

Spring is pouring out all over. Nice weather for the ducks, but in many homes there is enough water to float a snoeking fleet. I was having tea and a chat with a friend of mine the other day when the sound of music from another part of the house caused me to ask: 'Is your youngster learning to play the xylophone?' 'Xylophone nothing,' growled my friend. 'That's the rain leaking into the basins we've put on the kitchen floor.'

A moment later a harder downpour sent a long trickle through the dining-room ceiling into my cup. 'Drink up,' said my friend, cackling. 'Your tea'll get cold.'

It's no joke. The leaking roofs, I mean. We've just had the Asiatic 'flu, now I suppose we're in for another round of colds.

Along the Cape Flats the poor will be wading through the ruins of their hovels when the rain holds off for a while. To say nothing of Windermere. More charity, more discarded blankets and clothing. No improvement in the housing situation.

* * * * *

People are blaming the weather on the nuclear explosions. Some scientists have denied that hydrogen bomb tests cause disturbances in the weather, others say that they do. Whatever they do to the weather or not is unimportant in comparison to what they do to people.

A Japanese scientist said the other day that if bomb tests are continued, the Japanese people will be extinct in ten generations.

* * * * *

As the ancient Phoenicians would have it:
'Take war away from the earth,
Banish all strife from the soil;

Pour peace into earth's very bowels,
Much amity into earth's bosom.'

Up my alley, *New Age*, 10 October 1957

Brother, it's hotter here than the booster jet of an ICBM [intercontinental ballistic missile], and I guess there's a boom in the soft-drink and beer business. Anyway, everybody has a fried look about them. I don't know how the crowd that gathers around the gospel grinder on the Grand Parade can stand it … the heat, I mean. To say nothing of the stuff he hands out.

Well, I couldn't resist the temptation of stopping by and lending an ear to the bible-puncher (I'm allowed to attend religious gatherings) and what I got was a long line all about pie in the sky.

The gospel guy stood there with the sweat dripping all over the front of his jacket, telling us all about the good things to come. He got around to the love of man for man, and that set one of the audience to remark loudly: 'What about apartheid?'

Well, the bible boy just gives him a look, as if he was committing sacrilege, and goes right on plugging away.

Come now, pal. Why didn't you answer the man's question?

Anyway, me, I'll have my pie down here, thank you.

Up my alley, *New Age*, 28 November 1957

Trigger finger

The pictures in the press of the muscle-bound cop who entered the 'Mr Universe' contest in London drew the attention of some of the boys on Hanover Street. They examined the pictures, looked at the muscles.

'So that's what hit me,' said one of the boys, fingering a scar on his shaven poll.

'Hell,' said another, 'the — law don't need so much muscles. All they need is a good trigger finger.'

Up my alley, *New Age*, 31 October 1957

I have an idea that very few people raised a cheer of welcome when the cop with 'exceptional zeal' arrived in this town.

After reading of his exploits I wonder whether Sergeant Arlow hasn't been booted down here to a quieter climate because even his bosses think his zeal is a bit thick, even for them.

I'm sure this triggerman with thirteen African notches on his gun will feel somewhat unhappy in our quiet town and he will miss the exciting atmosphere of the Golden City where he made those thirteen donderse kaffirs bite the dust.

Apart from having shot down those African suspects, his record states 10 000 arrests. I wonder how many for pass offences.

A character like this should be transferred a century back to the raw towns of the wild and woolly west, instead of to Cape Town. I'm sure he would be much happier wearing a sheriff's star than the police Good Service Medal.

And what are the other incidents connected with Sergeant Arlow's zealous record? Among other things:
- At the time of the Lady Selborne baton charge on women, it was Sgt Arlow who dragged Dr Tsele into the police van after he had been handcuffed and beaten semi-conscious.
- It was Sgt Arlow who had phoned the police station prior to the baton charge to say he was sure the women were breaking a municipal by-law and asked for more police to be sent to the scene.
- It was Sgt Arlow who locked an African suspect into the boot of his car.
- It was Sgt Arlow who was present recently at the arrest of three Africans suspected of robbery. One of them died in the cells.
- It was Sgt Arlow who arrested a former magistrate, Kirschner, and forced him semi-clothed into a pick-up van. The magistrate was later awarded £2 000 damages for wrongful arrest.

Up my alley, *New Age*, 30 July 1959

The cry that sounds something like 'Baaaambooooo' is becoming well known in Windermere. It is the signal passed from street to street, warning that the police are approaching. Police raids are a regular occurrence in that part of our fair Peninsula. It is a common sight to hear police vans storming up the streets and unloading their armed freight, white and black, to scatter the populace and descend on houses under the pretext of searching for liquor.

South Africa is becoming well known for the work of its police force. Whether it is for passes, liquor or home-brewed beer, the cops always find great pleasure in going on a raid. It's great to be able to wave your gun or brandish your club under the noses of unarmed people.

I was standing on a corner in Darling Street when a patrol van swung past and pulled up beside a hawker who had parked his barrow at the kerbside. A red-faced cop stuck his head out of the window of the van and bawled at the fruit vendor to move on. The hawker reluctantly made preparations to leave the spot. Then one of the other cops said something to his pal, and the latter stuck his head out again and said: 'Awright, stay where you are, but give us some fruit.' The hawker sullenly flapped open a large paper bag and filled it up, handed it over and watched the van drive off. I could guess what was going on in his mind.

Up my alley, *New Age*, 27 June 1957

Conveyor belt

In factories everything is turned out on a conveyor belt. The other Saturday morning I looked in on the magistrate's court and saw money being made – not on a conveyor belt – but pretty much like it.

The dough is made by the state, of course.

The dock is packed so tight with the Friday night haul that I bet a louse from a jail blanket wouldn't find a place for a meal. And the court orderly strolls between the dock and the bench calling out the charge and the sentence like a stuck gramophone record.

'Two pounds or ten days. Two pounds or ten days. Two pounds or ten days.' When one batch has been cleared, the next follows, squeezing into the dock. 'Two pounds or ten days. Two pounds or ten days.'

From there to the underground and out through the studded gates for those who have coughed up with their fines. For those unable to come across with the moola, the steel prison delivery van is waiting, and the cops yell and push the human freight into it, packing them in like jam in a tin can.

Said a white woman watching: 'They're treated just like cattle. Just like cattle.' Black cattle, lady.

Up my alley, *New Age*, 21 November 1957

I dropped in at the magistrate's court where lots of people go to rest their tired corns, where I was due to appear anyway, and was very impressed by a prosecutor's poetic form of address to the accused.

It went something like this:
Dieklagteisdatjydronkwasindiehoofstraatwynbergskuldigofonskuldigtoepraatman praatman kom kom praatman.

Nuff said.

Up my alley, *New Age*, 2 July 1959

Stark message

'I regret to inform you that your husband died in this institution on the 14th July and was buried on the 16th. Please inform us what should be done with his property.'

This stark message received by the relations of a dead prisoner illustrates the callous method of the authorities in dealing with the families of those who die in jail.

No word explaining the circumstances of the man's death. No offer to deliver the body for burial by the family. Just the grim notification that he had died and had been buried.

Such was the letter received from the Rawsonville, Cape, farm jail by Mrs Johanna Cupido of Kensington, informing her that her husband Shadrick Dennison was dead.

Typewritten in Afrikaans on an official letterhead the letter said: 'Greetings, I regret to inform you that your husband, Shadrick Dennison, died in this institution on 14th July 1959, and that he was buried on the 16th July. Please inform us what should be done with his clothes, whether you will call for them or whether it should be sent. His property is as follows …' Then a list of the prisoner's personal effects.

From the postmark it is clear that the letter was not even sent until six days after his death.

'Couldn't they even let us know so that we could arrange the funeral ourselves?' asks the grief-stricken Mrs Cupido. 'And couldn't they even tell us what he died of? Someone who saw him in prison only a week before said that he was perfectly fit.'

I phoned the Rawsonville farm jail for information and was informed flatly, 'No one has died here during the past weeks.'

I checked out the facts and phoned again. This time the death was admitted.

'What did he die of?' I asked.

'Heart failure', was the reply.

Died in jail – family was not even told the cause, *New Age*, 30 July 1959

Phooey

While visiting the local labour offices the other day I was accosted by a sourfaced female member of the master race, mumbling to herself as she stuffed a wad of unemployment benefits into her bag.

'You ought to see them inside,' quoth she. 'Who?' I asked.

'The sunburnt ones,' she snapped. 'Those playing white. They are your enemies. Not the government. Me, I'm a Nationalist, I support apartheid, but just look at those people, they're not white.'

'What about their identity numbers?' I scowled at her. 'They're supposed to produce them.'

'Yah. Their cards might have W for white on them, but they ought to produce their mothers and fathers, too. Then you'll see. They are your enemies, they and the agitators.'

With that she stalked off.

PHOOEY!

Up my alley, *New Age*, 4 June 1959

A lot of people just can't get out of the darn habit of calling Africans 'Jim' or 'John' when those aren't even their names.

A friend of mine whose name is Gladstone was strolling in town the other day when a European character behind him called, 'Say, Jim, wait a minute.' Gladstone just keeps on going and this other character keeps on hey-Jimming behind him. So Gladstone turns around and says: 'You talking to me?'

'Sure, Jim,' this character says. 'Where is Plein Street?'

'How d'you know my name is Jim?'

'Why, I just guessed.'

'Well,' says Gladstone, 'You just guess where Plein Street is.'

Up my alley, *New Age*, 5 December 1957

Home to the bergies

The Battle of the Bulge has started again. This time the offensive has been launched on Devil's Peak. A Catholic priest is campaigning to have the name changed to Christus Peak, and even led a pilgrimage to the top to erect a crucifix. Came the Dutch Reformed Church with a counter-attack. 'A Catholic invasion,' they growled. 'Aggression!'

A communiqué from neutral sources stated: 'It's all wrong. The name isn't Devil's Peak at all. It's got something to do with "Duiwe" – "Doves".'

No, said another authority. 'It started with Van Hunks sitting down to a smoking contest with Old Nick himself.'

'It wasn't Van Hunks,' somebody else told me. 'It was Van Tromp.'

I'm getting all confused. Van Hunks, Van Tromp, Van Diggelen, Devil Shmevil. What's all the fuss about? There's no gold in that thar hill.

Whether they call it Devil's Peak or Christus Peak, or Pike's Peak, or Hill 1957, it'll still be home to the bergies who have no place else to live.

Up my alley, *New Age*, 26 December 1957

19

Me and 'cultcha'

The glory is departed. Are the days (or nights) of the good old commercials, kwelas and 'tickey-draaie' gone forever?

Back on the beat of my favourite boulevard I climbed the flight of steps to the dining room of a new restaurant on Hanover Street, just to rest my ankles and drink a cup of China. I took a table near a motley collection of teenagers who were sipping gingerbeer, their feet wrapped around the legs of the chairs, and I flapped my ears just to hear what I could hear.

Somebody slipped a sixpence into the slot of the jukebox, the coin went down into the bowels of this infernal machine, a record rose up onto the turntable and the next minute I was assailed by a certain Mr Presley yelling something about a 'poor teddy-bear'.

The teenagers immediately went into a frenzy of contortions and wiggles in the available floor space.

The owner of the diner has adopted a somewhat philosophical attitude. 'You can't please everybody,' he told me. 'Some people want to eat in quiet, and some want the jukebox going all the time. These youngsters are some of my best customers.'

When Mr Presley was through, I tried to bring the conversation down to the normal tone of voice, but found myself competing with an 'artist' by the name of Little Richard.

'I let them enjoy themselves,' the owner said. 'Otherwise they'd just be hanging around the streets. They might as well spend their time here.'

Not that he made any profit out of it, he went on. Some of them preferred to invest all their sixpences in the jukebox rather than buy a glass of milk.

'What d'you expect,' he yelled above the beat of the rock 'n roll. 'They don't get a chance to develop their tastes. All they get fed on is the movies and this stuff.'

By the time I had finished my tea I was 'all shook up'.

Up my alley, *New Age*, 13 February 1958

Tommy's girl
Rock 'n roll fans here in Cape Town have been going mad over Britain's contribution to the world of rubber-jointed gyrations and hot guitar, Tommy Steele. He even shared the headlines with Strijdom and [Sir De Villiers] Graaff. But write-ups of the Steele welcome in the local press still puzzle me a bit.

At the Sea Point hall where Thomas made his first appearance, the papers said that there gathered outside 'a constant crowd of teenagers and non-Europeans', and '200 teenagers and 100 coloured people'.

They didn't say whether the 'non-Europeans' and 'coloured people' had long grey beards, but from my knowledge a very large section of my younger brethren are of the fraternity of the jeans and leather coats and stovepipes who are as ardent fans of the gentlemen with the mops of hair and the guitars as any of their ilk on the other side of the Colour curtain.

Up my alley, *New Age*, 20 March 1958

One papa who seems to be hit up about his daughter's appearance in the … show for NEs [non-Europeans] is the old boy who has written to Doc Dönges and Div [De Villiers Graaff] about it.

At the same time the dress designer for the show seems to have gone to a lot of trouble to explain that the costumes worn by the chorus are quite presentable for use before non-white audiences.

I guess stern-minded Puritans would want all chorus girls to be regaled in the neck-to-shin costume á la DRC [Dutch Reformed Church]. But as a coloured young lady who used to be an artist's model for both white and non-white painters said to me when I spoke to her about the business:

'What have Tommy's girls got that I haven't?'

Up my alley, *New Age*, 3 April 1958

More rock 'n roll
So you like Elvis? … Well, just out of the army, he made two wiggles and sang two songs on TV … And for this performance he received a sum of moola that could have paid the salaries of 25 school teachers in the States, 42 ministers or 63 farm workers … It could have provided a year's training for about 30 nurses or for a year in college for 125 youngsters, or fed 3 000 children for a year.

And we talk about Jayne Mansfield's statistics!

Up my alley, *New Age*, 27 April 1961

And now Deputy Sheriff Blackie Swart is going to deal with ducktails himself. He's even going to bring up in Parliament a Bill that will solve the problem. Like all the legislation we've had, it will pass the buck on to the people – this time, the parents. They're responsible for the goings-on of young hooligans, says Blackie.

This Bill and the banning of Terry Dene will curtail the growth of demonstrations of hooliganism apparently associated with rock 'n roll music … Blackie hopes … in the same way the pass laws and deportations are supposed to prevent crime amongst Africans.

But our young folk must have something to replace rock 'n roll, Blackie? What's it going to be? A travelling choir of the DRC?

Up my alley, *New Age*, 3 April 1958

Night out

The other night I had occasion to find myself in the company of several local celebrities, in the lantern-lit lounge of a nearby nightery. All this was in aid of listening to Negro journalist Bill Gordon deliver himself of his impressions of the dark continent.

Flanked by an eagle-eyed hombre from the State Department and a gent described as a 'political officer of the US Embassy', Billy-boy sailed very carefully in the middle and refused to get his feet wet. 'I am not here to say what is right and what is wrong,' quoth he.

The evening went off with everything hunky-dory as far as the Westerners were concerned. The jazz played by combos headed by Messrs George Kussel and Morris Goldberg and assisted by trumpet-man Banzi Bangani was supposed to have been jazz as played in SA. Instead it sounded just like jazz as it is played 'back home' in the USA.

Which probably proved to the happy Americans that, apart from Coca Cola, they have got some foothold here.

Several numbers were rendered – render meaning to tear apart.

Even penny-whistler Frank Sitole forgot that his instrument had become practically hundred-percent African, and gave a strictly down South blues number – very beautifully played.

Music maestro Dan Ulster's single item, Liebestraum, was wunderbar. It had everybody listening.

* * * * *

African nationalism, said Bill Gordon, was running over this continent like a burst dam. The mighty flood needed to be directed into the right channels. Warning: The non-whites should be careful to choose the right leaders.

He didn't mention what the right channels or leaders were.

Having expressed in the press his due shock at the Windermere slums, this gentleman, who is the editor of an all-Negro daily paper, left for Pretoria, where he promised he would visit that greatest tourist attraction of all – the Treason Trial.

Crack of the evening: Mr Gordon was introduced by Dr Van der Ross (rhymes with brass) as the editor of the *Atlanta Daily Worker*.

Pleasant journey, tovarisch [comrade]!

Up my alley, *New Age*, 29 January 1959

The coons

We're heading for the last round-up of 1957 and please don't tell me it's too early to talk about it. The subject was brought up by a certain party who has been growling to me about the racket the coon bands are beginning to cause at night, now that they're getting into the rehearsal stage. Well, that is a sign that we're heading for the 'big days'.

I guess my friend's complaint (and I bet there are others with the same) will be one of those things that usually starts the controversy which crops up at this time of year. Are the coons degrading, or not? Should they be abolished, boycotted, ignored, etc., etc.?

I've heard so many arguments about the matter, and I guess you have too, that I might as well put in my penny's worth.

The way I see it in a nutshell is like this: A people's cultural level can't be divorced from their economic level. One has a bearing on the other. So folks with lots of money and leisure have the opportunities of raising their cultural level, and folks who are poor don't get a chance to develop, so they are only able to appreciate culture of a lower type.

The characters who are yelling about getting rid of the coons because it reveals a very low standard of culture and so on have got hold of the wrong end of the stick, I think.

The big job is to raise the economic level of the people, with it their cultural standards will go up, and the coons will die out.

So there. Me and cultcha.

Last New Year's Day I saw a coon with a picture of Herr Strijdom sewn to the seat of his pants. That's one coon whose side I'm on, anyway.

Up my alley, *New Age*, 5 December 1957

Liedjie for the masters
We are not surprised to hear that 'provisions will be made for non-European participation in the Union Festival 1960, within the framework of Government policy'.

Fifty years of Union based upon the oppression of the non-white peoples may be worth celebrating by the racialists and white supremacists, and 'within the framework of Government policy' undoubtedly means that certain Uncle Toms will be allowed to extol the benevolence of their white masters. No doubt the CAD [Coloured Affairs Department] and good boys among the African chiefs will feature prominently among these revellers.

Up my alley, *New Age*, 27 November 1958

At a recent meeting of the local Festival Committee there were no coloured organisations present, and I believe that the Eoan Group has also turned down participation.

With such a strong cultural body out of the show it looks as if Dr ID [du Plessis] will probably go a-fishin' and hope that he lands a coon band just so's he can save some face.

Up my alley, *New Age*, 17 September 1959

A summit meeting ... has been called by the CAD's Dr ID for the top brass of the coon carnival ... The doktor is trying hard to warm up the cold war that is developing among the non-whites over the ... festival, and this might be his first attempt to get at us blacks, no matter what.

The authorities are anxious to make known the cultural and sporting progress of the non-Europeans during the festival. Nothing is said about political and economic rights.

That is enough reason for us to stay away, but no doubt Dr ID will find some poor sap who will sing a liedjie for the masters.

Up my alley, *New Age*, 4 February 1960

Song and dance

Local boy who has made good is Johaar Mosaval, the coloured dancer back in South Africa from the Royal Ballet Company and at the moment guest dancer in another local boy's production, 'Pink Lemonade'.

Crowds have been flocking to see Mosaval backed up by the Eoan Group's ballet corps and have come back with high praise for a terrific performance.

The group has done much to promote talent in the community and we are all looking forward to further triumphs in all branches of the arts. But lately there have been mutterings in the background about the high-handedness of certain officials resulting in signs of dissatisfaction in the ranks of the membership.

The old light-skinned and dark-skinned question seems to be cropping up, too, particularly around a certain young lady said to be an outstanding dancer but who hasn't been given a chance to move higher up because she happens to have that kinky hair and dark skin.

We don't know whether all this is on the level, but where there is smoke there is probably a fire, and for the good of progress we hope that the group will be able to pour cold water on it and continue with the good work.

Up my alley, *New Age*, 11 June 1959

Of course, the Eoan Group did not get an invite to help in the formation of the State Opry. Whoever heard of us blacks being able to take part in anything guwermental, unless it is strictly in accordance with ye olde apartheid. No matter how good we can sing *Traviata* or *Bohème*.

Besides the group turned down the Coloured Affairs Departments dough, didn't they? Which is more than can be said of the Cape Malay Choir Board. This corpse – sorry, I meant, body – interviewed their Life President recently (none other than Dr ID du Pie) to shake an extra 1 000 quid out of the petty cash, so that they can hit the road around the Union singing folk songs.

All I can say is that the Malay community and their folk music need better treatment than this.

Up my alley, *New Age*, 22 September 1960

Movies

A reader wrote and asked, 'Do you like to go the movies?' so I took off and went to see a picture running the black belt in the Peninsula at the moment.

It turned out to be one of those 'let's be nasty to the Reds' things. You know, the kind of stuff they turned out during the war full of bad Germans, only this time they've substituted Russians for the Nazis.

Dana Wynter is a juicy piece – a bit on the scraggy side – who is sought after by the Red wolves lusting after her nearer the bone. She's a Fräulein (that's the name of the picture, too) whose professor daddy was blown up (probably by a Russian bomb) at the end of the war.

When the Russians come Miss Wynter has the time of her life trying to save herself from a fate worse (?) than death. The Reds are slavering beasts (from Mongolia?), sweaty and with no hair on their heads. They are idiots, of course, who don't know what cigar cutters are used for.

One of them tries to use 'diplomacy', even proposes marriage. But, no! Not for Dana.

Enter the hero. Yankee, of course (Mel Ferrer). All the Yanks in this film are clean-shaven, nicely dressed, and not a nasty word spoken. Lots of cigarettes, chewing gum and chocolates.

But Dana is suspicious of Mel, too. Is he also on the make?

She must be suffering from a complex.

Well, after dodging lots of things, including a house of ill-fame (one doesn't know who is stupider, Miss Wynter or the Russians), she is rescued by Mel from being on the run for the rest of her life, after being convinced that he is on the up and up, and after being let down by an old flame who has found a meatier morsel.

There is a Negro GI too (James Edwards) who seems to go to lengths to aid this damsel in distress, but of course he's black and, what with the Immorality Act and all that, he doesn't stand a chance.

An overseas viewer states that the screen-play was written by one of the informers before the Un-American Activities Committee. COINCIDENCE?

Up my alley, New Age, 10 July 1958

Feeling like time off from the usual grind I visited the local flick and sat through several reels of *Men in War*, which recalls how the brave Yankees got mowed down by those treacherous Koreans, who, according to this picture, almost always shot you from behind.

Following the remnants of a combat group picking their way along tedious miles of celluloid, one got the impression that negro actor James Edwards is purposely disposed of early in the picture just to save him hearing Koreans racialistically referred to as 'gooks' in practically every second line of the ensuing dialogue.

And just to show there was no ill-feeling against Mr Edwards, a sick white soldier whom he supplied with two ACPs [pistols] is made to gulp on hearing of his demise: 'He was my friend.'

In the final reel a 'gook' gun emplacement is adequately dealt with a flamethrower, accompanied by the appropriate shrieks from those 'gooks' inside being roasted alive.

The picture at least gave the impression that war, no matter whose side you're on, is an ugly business.

Korean soldiers, I discovered for the first time, also carry automatic pistols in their caps, so that when they placed their hands on their heads in surrender, they could snatch them out and mow down the opposition in a manner contrary to the gentlemanly rules of mass murder.

Up my alley, New Age, 12 March 1959

20

'Why must we move?'

'If Verwoerd and his people don't want to live with us, they should take the next rocket to the moon. Why must they come and throw us out of our houses?'

This statement was made last Friday by a coloured woman in Leeuwenhof Road, Tamboerskloof, where the entire coloured community of 'Germantown' has been ordered to get out as the area has been declared white.

Another woman in the same house said: 'Going to the moon is too good for Verwoerd. He should be made to suffer like he has made us suffer, slowly and for a long time.'

Altogether, nearly 1 000 non-white people in 'Germantown', Tramway Road, Sea Point, and Stony Place, Newlands, have been told that they are at present living illegally in a white area and must make arrangements to remove themselves as soon as possible.

The places where they live are non-white enclaves in the Table Mountain area, proclaimed white in a proclamation in the *Government Gazette* of July 5, 1957, which gave non-whites two years to move.

The coloured communities have for the most part been living there longer than the whites, and their period of residence stretches back more than 100 years. They did not penetrate into existing white areas. It is the whites spreading outwards who have surrounded them.

BUT UNDER THE GROUP AREAS ACT, IT IS THE NON-WHITES WHO WILL HAVE TO GO, WHILE THE WHITES TAKE OVER THEIR HOMES.

'Where are we to go?' one housewife after another asked … There is no alternative accommodation available for these people, as there is already a shortage of 12 000 houses for coloured people in the Cape Peninsula.

'And where are we to find the money to move? Where are we going to find schools for our children? What is the point of it all?'

The latest moves are creating race hatred where it never existed before.

'There has been no opposition from the whites in Sea Point against the non-whites here,' the Reverend Tattersall, of the Church of the Holy Redeemer in Tramway Road, told *New Age*.

'Seventy-five per cent of my congregation is white and 25 per cent non-white, but our services are mixed and we have never had any complaints.'

'White boys and coloured boys serve at the altar together. There has been no pressure from the whites for this removal.'

The white King's Road school is cheek by jowl with the coloured school in Tramway Road, only a wire fence separating the two playgrounds. According to the Nats, this is the sort of thing that leads to friction and must be prevented.

According to the people on the spot, however, there has been very little trouble and there have never been any fights between white and non-white school-children.

The white children always tried to help the non-white children. Some of the equipment of the non-white school has come from the whites, and the surplus from the white school-feeding scheme was given to the non-white children. Pencils, rubbers and toys were freely passed through the fence by both sides.

Similarly a European woman in Leeuwenhof Road, 'Germantown', told *New Age* that there had never been any unpleasant incidents between white and non-white in her area. She has non-white neighbours.

Asked for her opinion on the removals, she said: 'Well, I believe there should be separate living areas for white and non-white.' But she admitted she had moved into her present home, which is in the heart of the non-white area, only two months ago.

'Germantown' is a well-developed residential area in beautiful surroundings, within a stone's throw of the Administrator's residence, Leeuwenhof.

White and non-white have lived there side by side in amity for over 100 years. 'We are not the shebeen type,' one coloured woman told *New Age*. 'Nobody has any reason to complain about us.'

In Newlands, however, the whites have got up a petition calling for the removal of the non-white community in Stony Place, which is on the mountain side of Newlands Avenue. The whites alleged that the behaviour of the non-whites was 'becoming intolerable' and complained about brawls on Friday nights.

Their spokesman added, however: 'Any impression that we favour the Group Areas Act is quite wrong. We seized on the Act as a sure way of getting rid of elements that have made life in the area almost intolerable for us. In our petition we made it clear that their being coloured had nothing at all to do with the matter.'

Last week, in all the threatened areas, the coloured people were in a state of turmoil. Some of the tenants in Tramway Road had been given notice by their landlords, Ilford Investments, to vacate the premises they occupy by October 31, 1959.

According to press reports, Ilford Investments has twice applied to the City Council for the area to be rezoned for flats, but their applications have been turned down. If the population is removed in terms of the Group Areas, however, it is possible the Council might allow the rezoning plans to go through.

Residents in Stony Place, Newlands, have applied to the Group Areas Board for an extension of time for their removal, but their applications have been refused. A few of the householders in 'Germantown' have been granted an extension of a year in which to make arrangements for the sale of their properties.

In Tramway Road a meeting was held in the church hall last Thursday night at which it was decided to send a deputation to the Deputy Minister of the Interior, Mr PW Botha, to ask for an extension of time so that the people could make arrangements for alternative accommodation.

Mr M Thomas, the chairman of the coloured tenants' association, said: 'Even if we have to walk away the soles of our shoes, we must try to find other homes. We must remain within the law. As church people, we do not want to go to prison.'

Members of the SA Coloured People's Organisation and the Liberal Party who were present were not allowed to speak, one of the organisers on the platform stating at the outset: 'This is not a political meeting and we do not want to hear outsiders who have come here tonight to inflame us.'

Two members of the Special Branch were present at the meeting.

A statement issued by SACPO said that 'the callous treatment of the coloured people of Sea Point is an example of the fate of thousands of others under the notorious Group Areas Act unless the people take a militant and determined stand in defence of their homes and their rights.

'It is further proof that no apartheid law or practice can be applied justly, but lead only to hardships and disaster.

'The SACPO will do everything to assist the people of Sea Point to defend their homes, and continue to rally the coloured community against all forms of apartheid and discrimination.'

'Why must we move?', *New Age*, 1 October 1959

What with the hustling and bustling going on to prepare that place in Parliament Street for the opening this week, people are asking what more the Nats can do to the non-white people. They seem to have scraped the bottom of the barrel as far as discriminatory legislation goes, but you can be sure that Herr Dr Verwoerd has a few more tricks up his sleeve.

What they won't be able to do is to pass an Act of Parliament to bring back to life the two coloured men who killed themselves as a result of the Group Areas Act.

The suicide note found in the pocket of Joseph Bougardt of Tiervlei said: 'Group Areas is the cause of my doing away with my life. My property will be taken away from me. I have struggled to get it paid off, and I know that I will never get my money back that I paid for it.'

We hope that Dr Dönges sleeps well.

Up my alley, *New Age*, 14 January 1960

21

Christian National Education

'It is our duty to see that the Coloureds are brought up under Christian National Education.'
From a National Party pamphlet on Christian National Education, 1948

The Cape Provincial Council last week adopted a motion calling for the transfer of Coloured Education from the Provincial Administration to the Central Government. This will mean that education for coloureds will be regulated and controlled by the government in the same manner as is the education of the Africans by the Native Affairs Department.

Bantu Education has been instituted to educate the African for his 'proper place' in the Nationalist-controlled society. The African people are well aware of what that education means – the acceptance of an inferior status as hewers of wood and drawers of water.

With coloured education likewise controlled by a Coloured Affairs Department, and the introduction of separate universities, everything will be set for the 'brainwashing' of the future generations of the non-white people.

The Nationalist Government always makes rosy promises before introducing their pernicious legislation. Every piece of legislation is explained in admirable terms and carefully white-washed. But the people of this country have come to realise fully that the Nationalist promises are like pie-crusts and the white-wash is inadequate to hide the dirt underneath.

It is quite certain that the coloured people will not be bluffed by Nationalist propaganda about the benefits of Government-controlled education.

Mr JW van Staden, Nationalist MPC for Malmesbury, who introduced the motion in the Provincial Council, seemed to put his foot in it at the very outset.

First he tried to give the impression that the plan was entirely a matter of finance; then he handed out the old Nationalist line which we have heard time and again: 'We want to give the coloureds a place in our country, with their own minister. We whites let the coloureds be educated and what place have we given the coloured people? If you do not give a man a place he becomes an agitator and a communist. We want to give the coloured man a place in his own sphere.'

There were over 1 000 church schools in the Cape, Mr Van Staden said. The country's traditional policy of apartheid was being sabotaged in them.

All this implies that the true motive behind Van Staden's motion is the extension of the Nationalist's apartheid philosophy to the textbooks of the coloured scholars and students.

Having laid the basis for the economic enslavement of the coloured people by way of the Group Areas and the Industrial Conciliation Acts, the Nationalists are undoubtedly preparing for onslaughts on their intellectual life.

Up to the present education for coloured children has been no different from that given Europeans. Syllabuses and public examinations are the same for both sections. There exists, however, wholesale discrimination in the expenditure on education for coloureds and Europeans. …

In 1955 there were 28 000 more coloured children than Europeans at school: expenditure for Europeans was £55 per child, and for coloureds only £21 per child. During the 1956–57 financial year £5 800 000 was spent on coloured education as compared with £12 million on European education.

There exists also a great disparity between the salary rates of European and coloured teachers. There are only two training colleges in the Cape for coloured teachers holding the senior certificate. Compulsory education for coloureds exists only on paper and, because of the lack of schools, has not been put into practice.

With the transfer of coloured education to the Government the standard and quality of education for coloured children is sure to be lowered.

In recommending that coloured education should be transferred to the Government, the Nationalists are not following the advice of their own Coloured Education Commission, which made no such recommendation in its report issued last year.

Nor did the Commission make any plea for a special type of coloured education qualitatively or quantitatively different from the ordinary connotation of the term education. 'Such a point of view', said the Commission, 'could hardly be defended in a country which is democratically governed.'

The Commission added: 'Where, therefore, in this report we use the term education, it is on the assumption that it refers to education in schools for coloured pupils, and not to a special kind of education.'

The report did, however, accept that the fate of the majority of the coloured people would be to perform manual labour in industry and agriculture, and inferred that the main aim of primary education should be, in addition to teaching the three Rs, to give 'instruction in handwork which will contribute towards improving their manual skill in general'. In this way it came perilously near recommending a special 'coloured education'.

Knowing the way the Nationalists have dealt with the reports of their own commissions, like the Tomlinson Commission, there is, in any case, no guarantee that they will not drastically alter the recommendations of the Coloured Education Commission to bring them in line with Christian National Education.

The statement on the purpose of Bantu education made by Dr Verwoerd may easily apply also to the coloured people: 'There is no place for him (the Bantu) in the European community above the level of certain forms of labour.'

Conferences of teachers' organisations have been vociferous in their condemnation of any sort of 'colouredised' education and control by the Coloured Affairs Department. The time is now at hand when the teaching profession must seriously consider what positive action should be taken to frustrate the plans of the Nationalists.

The question of coloured education is now being clearly placed on the level of all other political issues affecting the non-white peoples and it behoves both teachers' organisations and other political bodies to seriously consider joint militant action against attempts to enslave the minds of our children.

> Christian National Education for the coloured people, *New Age*, 13 June 1957

22

Elections for the 'coloured representatives'

The first two pieces in this chapter are not by La Guma. They have been included because they are part of the New Age *coverage of an unusual topic – black South Africans voting in 1958 – and they link smoothly with La Guma's observations in the rest of the chapter. The first piece is unattributed. Barney Desai, who wrote the second piece, was one of the leaders of SACPO together with James and Alex La Guma, Reg September, George Peake, Stanley Lollan, Cardiff Marney and others.*

The annual conference of SACPO held last weekend unanimously decided to contest seats under the Separate Representation of Voters Act. The conference decided to include treason suspects amongst its candidates as a challenge to the Nationalists.

The resolution said, 'We are not impressed by certain people who have already indicated their intention of standing for Parliament. It is strongly felt that (a) four candidates be selected from persons who have already suffered and sacrificed on behalf of the liberatory movement, (b) SACPO in collaboration with the allied Congresses be delegated to screen and select such candidates, (c) campaigns on their behalf be conducted by the entire people's movement.'

The decision was taken in consideration of the primary task of defeating the Nationalist government, and will bring SACPO policy in line with that of the other Congresses.

SACPO to fight elections, *New Age*, 26 December 1957, unattributed

Mr Pieter Beyleveld, President of the South African Congress of Democrats and one of the remaining 95 treason trialists, will stand as a coloured representative for the Cape Peninsula (Skiereiland) seat in the forthcoming elections under the Separate Representation of Voters Act.

Mr Beyleveld was expressly invited to stand by the South African Coloured People's Organisation, who announced its nomination in a statement headed: 'The fight is on. The Nats must go.'

The SACPO statement says: 'The nomination of Mr Beyleveld and his return to Parliament will be of nation-wide significance. It will be a dynamic challenge to white baasskap and the brutal oppression of the Nationalist Government. It is a positive rejection of the idea that the coloured people seek their future in the bankruptcy of the United Party, and finally Mr Beyleveld's nomination by SACPO is a militant and progressive action in opposition to the sterile theorising of the Unity Movement and its boycott allies.'

Support for Mr Beyleveld's candidature has been widespread and includes Chief Luthuli, president of the African National Congress, Dr YM Dadoo, banned Indian leader, Dr GM Naicker, president of the South African Indian Congress, Mr Alex Hepple, MP, leader of the SA Labour Party, and Mr LB Lee-Warden, MP, African Representative for the Western Cape and also one of the remaining treason accused.

The SACPO statement continues: 'Now that our candidate is in the field and the fight is on, we appeal to all democrats to rally around our election campaign and render every possible assistance. We require 200 volunteers to canvass the electorate from now until election day. We have opponents who have a formidable machine and can only be defeated through the hard work of SACPO members and the full assistance of the other Congresses.

'The Freedom Charter which is the accepted programme of our organisation will serve as the basis of Piet Beyleveld's election manifesto. Among the principles of the Charter are these points:

- Every man and woman shall have the right to vote for and to stand as a candidate for all bodies which make laws.
- All national groups shall have equal rights.
- The doors of learning and culture shall be opened.
- There shall be houses, security and comfort.

Our candidate completely rejects the type of representation which denies the franchise to the bulk of the people. He will fight for the right of black people to sit in the House of Assembly. He will be the voice of Congress in Parliament', the statement concludes.

Desai B, 'The Nats must go' – SACPO, *New Age*, 30 January 1958

'Vote vir ou Piet'

Election time and all the hullabaloo that goes with it is on hand in the Cape. I can see hard work ahead for a lot of people, and, dear reader, if you have time to spare, report for duty. Canvassers. Canvassers. And yet more canvassers.

If this campaign goes like others I have participated in, I shall ask the editor to promote me to the position of War Correspondent.

Up my alley, *New Age*, 6 February 1958

Mr Piet Beyleveld ... will address a mass election rally in the City Hall, Cape Town, this Sunday ....

This will be Mr Beyleveld's first public appearance since his arrest on allegations of high treason in December 1956. The Supreme Court, Johannesburg, granted a variation of his bail conditions, allowing Mr Beyleveld to address meetings in connection with his election campaign, provided that he submitted a copy of his speech to the Special Branch 24 hours before each meeting.

The mass meeting, which will be addressed by leading members of the South African Coloured People's Organisation which nominated Mr Beyleveld, and national speakers from other Congress organisations, takes place a bare 11 days before the elections under the Separate

Representation of Voters Act are held on 3 April. It is the culmination of intensive canvassing of voters and propaganda work in the constituency, and it is expected that a great number of people will be present to hear their candidate for the first time in public.

In spite of the fact that Mr Beyleveld has not been allowed to address meetings, a great many of the voters canvassed have expressed their support for him.

…

In an interview with *New Age*, Mr Beyleveld said: 'It is becoming clear that large numbers of coloured people are turning away from the old idea that they are an "appendage" of the white people and are expressing more and more their determination to take their place as free and equal partners in a free South African society. This election campaign is helping to carry the Congress message of equality for all to the coloured people, and the principles of the Freedom Charter have reached the homes of thousands. The coloured people are beginning to cut loose from the United Party strings which have bound them for many years to its policy of white guidance and racial inferiority.'

Beyleveld to speak this Sunday: Mass rally at City Hall, *New Age*, 20 March 1958

Canvassers are finding warm welcomes from voters who have readily affirmed their backing for the Congress movement after having received Mr Beyleveld's election manifesto.

One voter told SACPO's canvasser: 'I and several of my friends have discussed this election in the train on our way to and from work, and we have all decided to vote for Mr Beyleveld. We are going to vote for him because he too has experienced some of the bitterness that non-Europeans have to endure under this Government.'

The areas in the Cape Peninsula are being flooded with handbills as the canvassers go out to see the voters, and big posters bearing Mr Beyleveld's picture and the slogan 'Equal rights for all' are appearing on walls and shops all over the Peninsula.

Mr Reg September, general secretary of SACPO, said that the key to the Congress election victory was the number of voters the election organisation was able to contact. 'There are 8 000 voters in the constituency. If we are able to canvass them all, then our success is assured. But we badly need more canvassers.'

Volunteers are asked to assist with canvassing and to work on election day, to report at the offices at 1 Roger Street, Cape Town, or to phone 2-6956.

Coloured elections: Growing support for Congress candidates, *New Age*, 13 March 1958

Rose-coloured glasses

The 'Unity Movement' mob, looking at the parish through rose-coloured glasses, are inundating voters with lengthy screeds which, after close study (use a microscope), tell them not to vote for 'dummy representatives'.

The question I am asking is: Are they going to boycott the City Council elections, too?

Ah, ah, they will say. There we have direct representation. Direct? asks I. When thousands of people in the municipal housing schemes have been taken off the roll? And what about the Africans? Can they vote? And with the City Council loaded against any progressives. (Same as in Parliament, mind you.) Isn't this also dummy representation?

But, of course, we have to look after representatives Holmes, Viljoen and Schroeder. Anyway, they are carrying out the policy by boycotting inside the City Council.

Question two I'm asking the 'Unity' teachers. Are you going to boycott the schools if education is handed over to the CAD, probably after April Fool's Day? If you don't, you'll be 'working the machinery of oppression'. What?

Oh, I see. You're not going to boycott? It depends what you really teach the kids in the classrooms.

But isn't that what also applies to the African and coloured representatives in Parliament? It depends on what they say in the House?

And why were the boycott canvassers telling people who insist on voting to vote for Beyleveld?

Up my alley, *New Age*, 3 April 1958

Wow! Lieutenant Mouton must have put his foot into the Unity Movement's wide-open mouth when giving evidence about an allegedly illegal meeting they held at Genadendal during their recent boycott campaign.

He said he didn't regard the speeches made by Wessels and Coy as political. 'I did not regard it as a political meeting.'

Or did he hit the nail right on the head?

But in spite of Lootenant Mouton, the UM boys, I hear, consider this case to be their Treason Trial.

Up my alley, *New Age*, 1 May 1958

44 per cent poll

The small poll and the slowness of the voting in the coloured people's first election under the Separate Representation of Voters Act on April 3 contrasted with the amount of activity, enthusiasm and noise that went on around the polling booths as opposing groups vied with each other for the support of the voters.

At all the six polling stations in the Peninsula there were identical colourful displays of banners and placards of the three candidates and the boycott movement, and all the hurly-burly that goes with elections.

The estimated 44 per cent poll at the end of the day was the result of many factors, among them the apathy, disgruntlement and disgust of the coloured people, and the inconvenient day chosen for the elections. Thursday was pay-day, just before a long weekend. The Muslim fast also prevented many evening voters from going to the polls. It was estimated that the boycott movement had influenced about 10 to 15 per cent of the electorate, and that another 2 000 voters could not be traced. Taking also into consideration that polling by coloureds, when on the common roll, was never more than 60 per cent, observers have set down the effect of the boycott as negligible.

In the Eastern Cape (Outeniqua) constituency polling was also slow, but the percentage of votes cast was higher in the Port Elizabeth–Uitenhage district where the bulk of voters are concentrated. In this area there was little sign of boycott activity.

Polling was also quiet in Boland and Karoo.

In Athlone, where there are 1 600-odd voters on the roll, 200 had voted by lunch-time and 500 by 5 p.m. The number increased towards the evening when candidates' cars transported many to the polls and others came to the booth on their own. The percentage there is estimated at 50 per cent of the effective voters.

All day barkers kept up a steady barrage, and the slogans ranged from 'Vote for Bloomberg, the skollie boys' friend', at the Drill Hall, to 'Boycott Bloomberg, vote for Beyleveld' at Athlone. At Athlone a man walked to and fro all day shouting betting odds, '11 to 10 on Bloomberg, 10 to 1 on others.' The odds, according to him, rose against 'the others' later in the day.

The Anti-CAD supporters stood quietly by with their banners and placards, calling for a boycott of 'dummy elections', but showed signs of impatience towards the end of the day when the polling increased.

At the Drill Hall, Cape Town polling was heaviest, growing during the lunch hour and after working hours. In all, 1 208 voted here – about 50 per cent of the available voters – and election day helpers and barkers went all out in their efforts.

Police intervened in a minor dispute between the supporters of Piet Beyleveld and Bloomberg after the Treason Candidate's helpers complained that the opposition was using a megaphone.

The presiding electoral officer ordered the barker not to use the megaphone. Police also spoke to some of Bloomberg's helpers who were accused of intimidating voters coming to the polls.

The third candidate in the Peninsula, Mr Louis Kellner, seemed to have little support throughout the day.

On the whole the competition between the helpers of the rival candidates appeared to have been conducted on a friendly basis, perhaps due to the fact that they had a common enemy in the boycotters.

Several voters in Athlone and Salt River complained that the boycott supporters behaved in an insulting manner towards them, but the rest simply ignored the remarks made by the Unity Movement adherents. At the Drill Hall the boycotters made no attempt to interfere with the voters beyond standing with banners reading: 'The people have no candidates.'

A significant feature of the election was the big fleet of flashy cars which served Bloomberg, but the pre-election canvass had shown that a number of voters were planning to use his transport to the polls and vote against him when they got there.

At the end of the day, when the last voter had made his cross on the ballot form, one thing had emerged clearly: that the coloured people had not been completely shaken out of their apathy, and that there was room for a lot more political work to raise their political consciousness to the highest level.

44 per cent poll in coloured elections, *New Age*, 10 April 1958

'Onse Abe'

Saw a picture of a top hat in the local daily the other day. Nice grey one, too. Not that I fancy top hats.

None other than 'Onse Abie' Bloomberg, posing for the camera at the Ascot race-track in England.

I wonder what those poor, kicked about, hard-working, below-the-breadline voters think about it.

Up my alley, New Age, 3 July 1958

I wonder how many of the 3 000-odd voters who put 'Onse Abe' Bloomberg into Parliament are company directors or have shares in high finance, but if there are any, I guess they are probably satisfied with their representative's speech on their behalf in the House.

'Onse Abie' seemed to be beside himself with congratulations for Tom Naudé's budget. No increase in company taxes. Bravo!

But what about the thousands of coloured people who are not company directors? 'Onse Abe' seems to have forgotten the people who put him into Parliament the minute the election results were announced. No criticism of the effects the Budget would have on the ordinary coloured man. Oh, no! Nothing about those already living below the breadline. Oh, no! Nothing about millions spent on apartheid and very little on the people's welfare.

Well, what are the voters for? I hope they'll remember Abie's budget speech the next time he comes around to put them to use again.

But, I forgot. Abie's election helpers did boast about the fact that the boss was the director of sixty-odd companies.

Up my alley, New Age, 31 July 1958

I suppose one and all [of the 'prominent' characters who appealed to voters on behalf of 'our old and tried friend'] received a pat on the head from Abe for commending him to the suffering (sorry, suffrage) of the voters.

But to find a trade unionist, Edgar Deane, signing a letter for a member of the boss's party, and Cissie Gool, one-time styled as the Joan of Arc of the coloured people, following suit, makes one wonder how much longer the people are going to allow the wool to be pulled over their eyes.

Up my alley, New Age, 27 March 1958

23

Ah, dis die economic boycott

About sixteen members of the Security Branch of the CID stopped *New Age* reporter Alex La Guma, Mr R Segal, editor of *Africa South*, and Mr Joe Morolong of the ANC in the Nyanga Location last Friday night and seized 3 000 boycott lists. The three men were later charged with being in the location without a permit and released on bail of £2 each in the early hours of Saturday morning. Mr Segal (whose passport was seized on Monday as a reprisal) also faces a charge of carrying an unlicensed firearm.

At about eleven o'clock at night a car loaded with Security Branch men raced after us, hooted and forced us to a halt at the side of the road. They piled out, surrounded our car, and told us to wait.

About ten minutes later several cars pulled up, also crammed with plain-clothesmen, who climbed out, surrounded us in a body and peered at us curiously as if we were creatures just landed from outer space. There were sixteen of them, and it did not look as if they had come from their beds.

Torches flashed on to the back seat. There were a few brown-paper packets and a number of collection boxes. Hands tore at the brown paper, and a voice said triumphantly, 'Ah, dis die economic boycott.' The detectives seemed very excited.

We were then each allocated to a police car and, wedged in by detectives, drove in convoy along the dark and silent roads to the Philippi Police Station.

In the station police-constables, unused to catches of this kind, came to stare through the windows. Mr Segal was removed to the Europeans Only side.

Several detectives stood with Mr Morolong and myself watching us with hawk eyes. We smoked and chatted, watched a first-aid man treating a Friday night casualty.

A security man came in carrying the packets of leaflets and said to his man: 'Count.'

'All of them?' asked a surprised detective. 'One by one?'

'One by one.'

They counted the leaflets on their fingers. Somewhere in the background another detective said: 'Tonight we've got Up My Alley with us.'

While they counted the 3 142 leaflets, the desk sergeant produced the charge sheet. He told us that we could pay £2 admission of guilt, but a security man stopped him and said that we had to be charged.

I was searched first and, after emptying my pockets, one of them looked through my property. He decided that he was going to keep an invitation to the 47th Annual Conference of the Teachers' League of SA, my reporter's notes and list of phone numbers.

We waited for some time, while a local character strolled in and sang rock 'n roll and sentimental songs on his guitar much to the entertainment of some of the police.

A detective examining a leaflet sneered, 'Who heard of a kaffir smoking —?' naming an expensive English cigarette. The desk sergeant looked at us and said, 'Why don't they b'ycott wine and brendy, huh?'

Mr Segal, in the meantime, was being questioned by the Special Branch detectives.

After that we were each loaded into a car and, accompanied by detectives, driven to our respective homes which were searched for boycott leaflets. Three plain-clothes men spent an hour in my house, found nothing and left, taking me with them to the central police station in Cape Town. This was about 2 a.m. and I spent another hour hanging about a corridor for no apparent reason.

After a long wait I was handed over to a uniformed constable who put me into a van and drove me back to the Philippi Police Station. I had an idea that the Special Branch had given up the night's investigation for I saw neither hide nor hair of them for the rest of the night.

At Philippi they locked me up with five other Africans and Mr Morolong who had arrived previously.

I had been given a pile of blankets and two sleeping mats and was just in the process of executing my fourth flea an hour later when the cell was unlocked and Mr Morolong and I were called out and taken back to the station office.

There we paid bail of £2 each and were allowed to go. Mr Segal was allowed bail of £5. The time was 4.30 a.m.

Mr Segal and I appeared in the Wynberg magistrate's court on Saturday morning and were remanded to June 22. Mr Morolong appeared in the Langa Native Commissioner's Court and was remanded to July 3rd.

New Age reporter, *Africa South* editor arrested, boycott lists seized,
New Age, 18 June 1959

24

'Coloured Affairs' and Uncle Toms

The Afrikaner saw the coloured man as a good neighbour, said Herr Botha, Unter-Minister of the Interior, but good neighbourship required proper boundary lines.

Of course Herr Botha implies that the Afrikaner should decide how far away his neighbours should live, and where. One can be a good neighbour if one lives in a camp somewhere out in the country miles away from the luxury flats of the master race.

And job reservation was justified to protect the whites in the interests of racial peace and a Christian state!! And the coloured people must be protected from the Africans, via Group Areas and the aforesaid job reservation.

Private enterprise and business competition can go on among the whites, but non-intervention from the others. They can strangle themselves in their own areas – provided they can raise the cash to go into business.

All this met with applause from the Botha boys, but what it all proved was that the people against whom the coloured population need the most protection are the Nats.

Up my alley, *New Age*, 5 March 1959

UP's 'Race Federation'

If you see me going around with my jaw hanging, it is not because I want to air my tonsils. It is because I have not yet recovered after hearing the UP's 'race federation' explained once more.

After several versions, this last one is presumably meant to throw light on the subject. Anyway, believe it or not, the heaven on earth which Div's boys are promising us is one in which a so-called mixed area can have a white–coloured parliament, and an African parliament.

The next explanation might well include a Japanese parliament, and Chinese parliament and possibly a parliament for 'other Asiatics' and sundries.

And just think of all the jobs there will be floating around. Foreign ministers and ministers of information, etc., etc., etc., all bumping into each other and getting their portfolios entangled.

I swear it would be enough to drive even the Liquor and Licensing Board to drink. Which reminds me that even the Minister of Justice, present one I mean, seems to be getting tired of the surreptitious manufacture and consumption of alcoholic beverages and has given all and sundry to know that legislayshun will be introduced to remove certain restrictions on the brewing of 'kaffir beer'. Or does this just mean that the boys in khaki or new blue will just be a little more polite when knocking people when on a midnight raid?

But if coloured parliaments and Colouredstans and all-coloured casts are going to be thrust upon us – Oh, no! Don't please let us now have an all-coloured film. And I'm not talking about Technicolour either.

It's this film that the Eoan Group has been asked to consider starring in. 'Carmen of the Cape', too, it's going to be called. Poor Mr Bizet. He must have turned in his grave when Hollywood turned out *Carmen Jones*. If it happens again, the old boy will surely be feeling right uncomfortable.

Then, believe it or not, the setting of the Cape project will be in a fishing village. It's a Bloom-ing shame. Let's hope the Group plugs for the film to be made in black and white, if they agree to taking it on, even if it must be called 'Carmen of the Cape'.

Up my alley, New Age, 22 February 1962

Colouredstan

A wise bird in the queue at the Cape Town station caused a burst of laughter the other day by asking the ticket-clerk for a single to colouredstan. It turned out he was going to Bellville South, which Nat circles are hoping will become one of the separate coloured municipalities.

What lovely new ideas Colouredstans and Bantustans must be giving the tourist traders. You can imagine the big bright posters showing the mayor of Athlone or Elsies River or Bellville South with his ball and chain of office against the picturesque background of the municipal housing schemes, and the Bush College.

And the gay slogans: Visit sunny South Africa. Special tours through Colouredstan. Apply for permits at the CAD. Warning: Anybody found in Colouredstan without a permit – £2 or ten days.

And what of the occupiers of white spots in Colouredstan? Will they become honorary citizens, or will they be classed as stateless satellites? Will they be citizens of the metropolis and non-citizens of the state within a state?

It is all becoming curiouser and curiouser. Like debarring Jap swimmers from a non-white swimming pool. That is the latest development in the saga of the Nipponese swimmers. After some members of a non-white swimming team were 'allowed' – thank you, very much – into the Newlands pool to watch the Japs, it makes the head whirl.

All this has sent theatrical producers into a dither, too. Because some scaremonger has passed it around that henceforth no production of *The Mikado* will be allowed without permission from the Minister of the Interior, countersigned by the Group Areas Board and censored by the Population Registrar.

Up my alley, New Age, 8 March 1962

What a shame! Us bruin mense won't be getting our own special kleurling theatre for a long time because it's all tied up with our very own special kleurling juniversity, since one of the factors for the 'development' of the theatre is the music faculty of the juniversity, and the mean ole City Council won't give the Government the land in our very own coloured group area to build the damn juniversity.

That means the opening grand opera 'Daar Kom die Alibama', written and composed by the staff of the CAD and featuring the Council of Coloured Affairs, will have to be put on ice.

Another hitch in the programme I hear is due to the fact that Unter-Gauleiter Botha can't find any volunteers for the chorus, or maybe they are too shy about having their names put up in lights.

Up my alley, *New Age*, 30 July 1959

Big Chief Buttonhole

I see that Mr [George] Golding [president of the conservative Coloured People's National Union (CPNU)] spent the Easter weekend morally re-arming himself in Johannesburg. He brought some of the boys with him from Cape Town, and no doubt a good time was had by all. Apart from weeping on each other's shoulders and saying how mistaken they'd been all along, and what nice boys they'd be in future, they saw a movie too.

But what Moral Rearmament really tries to put across is that there is no necessity for the oppressed people to struggle for their rights; that the class struggle between capital and labour, the bosses and the workers, is unnecessary. Everybody should look into their hearts and decide to be good boys.

Imagine Dr Verwoerd deciding that, really, there shouldn't be pass laws. Imagine the big industrialists and farmers deciding that they were doing a bad thing by mercilessly exploiting the workers. Imagine the great imperialist powers breaking into tears and deciding to end colonial oppression.

What Mr Golding and his ilk need is some mental rearmament.

Up my alley, *New Age*, 9 May 1957

When I left Cape Town last week Big Chief Buttonhole had just held a big indaba in the vicinity of Woodstock and got all minstrels to compose love-songs to various people who have been implacable enemies of the coloured people, and the non-Europeans in general.

One of Mr Golding's troubadours sang a serenade to Group Areas boss Van Rensburg. Another sang of the heroic deeds of Dr ID du Plessis [head of the Coloured Affairs Department]. Various other minstrels strove to outdo each other with praising their state of inferiority.

And what I consider an outright insult to the coloured people is GJ's [Golding] blaming them for the strained relationship between themselves and the Nats.

So, according to GJ, the government can push us around for as long as they like, and we're not supposed to raise hell. Or are the coloured people responsible for the Group Areas Act, the Separate Representation of Voters Act, and all the other laws that are pushing our heads into the mud.

I have a good idea that George's campaign to end the 'cold war' with the Government also involves a lot of cold feet.

Up my alley, *New Age*, 16 January 1958

Uncle George's CPNU held their conference in Bantustan recently, no doubt to show delegates what a coloured Group Area might look like one day.

Struck suddenly with the idea that South Africa's rulers will be multi-racial 'in the foreseeable future', Uncle George recommended that his boys prepare for this by taking advantage of the 'privileges offered us in the economic field by the Group Areas Act'.

Like trying to oust Indian cinema owners from coloured areas? George's dream of multi-racial rule is probably one of himself as President or something of Colouredstan ... with Meneer Botha as his Makulubaas.

Up my alley, New Age, 15 October 1959

Uncle George, GJ Golding to you, has been panting and perspiring in Port Elizabeth in attempts to eat the polony at both ends at the same time.

No coloured MPs – the brown folks will vote commie – he said. But Herr Doktor Verwoerd shouldn't have repeated it so loud so soon. Give us a chance to grow up first before we get our own MPs, says Golding, but put us back on the common roll, and the Group Areas Act is OK, except you ought to administer it carefully, and job reservation is lousy.

After this Christmas pudding, no doubt the fruits of moral rearmament, it is little wonder that Uncle George is becoming less and less digestible with the coloured community.

And even that didn't rate him an invite to meet [visiting British Prime Minister Harold Macmillan], along with other pro-Government flunkeys and ja-baas-boys.

Up my alley, New Age, 12 January 1961

CAC

I predict an outbreak of hostilities soon.

With the announcement that a brand new [Union Council of Coloured Affairs (UCCA) or, in short, the Coloured Affairs Council] CAC will be unveiled next month, political bayonets are being sharpened and sights lined up on any of us Cullud folks who dare desert to the Nationalist trenches.

I'm still waiting to see who would dare – and I could make a few off-hand guesses, too. I guess there are still a few appendages willing to hold out their caps for ten quid a month, which is what the Government will pay.

And although this thing isn't the be-all and end-all of coloured politics, it will be interesting to see what amount of cooperation and unity will be shown on this issue.

Up my alley, New Age, 28 May 1959

'Dummy will give all answers,' says a headline in a local paper. It might tell Under-Minister Botha where to find candidates for his Coloured Affairs Council.

Up my alley, New Age, 13 August 1959

The UCCA-lele band of Unter-Minister Botha and Secretary for Coloured Affairs, Dr ID du Plessis, [still] awaits 15 more appointed instrumentalists before the first performance.

It might also be interesting to note that one of the Council ... is a museum attendant. He will no doubt take great care of the rest of the rare specimens.

Up my alley, *New Age*, 26 November 1959

We mourn all the dead of Sharpeville and Langa. Whereas the Union Council of Coloured Affairs stood in silence only for the chauffeur, the late Mr Lombaard, who died tragically in Langa. We wish to point out to all, including his bereaved family, that in the final analysis he was as much a victim of the pass laws as all those who were shot down by the police in the two locations.

At the same time I wish to convey to the Lombaard family, on behalf of the many African people of Langa location who asked me to do so, their heartfelt sympathy with them in their loss, and to express the hope that the death of Mr Lombaard will be a greater inspiration for the coloured community to join with the Africans in the struggle against the hated pass laws which have brought so much tragedy to this country.

Perhaps a suitable inscription on the tombstones of the Sharpeville and Langa dead could be this quotation from Verwoerd's speech at Meyerton: We intend to do what is just and right as a Christian nation in dealing with people and fellow men in this country of ours.

Up my alley, *New Age*, 31 March 1960

Members of the UCCA at the 'hurriedly arranged' meeting with Mac[millan], the British Prime Minister of course didn't mention the fact that they had not been elected by the coloured people and that the majority of them had been appointed by the Government.

Under the shadow of Baas Botha and Dr ID, the chairman of the Council dished up the usual porridge about 'separate development' and 'parallel lines' and thereafter everybody joined in 'Die Stem' and then adjourned to collect Mac's autograph.

After having seen that he met Bantustan chiefs and handpicked coloured boss-boys, Herr Doktor Verwoerd might think that he has done his duty by introducing Mac to the non-white 'leaders', but we wonder whether the British Prime Minister did not leave with a feeling of having been led up the garden path – not only at Kirstenbosch.

Up my alley, *New Age*, 11 February 1960

Of course you must have heard of people being struck unconscious by lightning. But there are also people who are struck senseless by a brainstorm. For instance, take Broer Saleh Dollie, chief autograph hunter of the UCCA. Not satisfied with Verwoerd's Bantustans, Brother Saleh wants to out-Verwoerd Verwoerd. How?

Divide the whole African continent into two, says he ... Southern Africa shall consist of the Republic, the protectorates, Basutoland, Swaziland and 'if possible' Angola and Mozambique. Then, continues this recipe, let the north have a black government and the south have a white. Those people who want to live under a black government can move north and those who want a white can move south.

What's more, says Saleh, 'It will be interesting to note the reaction of the coloured and Asian communities.'

That's not all. This, says Brother Saleh with gusto, will solve their problem.

Ya-Allah-ha-il-Allah (sic). But going from one oh-dear to another, people down here are still chuckling over Cape Town Councillor Jerry Ferry's master plan (how many more are still forthcoming?) for turning at least some of the coloured people white.

Let all of them who have a high standard of living and conform to the standard of Western civilisation toddle along to the Pop Registration and ask to be classified Honorary White Citizens.

Brother Ferry, you're mistaken. It's not Western civilisation we need, it's money for pig-iron.

But pig-iron or no pig-iron, if you'd have been able to drag yourself out of bed early enough last Sunday morning and staggered over to the radio, twiddled the knobs and listened, you would have heard Radio Colouredstan – Die Protea-Program, according to Meneer [Albert] Hertzog – on air for the first time.

Complete with Negro spirituals too, so it looks as if the white man's music will be confined to its own group area. And not even a corny crack á la Eric Egan [the radio comedian].

The next thing we'll have will be of course a programme for the Indian community, one for the Chinese, one for Miscellaneous — and no doubt, one in Japanese, called Radio Jokyo.

Up my alley, New Age, 8 February 1962

Yours truly was contemplating application to the Council of Heraldry to trace my family tree with the hope of acquiring the long-lost family coat of arms. But some wet blanket has informed me that in my case it should be done through the Council of Coloured Affairs instead.

This has made me feel most rampant and I have a good mind to take up my bar sinister and go out and knock somebody over his crest into a position couchant.

Which is probably what members of the Malay Choir feel like doing after having been given the order of the boot from the Pretoria City Hall. Maybe they should now ask the Coloured Council to help them become honorary white citizens and then try the Pretoria swimming baths.

But I bet there are many members of the choir cursing themselves for having helped to raise shekels towards the Pretoria Voortrekker Monument and celebrate the Union festival.

Nay, not even the runnings around and salaamings of Boeta Saleh will change the fact that there are certain places the sacred atmosphere of which is reserved for die volk, and no matter how well you can sing 'Rooi Rose', you are only fit for a 'suitable place on the showgrounds'.

Unless, of course, you come from Japan and get an exemption from the colour-bar. Like those Japanese swimmers who were given a treat of boerewors in Worcester the other night.

I bet there was more than one ware Nasionalis who had to take a leaf out of the rooinek's book and 'grin and bear it'.

Yet I don't know whether to congratulate or growl at the powers that be for lowering the boom on the Chinese Moral Rearmament delegation. One would have thought that there would have been a wild hip-hip-hooray for the pedlars of anti-communism from the orient. But, nope, so solly, anti-communism it seems must also be accompanied by a white skin.

So there you are, it means that now I won't be able to go to Formosa for the international mah-jong tournament.

The whole business is beginning to look like a ©-&!!% Chinese puzzle.

Up my alley, *New Age*, 1 March 1962

Whose banner?

A newcomer to the newspaper world is *Die Banier*, a ten-page monthly printed in Stellenbosch, and with its offices in Salt River, Cape Town. Glancing through its pages it would appear that *Die Banier* is directed towards the coloured community, and more particularly those in the countryside. Many of its letters are from readers outside the urban areas, and it is printed almost entirely in Afrikaans, which, we could presume, is preferred by the country readers.

According to Dr RE van der Ross, one of the contributors who is closely connected with the paper, *Die Banier*, was launched, after consultation with some coloured people, in order to provide a medium through which the community could express its views 'in a courteous manner', and to provide a forum for discussion and a closer relationship between white and non-white. The paper would not be bound to any 'party political line', he said.

Why is *Die Banier* printed mainly in Afrikaans? Because, according to Dr Van der Ross, educational work must be done among the Afrikaner people, too, in order to show them that the coloured people deserve consideration and to show them that they 'have a growing potentiality'.

To show further how 'non-political' it is, this paper has been accepted by the Provincial Library Services for free distribution to coloured schools.

Closer examination of *Die Banier*, however, reveals it in another light. Since there is no editorial column one can only assess the policy of the paper from its content and the amount of space allotted to the various contributions.

On the front page of the second issue (January 1960) appears a three-column attack by a contributor on *The Torch*, the Unity Movement weekly, for defending the Chinese communists in the China–India border dispute.

'The facts are that Communist China brutally trampled the people of Tibet underfoot. Also that the Chinese communists violated the borders of India and occupied Indian territory. Both are examples of total and brutal aggression … Is this democratic? Perhaps for the communist bosses of China, but not for us!'

So we can take it that *Die Banier* is strongly anti-communist. A further forty-odd inches inside are allotted to a report of the Kleurlings-Volksbond conference at which a guest of honour was Dr JG Meiring, Rector of the apartheid coloured University College at Bellville, who also spoke at conference.

Pleas for coloured nationalism and responsibility in their own areas were made, and cooperation with the authorities pledged at this conference. Condemnation of the economic boycott was thrown in for good measure.

Other well-displayed contributions and letters defend the Coloured Affairs Department.

Half of the front page is devoted to an article by the Afrikaans author Mr WA de Klerk, explaining why the coloured community appear to be turning their backs on the Afrikaans language (and hence on the Afrikaner people). Mr de Klerk calls for a more 'Christian' attitude towards the coloured people.

Further examination of this 'non-political' paper reveals that it is well-supported by advertisers, the majority of whom also feature on lists being distributed by organisers of the Congress economic boycott.

According to Dr Van der Ross again, these firms were approached so that in helping to uplift our people they also uplift themselves 'by taking into account the tremendous potential of coloured and African people as customers'.

All of this is of course outside of party politics and 'non-political', for we are assured that the supporters of *Die Banier* would not accept a Nationalist Party 'set-up' and stand only for 'partnership of some kind.'

It is surprising, under the circumstances, that the official editor of *Die Banier* is none other than Mr Aart Kaptein, a prominent feature writer for the Nationalist daily *Die Burger*.

It might be argued, of course, that none of the contributions to this 'non-political paper' reflect the views of the editorial board. But if so, then what does?

The coloured people as a whole would like to know for whom does *Die Banier* wave!

> For whom does *'Die Banier'* wave? 'Non-political' coloured paper edited by a Nationalist, *New Age*, 25 February 1960

I see that Boeta Saleh Dollie, other members of the Council for Coloured Affairs, like Broer Willie Louw of Noordgesig, and Uncle Geo J Golding and all are now soliciting. For adverts in *Die Banier*.

Backing up *Die Banier*'s wheedling and whining – (us coloured ain't second class) – Uncle Tom Swartz, chairman of the third-class stooge CCA, even states that the ideals the coloureds have set themselves 'are ideals of peaceful evolution in the democratic sense'.

Wragtig! So that's why he was democratically elected chairman of the democratic CCA.

Uncle George hiccups that the CPNU defends the standpoint that the coloured people form an 'inviolable union' with the white community.

Tut, tut, George. You're committing treason. According to Baas Verwoerd, you're not even an appendage anymore.

And it is no recommendation to read or advertise in *Die Banier* when Boeta Saleh proclaims that *Die Banier* can be assured of our loyalty. 'We stand united because we pursue the same ideals.'

With all these hawkers peddling the coloured people to big business, it's no surprise *Die Banier* has to dump its thousands of unsold copies on the school-children.

And there should also be quite a few frowns within the coloured convention movement at the sight of Dick van der Ross plugging this rag, which obviously supports bodies and corpses rejected outright at Malmesbury.

> Up my alley, *New Age*, 19 April 1962

So what do you know?

So what do you know? I wake up the other morning and I find that I have my very own Minister [in the newly announced post of Minister for Coloured Affairs]. For your information, PW Botha by name. The Guwerment having decided that I need somebody to look after my affairs, they name this bird, and here I am, stuck with him.

It is not enough that I should have my ever-loving wife, the Minister of Justice and now and then the State Prosecutor, to look after my affairs. Oh, no. I must have this geezer, too.

What is more, the Department of Revenue sends me a buff form which says I must help to pay for Herr Botha's bread and water.

It's enough to make a man want to rise up in revolt.

Up my alley, New Age, 10 August 1961

25

Langa 1960

In a superb demonstration of unity, courage and determination, the people of Langa last week scored a smashing success in their struggle against the pass laws.

From ... Monday, March 21, when the Pan Africanist Congress launched its anti-pass campaign, until the weekend, the stay-at-home was solid.

Thousands of African workers began gathering at Langa and Nyanga at dawn on Monday morning ... The demonstrations were preceded by well-attended meetings at both centres on Sunday, where speakers from the Pan African Congress had outlined their plans.

A large group of the demonstrators at Nyanga began the three-mile march to Philippi Police Station just after 6 a.m. They walked along silently, in small groups of five or six.

By seven o'clock some 1 500 had gathered outside the police station, several hundreds in the grounds and the others closely packed on both sides of the road.

The demonstrators were quiet and well-disciplined. No badges or banners were displayed.

Fifty white and 100 African police, under the command of Major Rheeder, stood by at Philippi and another large force had been mobilised at Langa.

Many of the police were armed with Sten guns and others carried riot sticks. Two Saracens were parked in the rear courtyard at the Philippi station.

The police, however, confined themselves to keeping the road clear for passing traffic and there were no incidents.

Spokesmen for the crowd explained that the people had come to be arrested, as they had all left their reference books at home.

The police did nothing until after 9 a.m., when Major Rheeder announced that all those who had no passes and wished to be arrested should come forward.

The entire crowd surged forward. There were isolated cries of 'Masihambe Zonke!' – 'Let us all go!' – but for the rest the people pressed forward silently, but determinedly.

Queues were organised quickly and the men waited quietly for their turn to enter the police station.

Large numbers were still waiting their turn at noon, with hundreds still to be dealt with crowding the inner and outside courtyards.

No arrests were made. The demonstrators had their names and addresses taken and were warned to appear at the Wynberg magistrate's court next Tuesday, March 29.

Groups of demonstrators, when asked whether they would go to work on the morrow, answered with a unanimous and resounding 'NO! We shall stay away from work for as long as necessary, until we get our demands.'

When asked what they intended to do when they appeared before the Magistrate, they replied with the slogan: 'No bail. No fines. No defence!'

A spokesman for one group stressed that the struggle was non-violent. 'Our struggle is a peaceful one,' he said. 'We do not want violence.'

No workers presented themselves for arrest at the Langa Police Station, although several thousand gathered early in the morning at New Flats – the so-called 'bachelor' quarters.

The crowd dispersed after the police asked a young student leader of the demonstrators to ask them to do so.

Two minor incidents were reported to have occurred at Nyanga, neither of a serious nature.

A bus travelling to the Epping factory area found itself unable to enter Vanguard Drive because of a large crowd of demonstrators blocking the turnoff. The bus took another route.

A small road-block, consisting of a low wall of heaped-up sand and boulders, had been constructed during the night across the road leading to Nyanga from the national road turn-off. The road-block was removed by the police.

These were the only incidents until ... rioting broke out at Langa in the evening [and] at least five people were killed and an unknown number injured during a night of clashes between the people and the police ...

The trouble started when police arrived at a peaceful mass meeting called by the Pan Africanists at the New Flats at 6 p.m. The people were unarmed, as they had been specially asked not to bring any weapons. About 6 000 people were present at the meeting.

As all meetings had been banned under the Riotous Assemblies Act, the police tried to break up the meeting. Members of the crowd told *New Age* they heard no order to disperse, and they deny emphatically police reports that firing first came from the crowd. The police launched an attack with batons and shortly afterwards started firing on the crowd.

As darkness fell, the incensed people hit back. Police were stoned and buildings were set on fire. The labour bureau, administrative offices, library, market hall and schools were gutted.

Saracens and armoured cars were operating in the township throughout the night, and bursts of firing were heard. Army units were called in to help the police.

On Tuesday morning a tense atmosphere persisted in the township. The police were going from door to door ordering people to work and beating those who refused. There were reports of people being lined up and herded to the station [and onto the trains into the city at gunpoint] like cattle.

We ourselves saw a man whose face was streaming with blood after being beaten by a policeman.

Sporadic bursts of shooting continued to take place. Soldiers in the township made no secret of the fact that they were ready to 'shoot kaffirs'. We heard a number of disgusting remarks from them. One soldier said to us as we went by: 'I hope the kaffirs kill you.' The streets were crowded with tense, sullen people.

But when these tactics threatened to provoke a new explosion of violence, the police campaign [to drive the people to work at the point of the gun] was abandoned. It had proved ineffective in any case. Some of the workers forced out of the township got off the trains at stations along the line and did not go to work. Others took advantage of the opportunity to visit workplaces throughout the city and persuade their fellow-workers from other centres to join their stay-at-home and make it solid.

One after the other, workers at the docks, on construction sites and at the coalyards downed tools and went home. By the end of the week there was hardly an African worker to be seen in town. Milk, bread and newspaper deliveries were disrupted. Industry and commerce expressed their alarm.

Nyanga township, where most of the site-and-service workers live and which has been the scene of the most intensive and sustained pass raids during the past year, was in a state of siege the whole week.

Road blocks were thrown across the streets — barrels, slabs of concrete, felled trees — so that during the whole week the buses were unable to run and there was no transport to take the workers to town. To escape police attention, many people went to live in the thick bush surrounding the township, and the ridges of all the hills were lined with sentinels to give warnings of police approach.

In both townships, the permit system broke down completely. The huts at the entrances were not manned, and in some cases were completely flattened to the ground.

The police maintained a strong guard round the administration offices, and their Saracens and riot vehicles were drawn up laager fashion before the police stations. Occasionally heavily armed groups of police would make a quick sortie through the streets in a Saracen.

But for the rest it was the people who were in control. It was they who kept a check on the entrances and escorted visitors into and out of the townships.

It is only fair to mention that people of the wrong skin colour were not given a friendly reception in the townships last week, and anti-white hostility was very evident. After the police shootings and beatings at Langa and Sharpeville this is, perhaps, not very surprising. By the end of the week even the PAC leadership had become embarrassed by it and announced that they were taking steps to counteract it.

The PAC 'surrender' campaign continued fitfully through the week. On the Monday [as noted], 1 200 names were taken at the Philippi station of Africans who had left their passes at home and surrendered themselves at the police station to be arrested [and] none surrendered themselves at Langa, their leaders alleging that when they tried to do so, the police threatened to shoot them if they came anywhere near the police station.

During the week, two groups of Africans from Langa then tried to surrender themselves at the central police station at Caledon Square in Cape Town. On the first occasion on Wednesday about 100 were taken into custody and appeared in court later in the week.

On Friday a further 2 000 Africans from Langa, regardless of the Government's ban on gatherings under the Riotous Assemblies Act, demonstrated in the street outside Caledon Square and demanded to be arrested.

Their leader, Mr P Kgosana, who is PAC regional secretary, together with Mr Patrick Duncan, of the Liberal Party, interviewed the Commandant of Police, Col. IPS Terblanche.

New Age is informed that Mr Duncan suggested that the pass laws should be suspended for a period of one month, but Mr Kgosana replied that this would not satisfy the people, who were demanding the complete abolition of the pass laws.

Col. Terblanche said consideration would be given to the representations which had been made to him. In the meantime, the demonstrators would not be arrested, and the police requested that they disperse quietly and go home. The police provided a loudspeaker to enable one of the leaders to address the crowd and pass on this message.

The people then marched in a procession over a mile long back to Langa where they again presented themselves at the police station and asked to be arrested, but again they met with refusal.

The next day the Commissioner of Police, Gen. Rademeyer, announced that he had issued an instruction that until further notice no arrests would be made of Africans who were not in possession of their pass books.

Even the 100 who had appeared in court earlier in the week were released and told that the charges against them had been dropped. Charges were also dropped against the 1 200 who had handed in their names at Philippi when the campaign started on Monday.

Over the weekend plans were being made for further demonstrations against the pass laws, but PAC leaders would not reveal what they were.

Who are the PAC leaders in the Western Cape? Chairman of the region is Mr Christopher Mlokoti, aged 32, a garage worker. *New Age* was unable to interview him as during the week he was taken into custody by the police. He lives at Nyanga.

Secretary of the region is Mr Philip Kgosana, aged 21, whose home is in Pretoria but who was registered at the University of Cape Town this year to do his second year BCom.

He and five other students threw up their academic careers to take part in the PAC campaign. In an interview with *New Age*, he said: 'We shall not call off the struggle until the pass laws are abolished.'

Asked about the next stage in the campaign, he said: 'The word must come from Mr Sobukwe. He must speak, even if he is behind prison bars.'

Mr Kgosana said the PAC was prepared to cooperate completely with the ANC and other organisations in the anti-pass campaign. Asked what non-Africans could do to help the campaign, he said: 'They must stay at home.'

> La Guma A with F Carneson, Langa's night of terror, *New Age*, 24 March 1960, and
> In Cape Town last week Africans ruled the townships, *New Age*, 31 March 1960

26

State of Emergency

What a calamity the Emergency has been – for Afrikaner Nationalism!

Others suffered, as the Nationalists did not, in their persons and property. The 20 000 detainees, their wives and children, employees and employers, all suffered an injury.

Many of us have been ruined financially. Some lost their jobs and are still out of work. Some have seen their businesses and professions go down to the point of bankruptcy. Some have been uprooted permanently, and are forced to make new homes, carve out new lives for themselves and their families.

All of us suffered arrest without warrant, imprisonment without trial. We have been humiliated, brow-beaten and pushed around by a hateful police tyranny. We have had police snoopers standing about, listening to our conversations with wives, husbands and relatives.

We have been locked up, in some cases for 22 hours a day, in stuffy, badly-lit prison cells. We have slept on thin mats spread on bare boards or on concrete floors. We have had to relieve ourselves in open buckets standing in the cells. We have been herded like cattle from one place to another, always under the watchful eyes of warders or police.

Many were interrogated and expected to answer questions about their private lives, their friends and associates, their opinions and political ideas. Most of us refused to answer these questions, but always we were haunted by sickening uncertainty: how long would this last, would we end up in a concentration camp, when would we rejoin our wives or husbands and children?

The trials of our families were even worse than ours. They could not know what was happening behind the prison walls, while we did manage to smuggle in newspapers occasionally and pick up news here and there. If their detainee was the breadwinner, they had to get their food, clothing, rent and money from friends or organised assistance. Many of them travelled hundreds of miles every week just to spend 20 or 30 minutes with their detainees, of course under the eyes and ears of the political police.

Among the losers must also be counted the shareholders, whose shares went rocketing down to the extent of £600 million or so. I don't suppose that they ate or drank less, or sold their jewellery and big cars, and we need not waste much sympathy with them. But they too were victims of the Emergency in their own way.

Yet, I repeat, the Emergency was a calamity for Afrikaner nationalism. Perhaps also for the Afrikaner people because they have allowed themselves to be mixed up with Afrikaner nationalism and the Nationalist government.

During all the months of our imprisonment, the only white officials, political police and prison warders with whom we had anything to do were Afrikaners. We realised as never before that the Police State is manned from top to bottom by Afrikaners.

This is a very heavy burden, perhaps an unmerited one, that the Afrikaner people have to bear. For we know that the State and its officials are there to protect the wealth and privileges, not just of Afrikaners, but of the entire class of property owners. We know also that it is the English, and not the Afrikaners, who own by far the greater part of the wealth in the mines, factories, banks, and big companies.

But it is the Afrikaner people who have taken over the machinery of the State. They are the ones who frame its policies, direct its activities, and carry out the orders of the government. So in our minds, as in the minds of countless others who suffer daily oppression under the colour-bar, a connection has been formed between the Police State and the Afrikaner people.

The Afrikaner has obtained a monopoly of political power and of the fruits of power. But he has had to pay a terrible price for his victory. To gain his political kingdom, he has turned the rest of the population into opponents and – as regards many hundreds of thousands of people – into determined, bitter enemies of his rule.

Ours is a multi-racial, multi-national society. No one race or national community can lord it over the rest for long without plunging our country and its entire population into disaster. It is this fact that the Nationalist Government has chosen to ignore, Yet the hard, stubborn fact remains.

We detainees were reminded of this fact on every day of our imprisonment. We ourselves formed a multi-racial, multi-national community. Black, brown and white, men and women of different races, languages and religions, we shared the same fate and for the same cause.

Though segregated inside the jails according to race and sex, we saw or heard our brothers and sisters in adjoining yards and cells. Who of us can forget the deep-throated, many-voiced chorus that swept upwards every night from the packed cells of African detainees, over the walls, into our cells, and upwards to the starry skies?

We heard and sang in a great united community, not only of political prisoners, but of the entire population of oppressed South Africans. And we rejoiced that we shared a common fate with our brothers and sisters of all races and nationalities. For, as has been said, when laws are unjust the only place for an honest man is in prison.

What a calamity the Emergency would have been for the people if only black men had gone to jail! Those of us who were coloured, Indian or European knew that in the eyes of the State we were as dangerous to Afrikaner Nationalism and its Police State as were the Africans. And we would not have wanted it otherwise. In the multi-racial, multi-national community of political detainees lay the guarantee of the future, free South Africa.

We knew that we had been jailed because we had rejected a social order that violates every moral and religious law, that dooms people to poverty, ignorance and oppression because of the colour of their skins, that has become a key-word among the nations of the earth for brutality and disregard for human rights. We were in jail because we demanded dignity and respect for all South Africans.

Knowing this, we have come out of the jails stronger, more determined than before. The Nationalist Government has banned our organisations. We shall organise again, wider and stronger than ever. The Government jailed our leaders. We shall throw up new leaders to take their place. This is what we said in the jails, and this is what we will do!

We say this without bravado, but in the light of cold reason and an objective weighing up of all the factors. We know that the Nationalist government has all the armed force on its side, and that we have none. But we have a weapon that is far greater than their Saracens, their machine guns, their planes and armour. We have right and justice and the people on our side.

We have seen through the Emergency and know it for what it is – a gigantic swindle. Twenty thousand men and women jailed illegally, even though there was a 'law' to deny us our rights, and only a few of us have been brought before the courts and charged with an offence! When the State is forced to throw aside its cloak of legality, and to surrender every claim to moral action, it is doomed no matter how much physical force it may command.

It is they, the Nationalists, and not we, the people, who have lost ground. They have been isolated, here in South Africa and beyond our borders, in the rest of Africa and of the world. We, who stand for a free, equal society of all South Africans, black, white and brown, have gained enormously in fellowship, in confidence and in allies.

We detainees could feel the sympathy and support of the people coming to us through the prison walls. This feeling helped to keep our patience proud, our rebel thoughts unbowed. We knew of the many hundreds of people outside who collected money, food and clothing to support our families. We knew of the rising tide of indignation that forced the police to release detainees, in small batches or one by one, until the Emergency itself had to be brought to an end.

There will be more emergencies, and real ones too, if we fail to mobilise and organise the goodwill and support for our cause against the Nationalist Government. Our rulers have proved themselves incapable of solving South Africa's problems, of making friends, of responding – except by force and more oppression – to the challenge of Africa and the demands of our age.

Therefore, we ex-detainees say, the Nationalist Government and all apartheid policies must go. And we dedicate ourselves to their overthrow and to the creation of a new society in which all of us, whatever the colour of our skin, shall be free to live, work and play in dignity and peace.

The Emergency was a crisis for Afrikaner nationalism, *New Age*, 8 September 1960

Brickbats and bouquets

Except for the loss of six pounds in weight, a few more grey hairs and a very strong dislike for mealie-pap and beans, yours truly is once more in circulation and being nasty to the Nats.

Before preparing the brick-bats, however, it is necessary that a whole pile of bouquets be handed out. And they go to all those who kept the old flag flying throughout the State of Emergency; to SERF [State of Emergency Relief Fund] who kept our families happy, and to the donors who contributed to that fund in order that the home-fires go on burning, to the many voluntary workers and the car owners who saw to it that detainees received regular visits from their families, and to one and all who helped to make the detention of hundreds of freedom fighters worthwhile.

I have also been asked to pass on a bouquet to warders of Worcester jail who kept us well informed on the All Blacks tour, and the prison cook who tried his damnedest to make the SOS (same old s—t) look less like it.

No bouquets for Roeland Street gaol.

When it comes to throwing bricks, all we can say is confusion to the Nats, the SB [Special Branch] and all those nasty types who think that democracy is a belly-ache and that it can be got rid of by large doses of State of Emergency.

Uninteresting characters I have met:

Goateed 'General de Wet', the Roeland Street warder who stalked up and down the lines of detainees and snarled: 'I'm looking for a boy to clean the yard. And I don't want a &XOS§ communist!'

And his colleague who, whenever there were complaints that the latrine buckets were overflowing, could only bawl, 'Well, do it in your @-*S<X pocket.' Another, when told that the blankets were too scanty, had the stock reply of, 'Stand on your head and cover yourself with your crap.'

Gestapo humour!

Then there was the long-term convict who, when snapped at by a warder to knock some detainees around with his broom if they got in his way, replied with dignity: 'I will never do that. These people are fighting for me too.'

Of course, I must not leave out the Special Branch dick who looked in at the exercise yard in Worcester and said somewhat wearily to his pal who was chatting to me: 'It's no use talking to him. He'll just put it in Up My Alley.'

Such is fame.

A final word must go to the many coloured people who rallied to the common cause of the African people during the heroic days preceding the State of Emergency, in spite of the so-called 'leaders' who signed a public statement calling them off from the struggle: these Nationalist toadies must be rejected quickly and once and for all. The time has come for our people to seriously assess their relationship with the struggle to liberate South Africa and the rest of the continent. Our place is with the active forces of progress so that we can honestly claim that we deserve our place in the sun.

Now I must stop Pratt-ling and get down to work.

Up my alley, New Age, 8 September 1960

The missing men of the emergency
What happened to the thousands of Africans who were arrested for so-called pass offences under the notorious section 4(b) of the Emergency Regulations, and held without trial in an open court?

What has happened to those who, up to today, are still missing? *New Age*, probing into the story of one of these men, uncovered a pattern which must apply to hundreds of so-called idlers and vagrants arrested in the Western Cape.

It is a story of:
- 'drumhead' courts established in the local prison;
- summary 'sentence' to distant jails;
- transportation in chains;
- parents hopelessly searching for missing sons.

In an interview with *New Age* a young man, WH, 19 years old, said that he had been arrested in the middle of May for not being in possession of a pass. His protests that he could produce one were ignored and he was removed to Roeland Street jail. There he joined hundreds of other African men held for similar offences.

A special court established under the Emergency Regulations had been set up in an office in the jail and the prisoners were taken in one by one.

'After I had been lying in Roeland Street for about eight days I was taken into this room,' WH said. 'There were men in plain clothes inside, and one of them who was a magistrate said I was being sent to Makousvlei.

'Many other men were treated in this manner at the time I appeared before this court. I think about 180 to 200 men were sentenced that week.

'Afterwards we were driven in a lorry to the railway yards outside Cape Town station and loaded onto a train,' WH continued.

'We were handcuffed and wore leg-irons and stayed like this, sitting up in the ordinary day-coaches, for all of the three days the journey lasted.

'It was very uncomfortable. For meals on the train we were given a piece of bread and some water three times a day.'

Their destination turned out to be East London and they were taken to Fort Glamorgan jail which is just outside the city, near the sea.

In the meantime the mother of WH was trying frantically to get news of her son. At Roeland Street prison she was told that he was in good hands and being well cared for. There was no necessity for her to bring warm clothes. Later she was told he had been moved to Worcester jail but he was not there.

For this mother WH had simply disappeared.

'For the two months during which I served at Fort Glamorgan the jail remained crowded,' WH went on. 'Most of the prisoners were young men, but I also saw boys of about 16 or 17 years old.

'Those found to have been born in the Reserves were moved from Fort Glamorgan to jails near their respective places of birth. As a result I was separated from many of the prisoners who had come there with me.

'There was one old man of about 60 who was ill. He was transported to Fort Glamorgan with me, but I did not see him again after we arrived there.'

WH served at Fort Glamorgan for two months.

'The work was very hard,' he said. 'Many of us were sent to work in the quarries and on the prison farmlands. Others worked in the piggeries looking after pigs. I was set to painting ships in the harbour.'

After two months WH reported that he was ill and could not work. He said the prison authorities refused to accept this and sentenced him to one day solitary confinement and the loss of three meals.

The next day WH was released.

'I was given a rail warrant and two loaves of bread for the journey.

'When my property was handed to me my shoes were missing. I arrived at home barefooted.'

WH is now reunited with his family. But there are still men who have not returned home. The State of Emergency is over, but families still wait anxiously for news of sons and husbands who disappeared into the police net months ago and have not been heard of since.

One of these is Mrs Lily Vangqa of Langa whose son Richard was detained under the Emergency Regulations and who is still missing.

Richard Vangqa, 36, left to work in the Transvaal last year. In January he wrote to his mother stating that he would be returning to Cape Town. The only news of her son Mrs Vangqa received after that was when she saw his name in the Eastern Cape list of detainees in a local newspaper on May 6. His whereabouts to date are unknown.

Believing that Richard might have gone to the Transkei before setting out for Cape Town, and had been arrested there, Mrs Vangqa wrote to her relations there hoping they could trace him.

They had not seen Richard either before or after the State of Emergency. At the moment Mrs Vangqa is still hoping that enquiries at the Ministry of Justice will bring her son back.

In the meanwhile Richard Vangqa is still missing. He is one of the Missing Men of the Emergency. What has happened to him? Have all the detainees been released?

The missing men of the Emergency, New Age, 29 September 1960

SACPC Statement

'The events in South Africa since March have revealed that the era of white baasskap is drawing to a close and that the victory of the oppressed millions of non-white people over apartheid and racial supremacy is clearly inevitable,' says a statement issued by the South African Coloured People's Congress.

The upholders of white supremacy, amongst both the Nationalist and United Party plus their respective supporters, have been saying much recently about a new 'deal' for the coloured people. This has been done with the hope of wooing our people to their side in the defence of so-called 'Western civilisation'. There has been talk of spending more money on the coloured people, of franchise deals and coloured senators, and of regarding us as the 'natural allies' of this Western civilisation.

The coloured people must reject these overtures as efforts to seduce them from the struggle for full democracy in this country. The coloured people can never be the allies of the oppressor. The continent of Africa is aflame with the burning desire for economic, political and social equality for all people irrespective of race and colour. And the time has come when, once and for all, such must be the demands of our people, too.

'We want no more concessions! We want no more crumbs from the table of white baasskap or segregation with justice! In the new situation which the country faces we want no separate representation, nor to make use of it as a means of stating our grievances. The political developments since March have clearly indicated that nothing short of full and equal participation in the government of South Africa will satisfy the non-white people.

'The only "new deal" for the coloured people must be the total removal of the colour-bar from all walks of life for all people who inhabit South Africa.

'The coloured people of South Africa to which the SA Coloured People's Congress speaks have also a part to play in the liberation of the non-white people,' says the statement.

'During the eventful days of March large numbers of the coloured people rallied to the call of the CPC to support the African people in their struggle, and particularly to observe the day of mourning for the dead of Langa and Sharpeville.

'At the same time, however, certain "leaders" of non-European unity, hiding behind the screen of "principles" and the condemnation of "adventurism" and "opportunism", maintained a cowardly silence in the face of the militancy of the people and could offer no positive, honourable or decent policy to the coloured people in relation to the struggle then being waged. Their silence was strictly maintained throughout the state of emergency. It was only when the danger was past, that they started once again to pay their usual lip service to the "struggle for full democratic rights".

'Other so-called "leaders" had the audacity to dishonourably call on our people to withhold their support from the Africans, and, more as an afterthought, asked them to donate towards the relief of the besieged Africans, thereby hoping to salve their consciences by attempting to place our people in the position of a charitable organisation instead of an oppressed community whose place was and is in active alliance with others struggling for the common cause of democracy and equal opportunities for all people.

'These so-called "leaders" must be rejected at once and completely by the coloured people.

'Those scattered forces which found cause in support of the African people then must sink their differences now in order to build up a powerful front against all forms of racial oppression to forge an active alliance of the coloured people with the Africans for the liberation of the non-whites of South Africa.

'The SACPC believes that at this stage in the history of the continent of Africa every effort must be made to create the greatest unity among our people to break down the social and political barriers which have divided us in the past, so that our people can make their worthy contribution, not only towards their own emancipation, but also towards that of the whole continent of which they are part.'

Coloureds should stand by Africans – says CPC: Nat. overtures rejected,
New Age, 15 September 1960

27

No to the white republic!

Die Republiek. Ja-nee.

According to the local English morning blad, Namaqualand voted as follows [in the whites-only referendum]:

NO 2 053

NO 2 686

YES majority 4 633

The electoral officer, no doubt, can figure that out. But perhaps it can serve as a mathematical picture of this crazy, mixed-up country where three million white people can run around polling booths wearing blinkers while 11 million non-whites who, by the way, also happen to live here, are ignored.

The majority of whites might have said JA! to Verwoerd's Reich, but there is a feeling in the air that the results from the places where people don't vote by making crosses on paper are still to come in.

It will be a resounding NEE!

Up my alley. *New Age*, 13 October 1960

'Together we can win freedom'

The African people welcome with open arms the call of the Coloured People's Congress to the coloured people to struggle side by side with the African people, says an open letter addressed to the coloureds by the National Action Council, the body appointed to carry out the action resolutions passed by the Pietermaritzburg All-in African Conference.

The Pietermaritzburg action resolution has a clause calling on the 'the Indian and coloured communities and all democratic Europeans to join forces with us in opposition to a regime which is bringing disaster to South Africa'.

The open letter to the coloured people is prompted by the giant meeting of Cape Town coloureds on the Grand Parade recently which resolved to line up with the African people in the political struggles of the next few months.

The letter says, 'We accept the coloured people as full and equal allies in the battle for freedom. We have waited and worked for this day. For, once the oppressed peoples of South Africa achieve full unity, victory will be within their grasp.

'Decades of white supremacy rule have shown us that racialism is the most powerful weapon used by our oppressors to divide us. White supremacy rule has herded us into separate ghettos; ruled us under different sets of restrictive regulations; applied the colour-bar with varying degrees of harshness; and has tried to spread the poison of race hatred into our ranks. These tactics were meant to divide us. Instead they have brought us together.

'The African people know full well the misery and poverty that job reservation will bring to the coloured people, for we suffer under the colour-bar in industry. We who have been uprooted from our homes time without number know the sufferings that the Group Areas Act will bring to the coloured people. The African people lost their meagre political representation in Parliament and now the coloured people are being threatened with the loss of the coloured seats.

'The Africans have always been the first to fall under the axe of the apartheid executioner; not far behind them the Government has lined up its next victim: the coloured people and the Indians.

'OUR ANSWER TO THE HATED POLICY OF RACE RULE AND DIVISION CAN BE ONLY BROTHERLY UNITY AND STRENGTH.

'The hated South African Government has never before been so isolated and shaky. The present state of crisis is caused by world condemnation on an unprecedented scale; deepening economic difficulties; and the mounting anger of the South African people.

'THE UNITY AND ACTION OF THE AFRICAN AND COLOURED PEOPLE, OF THE INDIAN PEOPLE AND DEMOCRATIC WHITES CAN BRING THE HATED SYSTEM TO AN END.

'The call of the Pietermaritzburg conference for nation-wide action to compel the convening of a National Convention to draft a new constitution was addressed to all South Africans. The Coloured Congress has the honour of having been the first to respond to the call with vigour and boldness.

'FORWARD TOGETHER TO FREEDOM!'

Africans welcome coloured support, *New Age*, 20 April 1961

Afrika Day

The people of the Cape Peninsula once again indicated their support for mass demonstrations on the eve of the Republic when an audience of over 5 000 who attended the Afrika Day celebration on the Grand Parade last Sunday gave enthusiastic applause to all references to demonstrations at the end of May.

The meeting, which was called by the Liberal Party, was addressed by speakers from the Congress alliance and other organisations.

'The coloureds are no longer prepared to allow the African people to struggle alone,' said Mr Reg September, Secretary of the Coloured People's Congress amid cheers from the audience.

Mr September said that the African people had called for demonstrations throughout the country on the eve of the Republic. 'The days when the coloured people stood aside will not be repeated.'

The Rev. Clive McBride, of the Anglican Church, said that the political, economic and social wolves must be chased out of God's flock. 'We say to the oppressors: "Let our people go." And at the end of May we will show them what we mean.'

In spite of a sudden downpour of rain the crowd remained attentive and enthusiastic. When former ANC member Elliot Nziba appealed for funds, a shower of coins rained on the platform from among the crowd.

Advocate AL Sachs, speaking on behalf of the Congress of Democrats, said that the white people must actively dissociate themselves from the policy of apartheid. 'Instead of grumbling about Verwoerd the white people should show their support for a national convention of all people at which a new constitution for South Africa would be drawn up,' Advocate Sachs said.

Those South Africans who had volunteered to fight for Tshombe in the Congo were traitors to South Africa, Advocate Sachs went on. Tshombe himself was a traitor to Africa, for he was the murderer of Lumumba.

Mr Peter Hjul, chairman of the Cape Liberal Party, urged the people to be ready when the call finally came for them to act. 'The Government is beaten,' he said. 'All it needs is a push.'

The meeting adopted a resolution pledging to work for a non-racial democracy for a national convention of all the people of South Africa at which the constitution for a new South Africa would be drawn up.

Other speakers were Messrs JCA Daniels and Hammington Majija of the Liberal Party, Mr Norman Daniels from the Coloured National Convention committee, Mr C Mase of the African General Workers' Union, and Mr Zollie Malindi.

A large contingent of Special Branch detectives made notes of the speeches.

Afrika Day meetings, *New Age*, 20 April 1961

Coloured People's Congress

Coloured people throughout the Western Cape are preparing for mass demonstrations at the end of this month. Directed by the SA Coloured People's Congress, which is working with the local Action Council, numerous committees established throughout the Peninsula are busy working in their respective areas, holding meetings and drawing more people into what has become the biggest political campaign undertaken by the coloured community.

In areas beyond the Cape Peninsula similar campaigning is under way. Officials of the CPC have stated that the current campaign for demonstrations against Verwoerd's white Republic surpasses the one conducted by the Franchise Action Council in 1951 when workers stayed home on May 7 in protest against the removal of coloured voters from the common roll.

The first leaflets in the present campaign were recently distributed throughout the Cape Peninsula and the country areas by hundreds of coloured volunteers.

'Prepare for May!' the leaflet stated. The coloured people were urged to prepare to demonstrate with the African and Indian people on the eve of the Republic should the Government not accede to the demand for a national convention.

The CPC said that over 40 000 of these leaflets were distributed in the Cape Peninsula. The same leaflet, translated into Afrikaans, was distributed in the country areas.

Volunteers reported to CPC headquarters that the message of the Congress had been well received. Many people had told them that families were stocking up extra groceries in preparation for the periods of the demonstrations. Other reports are to the effect that housewives doing their Saturday morning shopping have also been talking enthusiastically about laying in stocks of food.

In various factories in the Peninsula workers are discussing the campaign.

Shortly after the distribution of the leaflets the homes of several CPC executive members were raided by Special Branch detectives who were searching for documents connected with the forthcoming demonstrations.

The CPC has called upon the coloured people to stand firm in the face of police intimidation, and have urged them to ignore 'spineless' leadership. 'Freedom will not be given to you on a plate,' the latest message to the people from the CPC stated. 'White baasskap is showing signs of defeat. Stock up your food. Tighten your belts. The time has come.'

Coloured support for mass demonstrations, *New Age*, 4 May 1961

Muslim call for action

A call to support the mass demonstrations on the eve of the Republic at the end of this month was greeted with thunderous applause by 4 000 Muslims packed into the Old Drill Hall last Sunday.

As Mr MT Bardien, executive member of the Coloured People's Congress, rose from the body of the hall and walked to the platform to address the meeting, he was greeted with a storm of cheers and handclapping.

'The African people represented at the Maritzburg conference have called on all sections to support the demonstrations against Verwoerd's Republic,' Mr Bardien told the crowd. 'Let us down tools and stay at home from the 29th of this month.'

At this stage Mr Bardien's words were drowned by the great ovation which arose from the audience. Clenched fists were raised and fezzes waved in the air.

Mr Bardien said that shops should be closed and nobody should go to the cinema or ride on the buses.

The Drill Hall was packed with people sitting two to a chair, with hundreds lining the walls and squatting in the aisles. Organisers said that this was the first time that the Muslim community had gathered in such numbers to identify themselves with the struggle for freedom and equality for all people.

The meeting had been called by the Claremont Muslim Youth Association, the Muslim Youth Movement, Cape Vigilance Association, Al-Jaamia Mosque and other Muslim bodies.

Speakers called on parents not to give permission to schools to issue their children with flags and medals as part of the official Republic celebrations.

'Verwoerd has said he will give no concessions to us "inferior beings",' Imam A Haroon said. 'But the Koran gives all Muslims the right to stand up and fight. If we sacrifice we will achieve victory.'

Mr M Booley of the Cape Town Youth Movement condemned a qualified franchise. 'We demand one man one vote. Freedom to vote is the fundamental right of all men.'

The Muslim people refused to be intimidated by the authorities, Mr Booley continued. If anybody on the platform was intimidated, he would have the support of 70 000 Muslims in the Cape.

Sheikh Nazeem condemned extreme nationalism, whether it was white, black or Arab nationalism. All men should live together in peace.

Mr S Tofy called on the meeting to support the idea of a national convention of all races at which should be present, amongst others, Chief Luthuli, Professor Matthews, Robert Sobukwe, Nelson Mandela and Jordan Ngubane.

With one vote against, the meeting adopted a resolution stating that the happiness and well-being of all people of this country could only be assured when all people had a direct say in the making of laws and the distribution of wealth; that the laws should uphold the right of all people to social justice and freedom to live wherever they wished, to earn a living wage, to have access to all educational institutions, to move without restrictions and to contribute to the welfare and happiness of all the people of South Africa.

4 000 Muslims cheer call for action, *New Age*, 11 May 1961

George Peake

Members of the committee of the Coloured National Convention, including Councillor George Peake, were amongst a number of European and coloured leaders invited to the farm of Mr AH Broeksma QC at Stellenbosch last week to take part in talks on the political situation in the country.

Among the Europeans present were ex-Chief Justice Fagan, Prof. SB Cilliers, Prof. Nico Olivier, Dr Keet, Dr Steenkamp of the DRC and Advocate Schachat.

When Mr George Golding put in an appearance, several of the coloured leaders present wanted to leave, but were persuaded to stay by urgent representations from the convenors.

Mr Broeksma told the gathering that the Europeans present, broadly representative of white opinion in the country, were gravely disturbed at the racial tension in the country and wanted to urge the coloured leaders to call off the demonstrations planned to take place at the end of the month.

Mr George Peake replied that, speaking as a member of the Coloured People's Congress which was committed to taking part in the demonstrations, he felt the Europeans had nothing to fear. The demonstrations would be peaceful and nobody was threatened.

The CPC was not prepared to consider calling off the demonstrations and in any case had no power to do so, as the main decision had been taken by the Africans at the All-in Conference held in Pietermaritzburg in March.

Mr Peake said that if the Europeans present did represent white opinion, as they claimed, then they should make representations to Dr Verwoerd to call a National Convention of all races to discuss a new constitution, as requested by the Maritzburg conference.

This was the most constructive thing the Europeans could do to ease racial tension at the present moment.

Peake rejects white bid to call off strike, *New Age*, 11 May 1961

Government terrorists

As preparations for the demonstrations against Verwoerd's Republic intensify, pro-Government terrorist groups have been active in attempts to intimidate Congress members who are active in the organisation of the demonstrations.

Last week:
- a petrol bomb was thrown into the Maitland home of Mrs R Kara, whose son, Mohamed, is a member of the Coloured People's Congress;
- windows of the homes of three other members of the CPC were smashed by stones. All the incidents occurred during the early hours of the morning.

In a statement to *New Age*, Mrs Blanche La Guma said that she was awakened at 1 a.m. on Thursday morning by the ringing of the phone; when she answered it a man's voice, obviously disguised, asked to speak to Alex La Guma.

Mrs La Guma replied that he was not home, and the voice said: 'Tell your husband to watch his step. We are going to get him. You won't see him alive after tonight.'

The man, speaking in a deep voice and rolling his r's added, 'This is the Supreme Commander of the Ku Klux Klan.' He repeated this twice.

At about 3.30 a.m. Mrs La Guma heard the sound of a car drawing up outside the house. Two heavy thuds against the front wall followed, and then the sounds of footsteps running away and the car moving off. Mrs La Guma called her neighbours and it was found that two heavy stones had been thrown at the windows, breaking one pane.

Mrs La Guma's attempts to ring the local police failed as the station line remained continuously engaged. She reported the matter to the Athlone Police in the morning.

'I acted on the instructions of the Police Chief who has said that all threats of intimidation should be reported,' Mrs La Guma said. 'I trust that they will act speedily to find the culprits.'

'We refuse to be intimidated,' Mrs La Guma added. 'I have every confidence in the political work in which my husband is engaged, and we will not be intimidated by pro-Government hooligans.'

Neighbours have arranged to guard Mr La Guma's home.

A petrol bomb was thrown into the house of Mrs Kara in Maitland in the early hours of the morning of Tuesday, May 16. The bomb, made out of a wine bottle, crashed through the window, setting alight curtains, a carpet and a chair.

Mrs Kara and her two daughters, Fatima and Khadija, were sitting in the kitchen when they heard the bomb explode. When they rushed into the lounge they found a pillar of flame roaring up one wall. They managed to put the fire out with blankets and water, and called the police.

This incident occurred after members of the local action committee had been distributing leaflets about the end-of-May demonstrations in the area.

A statement issued by Mr Barney Desai, vice-president, and Mr Reg September, general secretary of CPC, stated that the attacks on the homes of CPC members were made by pro-Government secret organisations.

'We consider these to be acts of political vandalism, and naked intimidation aimed at persons involved in resistance to apartheid.'

The statement continued: 'Colonel Muir, Officer Commanding police in the Western Cape, warned that drastic action would be taken against intimidators. The fact of the matter is that our supporters are being intimidated.'

The CPC also said that members of the police force had been visiting non-white shopkeepers and threatening that if they closed in sympathy with the stay-home demonstrations at the end of the month, their licences would be withdrawn.

'We call on people to resist these Gestapo tactics,' the CPC statement concluded. 'We are confident that our people will stand firm and that these tactics of intimidators will not affect the course of our demonstrations at the end of this month.'

Govt. terrorists attack Congress homes, *New Age*, 25 May 1961

Convention preparations

More than 500 delegates, representing a major portion of the coloured community, will attend the Coloured National Convention starting on July 7, the secretary of the Planning Committee, Mr JCA Daniels, told *New Age* this week.

The Convention, which will be held at the Claremont Civic Centre, will be opened on Friday July 7 at 8 p.m. by the chairman of the Committee, Mr D van der Ross. Discussions will also be open to the public on Saturday, July 8, and on Monday, July 10. The Sunday session will be attended by delegates only.

'All indications are that all shades of political opinion among the coloured people will be represented,' Mr Daniels said. 'The Convention, the first of its kind held by coloureds, will be of historic importance, and will enable the community to define their future political direction.'

Mr Daniels said that final preparations for the Convention were being made all over South Africa. 'The recent banning of meetings has, however, affected the preparations, and the Planning Committee wishes to make a special appeal to all those who have not been contacted and who are interested in sending delegates to write to the Committee at PO Box 2864, Cape Town, for details.'

Items to be discussed at the Convention will include the franchise, a non-racial constitution for South Africa based on the Declaration of Human Rights, and the calling of a non-racial National Convention. Another item on the agenda will raise the question of whether coloureds should or should not have a special status in relation to other groups.

Asked whether the idea of a Coloured Convention had met with any opposition within the community, Mr Daniels said that large sections of the working people and many professional people supported the call for a convention. The only opposition had been voiced by the Non-European Unity Movement and Mr George Golding's Coloured People's National Union.

Final plans for Coloured Convention to open July 7, *New Age*, 22 June 1961

Coloured Convention

The attempt by the Minister of Justice, Mr FC Erasmus, to prevent the National Coloured Convention from meeting was a miserable failure.

In a magnificent demonstration of unity and determination, the delegates, banned from meeting anywhere from Cape Town to Worcester, moved into the countryside near Malmesbury and held their historic convention in the open air.

The authentic voice of the coloured people was heard, despite every attempt of the Government and the Special Branch to silence it.

Seated on blankets, car seats and tree stumps in a little valley on a farm near Malmesbury for one session last Saturday, and in a large shed on another farm for the final session on Monday, about 150 delegates representing the bulk of the coloured community came to the most important political decisions in the history of their people.

The Convention stated:

- That the coloured people refused any special status in South African society; but that all people should enjoy complete equality in a non-racial South Africa.
- Adopted the principle of universal adult suffrage based on one man, one vote – stating clearly that all people irrespective of colour must have the right to elect and be elected to the governing bodies of the country.

Convention confirmed the basic resolutions of the Planning Committee calling for the total abolition of the colour-bar from all walks of life, and the extension of full democratic rights to all people.

'On these principles there can be no compromise,' the Convention stated.

A continuation committee was formed, consisting of the present executive and representatives from the different geographical divisions of South Africa.

The primary task of the continuation committee will be to make contact with leaders of all other organisations and movements who support the idea of a national convention, with the view of calling a non-racial conference of all people of South Africa, as soon as possible.

Despite the anger of the delegates at the banning of the Convention under the Suppression of Communism Act last Friday, deliberations were carried out in a considered and statesman-like manner.

The greatest effect the Government's action had was to bring about a spirit of unity and determination among a people of varied political opinions.

As soon as the ban was imposed, organisers of the Convention got together to decide what to do. The decision was to find a venue beyond the areas in which the gathering had been banned, and it was agreed that Malmesbury be the place for this historic meeting.

On Saturday morning cars left Cape Town for Malmesbury. Initial arrangements to use a hall in the town fell through, but a local white farmer agreed to allow the delegates to use his property.

Convention started late in the morning and lasted until sundown. Commissions were appointed to formulate policy on various topics after discussion by the Convention.

Mr JCA Daniels, secretary of the Convention, said that although some of the delegates had not been able to take part owing to partial dislocation of the organisation as a result of the ban, those present represented the majority elected all over South Africa, and whatever discussions and decisions were taken reflected the broad will of the coloured people.

On Monday the delegates once more travelled by car to the Malmesbury area for the final session. A second farmer gave the gathering the use of a large shed, and seated on benches made of planks laid across metal drums delegates heard the reports of the different commissions, discussed them and took the final vote.

The Special Branch had by Monday got wind of the plans to move the convention to the country and spent a lot of time chasing around trying to find the venue. When the large contingent of detectives and police finally located the farm and walked into the gathering, discussions had already reached the final stages. The police did not interfere with the proceedings.

Convention also called for a Bill of Rights guaranteeing such things as:
- Freedom of worship, of association, of the press;
- The right to own property and occupy it wherever one wishes and can afford;
- The right to full education;
- The right to sell one's labour in the open market, or to withhold it if one so wishes;
- The right to travel freely through the country, and to leave and return to the country freely.

Convention said that with regard to civil rights, it stood for the abolition of all laws which discriminated against people on the basis of race, colour or creed, including the pass laws. Education should be free, integrated and compulsory, and all institutions of learning should be open to everybody. Parents should have the right to decide in which manner their children should be educated.

All restrictions on the right of the individual to enter trades should be abolished; the colour-bar in commerce and industry should be scrapped, and the principle of equal work for equal pay, irrespective of sex, be firmly entrenched in the statutes of the land.

The tot system, contract labour, child labour, compound labour and convict labour must be abolished. There should be a redivision of the land so that it could be developed to the fullest extent with the aid of mechanisation and State financial assistance. Suitable working conditions should be introduced in order to ensure those who work on the land of a good livelihood.

Participation in trade and commerce should be free of any race restrictions and merit should be the sole criterion of advancement in the economic sphere.

Group areas, job reservation, the UCCA, BAD [Bantu Affairs Department] and AAC were rejected in the strongest terms.

A resolution calling for the nationalisation of the mines, banks and primary means of production was defeated.

Thus ended a historic meeting of the representatives of the coloured community.

Coloured Convention outwits the government, *New Age*, 13 July 1961

Part 5
Cold wars

28

The picture in the parlour

In winter, the light coming through the lace curtains over the window made bright patterns in the shadowy interior of the tiny parlour. When the summer came, the light was brighter, coming over the small enclosed backyard with the washlines and the damp door to the alleyway. But always, the parlour was cool and shadowy. The light fell here and there on the crowded furniture: the worn sofa with the springbok-hide mat before it; the crocheted antimacassars on the chairs; on the cane hallstand. There were two glass domes containing two stuffed parrots on the hall-stand, as well as a motley of Victorian bric-a-brac. Most of the things belonged to my grandmother with whom we lived.

My grandmother ruled over the household and the parlour like a dark version of Queen Victoria. She had a stern but wide and kindly face and wore her hair in a grey-black bun.

On the wall of the parlour was a big, old-fashioned photograph in a gilt frame of my grandfather. I had never seen him alive, but he seemed to see everybody who passed through the parlour because he watched sternly from his place on the papered wall, his eyes sharp and a little curious, with his white sidewhiskers bristling and his bearded chin as hard as a plank above the starched rampart of his high collar.

This had been my granny's husband. In her youth, I heard, she had been beautiful, with her Javanese ancestry in her looks, and had worked as a maid in the House of Assembly of the Cape Colony. A very well-known member of the House wanted to make her his mistress, but she married this Scottish carpenter instead and bore him my mother.

My mother worked in a cigarette factory, while my father organised trade unions. So as a small boy with a fondness for lead soldiers and a supreme dislike for haircuts, I occupied the parlour most of the time, arranging my imaginary battles under the eyes of my maternal grandparents. 'Mama', as we called my grandmother, supplied me with regular doses of ice-cream mixed with ginger-pop, a mixture for which she herself had a strong weakness.

There was another picture on our parlour wall. This one was of a man in an ordinary cloth cap and a somewhat wrinkled suit, who stood on what looked like a cobblestoned quay on the bank of a river, with towers in the background. He had one hand in a trouser pocket and he seemed to be looking intently into the future. He did not have sidewhiskers like my grandfather, nor the high, hard collar. Instead, a little pointed beard above an ordinary shirt.

At first I did not know who this man was, but since the picture was in colour and the frame and glass were dusted and cleaned regularly, I knew that he must be somebody special.

After a while I was drawn to enquiring from Mama: 'Who is that Uncle in the picture?'

'Your father brought it from Russia, a place very far away,' she told me from her regal position on the sofa. 'He was a very important man. Now don't spill your ginger-pop on the floor, I polished this morning.'

'What's important?' I remember asking. 'People who do good things are important,' Mama said. 'But you will have to ask your father and mother to tell you more.'

So I asked my mother. I seldom saw my father, I remember. He was always away at what were called 'meetings'. My mother explained that my father was a follower of Lenin; that Lenin had been the leader of the great change in Russia which had done away with poverty so that people no longer need be poor.

'Are the Russians going to come here, too?' I asked. 'No,' my mother told me. 'Your father and others like him used the teachings of Lenin to show the workers in our country that they could achieve happiness for themselves and their children.'

'Will all the children have ice-cream and ginger-pop?' I asked. 'I suppose so,' my mother said. So the man in the wrinkled suit and cloth cap remained on our parlour wall, gazing out into the future. He remained there all the time we lived in that house. My father fought his own battles. He led strikes and addressed meetings. I remember seeing him under a red flag with a hammer and sickle on it. Once he went to prison and when I met him again at the prison gate, coming home, I remember I did not recognise him because he was wearing a thick beard. Only when he'd shaven, was he my father again. And all the time, one heard discussions of the teachings of Lenin. It was strange and exciting that the ideas of the man on the parlour wall could cause such debate in our country, so far away from his.

I grew up and passed through school, and still the picture hung on the wall. I was drawn towards meetings. As a lad I marched in processions and demonstrations. I bought a leather coat and cloth cap and romantically called myself a 'revolutionary'. When I joined the Young Communist League, my father lectured me on the honour and importance of being known as a communist. In the YCL we read Lenin's works and debated youthfully and fervently. We sold papers and pamphlets to curious people who stood in shabby doorways and wondered at the ideas we preached. I suppose because I was a somewhat enthusiastic Young Communist, I was recruited into the Communist Party.

When the Nationalist Government came to power in our country, the Party was outlawed. Many of my associates disappeared in disarray from the political scene; others remained firm. The security police hounded the communists, raided their houses, questioned them. Books and papers were hidden everywhere, in lofts, attics, gardens. But in our parlour the picture of Lenin went on hanging on the wall.

When I married, my father presented us with the picture along with some of his effects. It went up on the wall of the living-room of our new home, It remained there through all imprisonments and persecutions which I and my family endured. I think the police were too stupid to recognise the man in the picture.

Our little boys looked at it often and called him Uncle Lenin, as I had done in my childhood.

Forced into exile, whatever we could transport was packed up. The picture of Lenin went along in the crates with the books and clothes and household effects.

Now in London, far from our own country, the picture of Lenin, which my late father had been presented in Moscow in 1927, hangs again on the wall in the living-room. The same picture in the same frame, the same man in the workaday suit and the cloth cap, looking towards the future.

Recently my nine-year-old son, Barto, sat in an armchair and looked quizzically at the picture. After a while he said brightly: 'At school we have to address the assembly on a subject. My turn is coming soon.'

'What are you going to tell them about?' his mother asked. 'I am going to talk about Lenin,' he said.

Lenin in Profile: World Writers and Artists on Lenin. Moscow: Progress Publishers, 1975

29

Uncle Sam

The boys on Hanover Street were kicking their heels around the entrance of the Portagee's café when I rolled up for a packet of the old lung poison. After handing a couple of cigarettes around I joined the conversation. Topic: Hollywood's latest productions. The boys like fast-shooting stuff, guys with stubbly chins and dangling cigarettes and tied-down guns. The conversation was a little bloodthirsty, and I'm glad they don't allow tied-down guns in this town. Then one of them asked: 'You ever hear of a place called Cripple Creek, Colorado? And Tombstone? Funny names for towns.'

'I read in the paper about a place called Little Rock, Arkansas,' another added. So the conversation turned to what has been happening in Little Rock, and the United States went down several notches in the estimation of Hanover Street.

The general consensus of opinion turned out to be: 'What kind of a place is it where they have got to get soldiers to keep coloured kids out of school, and more soldiers to get them in? According to the pictures, the States is one place where everybody, black and white, gets equal treatment, and no trouble.'

'Just shows you,' growled one of the boys, spitting into the street in the true Western style. 'You can't go by the bio. Lot of — lies.'

* * * * *

And speaking about Little Rock, Arkansas, Louis 'Satchmo' Armstrong doesn't like what's going on there either. In fact he doesn't like Ike [President Eisenhower], and said so. 'The government can go to hell,' he trumpeted in comment. 'It's getting so bad a coloured man hasn't got any country.'

Louis cancelled his government-sponsored trip to the Soviet Union. 'If the people of Russia ask me what's wrong with my country, what am I supposed to say? If I ever go through with this trip I'll do it on my own.'

A radio station blackballed the great jazz man, but that didn't stop artistes Lena Horne and Eartha Kitt joining him in his opinions of God's own country.

Up my alley, *New Age*, 3 October 1957

I had a glimpse of Down South, USA, through the local papers.

In Texas, Perry Dean Ross, white, was convicted of murder and given a five-year suspended sentence for killing an 18-year-old Negro and wounding two school girls when he fired nine shots into a café.

In Alabama, Charles Hamilton, Negro, was found guilty of burglary and recommended for death in the electric chair because when he was arrested in a white-owned home he was found without his pants and shoes.

Justice seems to be based on colour in God's own country too. Au revoir.

Up my alley, *New Age*, 9 May 1957

In contrast to the brutal and savage lynching of a Negro who was hauled out of jail and murdered in the Southern states of America recently, there was the court trial of two little Negro boys accused of stealing melons.

Said the magistrate to the court: 'All those present who never stole fruit when they were kids, raise your right hands.'

Nobody, from the clerk to the sheriff and police officers complied. 'Case dismissed,' said his worship.

Up my alley, *New Age*, 14 May 1959

Negro students in the Southern States of the Land of the Free have spotlighted the fact that the USA ain't so free by means of their campaign of breaking the social colour-bar.

They've marched into Blankes Alleen [Whites Only] cafés and lunch counters and insisted on being served. They've sat down in Blanke seats in concert halls. In some cases they were arrested and in others they were put out of the various places they invaded.

But they laid bare the apartheid discrimination that exists in the country that boasts of being the leader of Western culture and civilisation.

Like the coloured people of SA, the Negroes of the USA are a persecuted minority. And we've got Blankes Alleen cafés and milk bars and theatres too, as well as a government that claims to lead Western civilisation in Africa.

Up my alley, *New Age*, 17 March 1960

American way of life
Reported in the *Daily Telegraph*, an overseas paper, is the story of a cemetery in Massachusetts, USA, which refused to bury an American soldier's Korean wife. A clergyman said the woman was refused burial 'because of the colour of her skin'. The Hillcrest Park Cemetery was a burial place for the Caucasian (white) race.

We wonder if the American met his Korean wife when he was in her country fighting for the 'free' world.

Up my alley, *New Age*, 2 February 1961

Now I've heard everything! The Yanks who specialise in Red bogey stories have given us hair-raisers about Soviet spy-rings, sabotage, subversion, commies running around with cloaks and daggers, and bearded men carrying bombs.

And along comes a Perfesser Ivy out of Illinois University and says, give an African liquor and you introduce 'wholesale communism' to South Africa.

This is the first time I've heard of Marxism-Leninism turning up in bottles, and wholesale at that.

All I can say is that if there's somebody with brains anywhere near Professor Ivy the next time he opens his mouth, I hope that person puts a cork in it.

Up my alley, New Age, 12 January 1961

Which reminds me that some Yankees are belly-aching over the large dose of Castro oil they have to swallow now that Cuba's big boy is in New York. Incidentally he has moved to the Negro quarter, Harlem.

VIVA FIDEL.

Up my alley, New Age, 29 September 1960

And the magazine *Time* seemed a little embarrassed about another friend of the Yanks. He is Boun Oum (I can never remember these darned names) who ousted the legal Laotian government with their help.

Time described him as 'a plump sybarite who in quieter times is fond of repairing to the French Riviera … at lunch in his headquarters (in Laos) his favourite companions turned out to be not candidates for the cabinet but girls from the Vientiane dance halls.'

Well, that sounds like the American way of life, doesn't it?

Up my alley, New Age, 12 January 1961

While I am writing this, Lt Colonel Glenn has not yet gone up or come down. In any case I wish him good luck. But I must say I have been having the jitters for his part all week, what with faults and repairs and postponements and cancellations.

Anyway, it is hardly likely that the Americans can carry Jim Crow, the colour-bar, or apartheid in other words, to the cosmos. But nevertheless a segregated 'Cosmos' does exist in Washington. It's the name of a fashionable club and this Cosmos has more than 2 000 members all of the upper crust of American intellectuals.

But it has been discovered that there is a distinct bad smell of racialism around the high-class atmosphere of the Cosmos.

A Negro was not admitted to the club. He is not an ordinary Negro who does not dare to cross the sacred threshold of the club. No, sirree. He is Carl Rowan and he is no less than the Assistant Under Secretary of State, besides being a writer and journalist who has received many national prizes.

He has all the qualifications of belonging to Cosmos – except one. The colour of his skin.

That President Kennedy was forced to give up his idea of joining the club might be a nice gesture, because it allows the big-shots of the US to put on airs about liberalism. It does not, however, hide the fact that nobody seems to be breaking his neck to see that civil rights are accorded to ALL negroes in the US.

Up my alley, New Age, 1 February 1962

Armies

And going from the cosmos to the Bomb, *The New York World Telegram* reported last November:

> 'The Canadian Army has issued these orders telling a soldier what to do if he sees a nuclear bomb explode: The soldier will inform his immediate superior and tell him what has occurred. If a bomb goes off in duty hours a certain number will be called. If it is during off-duty hours an alternate number will be called. THE SOLDIER WILL THEN FILL OUT THE APPROPRIATE FORM AND DISPATCH IT FORTHWITH TO HEADQUARTERS.'

Which reminds me of a significant ending to a fictional account of the end of the atomic holocaust called World War III. Asks a survivor of another: 'Who won the war?'
Reply: 'WE did. Not that it matters.'

Up my alley, *New Age*, 1 February 1962

Wednesday the 8th of May has passed unnoticed. But it was on this day in 1945 that Hitler's smashed and bleeding armies surrendered finally to the Allies, ending World War II. And since that day millions of the world's people have vowed that another catastrophe such as was launched in 1939 will never be tolerated.

But the pundits of imperialism seem to think differently. Hans Speidel, one of the very Nazis who surrendered in 1945, is at the head of the army of the North Atlantic Treaty Organisation. All ready to go a-shooting all over the world all over again.

Middle East

It all comes out in the wash. We learn that sensational documents showing how United States policy in the Middle East is closely linked up with oil trusts were presented in the US Senate and House of Representatives.

Senator J O'Mahoney, chairman of the Senate anti-trust and monopoly sub-committee, charged that 'gigantic oil companies, exercising the power of political and economic states in the Middle East, have had a hand in framing our foreign policy'.

A document from oil company files showing how John Foster Dulles worked with representatives of the Standard Oil Company of New Jersey, the world's largest oil trust, and other companies in formulating policy on the Suez crisis, was also presented by Senator O'Mahoney.

Up my alley, *New Age*, 16 May 1957

The Yankees can find an excuse for anything. And Mr Richard Nixon has been trying to take the place of Mr Dulles. If the Reds hadn't supplied Nasser with arms, says Tricky Dick, there wouldn't have been all this trouble in the Middle East. And of course the Yanks had to go to the aid of Lebanon to prevent 'the tactics of subversion to nibble away at the free and uncommitted world'.

The old, old story. Why doesn't Tricky Dick admit that the American and British oil companies have been soaking the Arab people dry for generations and that they just can't stand losing all that dough.

Eight companies control all the oil in the Middle East. Five American and three European. In one year, one of them, the Arabian American Oil Company, made a profit of $425 million, £125 million in our money. I guess in the opinion of Mr Nixon it's worth making any kind of excuse to hang on to all that dough.

And South Africa, those who are interested I mean, will no doubt be prepared to help deal with those terrible people who are trying to take away the Yankees' billions of dollars. We have one division which we can put in the field. Hurrah! And imagine all the non-Europeans who are going to join up in the event of a war. Millions of them. They'll simply flock to the recruiting depots to sign up as bootblacks and butlers and help to save the FREE world.

And when they come back there'll be special medals struck with Verwoerd's head on one side and a petrol pump on the other.

Up my alley, *New Age*, 24 July 1958

There is a story about Admiral Brown, commander of the US fleet in the Mediterranean, at the time of the Suez business.

It seems that at the time of the Suez invasion he received a signal from headquarters in Washington which read: 'Be alerted. We expect trouble in your zone.' To which the doughty admiral replied: 'I am alerted. Please advise which side we are on.'

Up my alley, *New Age*, 28 November 1957

Mister K

With the Russian coat-of-arms on the moon and Mister K [Khrushchev] in the USA, the Yankees will undoubtedly do their best to impress both him and the rest of the world with the achievements of the American Way of Life.

We wonder, however, how much different this 'way of life' is from the South African brand, for lately the papers have carried numerous reports of violence and crime rampant among the youth of America. The slums of New York have given birth to these murderous youngsters in the same way as the horrors of Johannesburg's shanty towns have given rise to spoilers, Msomis and other tsotsi gangs.

Whether in New York or Johannesburg, there is no doubt that the youth are being destroyed by a way of life whose basic principle is 'every man for himself and the devil take the hindmost'.

Up my alley, *New Age*, 17 September 1959

Thinking that I could get some first-hand impressions of an American on the visit of Mr K to the US and of the Russian rocket on the moon, I set course for the dockland and hove to windward of a crewman from the Yankee destroyer *Jonas Ingram*.

The conversation went something like this:

'Hullo, welcome to Cape Town.'

'Uh-huh,' replied our visitor exercising his jaws around one of Mr Wrigley's products.

'Seen the city yet?'

'Uh-huh.' His eyes gazed speculatively past me in the direction of a pair of well-filled black jeans.

'You got somebody big visiting back home. Mister K.'

'Uh.' The eyes followed the black jeans towards the horizon.

'You think the American people will go for him?'

'Huh?' without looking at me.

I went off on to another tack. 'What do you think about the Russian rocket on the moon?'

'Uh.'

Before I could proceed any further with this illuminating conversation he hauled up his anchor and sailed full steam ahead in the direction of the black jeans, leaving me wondering whether I should have brought an interpreter with me.

HUH?

Up my alley, *New Age*, 1 October 1959

30

Sputnik

Everybody is talking about the satellite these days. From top politicians and scientists to the little man in the street. I was in a shop the other day and there the hangers-around were talking about it. They didn't seem to know what it was all about, but one of them expressed the opinion of millions of others.

'The — Russians can do anything.' Of course there are sceptics. On a radio quiz last week an entrant denied that there is any such a thing as a man-made moon circling the earth. He just didn't want to know in spite of the radio chap's efforts to convince him.

A friend of ours in Cape Town tried to get hold of an astronomer to lecture on the subject. Two of the leading ones were too busy or had other engagements. The third star-gazer, who claims membership of the Astronomical Society, answered the phone.

'Can you deliver a lecture on the satellite?' inquired our friend.

'What satellite?'

'The Russian satellite.'

'Oh, that?' growled the star-gazer. 'It's a hoax. It's the easiest thing to perpetrate a hoax like that.'

'But are you prepared to speak?'

The star-gazer wanted to know who for and was told Congress of Democrats. Said the star-gazer: 'I'm not prepared to speak to any congress or any democrats!'

I bet the only stars he's seen were launched in Hollywood.

But the local boys are convinced.

The reports are that the fah-fee punters on Hanover Street have been putting their pants on 'Moon' all week.

And the local pub has evolved a Sputnik Cocktail. Two-thirds vodka (for the Russians), one-third five-star brandy (for outer space), a dash of bitters (for the Yanks) and BOOM-POWIE!!! you're launched.

Johnny, of Johnny's Parcels, is happy too. Said he to a member of the Special Branch the other day: 'Say, I'm feeling fine. Every time the satellite goes over I raise my right thumb.'

The dick didn't get it. Beep. Beep.

Up my alley, *New Age*, 17 October 1957

I have heard that the next satellite will be launched by the Russians on November 7. I have also heard that the Americans are going to launch theirs on November 5. There'll be thousands of them going up all over on that night.

And I wonder if the Soviet legal expert really did say it was the earth's fault if Sputnik was violating the air space of other countries, because it was revolving in Sputnik's orbit, and not vice versa.

I bet the chap who translated the piece from the Russian newspaper knows as much Russian as I know Siamese, or maybe he might have been reading the laughs page.

I was having a chat with a friend of mine the other day, and of course the conversation inevitably turned to Sputnik. My friend is a very religious gentleman and also hands the plate around in the church.

He did not agree with launching satellites, going to the moon, exploring space, etc.

'Man is interfering with God,' he said firmly. 'There are things that man dare not touch. The stars, the heavens and all in it are God's. Let us beware lest He smite us with hell-fire.'

I tried to explain that such things as the moon and the planets and the stars exist, and just as we have investigated things on earth and acquired knowledge, so investigation of space would extend our knowledge.

'We are interfering with God,' he insisted.

Well, I'm afraid I couldn't convince him. But a second later his little son dashed in and began running round and round the table shouting, 'Beep-beep. Beep-beep.'

Up my alley, New Age, 24 October 1957

A joker around here said that thus far the most effective sales-talk for socialism has been [beep-beep]. Incidentally, Sputnik means somebody who accompanies one on a journey, a fellow-traveller.

Up my alley, New Age, 19 December and 24 October 1957

So the Americans have been caught flat-footed again. Big politicians in the States might try to make excuses for not being able to beat the Russians to the draw when it comes to launching satellites, but the little people will remain convinced that the Russians have got what it takes.

The dog-in-the-moon had everybody gasping when the news first hit the headlines.

A worker in the train coming to town: 'Wat reg is, is reg. Hulle maak die Americans klaar.'

Another worker: 'The Yanks talk big, but the Russians do big.' The ticket examiner: 'Jong, maar die donderse Russe is slim.' And somebody else cracked: 'I'm going back home to see whether my dog's still there.'

All over town people have been talking about Little Lemon. 'Shame,' said an old lady. 'He must be very brave …'

Some dog lovers have started howling at the moon over the dog up there.

But I seem to remember that only a few weeks ago surgeons were transplanting the hearts and lungs from one dog to another in experiments. Nobody howled then.

Take it from me, it's a case of sour grapes.

Another bloke I know had a suggestion.

He said: 'Let's put Strijdom in a satellite and send him up for good.'

Up my alley, New Age, 14 November 1957

So you want to be a spaceman, huh? ... Well, boetie, you'll have to becomes Springbok first ... According to 'an Afrikaner's' description of Yuri Gagarin [the first person in space], reported in *Die Burger*, he looked as handsome as a Springbok centre! ... That's about the highest you can rise in the estimation of Afrikanerdom! ... So that – if we had only beaten the Russians to it – the launching of our own spaceman would have been broadcast to the world something like this ...

We are now taking you over to Ellis Park for the launching into space of South Africa's first cosmonaut, Springbok centre Japie van der Gargargle ... The referee has just come on to the field and the crowd is going wild ... And here comes our hero, walking across from the dressing rooms ... He is wearing a new green and yellow jersey, the famous Springbok colours, and waving to the crowd ... The whistle goes for a scrum, Van der Gargargle is just outside the 25-yard line, it looks as if he's going to score a try ... The crowd is cheering their heads off ... Yes, ladies and gentlemen, history is being made today ... There's two minutes to go before the final whistle and the referee is starting the final count-down ... And there he goes ... A bottle flung from the Malay stand has just struck Van der Gargargle's noodle and he is really seeing stars.

Up my alley, *New Age*, 20 April 1961

31

The hot, grey streets, the blistering tenements, the foul alleyways (Why I became a communist?)

Many things pass through my mind when I try to pin-point all the events and circumstances which brought me into the ranks of the world's communists, in particular into the party of our own country South Africa. Perhaps I was influenced within the circle of our family – certainly that had something to do with it. On the other hand there were independent experiences which made me as an individual more and more aware of the necessity to change the face of our country.

I was born in District Six, that area of Cape Town into which crammed thousands of families of the coloured working class. Its slums stretched from the slopes of Table Mountain to the sea where the sewers belched their vomit into the Atlantic and where we as children splashed in the foul water during the hot summer holidays. It was the cheapest outing for the poor, picnicking on Woodstock Beach, a stone's throw from the municipal dumping ground and the outlets of the sewerage system. Everybody came down out of the hot, grey streets, the blistering tenements, the foul alleyways.

My first recollection of life seems to have been an alleyway. It faced the front window of our house and it was always piled with overflowing dustbins that left most of their contents behind in pools of stagnant water, so that we breathed a horrible odour of decay all the time.

My mother worked in a cigarette factory and my father was a trade union organiser. I was cared for during the day by my grandmother who looked like a mahogany version of Queen Victoria. I seldom saw my father – he was always at what was described to me as 'meetings'. Most of the family income came from my mother. Then my father started organising tobacco workers in Cape Town and my mother was fired for being his wife. Those were hard times, I remember. There was an old grocer in the district who used to give us parcels of provisions because he sympathised with the working-class movement.

I was about six years old when my father went to prison for leading demonstrations of unemployed. I remember going to meet him when he was released ten days later. I could not recognise him at first because he had grown a beard during that time.

One day my mother took me to the circus. It was an incredibly exciting prospect, seeing the animals in their cages as we made our way towards the big-top, the coloured flags, the balloons, the gay, noisy music beating on eardrums. But once inside the vast tent I had a peculiar experience. I discovered that I had no idea what most of the performers in the ring were doing because they had their backs to me all the time. When I asked my mother why this was so, she had to explain to me that we were in the seats for 'non-Europeans' and that the white people were given the best view of the performances.

I never went to a circus again in South Africa. The next time I ever attended a circus performance was when I was a man of forty-three years and went to see a show in Moscow. I could see everything the performers did, and I recalled a little sadly a small boy in South Africa who had only seen the backs of the clowns.

At school

All my youth was spent in the slums of Cape Town. I went to school on the hillside above the city and in the afternoon I and my friends would come down again into the smelly environs of District Six. I recall a few faces from the past. There was Daniel a jolly black boy with a smile full of white teeth. We were great chums. Somewhere along the line we drifted apart. When I met him again years later he had turned into a gangster and was continually in and out of prison. I remember the girls we used to chase along the streets. There was Habiba, a beautiful member of the Muslim community. She was my favourite, with her great eyes and long, straight black hair framing her olive-skinned face. Again, many years later, when I was canvassing for an election, I knocked on the door of a municipal voter, and when it was opened, there was something which had been a woman looking out at me. Matted greying hair was untidily wrapped in a kerchief, the face had fallen into loose wrinkles, prematurely aged, the rotten teeth smiled curiously at me above the body that had collapsed under greasy clothes. She smiled at me from a background like a dark cavern full of smells. It took me some time to recognise the eyes in the ravaged face. It was Habiba, but not the beautiful girl I had known when I had been a young boy chasing her on the streets. Grim life had destroyed that Habiba. Now there was just a hag whose eyes I recognised and who recognised me.

The grinding misery of the slums destroyed our people, blighted their lives before they had time to grow up. On the street corners the children shot dice and the dagga cigarettes passed from mouth to mouth. In the lamplight the razor-edged knives flashed and the blood mingled with the spittle and the rivulets of stagnant black water.

I read *The Iron Heel* and saw in Jack London's 'people of the abyss' my own community ground down under the weight of poverty, oppression, ignorance. Could it be that oppressed people all over were the same? In *The Ragged Trousered Philanthropists* I saw our own working men. These books moved me more than the set books we were given to read in school. I wasn't interested in *The Adventures of Maurice Buckler* or *Micah Clarke*. At second-hand bookstalls I found the *Trial and Execution of Sacco and Vanzetti* and *The State: Its Origin and Function* by William Paul, from the old Socialist Labour Press.

Threat of war

While I was in high school the Spanish Civil War was on. The news in the South African press was scanty, but some of us followed it. There was a period of restlessness. You wanted to get through school in order to enter a more dynamic world. After high school I turned away from further education because it appeared that life held more serious things than more certificates based on knowledge that had little to do with reality.

Nazism was overrunning Europe. I knew about the stupid system that turned my own people into strangers in their country. We were continually reminded that we were 'Non-Europeans Only'; in Europe they were butchering Jews and gipsies, and Hitler called us 'sub-humans'. We were all one, because we were all being persecuted, and they were fighting in Europe. I wanted to fight the Nazis, but when I left home to join the armed forces the recruiting officer found me underweight and too skinny. But one could still gain experience in struggle here at home. At the local Labour Bureau I asked for a job in a factory. I wanted to know what it was like to be a worker, so I went into this place that manufactured metal containers. All day long the conveyor belts clattered and roared and the shiny tin cans marched past like regiments of soldiers. In front of the pounding machines girls and women sat as if welded to them, while we, coloured and African boys and men brought the sheets of plate which they turned into cans. There were women who had had their fingers pulped off under the crashing die-stampers. The boss generously gave them a job for life at about four pounds a week. Once our blood froze when a man screamed above the roar of machinery as his arm was caught in a machine. At the waxing tables women perspired in the hellish heat. The highest paid workers got about five pounds a week.

At lunch-time I found myself talking to the workers. I seemed to have become a great talker. I talked about lots of things, I remember. International news, South African politics, the colour-bar. Some of the workers viewed me with curiosity. They asked me whether I was a communist. Certainly I was a member of the trade union. Was I a communist? I must have been telling them things, explaining situations, in the manner of a communist.

Given the sack

Then one day the trade union made demands which the bosses did not accept. There was talk of a strike. The trade union wasn't very strong and the bosses acted quickly. Certain workers were no longer needed. Men, women, coloured, African, found themselves without jobs. They were members of the trade union committee and other outspoken workers. Among them was myself.

I worked for a while in the drawing department of a commercial firm, reproducing blueprints on a copying machine. There were other coloured men working there too, but they were messengers or served the tea to the white staff. The whites referred to them all the time as 'boys'. They were married and had families, but they were still 'boys' in the eyes of the whites. One of them had worked for that firm for twenty-five years and the managing director presented him with a watch. The heads of department looked on condescendingly and he was promoted to head messenger. But he was still referred to as a 'boy' thereafter. All the time my gorge rose. I used to encourage the 'boys' to attend meetings on the Grand Parade in Cape Town, where the Communist Party held lunch-time talks. The whites in the firm looked at me with suspicion. Somehow they carefully avoided coming face to face with me. Perhaps I wasn't quite like the other 'boys'.

One day I realised that while I had been encouraging my mates to take more interest in those things which were keeping them in that position of indignity as second-class people in this their own motherland, I could do more myself. I was 22 years old. Perhaps I remembered the little boy who could not see what the performers were doing that time at the circus; or Daniel and Habiba, or those factory girls with their fingers cut off, or the hard life of my parents.

Around the corner from where I worked was the office of the Communist Party. A little nervously I climbed the narrow stairs. What responsibilities confronted me? It wasn't as if you were going to join a football club or a benefit lodge. That was when I first joined the Young Communist League. The next year the Nationalist Government came into power and started making dire threats against the communists. I transferred from the YCL into the ranks of the Communist Party.

> La Guma A, Why I became a communist?, UWC-RIM Mayibuye Archives, Alex La Guma Collection, MCH 118-2-5-8. Also published under the pseudonym 'Gala' in *African Communist* 89, 2nd quarter 1982: 49–52

Part 6

The ordinary or garden Nat (ruling-class politics)

32

Herr Doktor Verwoerd and Nationalist small-fry talk

So the Nats are back again. A lot of people have been hoping they'd get in again, and I don't mean their supporters only. Some non-whites have expressed the opinion that with a lot more oppression the people would decide to wake up and get down to fighting back. Force begets force. That may be so. But oppression can also become so powerful that it becomes pretty difficult to resist. And people can become so demoralised under the weight of the load that it takes years for them to get around to raising a finger to throw it off.

I've heard some saying, 'The people will be forced to organise.' But if they weren't enthusiastic about it when they were given the chance to, they might find it hard to shake a leg under increased difficulties.

Anyway, my old school motto said, through difficulties to success. I have no doubt that the bulk of the people will take it up and put it into practice.

I always wondered how the mind of the ordinary or garden Nat worked, and mingling with the crowd waiting for the election results I had the opportunity of acquiring a few examples of what is probably typical Nationalist small-fry talk.

'Up the Nats!' howled a character in a brown sports-coat every time they won a seat. 'We'll show the bloody kaffirs!'

'Strijdom, Strijdom! To hell with Nkrumah and Nasser!' screamed another somewhere else in the street.

Come to think of it, that kind of political thought is not confined to the lower level of the Nat ranks. I seem to have read of cabinet ministers talking in the same vein.

A youth in a leather jacket and jeans, and long blond hair started yelling counter-slogans: 'Up with the ducktails. We want rock 'n roll!'

Lord help us from these extremes.

* * * * *

As I said last week, the Nats wouldn't be satisfied with the Johannesburg City Council's commission of enquiry into the Dube riots.

Herr Doktor Verwoerd confirmed same by telling the voters of Hartenbergfontein that if the Council did not change its attitude towards the Africans, he would be compelled to take over responsibility for 'Native' policy in the city.

It looks as if the fate of all local authorities is in the balance. We will probably be saddled with Nazi-like 'gauleiters' to keep a watchful eye on us if the city fathers don't play ball.

* * * * *

The Nationalist paper *Die Burger* carried an apt cartoon last Friday when the final results were known. It pictured a grave-digger's hand holding a shovel, rising out of a swamp.

Very prophetic of South Africa's future under the Nats.

Up my alley, *New Age*, 24 April 1958

The thousands of Africans who bear the scars of baton charges and who have prison records because they didn't possess a scrap of paper must have wondered at the sudden change of heart that came over the perpetrators of their suffering during the period preceding the days of protest at election time.

Everybody who would be good children and behave themselves and go to work like nice little slaves would receive a pat on the back from our warm-hearted cops. They were even offered free rides in UDF [Union Defence Force] transport.

Never before had the Africans been offered such kind consideration. Never before did the Africans need more protection than they did this week. There was a big bogey waiting around the comer to gobble them up.

But the pie-crust promises must have given a lot of people indigestion, because all the nice words were spiced with lots of threats too. Nobody in their right minds could fall for the Strijdom–Div combination.

It all reminded me of the little rhyme which starts: 'Will you come into my parlour said the spider to the fly …'

Up my alley, *New Age*, 17 April 1958

Parliament

Now that parliament has shut down and the Parliamentarians have shut up, one can turn back the pages and have a look-see at what has been said by our lords and masters over the last few weeks.

A lot of the stuff makes me shudder. Said the pundit of job reservation, Senator De Klerk: Job reservation should be seen against the background of how white workers were being pushed out of certain industries. The survival of white civilisation was at stake.

Example: six elderly and handicapped white lift operators in Johannesburg had been discharged and replaced by Africans.

* * * * *

The GG, Dr EG [Governor General, EG Jansen] said business was looking up. I could just imagine him rubbing his hands.

Proclaimed he from the Throne: 'The mining industry has experienced a prosperous year … The past year was again a favourable one for agriculture … Once again there was an appreciable export of surplus supplies which contributed materially to the national income.'

The African miners probably got a little more mealies for supper. The farm labourers one lash less from the overseers. And the canning workers are expected to donate heartily towards the national income by accepting cuts in their pay.

* * * * *

The Lord High Executioner, Blackie Swart, said his piece, too. Probably stuck his thumbs in his gun-belt and scowled around the House when he said that ascribing the crime-wave to the so-called frustration of the Bantu as a result of Government policy was tantamount to saying that it was not the criminals' fault but the Government's.

No comment.

* * * * *

And of course there was the Great White Chief himself, also referred to by the lawless and disrespectful elements as 'die Kaffir Koning'. Dr Verwoerd's noble contribution was that he had been informed by the NAD [Native Affairs Department] that feelings between its officials and Africans were better than had existed before.

Hence Zeerust.

* * * * *

All of which reminds me that a Johannesburg engineer has invented a new type of pressure stove which works by means of a special chamber which generates hot air.

Up my alley, *New Age*, 20 February 1958

Herr Doktor Verwoerd, PM

There's a big fight coming off, if my guess is right.

With Baas Strijdom out of action and all the signs showing that he might be out for keeps, you can bet that the other jackals will be snapping and snarling for leadership of the pack.

The papers tip Verwoerd, De Klerk, Swart or Dönges as the next Führer.

I'm hoping they chew each other to rags.

Up my alley, *New Age*, 23 January 1958

Le roi c'est mort! The king of apartheid is dead, and it looks as if the country will be saddled with the high priest himself. I never had any bets on who was going to take over, but if Herr Doktor Verwoerd gets the driver's seat a lot of people are expecting fireworks. Others don't give a darn who's boss.

An old Indian merchant told me: 'I've been in South Africa since 1916 and four Prime Ministers have died since then. None of them did any good.'

An African in the street, when he heard of Strijdom's death, said to me: 'Swart or Verwoerd or Dönges, how can we have a preference for any of them?'

Six of one and half-a-dozen of the other.

Anyway, with Verwoerd as Prime Minister the African women will have the right man to march on the next time they decide to advance on the Union Buildings.

But I guess Herr Doktor won't be around either when they get there.

Up my alley, *New Age*, 4 September 1958

There are probably umpteen reasons why people expect a tightening of the apartheid screws now that the great white Chief, Herr Doktor, is PM but now that I've heard the reason given by a gent down here who is an estate-agent-cum-astrologer, I've heard everything.

He's born on September 1, he told me, and Verwoerd on September 8. That puts both of them under the constellation Virgo. 'We are noted for our tenacity, our unwillingness to compromise, we love power and we are not popular. Therefore Verwoerd is sure to push apartheid in a big way. And,' he added, 'that's what makes me a high-pressure salesman.'

'Well,' said I, 'if we have to go by the stars, then things look pretty ominous. How's business?'

'Lousy,' said he.

* * * * *

REPEAT PERFORMANCE: If my memory serves me right, what PM Verwoerd said last Wednesday night has been said before. Listening to the usual platitudes about God's will, cooperation, justice for all, and the unique problems of our country, I wondered whether the same speech isn't handed down from Prime Minister to Prime Minister, and just dressed up in the accent of the one who puts it across.

However, Doktor Verwoerd has a sense of humour, too. 'The policy of separate development is designed for happiness, security and stability ... The welfare of the worker and the security of his daily bread is a prerequisite for the happiness of a country ... It is my desire to contribute towards this.'

But then, those jokes are pretty stale, too.

Up my alley, *New Age*, 11 September 1958

Baas Verwoerd has just been given a degree of Doctor of Laws by the Potchefstroom University ... Well, he's had a lot of experience with laws ...

Mostly of the unsavoury kind.

Up my alley, *New Age*, 4 May 1961

The man in the street got the first jolt from that Budget when he tried to present 1/6d for a packet of 20 cigarettes last week and found that they cost 1/10d. To say nothing of the boys at the pub when they bellied-up for a snort of that old firewater.

It looks as if the habitués will have to go on the water-wagon, and give up smoking.

But the biggest jolt has come to the Africans who find their poll tax increased ... with more increases to come!!!

Of course, chiseller Tom Naudé didn't think of even advising employers to jack up the African's pay. Oh, no. He's a farmer's boy, and a pal of the money mob, too.

You've got to pay for your education, said Tom.

What education? The kind that Herr Doktor Verwoerd said will not mislead the African by showing him the green pastures of European society in which he was not allowed to graze.

Up my alley, *New Age*, 24 July 1958

And it is probably in conformity with Herr Doktor's Christian National Education to distribute to Afrikaans high schools a 'Voorligting vir Standerd VI'.

This Information for Standard Six says, 'Whites must so live that they shall not sink to the cultural level of the non-whites. Only thus can the Government remain in the hands of the whites.'

We would like to see what kind of vice, sorry, advice, is distributed to the African high schools by the BED [Bantu Education Department].

Up my alley, *New Age*, 27 August 1959

Sitting up on a tambuti table presented to him by a chief at a Bantu Authorities inaugural ceremony somewhere up north the other day, the Minister advised as follows:

'The elephant is big and has a thick skin, and all big chiefs should also have thick skins in order to withstand the spears and arrows of insults heaped upon them by our benign and kindly Nationalist government. The Big White chief, Dr Verwoerd also has a thick skin and many wastepaper baskets in which he deposits the advice of liberals, the communists and the kafferboeties. But it is not fitting that chiefs such as you should also have wastepaper baskets such as Dr Verwoerd has. Does the jackal or the hyena have a wastepaper basket? No. Does the rinkhals and the mamba have wastepaper baskets? No. Therefore I am going to call on my secretary to present you with presents more fitting. These lovely briefcases inscribed with your names, in which you may carry the orders issued by the well-beloved Bantu Administration Department. Hallelujah.'

My private telescope might have got the speech all wrong, but the local newspapers did say that briefcases were presented to a couple of chiefs up in Zeerust. One of them even said in thanks: 'We are your children. Lead us and we will try to crawl.'

They don't have to try. They're doing it already.

Up my alley, *New Age*, 13 August 1959

All we need now is for Herr Doktor to divide up the air into black and white. Having thought out grandiose schemes for the partition of this fair land of ours into black and white blobs, some over-enthusiastic Nats are not satisfied with just that. No, they long for a life on the ocean wave and want to send apartheid to sea. It is now possible (!) for the Minister of Lands to reserve for the use of any racial group 'the whole of the sea or any specified portion of such sea'.

It's easy. You mark off the Indian Ocean and the Atlantic in sections up to three miles out and put up floating signboards saying 'Nie-Blankes Alleen' or 'European Gentlemen. Please Stand Close In'.

The taxpayers will be asked to contribute to the building of separate harbours, special ones for shipping from India, Japan and the East. Ships from white countries will unload their non-white crews at a Nie-Blanke port and proceed under their own steam to a white one.

It might be a good idea for the Minister to add to his title and call himself the Minister of Lands and Sea. On the other hand I hear that a feud has arisen between him and the Minister of Water Affairs, who thinks the job should have come his way. This might lead to a serious crisis in the Cabinet and Herr Doktor Verwoerd is contemplating appointing an Under(water) Minister to solve the problem.

The biggest problem I suppose is how the State Information Bureau is going to explain the ridiculousness of sea-apartheid overseas, where I am sure all must be spluttering, along with us, at the depths to which racial prejudice can sink.

Let's not accuse them of being up in the air, they might want to start on that too.

Up my alley, *New Age*, 26 February and 20 August 1959

New Year's weekend went over with a bang accompanied by the usual festive spirits, thick heads and furry tongues. And thrown in with the sincere good wishes received from friends, there were also the platitudinous expressions from our beloved Prime Minister, Dr Verwoerd.

Begging the two white sections to forgive and forget and sink their differences, Herr Doktor studded this New Year pudding with poetic raisins about high mountains and blue skies and wide veld and trees and wildernesses. It sounded almost as if he had got his copy mixed up with a brochure issued by Cook's travel agency.

Very little, if anything, was said about the black people, and their problems. But then Herr Doktor has got it all worked out and I guess very little needed to be said.

The problems of the non-white people will be solved by that one word – Apartheid – and no doubt Herr Doktor will show his goodwill in a practical way by attempting to supply us with more stiff doses of the mixture this year.

Up my alley, *New Age*, 7 January 1960

Go man, go

Looking over the shoulders of two ladies to find out what they were scanning so excitedly, I discovered that they were Prince Charles fans. He'd just been given the handles of Prince of Wales, Lord of the Isles and a list of other titles as long as my arm, and they were simply drooling over it. Poor Elvis Presley, why did the army have to get him?

In this age of national independence and republicanism, even the Strijdom [and Verwoerd] kind, the feudal trappings that still dangle in the eyes of the pukka Englishers stand out like boils on a blonde's back. There are still lots of suckers even amongst us poor blacks who insist on pictures of Her Majesty, the Dook and the kids around the walls in their homes, probably with the unconscious hope that they could use their influence on the Herr Prime Minister.

I don't like Strijdom [and Verwoerd] either, but can't we remember that the Empire or the Commonwealth as we call it now was built on the blood and sweat of us niggahs.

Up my alley, *New Age*, 7 August 1958

Me, I'm all for a Republic … The kind that says for the people, by the people … And I'm not a republican because I'm jealous of what Henry VIII and King Solomon had.

Up my alley, *New Age*, 8 May 1958

The [anti-republican, English-speaking] citizens of Maritzburg at least weren't prepared to hand over the keys to Herr Doktor Verwoerd and ticker tape was replaced by fireworks, teargas and custard pies.

However I am not prepared to support the jingo slogan of 'Go Home, Dutchman' directed at a citizen of the country, even if he is the PM and stormjaer-in-chief of the Nationalist Party. Not that I don't want Verwoerd to go home; but I've nothing against the Dutch.

Up my alley, *New Age*, 10 September 1959

Herr Doktor will no doubt tell the world that his Republiek has come by the will of God. However, a gentleman who calls himself 'King of the World' and considers himself a prophet, too, wrote to us, saying: 'Their republic is against the logic and God made the logic. King Pharaoh made skelm, crook laws and God dealt with him and his spirit left off out the body and his spirit shall feel the heat of hell with other skelm crooks likewise.'

Do you believe in prophecy?

Up my alley, *New Age*, 13 October 1960

The first chance I had after hearing the news [that South Africa was out of the Commonwealth] I dashed out and bought myself a large bun and cold drink – believe it or not – by way of celebration ... Papa Verwoerd had got the old frozen shoulder ... But what made a lot of people gape was that he was amazed, surprised, astounded etc. that folks don't love him and apartheid ... Talk about a stubborn ole mule going through life with blinkers over dem eyes.

Up my alley, *New Age*, 23 March 1961

I hear that [he] is just a leetle bit browned off because visiting Britisher Cliff Richard got a bigger and better hand here than Herr Doktor got in the rock 'n roll yodeller's home country ... Probably because his new theme song 'Hi, neighbour' didn't make the hit parade ... Of course he did get the traditional rock 'n roll acclaim ... Go man, go ... Awfully stuffy folks, these Britishers.

But it was Ma Verwoerd, out on a shopping spree, who stole the show while examining some materials ... I don't know anything about colours, quoth she.

Up my alley, *New Age*, 16 March 1961

Only suggestion I can make to Herr Doktor [to help him get over the knock is for him] to answer an ad seen in the local daily ... It says: 'Hypnotism. Stop worrying. Face each new day confidently and fearlessly. Be yourself again through a course of Hypnotism ...' The country would, I bet, be better off if all the Nats went into a state of suspended animation ... Permanent.

Up my alley, *New Age*, 6 April 1961

Henk's craziest show on earth
BAD man De Wet Nel seems to be a very agile mental juggler. In fact he deserves his name up in lights in Henk Verwoerd's Craziest Show on Earth.

Latest tossing around of words and arranging them into reasoning that could only suit him and his pals was done in the Eastern Cape where he prevented the whites from throwing chairs into the arena by explaining to them logically that apartheid is, and also isn't.

The Bantu areas were for the Bantu, he said, but they were also for the whites. The Africans were too stupid to do business, and needed the whites to do it for them, so the whites will stay, but the Indians will go, because the Indians create racial friction.

There have been no signs of anti-Indian feeling down there, though a lot of whites were arming themselves against Africans a while ago – but that, of course, is just by the way.

Little Nel's juggling inspired rounds of applause from the white traders, but what he just proved was that apartheid really means looking after the whites at the expense of the blacks.

The Africans are too stupid, the Indian traders cause friction, so the white traders will carry on as usual.

And I suppose Little Nel believes in free trade too.

Up my alley, *New Age*, 27 August 1959

South Africa's roving ambassador, Tommy Boydell, who should more appropriately be dubbed roving whitewasher for apartheid, has again added his ha'penny's worth to the drivel that Nationalist politicians like Makulu-baas De Wet Nel use as soft-soap.

Supporting the Makulu-baas argument to expel Indians from Bantustan, Tommy places the blame on Indians for causing friction between non-whites. Apparently blind from his own 'realism', Tommy did not appear interested in the fact that during the recent disturbances in Natal the Africans could have 'settled the Indian problem' as he says they want to do, but made no attempts to turn against Indians. In fact provocateurs who tried to create anti-Indian feeling were dealt with by the Africans themselves.

The African people might have fallen into the trap of racialism in 1949, but today it is different – thanks to the Congresses.

No amount of smokescreens or white-wash for apartheid by Tommy Boydell or De Wet Nel can disguise the fact that it is the racialism they preach that causes the chaos.

Up my alley, *New Age*, 10 September 1959

And said a headline: It's Dr Boydell Now … This knuckle-headed roving ambassador for apartheid has been given an honorary doctor's degree by the University of the Vrystaat … Conferred on him by the Minister of Education, Arts, Science, Social Welfare and Pensions …

Why didn't Serfontein just give him a pension?

Up my alley, *New Age*, 6 April 1961

Little Eric [Louw, Minister of Foreign Affairs] has been whining again. Oh, these bad people overseas. To kick back at December 10 Day of Conscience speeches, Eric made with the moans over the radio. Talk about other people stirring up hatred.

You shoulda heard him. Africans rioting in PE and DEVOURING a nun!

If that isn't stirring up hatred for Africans, I'll eat my hat. My best one.

Up my alley, *New Age*, 19 December 1957

Eric Louw need have no complaints about Independent Editorial Services in Washington, USA. In fact we believe he even helps by having the SA Information Service in Washington dish out their stuff.

A large technicoloured rubber stamp on the front of the IES Newsletter No. 9 prevails on editors and executives to see page 3, and there, nicely written up ready to go into any paper that falls for it, we have the facts behind the facts about this country:

'Anyone knows that the South African Government is a responsible group of serious and advanced men, facing a terribly serious problem with a coloured population outweighing the whites nearly 10-1. Anyone who has spent more than a few days in South Africa knows that there is no underfeeding, even among the people who won't work. As a matter of fact, the movies of the riots (in Cato Manor) show some women whose size was three times that of the average white woman.'

All this and a few more facts of life for Americans, who are also informed that 'South Africa was never Negro ... there were no Negroes when the Boers settled the empty lands long ago.'

Somebody's certainly working hard to fool all the people all the time.

Up my alley, *New Age*, 3 September 1959

One must admit, however, that the Nats do not lack a sense of humour, even though it might be considered of a queer type by us ordinary, common or garden insects.

Senator Verster's plea for a more 'humane' method of executing criminals sentenced to death could only come from somebody with the mentality of a butcher, although I know a few very nice people working at the local abattoirs.

While a lot of civilised people all over the world have been plugging for the abolition of the death penalty, Senator Verster is in favour of shooting instead of hanging.

And in case the firing squad is squeamish, let's have a modem labour saving device that will bump you off by pushing a button.

One doesn't know whether he has been infected by the trigger-happiness of some of our cops, but there you are. Senator Verster laboured and produced this squib, worth about £1 400 a year.

But then, I suppose that's what Senators have been appointed for.

Up my alley, *New Age*, 25 September 1958

By having the right ideas and knowing the right people, and of course having the right skin colour you can get an easy job as a senator. It's money for jam, ... or should I say hot air.

The Senate has adjourned for a month after sitting for 24 hours this session – they have nothing to do. And calculations reveal that the 24 hours cost the taxpayer £44 000.

Further calculations have revealed that each intelligent 'hoor hoor' uttered by some honourable member from Pampoen Rivier Sonder Skaamte costs us £1.

Just think of millions of poor blighters sweating day in and day out for much less than £1 per day.

Up my alley, *New Age*, 12 February 1959

An Afrikaans radio discussion on whether or not whites could do without non-white labour revealed very little new in white attitudes on the subject. Here are snatches from a playback:

Prof Celliers of Stellenbosch: I am in favour of territorial apartheid but to do away with non-white labour is not practicable in the foreseeable future. Seeing there are no Europeans to do the work in the meantime, and they will in any case be too expensive, white South Africa will have to make do with the next best thing, the coloureds. I want to live like King Solomon, if I can afford it. Why should people have to do without non-white servants?

Dr Scholtz: Do you think your descendants will always be able to live such a lazy and comfortable life?

Prof Celliers: Why not? We will always have the servants with us.

Up my alley, *New Age*, 19 February 1959

They never learn
They never learn.

Said JH Abraham, Nat MP for Groblersdal, at a gathering of the faithful in Bloemfontein: 'South Africa is our birthright. We did not steal it. We claimed it from the creator.'

Is this guy kidding?

Up my alley, *New Age*, 25 July 1957

And, there can be hardly any defence of Bantu Education now that Brainwasher Maree has finally set the seal on higher learning.

Referring to Fort Hare he said: 'Previously all colours were mixed up and all that was done there was to make black Englishmen. Under the new system Fort Hare will produce good Bantu.'

Up my alley, *New Age*, 8 October 1959

I've heard that in future graduates from the 'Bantu' universities will have their degrees following their names something like this: George Madala BA, BSc (Lapa side).

Up my alley, *New Age*, 7 May 1959

'If sickly liberalism triumphs in South Africa it will mean self-destruction for the Europeans, suicide for the coloured people and enslavement for the Natives under a chaotic policy of terror' – Dr Otto du Plessis.

Come on, Otto. That's not sickly liberalism you're talking about, it's apartheid.

Up my alley, *New Age*, 22 January 1959

Shooting off the mouth:

'Partnership is something that will never work.' – JN Malan, MEC.

Up my alley, *New Age*, [date unconfirmed]

'... Our non-Europeans here in South Africa are the most contented people in the world.' – Mr Van Staden, MPC (Nat).

'... Existing legislation in South Africa is ineffective to maintain the colour-bar in the nursing profession.' – Mr Viljoen, Minister of Health.

Up my alley, *New Age*, 20 June 1957

'... A house has been built for the chief (of the Mamathola) at Metz, and tents are available for the others.' – Dr Verwoerd.

'We must train our young police recruits both mentally and physically to maintain baasskap.' – Minister of Justice Erasmus.

A little more exercise on the trigger finger, boys.

Up my alley, *New Age*, 17 March 1960

'The ideal (of total apartheid) was there for future generations and the apartheid legislation of the present government would make it easier for them.' – Minister Erasmus again.

That's what I call being a super-optimist.

Up my alley, *New Age*, 10 April 1958

'The poor white problem no longer exists. If a person is still in the position of a poor white it is his own fault.' – PO Sauer, Minister of Lands.

Three cheers for job reservation.

Up my alley, *New Age*, 5 March 1959

I almost gave three loud cheers when Dr Diederichs said the other day that South Africa was heading rapidly towards socialism.

Then I remembered that Hitler had also promised his people socialism – National Socialism.

Up my alley, *New Age*, 23 April 1959

Said Baas De Villiers of Vasco: 'The government has already done much for the coloured people. It should be remembered that up to now they had had only one representative in a Senate of 90, and now they would have one in a Senate of 53.'

Up my alley, *New Age*, 3 March 1960

The mask is off! Dr ID [du Plessis of the CAD] really must have meant it when he said this week: 'It is true we cannot help those who want to be engineers, scientists and mechanics, but we can offer work which in no sense can be classed as dead-end jobs.'

Such as cooks, chefs, handymen and tree-pruners?

Up my alley, New Age, 27 November 1958

I see Dr ID is advertising for white-washers – not for the CAD buildings, but to enlighten the coloured people on the 'correct purpose and scope of the various departmental services and the measures relating to them'.

It will be interesting to see how his Information Service will wash the notices to quit under the Group Areas Act.

Up my alley, New Age, 15 October 1959

A minister down here says his church doesn't have apartheid, only separate congregations.

Sounds like the difference between baasskap and discrimination with justice.

Up my alley, New Age, 19 June 1958

Since Africans are not allowed to attend church services in white areas, the solution is to hold 'garage services', said the DRC Synod in the Northern Transvaal.

This is the only way to bring Christianity to domestic servants, they added.

Hallelujah!

Up my alley, New Age, 30 April 1959

Nat Senators seem ... to be most perturbed by the fact that they are not able to visit the Johannesburg zoo because non-Europeans go there in such large numbers.

There is a simple solution to the problem. I recommend a large wire enclosure and a special keeper. And a big sign over the gate: NATIONALIST SENATORS. DO NOT ANNOY.

Up my alley, New Age, 6 June 1957

A highly intellectual debate has arisen in younger Nat circles I see. The future of the new generation depends on its outcome. Are Volkspele sinful?

Nat YES: Couples have been seen to leave the floor two-by-two.

Nat NO: Women taking part wear long dresses and thick white stockings and bare legs could not be seen.

Dig those crazy cats, man.

Up my alley, New Age, 5 March 1959

As somebody told me, there are three degrees of dumbness. You can be just plain dumb, terribly dumb, or Strijdom.

Up my alley, New Age, 17 April 1958

St Peter and the Congress card
Our postal system always the victim of complaints about its service, will now be streamlined. According to the SA Postal Association efficiency will be increased by:
- Rather than a non-white postman in the vacant job of a white postman, a postal delivery service should be suspended.
- Objection was raised to a 'Native' having been used to relieve a European postman at Maraisburg. Steps have been taken to avoid a recurrence
- The employment of 'Natives' on mail officers' duty at Florida was objected to. The practice was stopped.

And what's more, the department said that steps will be taken immediately such 'absurdities' as non-whites doing whites' work were brought to its notice.

So don't grumble when your mail doesn't arrive in time.

Up my alley, *New Age*, 15 December 1960

So now we're going to have funeral apartheid. It's getting so that a guy won't be able to die without organising a protest about the way he's going to be buried.

A reader wrote to us the other day saying that he fears death if racial discrimination continues in after-life.

Well we get apartheid funerals, and ... apartheid graveyards are virtually the law, so we can only hope that St Peter carries a Congress card.

Maybe they'll get around to thinking up a way of extending apartheid beyond the grave one day. I wonder what part of hell the Nats will occupy?

But does it now mean that non-Europeans will have to have their tombstones done in black marble?

Up my alley, *New Age*, 6 March 1958 and 3 September 1959

And now a drive-in cinema will be opened down here with one half of the parking space for coloureds and the other half for whites ...

We've now reached the stage when even motor cars can't mix.

Up my alley, *New Age*, 4 May 1961

As far as I know there is no Act on the statute books introducing apartheid into counting, but at a law court last week I heard a magistrate addressing an African witness: 'Oh,' he said, 'you don't count the European way. You use your fingers and the moons.'

Up my alley, *New Age*, 31 October 1957

A coloured scholar came to me grumbling that he didn't like being forced to participate in the Afrikaans Taalfees. One of his objections: The Afrikaans translation for 'gentleman' is still 'witman'.

Up my alley, *New Age*, [date unconfirmed]

In Robertson, Cape the authorities wanted to accept the tender of a coloured contractor to do some building work, but the school board objected on the grounds that it wasn't fitting for coloured men to build a white girl's hostel.

Up my alley, *New Age*, 17 March 1960

It's so damn hot down here these days that even the sweat is sweating, which brings to mind that in Jo'burg African domestic workers at a school have been given permission to use the swimming bath.

There was no need for parents of pupils to worry said the Headmaster. 'The bath is chlorinated and filtered and the water is changed after the Natives use it.'

What, no DDT?

Up my alley, *New Age*, 10 November 1960

Advert in a Johannesburg newspaper: Situation vacant, middle-aged house-girl with references.

Up my alley, *New Age*, 17 September 1959

There they are again … Those adverts that offer jobs for 'slightly' coloured girls … At very coloured pay, I bet.

Up my alley, *New Age*, 23 March 1961

Returning from the Miss World Contest, Miss South Africa remarked huffily that she didn't know whether it had been a beauty contest or a political symposium.

Did some busybody perhaps ask her why she hadn't been called Miss White South Africa?

Up my alley, *New Age*, 10 December 1959

I bet you never heard of Sally Meyer. Neither did we until her name cropped up in the local daily the other day. For refusing to make tea when her employer told her to do so. Sally, who is a domestic, was fined R6 under the Masters and Servants Act.

I'm voting her Miss South Africa. Ah! Our South Africa.

Up my alley, *New Age*, 11 January 1962

The Automobile Association doesn't want roads through or near locations because African cyclists are a hazard, the smog is awful, and when the trouble starts the people stone the lovely new fishtails going by.

Perhaps the problem could be solved more simply by another apartheid law prohibiting Africans from buying cycles, lighting fires and picking up stones.

Up my alley, *New Age*, 24 November 1960

And if you're a cyclist just watch out where you pedal, pal. A Mr Theunis Theart received the awful label of 'hotnot boetie' because he cycled behind some coloured cyclists who were taking part in a road race recently.

The white cycling association in the WP also gave Theunis the order of the boot for three months. You can just imagine those defenders of herrenvolk sport telling Mr T.: 'On your bicycle, chum.'

Up my alley, *New Age*, 17 August 1961

It looks as if Jo'burg journalist Lewis Nkosi has come under the axe of the passport authorities and that he might not get to Harvard USA to take up his scholarship.

We have our fingers crossed for Lew, but it does appear that our benign rulers would like him to stay and develop along his own lines.

Up my alley, *New Age*, 15 September 1960

Permits to travel from province to province, permits to be in town, permits to enter locations, permits to rent a house, permits, permits, permits ... Now permits to play golf ... It has been well said that the traditional expression of this dear country of ours is, 'Did you got a licence?'

Up my alley, *New Age*, 16 March 1961

'Flame of Civilisation'

Much has been said about the contribution of the pass laws to crime in South Africa. Our jails are filled with a great number of 'criminals' whose only misdemeanour was that they didn't have a piece of official paper or a reference book in their possession at the right time. This whole country, in fact, has become a prison for millions of black people who have been condemned to the torture of reference books and passes.

Now the sword of condemnation must be pointed the other way.

I ACCUSE the Government and the whole pass-law system of a monstrous crime.

I ACCUSE them all of having been responsible for the death of those two Africans in Johannesburg who were burnt to death because they ran back into the fire to attempt to rescue their reference books.

I ACCUSE them, because they have been responsible for the life of terror in which an African exists, knowing that without a pass he is doomed to arrests and raids and beatings and imprisonment, separation from his family; a state of terror that made those two innocent men regard the possession of those two miserable reference books to be a matter of life ... and death.

Up my alley, *New Age*, 19 February 1959

The farmers have discovered that one-third of coloured children born on the platteland die before reaching the age of five. And all as a result of malnutrition and squalor.

I can't imagine the Farmers' Association weeping on each other's shoulders over it, but they were horrified by the discovery that if the death-rate wasn't checked, the platteland would soon have a shortage of labour.

That's all we're interested in, ou broer ... labour, labour, and more labour.

Up my alley, *New Age*, 19 June 1958

[And] it seems as if African babies are worth a flat 200 quid dead in this country. At least that is the estimated value of Baby Manjati, killed by a trigger-happy naval-rating during the siege of Nyanga.

And although the Manjati family is entitled to compensation, even though it won't replace one dead child, it is enough to make the blood curdle to hear the Government payment praised as 'humane and generous' – just as if a donation was being made to the SPCA.

A Race Relations Institute official, writing as if they were negotiating a cattle deal, also said 'a baby boy is of considerable value to an African parent … we feel it would be diplomatic and reasonable if some such gesture would be made'.

You can just imagine the book-keeping entry: To one baby shot dead – £200.

And I see that the Defence Force is changing from the old-fashioned Sten gun to a 'newlook' Nato-type automatic carbine.

Up my alley, *New Age*, 31 March 1960

The second suicide of a coloured man has thrown further light on the grim face of the Group Areas Act. No longer can the Nats hide [behind] the camouflage that any of their laws will be administered with justice. Legislation that drives people to suicide can be compared only with the most barbaric enactments of the Middle Ages.

But next year the 'Flame of Civilisation' will be carried through [South Africa] as part of the [Union] celebrations.

Up my alley, *New Age*, 26 November 1959

33

'Immorality': Says who?

Once upon a time Algernon Impala fell in love with a cockatoo in the Kruger National Park ... 'Tut, tut,' said Kerkbode Kudu. 'You can't do that. This liberal-humanistic tendency must come to an end. Separate development, old man. Separate development. Can't allow mixed marriages and all that, you know.'

... Algernon Impala was broken-hearted ... Kerkbode Kudu could be right, because I've never yet heard of an impala marrying up with a bird ... But I must still hear of a red or brown or black impala or horse or dog refusing to mate with a white one, just because of the different colour ...

Dr Malherbe's claim that God started apartheid is strictly for the birds.

Up my alley, *New Age*, 4 May 1961

A bird of pale plumage who passed himself off as one of those across-the-border coloureds tags onto a nut-brown maid and they do what is known as going steady. They are said to have dat ole black magic called love. Juliet seems to accept Romeo as a fair-skinned nie-blanke.

The next thing – up pops villain Immorality Act, twirling his moustache and cackling with triumph. Lover boy takes the high jump – six months.

But lover boy had this coloured gal, he mixed with coloured people, went to their parties, etc., etc., etc. Yet he prefers jail rather than admit he was coloured – to save his family from the 'stigma' of being labelled coloured.

What I'm trying to figure out is – was lover boy on the level? Was this true love? I leave it to you. It beats me.

Up my alley, *New Age*, 25 January 1962

The race classification orchestra has been holding its latest Pop concert here in the Cape, and its Danse Macabre has created panic in a number of homes. This time there was no pencil through the hair, or pinpricks, although everything was conducted in secrecy, but probings behind the leaves of the family trees of families who, according to Pop Register regulations, are too shady.

Some of the families have been referred to as play-whites and refugees across the colour-curtain. But whatever they might be, don't let's be nasty and say 'serve you right'.

They're just poor victims of South Africa's 'traditional policy'.

A lot of people are also waiting for the classification orchestra to hold a concert in the Houses of Parliament.

Up my alley, *New Age*, 27 February 1958

The miracle-workers in that mystifying dreamland called Government have now [also] turned a Chinaman into a white man, and saddled him with the prospect of trouble under the mixed-marriages laws, because his wife remains Chinese.

Up my alley, *New Age*, [date unconfirmed]

You must have heard the other one about this crazy mixed-up land of ours.

Here in CT a non-white woman had to look like blazes for a job as a domestic. All prospective madams turned her down because she was too white! She got a job eventually. It reminds me of the white slave racket.

Up my alley, *New Age*, 25 January 1962

And, overheard in court after a housewife was found not guilty of unlawfully using a European women's toilet on a railway station:

'According to your mother you are a European and your husband is a European. You are accepted by the congregation of your church as a European. In appearance you are coloured, but there is evidence that you regard yourself as European. I have doubts whether you are European or non-European, so I must find you not guilty.'

Phew!

Up my alley, *New Age*, 20 March 1958

Likewise and once again. A white woman got four months for bigamy. So what? It also turned out her second husband was an Indian. So the beak on the bench puts in another penny's worth after passing sentence by saying that now she and hubby might even be charged under that Immorality Act, and added another tuppence worth: 'I can't see you turning back now that you have lived as an Indian. Perhaps God will forgive you for your folly – I cannot.'

All this, like Parliament, has given me a bad pain in the neck.

Up my alley, *New Age*, [date unconfirmed]

'Why should you be
So unkind to me,
I'm feeling so blue,
Your broken-hearted Le Roux.'

No, that wasn't jazz singer Dolla Grant. But it could have been sung by the Minister of Water Affairs at a Nat jam session in Vaalharts during the election campaign. 'The Immorality Act makes us heartsore,' he groaned into the mike while die volk daar buite swooned. Fancy being broken-hearted over Frankenstein.

However, there's nothing wrong with the Act, Meneer Le Roux assured his audience. The only thing that broke his heart is that every time there was an immoral act by a white Afrikaner it appeared on the front pages of the English press.

Did the Water Minister imply that die volk should be a little more careful how they committed their immoral acts? Or that you can't stop immorality by legislation, anyway?

Up my alley, *New Age*, 29 October 1959

Whenever new ideas for apartheid are lacking and one is a coloured MP wanting to make a good impression and willing to lend a helping hand, the lack of ideas can always be compensated for by falling back on some worn-out old theme and trying to polish it up further ... I should say dirty it up further.

The Honourable Member Tot le Roux (rhymes with Karoo) was inflicted with a brainstorm the other day.

Let's have apartheid between coloureds and Africans now, he brayed. We can start with that most ignored piece of legislation, the old Immorality Act, and throw in Mixed Marriages as well.

'Coloured leaders', he said, have asked for it anyway. What coloured leaders, Mr Tot?

And, Mr Tot, is it any business of yours and your 'coloured leaders' who wants to marry whom? I bet nobody advised you on the choice of a wife.

And if an African wants to take up with a coloured girl (not that I care) don't you know it's because the 'present system of migratory labour' doesn't allow him to bring his own wife or girlfriend into the city from the territories? Or sends them away when they are here?

I can't understand the morality of a man who says immorality must only be punished if it's inter-racial. Apparently you can be as immoral as you like if you stick to your own kind. Is that what it says in the Bible?

You are trying to sell people's birthright for a mess of 'Hoor-hoors' from your pals on the Nat benches, Mr Tot.

One of the boys tells me that the breaking of the Immorality Act is part of the 'traditional policy' of apartheid.

Up my alley, New Age, [date unconfirmed]

[However,] none of the Nats have yet assured us that immoral acts are traditional – I mean the kind specified in the Act – but [the NP] has lately emphasised that other kinds of immoral acts are. It is traditional not to educate Europeans and non-Europeans in the same universities, and another South African tradition is not to increase the non-European vote, but to reduce it gradually.

Up my alley, *New Age*, 29 October 1959

A dominee, I notice, is at the moment recovering from shock after having conducted his own personal, private investigation into vice. Vice is not what the carpenter uses to hold fast his wood while he does the planing – it is much more gripping than that. Anyway, I am wondering whether the investigator is shocked about the vice, or about the percentage of die volk involved. Certainly young ladies from the platteland can become as much involved as a tootsie from somewhere else, so why discriminate?

Which reminds me that just recently, the columnist in Cape Town's *Die Burger* revealed that the Immorality Act has been a major topic of discussion with him over the festive season. Maybe alcoholic beverages loosened tongues and drove away them inhibitions.

But conclusions drawn at those discussions all seemed to have been: SOMETHING MUST BE DONE ABOUT THAT IM ACT!

Yea, truly is it written that the grass is greener ...

But for some birds, all roads are now leading to Durban. For the weather and the Indian Ocean? No! For bananas and mangoes? No! Take another guess. The most important product of dat Durban today seems to be de strip-tease.

It's enough to give any dominee a headache.

Conversation as reported in a Sunday newspaper:

Erica: I think I can do a better strip than Kathy. She hasn't got the body for it.

Rosallinde: I once worked for Kathy, and I'm not afraid of the competition. The challenge excites me.

Jeez. And I always thought it was just a matter of loosening buckles and buttons …

I must now tiptoe off to a secret parlour and join some of the mob in a clandestine game of – BINGO!

Up my alley, *New Age*, 18 January 1962

Must they add insult to injury? In Pietermaritzburg the magistrate expressed horror that a white man 'could stoop so low' as to break the Immorality Act with a non-white girl.

Shame! And yet we find so many, even bible punchers, quite willing to stoop when the opportunity presents.

Up my alley, *New Age*, 8 May 1958

Dominee Odendaal, literally caught with his pants down, was committing an offence, said the Judge-President of the Free State when he sentenced the assailants who took the law into their own hands.

The whole country is now waiting to see whether a prosecution will be instituted against the Dominee.

Up my alley, *New Age*, 13 August 1959

A tune, an adaptation of one of the old coon songs, is starting to circulate around District Six, and I'm waiting to hear it on New Year's Day, if it isn't banned by then. It goes something like this:

'Daar kom die predikant aan,
Hardloop, bokkie, hardloop …'

Up my alley, *New Age*, 31 October 1957

If I had the time, the energy and the money to waste on postage stamps I would send a large brick to the Reverend JJ Swart. Since I haven't any of these wherewithals I will content myself by just saying – Phooey.

The demented writings of Swart (I will omit the Reverend) are of the type that Hitler specialised in when referring to the Jews and other sub-humans and even his feeble excuse about the 'forgotten' paragraph does not help him out of the category of bone-headed racialists.

The 'mongrel' coloured people have contributed to the growth of South Africa and will continue to do so when JJ Swart and his ilk are late and unlamented.

However we wonder whether his words will be a deterrent to some members of his calling who do not seem averse to 'bastardisation'.

Up my alley, New Age, 26 January 1961

How crazy can we get?

After howling about the statue of the nude white couple over the Population Registration Building in Pretoria, there came an uproar from the same bigoted section because the nudes were being removed by Africans.

As somebody told me, some people's minds are so narrow, every time they think they overbalance.

Up my alley, New Age, 29 August 1957

So the censors have allowed what they have left of the film *Island in the Sun* to be shown in this here sunny land of ours.

In case you don't know, the original film included love scenes between Harry Belafonte (black) and Joan Fontaine (white) and marriages between white and half-caste characters.

Well, you can imagine what happened to it after it got into the hands of our Mixed-Marriages-and-Immorality-Act-struck officials. They cut it to ribbons, left out Dorothy Dandridge (black) altogether, and passed the scraps to the public.

It was released very secretly in PE, but curious (and disappointed) bio-fans made it a hit.

They should have asked for their money back.

Up my alley, New Age, 1 May 1958

Right in the middle of a showing of the film *Die Goddelose Stad* in a town upcountry, members of the audience, white, realised that it was not allowed to be shown to other members of the audience, coloured.

So they upped and demanded the removal of the nie-blanke crowd.

The pic, I heard, deals with the wrong-doings of white youth in Johannesburg and covers everything from dagga-smoking to knifings.

Perhaps this time it wasn't that ye censors were scared that us darkies would be evilly influenced by seeing such goings-on, but more that the seamier side of white life should be hidden from us.

Similar actions are performed by ostriches who shove their heads in the sand when they want to hide.

Up my alley, New Age, 13 November 1958

Do sharks prefer white meat? You'd better ask a shark, but it appears that the folks at Margate, Natal, think so. Because I've just seen a picture of anti-shark nets strung around the European section of the beach. All nice and fancy like something out of Buck Rogers. With the beauty queen of the South Coast splashing about by way of illustration that the contraption really works.

Anyway, they haven't bothered about safety nets around the non-European beach yet. That'll come later they say. The same old line. I suppose they're going to wait until Mr Shark finds out he can't get at the white meat and decides to sample the third-grade black.

I'm surprised somebody hasn't thought of erecting a similar sort of net to prevent contraventions of the Immorality Act.

Up my alley, *New Age*, 6 March 1958

A friend of mine has by careful reading of newspapers from all over the country discovered that the number of convictions for contraventions of the Immorality Act over the last six months of the year 1957 total to 988. SOMEBODY ELSE REMARKED THAT IT AMOUNTED TO A DEFIANCE CAMPAIGN.

Up my alley, *New Age*, 17 July 1958

34

Fishy business

Chaos is come again. This time to the Fish and Chip Shop Masters' Association. And it has been caused by the arrival off the coast of South West Africa of fishing vessels of a foreign power. The presence of such vessels in South African waters constituted a grave danger to the fish-and-chip industry, the fish-and-chippers claimed. There was a serious danger, furthermore, of the fish in our waters declaring an economic boycott (under the influence of the foreign vessels of course) and refusing to enter our nets.

An emergency meeting of FACSMA called at the boardroom of SNOEK (Strong Nets On Every Kabeljou) decided to ask the Minister of Justice to serve one of his surplus banning orders (if he can manage to find one) on the said foreign vessels, ordering them not to darken our muddy doorstep again – not for at least five years, anyway.

Another proposal asking the Government to extend the limit of our territorial waters from Walvis Bay to Walla Walla, Australia, was turned down as impracticable, as it would upset the passport department who are already experiencing difficulties trying to prove to would-be emigrants that Isipingo Beach, Natal, is just as good as Bondi Beach over there.

However, a full-scale advertising campaign is under way to encourage the population to eat more pilchards, and it has been suggested that the next winner of the female jukskei singles should be photographed pulling up her nose at a geelbek. If it did not affect her amateur status, of course.

A cable was also sent to the Foreign Minister at UNO: URGE YOU ATTACK THREAT TO FISH AND CHIP BUSINESS AS INTERFERENCE IN DOMESTIC AFFAIRS.

The following reply was received: BAIE JAMMER COMMA PRESIDENT GENERAL ASSEMBLY IS TOO SLIM.

This dereliction of duty angered several fish-and-chippers and one of them said he had a good mind to ask the Minister of Justice to order the Foreign Minister to resign from UNO.

However, a delegation which investigated the foreign vessel reported later that they weren't interested in fishing anyway, but were really making preparations to test a nuclear bomb in the area. This news was greeted with relief, but everybody had to agree that it was a fishy business, anyhow.

Up my alley, *New Age*, 28 September 1961

End of the world
Unlocking the door of my very own shelter the other day, I peeped out cautiously. The sun was shining brightly and the Slegs Blankes signs were sprouting gaily all over the place, and even Parliament was adding to the warmth in the air.

All of which went to prove that the end of the world had not come.

So much for the fortune-tellers, soothsayers, witch-doctors and star-gazers.

I hear, however, that the Yanks have climbed in and offered aid to the disillusioned dummies in India do-it-yourself kits guaranteed to replace the dough some poor saps decided to burn while waiting for the Day.

Anyway, you can't keep a good man down, as the Japanese acrobat said to the Minister of Interior, and I proceeded to read the morning blah over my breakfast cereal (also from America, called Non-Fall-Out Krispy Atomic Krunchies, send two package tops and you get a free rocket – one that works).

The news seemed to read as follows: 'Visitors to Kirstenbosch were surprised to see a troop of about 29 baboons near the contour above the Gardens on the Constantia side – about five minutes' walk from the popular tourist attraction.

'Except for Algeria, we in South Africa have the most difficult problem of adjustment between human beings and human beings,' said Mr Marais Steyn.

Further perusal of the paper failed to reveal what had been said by the others, but all this, as I afterwards discovered, was due to the fact that I was not wearing my specs at the time.

Anyway, a reader did point out to me the following by a Hollywood sniper commenting on l'affaire Frankie [Sinatra] and Juliet [Prowse]: 'There are two ways of becoming Queen of Hollywood. One is by way of the box-office, and the other is by marrying Hollywood's king.'

I have nothing to say on this matter, except that one should not underestimate Juliet's prowess.

And another item called news gives us to know that a lady who claims to be the spiritual 'bride' of long-dead George Bernard Shaw now claims to be expecting a baby.

I believe that similar things are happening right here in South Africa, and that the off-spring is likely to be baptised Independent Transkei.

And now, as the lady at the Shooting Club quiz said when asked how come the African population figures stood at 11 million and the white at 3 – 'I've run out of ammunition.'

Up my alley, *New Age*, 15 February 1962

Sea water

Finding myself suffering acutely from dyspepsia, heartburn, ingrowing toenails and feeling generally lousy, I decided to amble along to the beach and give myself a large drink of sea water.

Yes, you read me right the first time – SEA WATER. The stuff the ships sail on.

I'm not kidding. If you don't believe me, read the SA State Information Service digest of May 26.

It says there that sea water will soon be sold to the 'Bantu' as medicine.

QUOTE: 'For the first time sea water, a product which abounds in Natal (!!!???) is to be marketed and even exported. It will be sold in dehydrated form.

'Many Bantu believe that ocean water can do wonders. It can be used for anything from despondency to stomach ailments.'

So, because a lot of poor suckers live far from the sea, a gent in Durban, by name Mr Cox, who has been struggling for eight years to dehydrate sea-water, has at last found the golden formula.

The salt will be sold in nice plastic bags. Add half a gallon of fresh water, stir well and there you have it – right from the Indian Ocean, to be taken three times a day. Don't forget to shake yourself after each dose.

What's more – with every packet of salt – you will get a packet of sea-sand (purified), so by the time you've mixed the whole works you'll have a strip of Isipingo Beach all to yourself.

All Mr Cox has left out is a free bikini. No wonder they've introduced beach apartheid. This bird probably owns a monopoly investment in beaches.

Up my alley, *New Age*, 6 July 1961

Dead duck

My nose having this week taken on a delightful rose and luminous aspect due to my boil [acquired because of adhering to the potato boycott], I have been thinking of hiring myself to the City Council as a danger signal. I got the idea while standing on a corner the other day waiting for somebody, and suddenly noticed that all the traffic had come to a standstill in front of me.

Of course, it would be no use hiring out my nose to the Government since they aren't interested in danger signals. They would probably mistake it for the Red Menace and ban it for five years.

Well, as I was saying, I was standing on this corner waiting for this friend, and all the traffic having passed on after I had turned my head, when I noticed a character walking along the street peering at the ground.

'Hey, chum,' says I. 'Looking for something?'

'Bread and jam,' says he.

'Bread and jam?'

'Yes,' he replies. 'I read in the paper the other day that Senator van Aarde says that the streets of the Western Cape are paved with bread and jam, and when us Africans come here to eat bread and jam, we think we are white people. I'm looking for the bread and jam.'

I did my best to convince him not to take the utterances of Enlarged Senators too seriously no matter how intelligent these utterances may appear, especially when they come from Enlarged Senators who have been appointed because of their knowledge of the 'coloured races'.

A little later I felt a touch at my elbow and, focusing the beam of my smeller on another chap I discovered that he had a sack slung over his shoulder out of which came strange squawking sounds … out of the sack, I mean.

'Want to buy a chicken?' he muttered.

'Have you got the necessary certificates?' I ask.

'Certificates?'

'Don't you know that Minister Swart has introduced a law saying that if a non-white wants to sell a fowl he has first to get a certificate from two men of standing or from some official, and that the certificate must contain a full description of the fowl, its age and colour of its eyes, criminal record, if any, and that you are entitled to sell it? Tut, tut my man, carry on as you are and you're doomed to a life of crime.'

'Bah,' said this gent, stalking off. 'That means I'm a dead duck.'

Up my alley, *New Age*, 2 July 1959

Nice guy

A woman I never had the opportunity of meeting up with once described me to a mutual acquaintance as a real meany and the cruellest character in the pen-and-ink racket. And a blues singer in a night-spot once used this man's name as the equivalent of nastiness. So in order to salvage my reputation as an officer and a gentleman I am going to be nice and polite to everybody this week, and hand out bouquets all round.

The biggest bouquet goes to the non-whites of Cape Town for staying away from the opening of the festival of 50 Years of White Supremacy (there I go again being nasty – sorry). The handful reported present can have a raspberry.

And I can't be anything but nice to Herr Dönges for his budget. The kind, generous and lovable old boy. He's so inspired with that wise observation, 'the poor you have with you always'. So that there should always be poor and starving people around, he didn't bother to consider the Africans for a handout.

I could just hug him to death. Why, it strikes me I really must recommend to the Mint that they put his dial on the new decimal dough they're turning out next year.

And of course I just killed myself laughing over the wisecracks of the South African Police. Talking about shooting 'kaffirs' is just an ordinary sort of joke with them. I bet the good ones would make you split your sides.

It's a pity Baas Hertzog has banned TV. A programme by the cops would blow all the tubes.

And the coloured people are still cheering wildly over the speech made by Minister Serfontein at the 'university' at Bellville the other day. He said they could forget about ever getting the same things as the whites.

There, you see, I can really be nice to people.

Up my alley, *New Age*, 10 March 1960

Poor rich people

Tsk. Tsk. Tsk. So the crowd that gathered to welcome our Springbok heroes got a wetting. But why all the trouble to call out the fire brigade? All the cops needed to do was pull out their gats and start blasting … But then it wasn't Sharpeville or Langa and the crowd wasn't black … Just white South Africans come to give a boost to their all-white team captained by a Junior Broederbonder … So we can take it that water can't be wasted on black crowds … You can give naughty whites a ducking, but kêrel, when it comes to those kaffirs … just mow 'em down.

* * * * *

And talking about fire brigades, about R70 000 worth of pondokkies belonging to the poor rich people of Hermanus went up in smoke the other night ... This received the treatment of a national catastrophe by the papers and Soapy Williams, the Congo, and rands and cents had to take second place ... Undoubtedly there must have been tears in the eyes of the inhabitants of Cook's Bush, Pimville and Nyanga when they read the sad news of the suffering of this exclusively white holiday town where the only blacks are the kitchen help ...

And poor De Villiers Graaff's garage was burnt out too.

* * * * *

A Yankee professor said the other day that to give Africans access to liquor would result in the spread of communism ... A John Young, president of Western College for Women in Ohio, USA, has now said that the use of instant coffee by North Americans 'is a contributing factor to the spread of communism in Latin America' ... How come? 'Instant coffee is African coffee,' said Mr Young, and its use in the US has 'pulled the rug right from under' the economies of several Latin American countries ... The pulled-out rug then ushers in communism, according to Young.

* * * * *

And now that Judd Saxon is also going red hunting, all we need is for Juliet Jones to rescue sister Eve from a bearded Bolshevik and for Ben Bolt to beat up some glass-jawed challenger from behind the iron curtain ... Then our breakfast comics will conform 100 percent with the views of the Un-American Activities Committee.

Up my alley, *New Age*, 2 March 1961

Racketeers

THE SLOT MACHINE RACKET: Back in the old days of American racketeering, which became the subject of innumerable pocket novels, a flourishing business was the slot machine. 'The boys' walked into the ubiquitous drug store, planted a jack-pot, or a smut movie, or a pin-table machine in the place, and said: 'This here's our machine. Let the suckers fill it with their nickels. You get a percentage and we take the rest. You play ball and everything's okay. Get tough and we bust you wide open.'

Today the slot machine game has become a racket on a grand scale. The bosses are in Wall Street, New York, and the offices of the big oil companies, the lieutenants sit in the Pentagon in Washington DC, and 'the boys' are the green-clad marines and commandos.

The suckers of the Middle East have objected to being soaked of their hard-earned nickels. They have sweated in the oil-fields of the Standard Oil Company, Arabian American Oil, Kuwait Oil, Gulf Oil, and seen their dough leave the country. The greater part of the tonnage produced is in the control of the American companies. The great oil companies control most of the tanker fleets.

So when they decided to shake off the hold of the big-time mobsters, 'the boys' were sent in to cool them down.

The old days of diplomatic capitalism are gone. The gag about the 'civilising mission' of the Western powers has worn thin, and the strong arm is the order of the day. Said the *Cape Argus* (16/7/58) blatantly: 'The reason for American intervention, backed by Britain and France, is that [they] and West Germany, indeed Western Europe in general, cannot live without the oil of the Middle East ... Therefore when there is a serious risk of losing oil supplies they will, in the last resort, take action to avert their loss, whatever danger that action may imply.' The oil bosses cannot live, and they have shown that they have learned much from Capone and Luciano.

THE PROTECTION RACKET:

'You just keep payin regular and nuttin' happens to you, see?' The cigar-chewing hoodlum grins at the victim. 'You can't find the dough, and, why, somebody's liable to toss a bomb in dis jernt.' African poll tax will go up by 15/- with further increases after January 1, 1960. It's all supposed to be for the African's own good. But he didn't want Bantu Education, he didn't want a penny increase in bus fares, he didn't ask for slave labour and sweat shops.

Boss Naudé has other ideas. 'These taxes were reasonable when limited educational opportunities were provided for the Natives, but under the present circumstances ... the Natives will have to be prepared to pay higher taxes' (The Budget Speech).

'You just can't find the dough, and, why, somebody's liable to toss a bomb in dis jernt.'

THE ADVERTISING RACKET:

'Be like teen-agers, drink Soke!'

'Be like Superman! Eat Krispie Krunchies and all contain the same acetylsalicylic acid. Watch those muscles grow!'

Wedged in between commercial radio's interminable serials of unrequited love and the adventures of one of those ageless heroes, the announcer's stock slogans have become practically part of the lives of millions of listeners. To the man heading for the thirties, Soke is the elixir of eternal youth; to the man who smokes and LOVES it, Gaspers are a boon to the throat and chest; even the baby knows that Gripo is good for gripe.

A sucker, says the high-pressure salesman, is born every minute. Sometimes two a minute. So, in the era of shrinking markets the advertising man has risen to the status of a wizard. Sell those goods. Tell the suckers that Hisprin is better than Wisprin, but for heaven's sake don't let them know that they all contain the same acetylsalicylic acid.

So the suckers are caught in a maelstrom of propaganda that has been geared to convince them that it is fashionable to wear shoes two sizes too small. To the devil with corns, as long as I can look like my favourite star.

On the screen an insurance company convinces, by means of using African filmlet-stars, that the son of the poor African CAN BECOME ANYTHING! His future is assured by supporting us. See, there he is behind a big flashy desk in a big executive position. FORGET THE COLOUR-BAR. Why bother about it? With us your future is in the bag.

Well, it's time for one of those cool, smooth, Golddust cigarettes.

From the sidelines, *Fighting Talk*, August 1958

Wild west show

YESSIREE! Roll up, folks, and welcome to Hank Verwoerd's own genuwine Wild West Show. Right here we got the only real, live and kickingest Westerners in the ole Lone Rider Republic.

And just to show how well we like our Western coloured community, here's ole Buck Botha of the ole CAD Ranch to hand out, free, gratis and for nothing, a whole passel of ten-gallon Stetson hats all the way from Texas, our good neighbour.

Sigh-multaneously, folks, we got a whole stretch of territory lined up for these Westerners which will be their own stamping grounds called group areas. Yes, sir. And we got the Population Registration branding irons all nicely warmed up and ready to sizzle.

Just give me a breather, folks, while I hitch up my ole gun-belt. This here Sten gun is a mite on the heavy side.

Now to get back to business, ladies and gennulmen, as I was saying, this here Western show is in accordance with our traditions. None of them ornery inter-grationist rebel-yellers are allowed into this show. Nope.

Now step right this way, folks, and let me introduce you to our new style Western typist. Now tell the nice customer how well you use that there hammer and chisel, babe.

There, there, gal. Don't scratch. Heh, heh. She reckons ole man Hank is about as mean as a rattler on a granite wall.

Now right over here, folks, is a real and genuine job reservation. Complete with traditional Western handicrafts. Yessiree. Our Westerners can carve the best curios and dig the deepest holes in the Republic. They can carry water too, two buckets at a time.

Now right here is my ole buddy Six-gun Vorster of the sheriff's office. Real patriotic feller he is. Makes a speech in Randfontein the other day and says our young folks gotta be pumped plumb full of that mean ole patriotism.

I guess you all know what patriotism means. The only good darky is one in a group area, and the cop that's the fastest on the draw keeps the Government in longer.

Weal, getting the show back on the road, let me remind you that our Westerners ain't allowed to carry no six-shooter, see? Nope. That's reserved for them paleface shooting clubs.

But like I said, folks, it don't matter whether a 'Hottentot' is of Negro stock or not, these folks are still our honest-to-goodness dyed-in-the-wool Westerners. Juslaaik.

Up my alley, *New Age*, 7 September 1961

Veldskoenfontein

The election campaign in Veldskoenfontein is going great guns. In fact it appears that this is the only part of the Republic where the fever has caught on.

And what makes it more rambunctious is the fact that there are more candidates in the field than voters on the roll!

The thriving community of Veldskoenfontein – population nine – is agog at the goings-on. Never before has there been such activity. The five candidates are going all out to capture the four voters. According to the calculations of Meneer Van der Stoff, the National Bunion candidate, he needs three and five-sixteenths of the voters to get in.

The National Bunion Party is standing on a programme of free corn plasters for the Defence Force. In a speech delivered to two voters, a flock of ducks and a prize ass last week, Meneer Stoff said: 'The Defence Force does too much marching. As a result their feet are sore. How can they defend the Western world with sore feet? That is why I stand for corn plasters for all.'

At one stage of the meeting Meneer Stoff could not be heard because of the heckling from the ass.

Among the opposition candidates is young Japie Kameelblaar. He represents the Benighted Party and stands for the introduction of compulsory rugby for all whites. 'How can we defend white South Africa without rugby?' asks Japie. 'When I am in Parliament I will introduce a bill making it compulsory for all whites to become Springboks. In this way we will be able to defend our civilization. What's more, I will see to it that the rugby rules are published in both official languages.'

Another candidate is Corneels Kouwater, who is standing as candidate for the UXQ. Mr Kouwater recently resigned from the Nationalist Branch in Veldskoenfontein. Asked by a questioner what UXQ meant, Mr Kouwater stated that he did not know, but since he believed he should belong to some party and not stand as an independent, he had formed the UXQ all on his own.

Therefore the only independent in the field is Oom Donderweer, who claims to be 103 years old, and a victim of acute arthritis and short-sightedness.

Oom Donderweer claims to have seen parties come and go in Veldskoenfontein since the years of the first runderpes, and is therefore a man of great political experience. He is standing for the proclamation of Veldskoenfontein as a white Group Area and for the reservation of typists' jobs there for whites only.

NB. The only non-white near Veldskoenfontein lives 80 miles away and is 90 years old, crippled as a result of being run over by young Kosie Baljaar while the latter was on his way home from a braaivleis one night. Commentators in Veldskoenfontein say that it is not likely that this man will apply for a job as a typist in Veldskoenfontein.

The Nationalist Party candidate is Mej. Flo van Kopseer, the only woman in the field. Rumours passed around by the opposition say that Mej. Flo has been seen in the field much too often, and does not deserve the vote of any upright citizen of Veldskoenfontein.

However, as election day draws nearer and nearer, tension is mounting and it looks as if it will be a ding-dong battle on polling day. Although it is difficult to assess at this stage who will get the ding and who will get the dong.

(Nudes by Jannie Skerpkyker)

Up my alley, *New Age*, 21 September 1961

35

Pampoen-onder-die-Bos

From the Kommandant-in-Chief, Pampoen-onder-die-Bos Skietkommando, to His Excellency, Minister of Defence.

Edelagbare Meneer, – I am in receipt of the good news that we are going to have a wonderlike new army what is going to have lovely new weapons of the kind what shoots three hundred rounds a minute.

Allemagtig, but we will be able to shoot hundreds and hundreds of kaffirs.

Edelagbare, meneer, but there is a little trouble. We have got a sample copy of this new gun and we have been doing some practice with it last Sunday afternoon – with the permission of the Dominee, natuurlik – and that is where the trouble starts.

Old Koos van der Waterval, who is our oldest resident and therefore veldkornet in the Kommando, decided that he would be in charge of the gun. He will be eighty-three the day after next Stryddag, and, anyway, he took the first shots.

Meneer, I want to report to you this big trouble. As you said, it would not be a good thing for a farmer of Rouxville to handle such a gun, but old Koos said this is not Rouxville, it is Pampoen-onder-die-Bos. So he just blazed away. So I must report to you, as follows:

Killed in action: Three fowls belonging to Oom Akkerboom; two ostriches belonging to Meneer Groenkloof; one cow and one donkey (owners unknown); and prize bull, property of Tante Grietjie. Additional casualties: Jannie Warmbad, shot in agterplaas, and Gert Blesbok, wounded in big toe.

Your Worship, the Kommando is not so much worried about the dead and wounded. But, meneer, the trouble is this. All the parties affected are very cross, and now say they are going to vote for the United Party.

Except for Jannie Warmbad, who is going to vote for the Progs. So, meneer. You see this is the trouble. The Kommando had a meeting on the werf yesterday, and it was decided that we will rather stick to our voorlaaiers, because they are more traditional and go very well with our corduroy trousers and veldskoene.

Oh, yes. I must also report that Old Koos van der Waterval is in hospital suffering from the backfire of the new gun, and will be unconscious for a long time. So you can write him off from the election, too.

That is all I have to report, meneer. Please give our regards to Oubaas Verwoerd, and also his bulldog. The Kommando is very glad to hear that you had a good time in France.

Yours for our glorious cause, apartheid über alles. Heil! Gesper Wilderfontein, Kommandant.

Up my alley, *New Age*, 31 August 1961

Traditional sport

This time it was not chaos, but pandemonium which came to Pampoen-onder-die-Bos when the news broke that the patriotic community had been expelled from the International Soccer Federation.

The tidings arrived right in the middle of a meeting to decide on the colours for the next touring side. Red was out because Pampoen-onder-die-Bos would never dream of giving the impression that it gave the teeny-weeniest bit of support for that scoundrel Khrushchev. So it was black and white. Never in the history of Pampoen-onder-die-Bos had multi-racialism been supported.

Meneer Wilderfontein, who had a keen interest in all sporting activities in the community, said that their expulsion from the Federation was a great victory, because the Fed was dominated by a lot of blanket kaffirs and coolies anyway.

In any case soccer was a most un-Pampoen-under-die-Bos game and would lead to communism, seeing that countries like Hungary and Poland also fielded teams. He was all for rugby, said Meneer Wilderfontein. It was our traditional sport, like apartheid and skietkommandos.

Why, he continued, warming up after wetting his throat with a plug of biltong, he could trace the history of rugby as far back as his ancestor Cornet Willi Wilderfontein, who had played in Jan van Riebeeck's side against the Quoi-Quoin.

They had won two herds of cattle and the Pampoen-onder-die-Bos vineyards in that game, after young Willi had converted one minute before the final whistle. It wasn't their fault that the ref was Oom Jan himself, and the Quoi-Quoin were so uncivilised as not to know the rugby rules.

Returning to the issue of the colours, one of the members who was standing as an Independent in the selections, moved in favour of the Waring of the Green [Cabinet Minister Frank Waring was a Springbok rugby player] but was booed down in favour of the colours of the old Pampoen-onder-die-Bos Republic. Oom Wilderfontein was nominated cheer-leader, and agreed provided the club provided him with some genuine Springbok biltong.

At this stage Colonel Cholmondeley Paperbotham (Kaffir Wars, Retired), the only English-speaking resident of Pampoen-onder-die-Bos, stalked out of the proceedings, muttering that all this was definitely not cricket.

Up my alley, *New Age*, 5 October 1961

Heresy trial

Pampoen-onder-die-Bos was rocked back on its heels the other day when one of its leading citizens, Frikkie Mielieblaar, was arrested by the local Security Branch and forthwith dumped in the lock-up.

What was more astonishing to all Pampoen-onder-die-Bossers was, firstly, the fact that young Frikkie had for a long time been filling the honoured position of full-back for their rugby side, and secondly that he was being charged with heresy for advocating an equal number of black and white squares for draughtboards.

That such a famous rugby player as Frikkie Mielieblaar could be guilty of such a heinous and heretical crime was beyond words. In fact the population was struck speechless.

When the proceedings opened, the courtroom was packed, for Pampoen-onder-die-Bos had never had a heresy trial since 1666, when Veldkornet Peperbus was hanged, drawn and quartered for ogling the dominee's housemaid.

Opening the case for Pampoen-onder-die-Bos, Meneer Van Buffel, the Public Inquisitor, said that Frikkie had wilfully, feloniously and maliciously contravened chapter forty-three-and-a-half, verse eleven, of Ye Olde Witche Crafte Acte.

Meneer Justice Kosie Jeffries: Which?

Inquisitor: Yes.

Men. Kosie: What?

Inquisitor: No, which, your lordship.

Men. Kosie: What which?

Inquisitor: Witchcraft, m'lud.

Men. Kosie: Proceed, Meneer Inquisitor.

Under cross-examination young Frikkie admitted that he was a famous full-back for the Pampoen-onder-die-Bos Rugby Club. He had been awarded his Springbok badge. Yes, he had advocated equal shares of black and white for draughtboards because he understood that this was the only way one could play draughts. (Uproar in the court.)

Inquisitor: The prisoner admits his guilt, m'lud, but in mitigation pleads that he was led astray by malicious multi-racialists and the English press.

In his summing up Meneer Kosie Jeffries said that he was most astonished, bedaddled and bewildered that a famous rugby full-back, and a Springbok at that, could be led astray. Why, surely his long rugby experience should have thickened his skull enough to prevent foreign matter from entering it? Tsk. Tsk. Tsk. Frikkie was by no means an example to the Pampoen-onder-die-Bos race.

'Under these circumstances,' said Meneer Kosie, 'I have no alternative but to find you guilty of heresy and sentence you to two days in the stocks.' (Screams and tears from Frikkie's relations.)

Up my alley, *New Age*, 12 October 1961

That Bliksem Jameson

There was a feeling of great joy and jubilation throughout the ranks of the Pampoen-onder-die-Bos Smashionalist Party this week. They had won the elections. Oom Wilderfontien in a post-election speech said that the victory of his party was also a vote of confidence in the party slogan: 'We guarantee to smash the country'.

Of course it had been a ding-dong battle as previously predicted by the Pampoen-onder-die-Bos *Daily Blather*, but a few minutes before the polling station closed it had become quite clear who had got the ding and who had got the dong.

This was because the last man to cast his vote was Oubaas Turksvy, who came all the way from the far reaches of Die Hel.

Arriving at the polling station (which had been established at the Pampoen-onder-die-Bos municipal privy, the newest and most modern building in the district), Oubaas Turksvy was met by Colonel Paperbotham (Kaffir Wars, Rtd), leader of the Benighted-National Bunion Party coalition.

'By jove,' spake up the Colonel. 'I'm certainly glad you arrived in time, my good man. Here, let me hold your voorlaaier. Are you ready to vote for our disorderly advance towards disintegration?'

'Ag, man,' said Oubaas Turksvy. 'I didn't come to vote, man. I came because I heard that bliksem Jameson is up to his tricks.'

'Jameson?' spluttered the Colonel. 'Gad, man, the Boer War ended in 1902.'

'Wragtig. Why didn't anybody tell me, hey?' replied the amazed Oubaas. 'I'm going back home.'

But the old boy was unable to foil the horde of flag-waving Smashionalist supporters who hustled him into the privy yelling: 'Vote for us and help smash the country.' One of them even went so far as to put a penny in the slot so the Oubaas could vote, while others threatened that he would not be let out until he had shown them his ballot paper.

The result was that the Smashionalist Party won by the grand majority of one, and as Oom Wilderfontein said, it was a clear demonstration of the electorate's support for their policy of true Pampoen-onder-die-Bosism.

Oubaas Turksvy, however, left in a huff after telling the *Daily Blather* that the elections were a big fraud as he had been led to believe that Mafeking had been relieved.

Colonel Paperbotham (Kaffir Wars, Rtd) said that the Smashionalist victory only meant that the voters had been deluded into thinking that it was better to smash the country than to disintegrate it.

'But it is also a moral victory for us also,' whined the Colonel. 'After all we and the Smashionalists really believe in the same things.'

Thereupon he stalked off to his offices in the Pampoen-onder-die-Bos Mining Company, followed by young Japie Washbasin, his newly hired office-boy.

Up my alley, *New Age*, 19 October 1961

King Koos

Last Saturday night was Jazz Festival night at Pampoen-onder-die-Bos. This of course was quite a new innovation, but it all came about as a result of Basie Blesbok's trip to Alabama, USA, as a delegate to the annual convention of the KWW (Keep the World White).

The idea of a jazz festival certainly got the cool cats of Pampoen-onder-die-Bos latching on to that rhythm. Especially Oom Mielieblaar, who has been aching to render his own composition 'Concerto for Piano – White Keys Only'. This of course presented some difficulty as Oom Mielieblaar insisted upon finding a piano which had no black keys, and since it was impossible to find such an instrument in Pampoen-onder-die-Bos, never mind anywhere else, it was decided to ask the audience to shut their eyes when the Concerto number was presented.

Young Dirkie Agterplaas's Jew's harp solo was turned down as un-Pampoen-onder-die-Bos, and more consternation was caused when Mevrou Borstrok threatened to walk out if anybody so much as dared to suggest including the 'Indian Love Call' in the programme. She felt the same about 'Red Sails in the Sunset'.

However, the situation was saved when Gertjie Sonderswart suggested that gaps in the programme could be filled in with extracts from his own musical production, 'King Koos'. So it was decided that these and the piano concerto ('White Keys Only'), plus a good wallop of boere-musiek, should complete the programme.

But some of the gang from Pampoen-onder-die-Bos Jeugbond threatened to come around and wreck the joint if they were to be debarred from doing some rock-and-roll.

The Festival Committee, in a panic, agreed, provided that they wore corduroy trousers and Voortrekker kappies instead of zoot-suits and duck-tails.

So the Pampoen-onder-die-Bos Jazz Festival went off with a bang, to say nothing of the explosion which some saboteurs caused right in the middle of the white-hot rendition of 'Jail House Rock' by the quartet provided by the local Special Branch.

The only character who was disappointed was Colonel Paperbotham (Kaffir Wars, Rtd), who stalked out in the middle of the programme muttering that the Committee could have at least included 'White till the Sun Shines, Nelly'.

Up my alley, *New Age*, 26 October 1961

Springbok Rogers

There have been mysterious comings and goings throughout the week at the metropolis of Pampoen-onder-die-Bos. Every day the sleep of its residents has been disturbed by the crack of whips and the creak of ox-wagon wheels heading in the direction of the jukskei course.

The truth of the matter is that preparations have been under way for November 5. November 5 is Pampoen-onder-die-Bos National Day. And it all started way back when Guy van der Fawkes emigrated to England and got clobbered for trying to blow up the Houses of Parliament.

This also accounts for the strained relations between English-speaking Pampoen-onder-die-Bossers and the rest of the population, because it was felt that young Guy need not have gone all the way to England to find a Parliament to blow up. Others felt, however, that the critics did not appreciate the kind consideration of the Minister of the Interior who granted Van der Fawkes a passport.

Anyway, celebrations of November 5 at Pampoen-onder-die-Bos will take the form of a grand fireworks display and the launching of a rocket to the moon.

And just to show that there is no ill-feeling, the PODBATECOM (Pampoen-onder-die-Bos Atomic Energy Commission) was going to invite Colonel Paperbotham (Kaffir Wars, Rtd) to light the match that will launch the rocket into space.

But the Colonel made the embarrassing suggestion that the Minister of Foreign Affairs be invited to be the first passenger to the moon. The celebrations committee felt that Pampoen-onder-die-Bos had enough trouble over the Minister's stand at UNO. Sending him to the moon might lead to a demand for the expulsion of Pampoen-onder-die-Bos from space.

So the Colonel stalked out of the proceedings muttering that people just couldn't appreciate the fact that the best place for the Minister was the moon.

Therefore the honour of lighting the match will go to the oldest inhabitant of Pampoen-onder-die-Bos, Oom Van Der Waterval.

'Wragtig, man,' crowed Oom when he was told of the decision. 'You makes me feel just like Springbok Rogers.'

Up my alley, *New Age*, 2 November 1961

Radio Pampoen-onder-die-Bos

If you have patience and keep on twiddling the knob of your wireless set, you might, at some time or other, pick up Radio Pampoen-onder-die-Bos. The station is identified by its call sign, which can only be described as sounds made by an announcer trying to read the news through a gag.

When he succeeds in getting the gag off he will say: 'This is Radio Pampoen-onder-die-Bos. Here is the news read to you by Johannes Papegaai and brought to you by the kind courtesy of the Prime Minister.'

Of course, none of the news from Radio Pampoen-onder-die-Bos is biased or slanted like that of other stations. Certainly not. All news is carefully sifted, drained, screened, boiled, distilled and purified before being presented to the public. So that the news you get is really new.

There are also commercials thrown in between the main items, such as: 'Do you eat Hellfire Ice-cream? It's the best ice-cream on the market and guaranteed not to melt over the weekend so that you can safely buy it on Saturday and keep it till Monday and so commit no sin by buying it on Sunday.'

Of course there are some people who are hard to please and are always writing to the director of the Pampoen-onder-die-Bos Broadcasting Company about some trivial errors in the news.

Like Colonel Paperbotham (Kaffir Wars, Rtd), who sent a rather irate letter last week, saying: 'Your news about the Boer War is most misleading. The other evening you reported that kommandos were advancing on two fronts upon Stalingrad. I would have you know that it was Wellington who relieved Khartoum, not Gunga Din. Please get your facts straight. I find a definite tendency on the part of the PODBBC to slant the news.'

Meneer Van der Draadloos, the Minister of Posts and Telegrams, refused to comment and Colonel Paperbotham wrote another letter saying sullenly that in any case no news is good news.

Another example of the highly educational features on Radio Pampoen-onder-die-Bos is the weekly round-up broadcast direct from the United Nations. This feature consists of a technical hitch as a result of which nothing can be heard.

It is because of this feature that many overseas visitors to Pampoen-onder-die-Bos are amazed at how much the local Bosses know about foreign affairs.

As Oom Danie Wilderfontein said to one of them: 'Man, you people come here for two weeks and then go away claiming to know all about onse problems. We've been living here all our lives and we haven't heard a thing yet. Wragtig!'

Up my alley, *New Age*, 9 November 1961

Five Santa Clauses

Christmas comes but once a year and, believe it or not, it comes to Pampoen-onder-die-Bos too. But not until it has been thoroughly investigated by a Commission of Inquiry including the Special Branch, the Department of Immigration and the Minister of the Interior – all of Pampoen-onder-die-Bos, of course.

First to be heard by the Commission was Oom Van der Mielieblaar of the PODB Kultuur Vereniging who had strong objections to Christmas this year. Oom's evidence went something like this:

Chairman: You object to Christmas this year?

Oom: Ja, boetie. I hear this Father Christmas comes from somewhere near the North Pole. That's where Norway is, isn't it? Besides this Papa Christmas goes around in red. So he might be one of those Kommuniste for all we know. I think we ought to get our own Papa Christmas from the South Pole, then we'll have a whale of a time.

Next customer was young Japie Kakebeen, who was all for Christmas.

'All we have to do is have members of the Special Branch meet old Santa Claus when he arrives at Pampoen-onder-die-Bos and follow him around to see that he visits the white Group Areas only,' said young Japie. After all, he had written to Santa Claus to bring him a Sten gun for Christmas and he was looking forward to getting it.

The Commission of Inquiry later produced its findings and recommended as follows: 'After all is said and done, Pampoen-onder-die-Bos really can't afford to abolish Christmas or prohibit Santa Claus as an undesirable alien. However, to ensure that all sections of the PODB population enjoy the spirit of goodwill there will be five Santa Clauses this year. The regular one for die volk, plus others appointed from the BAD, the CAD and the AAD for the non-white Pampoen-onder-die-Bossers. The fifth one will be Mr Jackie Schnossel, who will be Santa Claus for the Yiddish community. Of course all of them will come under the strict surveillance of the Special Branch, while going around spreading joy along parallel lines. At the same time the SB will be asked to conduct widespread raids and seize all lists of requests for presents in order to see that no obscene, undesirable, treasonable and banned stuff is imported.'

In this way, said the Commissioner, Christmas would be celebrated in the traditional Pampoen-onder-die-Bos manner.

The only character who protested against this was Colonel Paperbotham (Kaffir Wars, Rtd), who stalked out muttering that he could at least have been asked to carry the bag for the English-speaking section because they had introduced Xmas hats and jingle bells to Pampoen-onder-die-Bos, anyway.

Which remark definitely sleighed the Commission.

Up my alley, *New Age*, 14 December 1961

Out of step

The good patriots of Pampoen-onder-die-Bos all flocked to Oom Van der Meilieblaar's sheep kraal last weekend for the annual stryddag and Covenant Day jukskei-cum-coffee-drinking competition. Of course, there was also a display of the Pampoen-onder-die-Bos internal security forces and speeches preceding the competitions.

The salute was taken by Veldkornet Kakebeen and the only person who caused some consternation was young Gertjie Blesbok, who was continually out of step during the march past of the PODB Hoërskool Cadet Corps.

However, upon being taken to task about it, young Gertjie explained that it was he who had been in step and that everybody else had been out of step. In fact, said young Gertjie, if he had been out of step, then he was only doing his patriotic duty by being in step while everybody else was out of step. Hadn't the Prime Minister said that in order to preserve Pampoen-onder-die-Bos civilisation, everybody should be out of step with everybody else, and that anybody being in step with everybody who was out of step was most un-Pampoen-onder-die-Bos, and deserved to be hanged, drawn, quartered and banned.

After puzzling over this, everybody agreed that they had never heard a more straightforward and illuminating exposition of Pampoen-onder-die-Bos policy.

In fact, in his speech delivered later, Oom Buffelfontein said that the PODB Government would continue to pursue this course until such time as it found itself down the drain, after which it would call on the Waterworks Department to come to the rescue. It was also the Government's policy to extend separate facilities and group areas to the United Nations, Oom Buffelfontein said. Since there were now so many African and Asian states at UNO, it had been decided to afford all these states the opportunity to develop along parallel lines. A Bill to this effect would be introduced at the next session of the Pampoen-onder-die-Bos Stadsraad.

This speech was met with applause and everybody adjourned for coffee and jukskei.

During the jollifications members of the Special Branch mingled with the crowd, taking notes and seeing that nobody pinched the ramrods from the skietkommando muzzle-loaders.

The only one who objected to the whole business was of course Colonel Paperbotham (Kaffir Wars, Rtd), who had been going around in a Father Christmas rigout selling balloons and fancy hats.

He left in a huff, muttering that this jukskei business was not cricket, and that the least Pampoen-onder-die-Bos could have done on such an important occasion was to have presented the Prime Minister, the Foreign Minister and young Gertjie Blesbok each with a lucky dip.

Up my alley, *New Age*, 21 December 1961

Christmas crackers

There was uproar in Pampoen-onder-die-Bos the other day. Cause of aforesaid hullabaloo (*geweld*) was a Christmas cracker which some skulker had put into Oom van der Mielieblaar's festive pudding.

The resulting bang blew the Oom's false teeth into his flagon of witblits standing nearby and Tante Grietjie's melktert bespattered her Voortrekker kappie, thereby adding sacrilege to treason.

Oom van der Mielieblaar naturally sent out a smoke signal for the local SB boys and they immediately cordoned off all roads in and out of Pampoen-onder-die-Bos.

Hoofkonstabel Klopperman, chief of the PODB law enforcers, was summoned from his holiday in the local game reservation and came back grumbling that he had just been on the point of nailing a black kudu which he intended turning into biltong, and Oom van der Mielieblaar deserved all he got for celebrating such an un-Pampoen-onder-die-Bos occasion as Christmas.

Anyway, what the Hoofkonstabel did was make an announcement to the effect that 'Everything is under control, jong. I will deal with these white agitators when I come back from my shooting practice.' Thereafter he returned to his biltong hunt.

Unknown to everybody this statement caused great consternation to Oom van der Mielieblaar himself, who had for a long time been contemplating doing something about the PODB House of Parliament for passing that disturbing Immorality Act.

The Pampoen-onder-die-Bos *Daily Wail* carried an editorial saying that setting off Christmas crackers was all very well, but at least the setter-offers need not have been so amateurish about it. They expected a better job next Christmas. While the *Daglike Skandaal* cried that the PODB Republiek was in danger, and called for the confiscation of all Christmas crackers in future.

However, the SB boys, disguised in Father Christmas outfits, went around wishing all and sundry the compliments of the season and handed out banning orders left and right.

Of course, the only one who was indignant about the whole business was Colonel Paperbotham (Kaffir Wars, Rtd), who muttered into his moustache that turning Christmas into Guy Fawkes could lead to a serious dislocation in the holiday excursions, and whoever heard of anybody eating plum-duff on the 5th of November.

But the last word was had by the Foreign Minister, who sent out a special message from his ostrich farm: These things never happened at all, so there's no cause for alarm, man.

Up my alley, *New Age*, 28 December 1961

Cloaks and daggers

We have just received the following advertising handout from the Pampoen-onder-die-Bos Fashion Centre.

- GREAT SALE NOW ON! Latest costumes for would-be saboteurs specially designed by experts. Visit our Cloak and Dagger department. We recommend our flak hats and capes, air-conditioned for summer work, and we have a limited number of fur-lined capes for the winter nights. They will keep you cosy.
- See our underground wear department. South African Foundation garments with secret pockets complete with information by Frankie. You should be WARING them today.
- For juvenile saboteurs we offer a wide range of pea-shooters, ray-guns, catapults and a special chemistry outfit complete with french chalk and plastic bottles.
- PS. We regret that all paint-sprayers have been bought up by the Public Works Department.

Up my alley, *New Age*, 24 May 1962

Foreign and un-PODB

Of course Pampoen-onder-die-Bos could not do without its annual bust-up, and this took place on New Year's Eve – although the singing of 'Auld Lang Syne' was omitted from the agenda as foreign and un-PODB. In fact, a Commission of Inquiry was immediately established to go into the matter of finding something more Pampoen-onder-die-Bosish to replace the ditty.

Anyway, if they didn't have 'Auld Lang Syne', they had a speech by the Prime Minister. This gent, full of national pride and the rest, and draped in the national flag, spoke on 'Onse Traditions' and said that the coming year would see Pampoen-onder-die-Bos a better place to live in.

The vote would be extended to all blanke Bossers over the age of fourteen since if the lads were entitled to firearms they were certainly entitled to vote. At all times the traditions of Pampoen-onder-die-Bos must be encouraged.

At the same time steps would be taken to prevent political fall-out which was polluting the atmosphere as a result of bomb tests carried out recently by elements who intended to introduce such foreign ideas as liberty, equality and fraternity. The matter of preventing the fall-out would be left in the hands of the students of Pampoen-onder-die-Bosch. (Applause from several volkspelers who flung their kappies into the air.)

'Next year negotiations will (hic) also be arranged with the PODB Department of Carpentry for the manufacture of several thousand ox-wagons with which to strengthen our laager,' quoth the PM. 'We will see to it that our borders are surrounded by wagons so that we will live in our traditional manner. In fact we might even call it the ox-wagon curtain.'

Interjection from Oom van der Meilieblaar: 'And what about the foot-and-mouth, meneer?'

PM crossly: 'What about it? It's our traditional disease, like black spots. You can't have your own foot-and-mouth and eat it, you know.'

This gave a sour note to the whole celebration and the PM went off with a pained expression to the Department of the Posterior. But he was given a good send-off with the singing of 'Vir hy's 'n vrolike kêrel', which Pampoen-onder-die-Bos claims was stolen from them by the British many years ago and converted into 'For he's a jolly good fellow'.

Once again the only guest present who objected was Colonel Paperbotham (Kaffir Wars, Rtd), who growled that the PM should have been given 'Hail Caledonia' for not referring even once to that very old Pampoen-onder-die-Bos tradition of piping in the ordered advance to H(aggis).

Up my alley, *New Age*, 4 January 1962

Part 7

Into exile

Part 7, including the contextual chapters 37–38 and 43–44, written by André Odendaal, attempts to provide a brief overview of Alex La Guma's experiences and writings after he was forced out of South Africa and into exile in September 1966.. This Part has been added to the original manuscript in order to enable readers, looking back nearly 50 years later, to have a sense of La Guma's extraordinarily different lived experiences after going into exile. Without knowing about the profound journeys he undertook as a revolutionary and internationally-recognised writer in the 19 years before his sudden death in Havana, Cuba in October 1985, it would be difficult to understand the full extent of the published fiction and non-fiction of this pioneering African novelist, and the wide range of influences that shaped his writings.

36

Love song

When I first saw my wife, Blanche, she was a thin, gawky schoolgirl with long, spindly legs, who delivered letters to me from her brother. I took little notice of her at high school, accepting the messages casually and handing back replies in return.

I knew she was on the school's hockey and netball teams, that she was a crack sprinter, could run like a gazelle and had brought back several prizes for the school – but these things did not impress me. Probably I did not impress her either.

When I had joined the Communist Party in 1949 I happened to be sent to help at a branch in the suburbs of Cape Town – and there I saw her again, a member of the same Party. They were proud of her because she sold lots of Party literature and could be relied upon to do a job of work. I noticed that she had filled out and was quite pretty.

We got along well together after that and always seemed to drift together at meetings and social functions.

Then the Party was declared illegal by the Nationalist Government and we lost touch with each other. I heard she was training to be a midwife.

Then one day we accidentally met each other in Cape Town's main street and I decided to marry her. I think she felt the same way because when I proposed to her a little while afterwards she immediately said 'Yes'. So we married in 1954.

Our first son was born in 1956. We named him Eugene Varlin, after a hero of the Paris Commune. He was nine months old when I was arrested for high treason having participated in the activities of the national liberation movement in South Africa. Blanche was not at home when the police took me away, she was out delivering a baby and I had to leave our own baby with his grandmother. I only saw her again when I and the 155 other accused were released on bail. The trial lasted four years and we saw each other during the court recesses when I returned from Pretoria, the capital. We were acquitted in 1960.

She was one of the most popular and well-liked midwives in the district where we lived and was kept busy all the time. But Blanche always found time for political work among women. She was one of those who organised and led a mass demonstration of nurses in Cape Town when racism was introduced into the South African nursing profession. She was local executive at the Federation of South African Women. She also loved to sing.

After the Sharpeville massacre in 1960 a state of emergency was declared in South Africa and I was one of those detained for five months. She visited me regularly although the prison was about one hundred miles away and she also had to see to the children and her practice.

Our second son had been born in 1959 – Bartholomew Vanzetti, after one of the two Italian-Americans executed in 1927. In 1961 I was again arrested for helping to organise a general strike against the declaration of the South African Republic. Blanche was always there at visiting hours.

In 1962 I was placed under house arrest for five years. I could no longer work but had to remain confined to our house and garden for twenty-four hours a day. So Blanche had to earn a living for our whole family. She never complained once.

Then in October 1963 we were both arrested. The police accused us of assisting the underground African National Congress and we were to be detained in solitary confinement until they completed their investigations and then brought for trial.

The children were at school when they took us away. They did not even let Blanche change from her nurse's uniform. At the police station the fascist plain-clothes men jeered and shouted at us.

Then we were separated. Fuming, I demanded to know what had happened to my wife. They took me to a local station and locked me in a cell alone. I paced up and down wondering where Blanche was.

Then I heard her singing.

The voice was unmistakable, coming across the stone yard and past the cell bars. She was getting in touch with me, trying to find me, hoping I was in the same building.

It was her favourite, 'Come Back to Sorrento.'

'…then say not goodbye,
Come back again, beloved.'

So I sang back in relief. We did not see each other all the time we were imprisoned but we went through our whole repertoire of love serenades and revolutionary songs.

On the morning of November 7, 1963 I heard her singing the 'Internationale', and joined her:

'We are but nought,
We shall be ALL!
Then comrades come rally
The last fight let us face …'

The police investigations collapsed and with profound relief I heard that Blanche had been released. I was charged only with being in possession of prohibited literature and was transferred to the awaiting-trial section of the local prison.

There Blanche visited me again, but only by strict permission, because the Minister of Justice had confined her to the district in which we lived and she could not leave it.

When I was given a suspended sentence I returned home to house arrest. In 1966 I was again detained under the notorious '180 day detention' law.

When I was released, on our comrades' advice, we departed from our homeland. We did this with regret, but Blanche and I look forward to the time when we will hear our favourite songs again under a free South African sky.

Alex La Guma personal scrapbook, A South African love song, *Soviet Women*, undated magazine cutting [1971], UWC-RIM Mayibuye Archives, Alex La Guma Collection, MCH118-4-1

37

The note in the roast potato

See La Guma B, 'A child is born', *New Age*,
2 August 1956 for her description of her work

Alex and Blanche La Guma had a close relationship that held despite the huge pressures put on them by what was called the Special Branch in the first 12 years of their marriage of shared activism. Blanche's memory of their early days together was more lively than the telling but low-key description provided by Alex in *Soviet Women* (an excerpt from which forms the previous chapter). She recalls, it was 'almost a classic romance. Alex was absolutely fun to be around with'. He asked her to marry him half an hour into their first proper date, played the guitar, sang love songs and recited poems to her:

> We had an active life together. We went to cinema quite a lot as he was especially fond of Westerns. We were also rock 'n rollers. It was the era when rock 'n roll and jitterbug came along. We'd go to a dance in the town hall of Athlone or a wedding reception where the band was playing the new music from America. The dancing was vibrant, Alex could easily pull me through his legs and turn me, and then throw me over his shoulders. I was quite thin and light, boasting a waistline of 18 inches. I enjoyed being tossed around.
>
> ... I appreciated Alex so very much. We worked hard at politics, but we also had great fun. He was warm-hearted towards me and later with our boys as well. His subtle humour was hilarious. I would kill myself laughing at some of the things he'd say in that dry way of his. (La Guma B 2010: 42–43)

After an engagement of two years, Alex the outspoken atheist and Blanche an agnostic got married on 13 November 1954 – in an Anglican church. It was for the sake of Blanche's parents, at the insistence of Jimmy La Guma. Blanche remembered, if you wanted support, there were 'certain things you do in the community'. One of those was getting married in church. Alex was arrested for the first time within a year. Given his precarious job at the often-banned struggle newspaper *New Age*, and that he was charged with treason soon after their second wedding anniversary, Blanche assumed the role of being the family's main provider. From a poor family, she first worked in a cigarette factory before doing a nursing course that came with board and lodging and a small stipend. After their marriage she worked as a midwife, walking long distances, taking the bus, or later cycling, to attend to her patients. She soon became well known, never charging the mothers-to-be if they could not afford the assistance, even for subsequent babies. The title of Blanche's autobiography, *In the Dark with my Dress on Fire*, came from an experience one rainy night, in a small leaking pondokkie on the Cape flats, when she arrived to find a woman lying on newspapers in a space too small for her to stretch out her legs. A squall blew out one of the two candles, and delivering the baby in virtual darkness she 'began to feel an intense heat on my bottom'. Her dress was on fire, but the baby emerged healthy. Besides having a good laugh at her expense when she got home, Alex wrote the episode into his novel, *And a Threefold Cord* (La Guma B 2010: vi–vii).

Blanche was an activist in her own right. After joining the Communist Party in the 1940s, she became an integral part of the left community in Cape Town, being one of the leaders of the protests against the 1957 Nursing Amendment Act which was part of the whole battery of legislative attempts to consolidate apartheid in those years. She was active in forming the Cape Town Nurses and Midwives Vigilance Association, organised secretly in hospitals, marched and wrote articles in the press that were 'smoothed off' by Alex[1]. Even as state repression became more intense, Blanche maintained an uncompromising defiance, which eventually led to her being listed for five years as a banned person in February 1962, like her husband. Her overt political activism included strong statements in the newspapers, her attendance at the Coloured Convention in Malmesbury, and being one of four SA Coloured People's Congress delegates at the secret meeting in Stanger in July 1961 attended by Chief Albert Luthuli and Nelson Mandela, by then operating underground, where the historic decision to embark on the armed struggle was approved. (See 'City housewife banned', Cape Times, 17 February 1962; La Guma B 2010: 79-81). In 1958, two bullets were shot through the window of Alex's study one night, the second grazing the back of his neck, leaving blood oozing through his hand onto his shirt collar. The La Gumas had no doubt it was the security police, even though Alex was left a note by 'The Patriots' who warned: 'Sorry we missed you. Will call again' (La Guma B 2010: 64–65).

Later, on receiving threats to Alex's life, Blanche was reported as saying, 'I have every confidence in the political work in which my husband is engaged, and we will not be intimidated by pro-Government hooligans'.[2] However, the situation by the mid-1960s was becoming intolerable for the La Gumas. It was clear that they would have to leave the country. Harsh state actions were causing disarray in the banned movements. Mandela and his fellow leaders were on Robben Island, having just begun their 27 years in prison. Vuyisile Mini, Alex's fellow Treason Trialist with the golden voice, had been hanged, singing as he went to the gallows. 'Hutch', Alfred Hutchinson, La Guma's fellow writer, whom he sketched and profiled during the trial, was one of many who had already fled the country. *New Age* was banned. The space for open activism was virtually closed down. While Alex was approaching his fifth year of being under house arrest or in detention, Blanche was herself restricted to the Wynberg district. She had to get the magistrate's permission to visit Alex once a month for 30 minutes in the inner city. Her midwifery practice collapsed. She noted that there were times when Alex was in prison when 'I didn't have any money. I had nothing, absolutely nothing. Not a crumb of bread' (La Guma B 2010: 109).

The stress of Alex being confined for years under either house arrest or detention – for long periods in solitary – had also begun to show. Though they had a good marriage and 'good understanding', with Blanche responsible for maintaining the family and being banned as well, 'the two of us together became too much for each other at times'. After four years of house arrest, Alex cracked. One night, in an incident never repeated, he started throwing things, hitting Blanche on the shoulder with a dressing table stool. Blanche thought he was having a nervous breakdown (La Guma B 2010: 122–123).

It was she who finally acted when the time came to leave South Africa. Comrades had warned them they were no longer being as useful to the movement as they would be in exile. But how to convey this to Alex who was then in solitary confinement under the 180-day detention law? Blanche thought hard about it:

> Eventually, I got an idea. I wrote a small note on firm paper: 'Think of leaving'. In bold type I wrote: 'Decided'. I boiled a small potato and, when it was soft, I inserted the note and smoothed it over. I gave the potato a quick fry in a little cooking oil until it was crisp and brown and then placed the potato into a pie and covered it with pastry. Alex liked potatoes and I knew he'd suspect there was something in that small, lonely potato.
> (La Guma B 2010: 128)

Alex found the note in the potato in the pie and agreed they should go, provided the local ANC leaders confirmed the instruction, which Zoli Malindi, the Western Cape chair, promptly did. But to leave by going underground with two children would be high risk. As banned people, they had to apply for permission to leave the country, with their trusted lawyer Himie Bernadt warning it would be an unpleasant bureaucratic process. The reply from the Secretary of the Interior on 11 August 1966 was to grant them one-way exit permits to leave South Africa permanently. Taking this route would mean they would lose their South African citizenship and become 'prohibited' persons in South Africa.

Mr JA La Guma
8 Helder Road
Athlone, CP

Sir,

> I forward herewith the Departure Permits Nos. P 03127 and P 03126 issued to you and your wife in terms of section 5(6) of the Departure from the Union Regulation Act No. 34 of 1955, to enable you to leave the Republic permanently, and have to invite your attention to the provisions of section 6 of the above quoted Act, which reads as follows:
> 6   Any person to whom a permit endorsed as provided in sub-section (6) of section 5 has been issued and who has left the Union for the purpose of proceeding to a place outside the union, shall –
>
> (a) if he thereafter returns to the Union be deemed for the purposes of section 2, to have left the Union without a valid passport or permit;
> (b) for all purposes become a prohibited person within the meaning of the Admission of Persons to the Union Regulation Act, 1913, (Act No. 22 of 1913), in the Union with effect from the time he so left the Union.

> In terms of section 15(1)(c) of the South African Citizenship Act, No. 44 of 1949, as amended, a South African citizen ceases to be a South African citizen should he, for purposes of admission to the Republic of South Africa become a prohibited person.
>
> Yours faithfully,
> Secretary for the Interior[3]

The La Gumas decided in early September it was time to go. The state made it as difficult as possible for them:

> In reply to your letter dated 15th September, 1966, I have to inform you that permission is granted you both to leave your home and the magisterial district of Wynberg to proceed to the DF Malan Airport on Tuesday, 20th September, 1966, in order to board an aircraft departing from DF Malan Airport at 3 p.m. en route to Johannesburg, and leaving Johannesburg at 7.45 p.m. on 20th September, 1966; in order to leave the Republic of South Africa permanently.
>
> This permission is granted subject to the following conditions:
>
> (a) You and your two children must travel from your home to DF Malan Airport via Settlers Way R8 direct;
> (b) You may not leave your home before 1.30 p.m. on 20th September, 1966;
> (c) When you arrive at the Airport you must produce your tickets at the Reception Desk, your luggage must be weighed and you must obtain your seat numbers. This must be completed by 2.30 p.m.;
> (d) Your plane leaves at 3 p.m. and until your plane leaves you may not communicate with any listed or prohibited person, except, in the case of Mr JA Guma, who may communicate with his wife, Mrs Blanche La Guma, and in the case of Mrs La Guma, who may communicate with her husband, Mr Justin Alexander La Guma.
> (e) You may not leave the precincts of the Jan Smuts Airport in Johannesburg while you are waiting to leave there at 7.45 p.m. on 20th September 1966, and you must not contact any listed or prohibited person, with the exceptions indicated in paragraph (d) above;
> (f) All other conditions of your banning orders must be strictly adhered to.
>
> Yours faithfully,
> CHIEF MAGISTRATE: WYNBERG, CAPE, AJ BARNARD[4]

The last hurdle was to get to the airport. Being associated with the La Gumas could get you in trouble down the line. Blanche's close friend, Dolly Wiid, said to hell with that; she would take them. Sticking to the strict instructions of the magistrate, they left home with Alex and the boys dressed in suits, 'the Special Branch waiting in several cars'. As banned people, the La Gumas could not speak to the neighbours as they left, but they were in the street waving. Then, 'As we drove to the airport in Dolly's car we saw a police car in front and two cars on each side'. At the airport it was the same thing, 'ten Special Branch men stood waiting', including the notorious bully and torturer Spyker van Wyk. A big crowd had come, but Alex had to stand 'facing the wall with his back to his well-wishers' in case he breached the regulations (La Guma B 2010: 129–130).

Then the La Gumas boarded the DC10 'jet' where they 'were guided to the rear of the plane where blacks had to sit in those days', before flying out into the blue from what for them had become a caged society (La Guma B 2010: 131).

Notes

1. See La Guma B, Nursing apartheid will ruin a noble profession, *New Age* 29 June 1957 and details in La Guma B 2010: chapter 9.
2. Govt terrorists attack Congress homes, *New Age*, 25 May 1961.
3. UWC-RIM Mayibuye Archives, Alex La Guma Collection, MCH 118-1-1-9.
4. UWC-RIM Mayibuye Archives, Alex La Guma Collection, MCH 118-1-1-10.

38

From canary cage to albatross wings

The era of exile starting in the sixties broadened the arena and scope of thinking and experience of thousands of South Africans in profound ways. Alex La Guma, caught up in this maelstrom of forced migration and the resetting of strategies, was no exception. Having not left his small home in Cape Town for 16 months at one stage, Alex's life changed dramatically after landing in London in late 1966. In the next two decades his routine became a whirl of activity and travel. He was soon gliding along the main travel arteries of the world, visiting dozens of countries as an internationally recognised writer and cultural and political ambassador for the liberation movement.

Exile and its challenges
The journey into exile of Oliver Tambo, one of La Guma's fellow treason trialists and hotel guests at the Fort prison in Johannesburg, vividly portrays the dramatic nature of the changes many exiles had to cope with. On 22 March 1960, the day after the Sharpeville massacre, the man who had been a maths and science teacher and planned to become a Christian minister, had been instructed by the ANC to leave the country to find and establish operational bases outside of South Africa for the banned liberation movement and to kickstart the mobilisation of international support. His first task was to slip across the border into Bechuanaland (today Botswana) and traverse unsympathetic colonial-ruled Southern Rhodesia (Zimbabwe), Northern Rhodesia (Zambia) and Nyasaland (Malawi) in a knife-edge journey of evading arrest, to reach Tanganyika (Tanzania) where he was embraced by Julius Nyerere, then leader of the Tanganyika African National Union. Tambo's first trip from this initial base was to Tunis via Nairobi and Rome. His biographer Luli Callinicos recalls:

> For the first time in his life, Tambo was exposed to the sheer cosmopolitanism of Africa. Here in the north, ebony blue-black men spoke fluent French and Italian, yet wore their dress of vibrant textiles, design, colour and stitchwork. Colonised as most unmistakably were, they were also located in a nexus where Africa met the Mediterranean and the Levant, the cultural product of centuries of vigorous trade, war and religious transaction. (Callinicos 2015: 262)

It was a culture shock that made Tambo realise the challenges ahead. Callinicos observes, 'He had now to reconstruct his identity in a world of new diversity' (Callinicos 2015: 262). As did his organisation. Exile added immeasurably to the rich texture of the culture and thinking of the ANC and its partner the SACP. The influence of decades of international networking and living was to be profound, and is one of the reasons the liberation movement was able eventually to politically outmanoeuvre and remove from power a regime with an insular, colonially rooted world view (see, for example, Odendaal 2022: 174–183).

In keeping with the ANC and SACP's ethic of connecting in a universal way rather than withdrawing into parochialism, Alex La Guma became one of the most prominent of the wandering exiles, frequently getting to visit, travel and work on five continents. Like a bird set free, the internationalist thinker of the 'Up my alley' columns of *New Age* now became an internationalist in a practical, cutting-edge cultural and political sense.

La Guma on the move

Things moved quickly for La Guma after he arrived in London towards the end of September 1966. In addition to finding a temporary job to write for radio and being appointed as spokesperson for the ANC in London, Heinemann in 1967 canonised his work by bringing out both an updated version of *A Walk in the Night* as well as his third novel, *The Stone Country*, in its prestigious Heinemann African Writers' series. At the African-Scandinavian Writers' Conference held at Hässelbly Castle in Stockholm that year, La Guma finally met Soyinka, Ngũgĩ and other top writers from the continent who had spoken so highly of *A Walk in the Night* on its debut in 1962. Ngũgĩ remembered 'the tall, serious and focused' La Guma of this time: 'In person, he dominated the discussions in Sweden much as his text *A Walk in the Night* had done at Makerere five years earlier'. At a party in Stockholm Ngũgĩ also saw the other side of La Guma: 'When some jazz music was put on, I saw Alex La Guma, on the floor, jiving. Yes, he could jive! He was free, the picture of one who loved life' (Ngũgĩ wa Thiong'o in Lee 2024: xi–xii).

In 1967 Alex attended, too, the third Afro-Asian Writers' Association (AAWA) conference in Beirut, together with Lewis Nkosi, Ruth First and Mazisi Kunene. As in other spheres of life and politics, progressive South African writers were becoming part of old and incipient global networks in their numbers. From now on La Guma truly boarded the international writing circuit, with the AAWA as the initial vehicle for his extensive travels and engagements (Lee 2024: 25).

To add to his running start in exile, La Guma was awarded the 1969 Lotus Prize for literature by the Afro-Asian Writers' Association, sharing it – as first recipients – with the renowned Palestinian poet Mahmoud Darwish, who went on to write the Palestinian Declaration of Independence in 1988, and To Hoai from Vietnam. La Guma travelled to New Delhi in 1970 to receive the award from Indian Prime Minister Indira Gandhi, appearing the next day in a front-page photograph and report in *The Times of India*. This was exactly eight years to the day after the *Cape Times* reported in 1962 that he had been listed, banned and silenced in South Africa. La Guma's citation acknowledged the 'high artistic merit of his work' and lauded his 'contempt for all forms of national and racial discrimination, social inequality, aggression and imperialist infiltration' (Alex La Guma personal scrapbook 1969). Some renowned literary figures followed him as Lotus prize-winners: in 1970, the poet and president-to-be Agostinho Neto (Angola); Ousmane Sembène (Senegal) in 1971; Marcelino dos Santos (Mozambique) in 1972, Ngũgĩ wa Thiong'o (Kenya) in 1973 and Chinua Achebe (Nigeria) in 1975 (see personal scrapbook: 1969; 1970a; 1970b; 1978). In the age of decolonisation and third-world revolution in the seventies, the wandering writer from District Six found himself in stellar company under the most unusual circumstances.

Afro-Asian Writers' Association and World Peace Council: La Guma and Soviet–Third World solidarity movements

At the Afro-Asian Writers' Association congress in Kazakhstan in 1973, La Guma was elected deputy secretary general of the Afro-Asian Writers' Association as understudy to Youssef El-Sebai, a best-selling author and one-time Egyptian Minister of Culture. La Guma held the position of deputy until 1979 when he became secretary general after El-Sebai was assassinated in a hostage-taking drama in Cyprus for his support for President Anwar Sadat. The AAWA was fully funded by the Soviet Union, and from 1967 onwards La Guma travelled to the Soviet Union several times a year, going from Moscow on to numerous other 'Third World' destinations. His participation in the anti-imperialist networks of the Cold War years was consolidated by his subsequent close involvement with the World Peace Council. Another Cold War vehicle for Soviet and Third World activism, the WPC rallied under the banner of opposing the proliferation of nuclear arms. Blanche remembers that the WPC president, Romesh Chandra, frequently asked Alex to accompany him on international trips. He was so busy with his unpaid work for the ANC and this solidarity work and diplomacy that, as in South Africa, Blanche again became the breadwinner during their 12 years in London between 1966 and 1978. She had started off nursing in London, battling to make ends meet, but a job as office manager at *Soviet Weekly* in London in 1971, where she was employed with several British communists, brought stability (see La Guma B 2010: chapter 21 for details). The La Gumas were by then deep in the Soviet solidarity camp, with Blanche saying she 'always believed in the rightness of what I was doing'. She emphasised that while the reality may have been different, the philosophy of communism and its basics, 'a job for everyone, bread for all, a roof over people's heads', was what she was working towards in South Africa as well (La Guma B 2010: 146).

By 1985, Alex La Guma's status within this network was such that he was awarded the Soviet Union's high honour the Lenin Peace Prize, formally known as the Order of Friendship of the Peoples of the USSR. In his acceptance speech, he said African and Asian writers 'would not stand idly by' in the fight against 'the forces of fascism, racism and oppression', and every effort had to be made to avoid nuclear war and the obliteration of the planet (Alex La Guma personal scrapbook 1969: 6).

Remarkably, almost paradoxically, in the same year that he won the Lenin Peace Prize, 1985, the French government recognised La Guma's literary standing by giving him a knighthood. He became a Chevalier des Arts et des Lettres. The Minister of Culture, Jack Lang, said the award was 'destined to recompense people that have distinguished themselves for their creations in the artistic literary domain, and for the contribution to arts and literary splendour in France and the World' (Alex La Guma personal scrapbook 1985b; 1985c; Obituary Alex La Guma 1985).

References

Alex La Guma personal scrapbook (1969) Lotus Prize citation and other cuttings, Alex La Guma Collection, RIM-UWC Mayibuye Archives MCH 118-2-1

Alex La Guma personal scrapbook (1970a) *The Times of India*, 18 November, UWC-RIM Mayibuye Archives, Alex La Guma Collection, MCH 118-2-1

Alex La Guma personal scrapbook (1970b) Youseff-el-Sebai, secretary general to UWC-RIM Mayibuye Archives, Alex La Guma Collection, MCH 118-2-1

Alex La Guma personal scrapbook (1985a) Typed report of award ceremony, UWC-RIM Mayibuye Archives, Alex La Guma Collection, MCH 118-2-1

Alex La Guma personal scrapbook (1985b) Jack Lang to Alex La Guma, 11 June, UWC-RIM Mayibuye Archives, Alex La Guma Collection, 118-1-2-1

Alex La Guma personal scrapbook (1985c) Alex La Guma to Jack Lang, 25 September, UWC-RIM Mayibuye Archives, Alex La Guma Collection, MCH 118-1-2-1

Callinicos L (2015) *Oliver Tambo: Beyond the Ngele mountains*. Cape Town: David Philip

La Guma B with M Klammer (2010) *In the dark with my dress on fire: My life in Cape Town, London, Havana and home again*. Johannesburg: Jacana Media

Lee CJ (ed.) (2024) *Alex La Guma: The exile years: 1966–1985*. Voices of Liberation series. Cape Town: HSRC Press

Ngũgĩ wa Thiongo (2016), foreword in Lee 2024, page xxii

Obituary Alex La Guma, *The Times* (London), 23 November 1985

Odendaal A (2022) *Dear Comrade President*. Cape Town: Penguin Random House

39

Vietnam 1973: A repetition of the pictures of Hiroshima and Nagasaki

The next four chapters provide a small sample from Alex La Guma's extensive writings, stretching to hundreds of published and unpublished pieces, on the many-layered journeys – political, literary and personal – that he undertook while in exile.

We see in them how he opened up new spaces in South African writing, and gain insight into how the life, thoughts and intellectual paradigms of this African world traveller were significantly expanded and enriched after his departure from home after four years in virtual solitary confinement. We see also how La Guma's social realist writings drew a great deal on his experiences and how he moved comfortably between his interlinked politics, cultural diplomacy and writing.

This chapter, in the form of an unpublished report of a visit to Vietnam that La Guma wrote to ANC secretary general Duma Nokwe while that epoch-defining war was still in progress, underlines very vividly how exile took him and many other South Africans to the literal frontlines of global events and politics during momentous times in history.

c/o ANC (South Africa)
49 Rathbone Street,
London W1A 4NL.
30th January, 1973

The Secretary General,
African National Congress (SA)
Morogoro, TANZANIA.

Dear Brother,

VISIT TO DEMOCRATIC REPUBLIC OF VIETNAM

While in Moscow on 9th January on my way from Cairo where I had attended a meeting of the Permanent Bureau of Afro-Asian Writers, I received a message from Helsinki asking me to participate in the delegation of the World Peace Council which would leave Moscow for Hanoi on 12th January. I had been chosen to represent Africa on the delegation, the other members coming from Europe, USSR, Latin America, USA, Asia. The delegation was headed by Romesh Chandra, Secretary General of the World Peace Council, who of course also served as the delegate from Asia.

The purpose of the delegation was to serve as eyewitnesses to the scene in the DRV as a result of the US attacks, and to present to the cities of Hanoi and Hai Phong the Lambrakis Medal of the WPC for 'courage and sacrifice in the cause of national independence' in accordance with the decision of the WPC Presidential Conference held in Chile.

In addition to the official delegation there was a member of the Soviet Peace Committee and an official cameraman to record the visit of the WPC delegation in the DRV.

We left Moscow on 12th January and arrived in Hanoi on 13th. We were received at the airport by representatives of the Vietnam Committee for World Peace, including its secretary Com. Van Hoang Tung.

Immediately on arrival in Hanoi it became obvious that the United States airforce had caused widespread and serious damage by its bombing during 10 days of December last year and over periods prior to that. The Gia Lam airport had been severely bombed, and areas around the airport and towards the city had suffered heavily. Bridges over the Red River were down and all traffic had to cross by the pontoon bridges erected by the Vietnamese Army.

While in Hanoi the delegation had the opportunity to view the devastation of large sections of the city, in particular the populated areas. It became clear that the US had not been concerned with military targets but had attempted to break the morale of the population by bombing populated quarters. During the period 18th to 29th December Hanoi had endured the highest concentration of bombing by planes, including B52 heavy bombers, in the history of the US engagement in Vietnam. We were told that a total of 700 sorties had been flown against the city in that period.

Most heavily attacked was the densely populated area of Dong Ba which includes the old and historic Kham Thien quarter which holds a population of 30 000 people. This section was virtually obliterated. The working-class quarter of Anh Dung was also attacked destroying 200 civilian homes, the primary and secondary schools which accommodated 1 500 children, the maternity centre and infirmary. Here we were told 125 people were killed and 126 wounded. Other residential areas attacked were Dai Lanh, and Anh Duong along the Red River. The university was hit and 150 students and others were reported killed. The living quarters at the local cigarette factory, the textile factory and noodle factory were also hit, as well as the International railway station.

The delegation also visited the Bach Mai hospital over which the Swedish Government had made strenuous protests. The US contention that this hospital might have been struck by the defenders' own anti-aircraft shells falling back was proved ludicrous. Practically the entire hospital is demolished and the area left a scene of bomb craters and piles of rubble. The only section left is the shell of the administration section and a few other rooms from which the staff now administers the hospital. The director of the hospital took us on a tour of the ruins and it was obvious that the hospital was deliberately attacked since there are no military installations or any target which could be described as military in its vicinity. The hospital lost all its principal departments like [gynae], surgical, dermatological, x-ray, [dietetic], pharmacological and blood; its entire store of medical supplies was destroyed as well as the catering section and the laundry. The electrical and drainage systems were shattered. Fortunately patients had been moved to the shelters when the alarms were given, but the hospital lost 28 of its personnel ... including 2 doctors, 6 nurses and 6 medical students.

We also visited Saint Paul's hospital which had also been damaged, but which had been able to attend to most of the air-raid casualties. There we were able to see several of the wounded, and this was a most moving experience and a testimony of the deliberate cruelty of US aggression. Many children had been wounded by anti-personnel bombs and the surgeons explained that operations to remove numerous pellets and fragments from bodies were the most difficult. The US also used anti-tank ammunition contained in 'mother bombs' which caused severe wounds.

At a small ceremony attended by representatives of the city administration, the Buddhist association, women and youth organisations, civilian defence, the People's Army, and the delegation, the Lambrakis Medal was awarded to Hanoi through its Mayor or Chairman of the City Administration, Tran Duy Hung. Each member of the delegation said a few words of tribute and solidarity. Due to the potential danger of attack all public gatherings had been stopped, although the Mayor assured us that the citizens would be informed of the presentation through their representatives and the newspapers.

The delegation went on a one-day visit to the port of Hai Phong. The journey took five hours by car and we were able to see the countryside between the cities. Here again villages had been damaged or destroyed by bombing. However such is the organisation of the people that roads had been repaired immediately the enemy planes had left so that transport was able to continue uninterrupted. We saw hundreds of people working on a dyke which had been damaged, and at that time most of the dykes had been repaired.

The outskirts of Hai Phong was a repetition of the pictures of the results of the atomic bomb attack on Hiroshima and Nagasaki. Acres upon acres have been turned in[to] rubble and twisted metal. Inside the city again the populated areas had been bombed. In the harbour extensive damage had been done but the defence had saved the main parts of the harbour and the city itself. The Polish Ship 'Josef Conrad' had its upperworks smashed by bombing and displays a huge hole where the bomb struck. Three sailors had been killed and several wounded.

At a ceremony similar to the one in Hanoi, the Lambrakis Medal was awarded to Hai Phong through its Mayor, Le Duc Thinh.

In Hai Phong the delegation also visited the Czechoslovak-Vietnam Solidarity Hospital and viewed the damage and saw several of the civilian victims of the attacks.

It was quite clear that the state of organisation among the people in North Vietnam had resulted in saving many more lives than had been lost. The participation of the entire population in the defence and air-raid precautions resulted in the preservation of the major parts of both Hanoi and Hai Phong and kept casualties down to a minimum. The system of air-raid shelters and civilian defence and the discipline of the populations are examples of both extreme fortitude and coolness in the face of the most formidable attacks from the most advanced technical weapons. Everywhere we went we found a cheerful people, smiling and chattering as they went about their duties, whether patrolling or clearing rubble or going about their daily routine. Nowhere was there a sign of war-weariness or loss of morale. While touring the cities the delegation was able to speak to the ordinary citizens, many of whom had lost relatives, friends, even entire families in the attacks, and everywhere was a determination to withstand the attacks should they continue and to finally win, but always the wish that they be left in peace to decide their own affairs.

The delegation had the opportunity of visiting the defence systems, namely an anti-aircraft company manned by civilians and the surface-to-air missile systems handled by the army. The anti-aircraft batteries we visited were composed entirely of young workers, the eldest of them 20 years old, and they all showed a magnificent skill in handling the advanced technical equipment. In fact this company had been given awards for their contribution to the defence of the DRV. The surface-to-air missiles were awesome and again skilfully managed by young soldiers.

During the visit the delegation spent some time in an informal talk with the Prime Minister of the DRV, Com. Pham Van Dong. Of South Africa he had this to say: 'If the world should continue to tolerate the shameful system of racism, then we would have made no progress.'

In the course of our visit the main concern pressed upon us was that while a ceasefire was welcomed, it should not be cause for relaxation on the part of either the Vietnamese people or the world community. It was now the time for the most extreme vigilance and maintenance of pressure on the imperialists to make sure that the end of the war remained permanent and that they be given no opportunity to resume activities either in Vietnam or anywhere else.

We also met the representatives of the Provisional Revolutionary Government of South Vietnam, and several former prisoners of the US and Saigon puppet government. The PRG representatives, Nguyen Phu Soai and Nguyen Van Tien, stressed the question of the political prisoners in the hands of Thieu and called for international activities to demand their safety and their release.

The delegation also met the Commission on US War Crimes at their headquarters in Hanoi and information given by them is attached to this report.

In particular there were many lessons to be learnt from the Vietnamese people, especially for those of us engaged in our own national liberation struggle. In particular the lessons that the entire people must be convinced of the justice of their cause, and must be drawn into mass participation in the struggle; the necessity for widescale organisation – in Vietnam people are organised in 'people's teams' on street level, then streets formed into quarters and quarters into districts and so on; then cooperation between the people and their elected representatives on local, city and national level; and their understanding of the military and political objectives of the struggle; the cooperation between the urban workers and the peasantry; and the understanding of their role in the international anti-imperialist struggle.

We believe that the example of the people of Vietnam touched the lives of all of the WPC delegation and that none of us were really the same persons when we finally left Hanoi. We carried with us the best wishes and expressions of solidarity from everybody whom we met, and warm greetings to all who are participating in the struggle in South Africa.

I shall be writing a further report for *Sechaba*, and hope that this short account will give you an idea of our experiences.

Please convey my best wishes to all, and greetings with the hope that all enjoy good health.

AMANDLA.

Alex La Guma

> ANC Collection LSM/0101/0045/06, National Heritage and Cultural Studies,
> University of Fort Hare

40

Visit to Vilnius

The Byelorussky Railway Station had the usual atmosphere of railway terminals: the islands of baggage, the loaded barrows, the groups around the cigarette kiosks, the last-minute arrivals pushing their way through to catch the rear coach at least, before the whistles blew. A woman with a bag of oranges puffed like a steam engine through the entranceway; young people in summer casuals and haversacks shrieked with excitement. We made it fairly easily, although our carriage was far down the train to Vilnius: the motors of the locomotive were humming, and the gray-uniformed women waited at the carriage steps. Soviet railways seem to be run by women; at least they blew the whistles, waved the flags, slammed doors and administered the journey, attended to the restaurant cars. Probably, they were locomotive engineers too.

A young *devushka* in the gray railway uniform examined our tickets and showed us where our sleeper was. In front of our compartment a man who would share it with us was already sitting on the tip-up seat in the corridor, reading a Nero Wolfe detective story in the English language. The doors were slamming, and we were off, dragging slowly along the station, out into the yards which looked like any in the world of railroads except for the Cyrillic alphabet signs, the wheels clack-clacked below us, and the blocks of flats in the distance passed from view, a frieze of cranes along the Moskva River and the city skimmed back out of sight as we gathered speed.

I prefer trains to airplanes – perhaps I am secretly terrified of those giant birds, wondering how on earth they managed to keep us in the sky. But you can ponder in comfort in a train, stretch out on a bunk or gaze through the window and watch *terra firma* pass by, the buildings, fields, smoke in the distance like Amerindian signals, faraway villages, mountains, life; time meant nothing, you need not hurry. In the Soviet Union the best train journeys I had made had been to Samarkand and once to Leningrad and Kiev.

A woman brought the bedding. There was another man besides the Nero Wolfe fan, who shared the compartment with us, but I saw little of him. The countryside swept past to the sound of quiet music from the radio fixed somewhere in the compartment.

You have to take your chance in the restaurant car on Soviet trains, it is a matter of first come, first served. We waited among the tables and crates of beer – now I knew where the *pivo* went that one found so difficult to acquire at hotels.

The first stop was Gagarin, the birthplace of the late cosmonaut. In the morning, when we were awakened by the young lady in charge of the carriage, the radio was broadcasting the seven a.m. news, and Byelorussia was passing by outside, flat and green, farmhouses and barns, a woman leading a cow in a field. The *devushka* of the Soviet railways brought us chai from the samovar that boils over a coal fire at the end of each carriage. The flat green fields swayed by, and we were crossing into Lithuania, but the landscape took no notice of borders and did not change – after all it is all the USSR.

* * * * *

Old and new

In the foyer of the Hotel Gintaras in Vilnius, local people waited with bouquets and tapestry scarves for relations who were about to arrive on visits from America. During the period of reaction thousands of Lithuanians had emigrated to settle abroad, and nowadays they or their children make a point of returning to their native home, if not to stay for good, at least to look and see, to touch the soil, tread the old streets.

Tearful reunions took place around us, receptions, hugs, kisses, the twang of the newfound North American accent mingling with the Lithuanian. A custom seemed to be to decorate the old relation with the embroidered sash or scarf. The decorative art of Lithuanian women artists includes the famous tapestry work. The women of Lithuania have been weaving since time immemorial, and the process of preparing the flax or wool for weaving took up much of the women's time, so that poetry and popular song actually arose out of this occupation. To this day in some villages it is the custom for a bride to present all wedding guests with linen gifts woven with her own hands. Modern artists owe their ability to harmonize contrasts of dark and light, smooth, rough, closed and open work to the ancient craft of their ancestors. The refined colours in tapestries spring from the ancient ability to make natural dyes from flowers, leaves, roots and bark, and metal ores.

Now even parcels in modern stores in Vilnius, I found, are tied with embroidered tape instead of ordinary string.

From this association with colour also, I daresay, springs the famous stained-glass work of Lithuanian artists, in both their formal and modern designs. It is impossible not to be attracted by the blaze of Lithuanian stained-glass work, the gifts of the hands which stretch back to the fourteenth and sixteenth centuries, and the stained-glass work in Kaunas must be seen to be believed: *Mother Earth* by Stoškus, *Harvest Home* by Galeškas, *Spring* by Morkūnas.

Vilnius itself is a combination of old and new: the medieval city with its narrow cobbled streets and courtyards flanked and surrounded by old buildings, the archways casting shadows, the dim interiors of old inns and wine cellars, cafés. The Nazis destroyed a lot of this, but the old city was built again as it had stood in the centuries old past. You can still climb the hill to Gediminas Tower that overlooks Vilnius, pass under ancient gateways, rub against old city walls.

At the shrine of Mater Misericordiae, Catholic old women knelt on the hard pavement to pray at matins and vespers in St Anne's Cathedral. Over a medieval gateway an altar of gold is open to full view through plate glass so that the faithful who cannot get inside may pray before it in the street. The curious, like ourselves, climbed the narrow stairs to see it close up: religion's golden-wrought images are not interfered with, the Catholic Church continues in its old way, as do others.

Around all this old history the new closes in; not only in the modern blocks of flats, the parks, and hotels, but in industrial and agricultural development. In the Soviet period entirely new branches of industry came to life: instrument-making and machine-tool industries, radio and electrical engineering and electronics. Lithuania produces computers and electric meters, radio and TV sets, vacuum cleaners, car compressors, agricultural machinery, and ship propellers.

In one of the squares we went to see an open-air production of Verdi's opera Aida. The whole front of a building, which we learned had been an army barracks, had been turned into a reproduction of ancient Egypt, all the colour and pomp of the opera was produced under the open sky. One evening we went to see an American film at one of the local cinemas – actually I had missed the film when it had been shown in London: *They Shoot Horses, Don't They?*

* * * * *

Pirčiupis's mother

That Sunday we drove down to Trakai with its old castle on the lake. It was a long drive, and on the way we turned off toward the Rūdninkų forest area. On the way our driver made the mistake of overtaking another car on a bridge, and there was the militia up ahead in their yellow squad car that some of the people call 'canaries', to wave us down.

The militiaman was very polite, saluting and saying, 'Good morning, comrades.' He called the driver out and said something about there being traffic laws in this republic that had to be obeyed. After this lecture he let us go on. You can get your licence clipped by the militia, and after three clippings you have a lot of explaining to do to the traffic authorities, and they might make you do your driving examinations all over again. In serious cases, of course, they might suspend a driver for a period, or for good. But the militia on the whole is never harsh, and I never heard anybody refer to them as the equivalent of 'fuzz' or 'pigs' or 'scuffers', as the police are called in some countries. Once I asked a friend to warn a slightly tipsy man on the street, and the man laughed and said, 'No, no, they're all right. They are *our* militia, people's militia.' Once I even proposed a toast to the militia – but one cannot push one's luck too far. Another friend told me: 'Why, if we had no militia we wouldn't be able to read or write our own detective stories!'

We drove on to the Rūdninkų area, and came on the site where the old village of Pirčiupis had stood – the Lithuanian Lidice. In the summer of 1944, the Nazis had swept down on it and mercilessly burnt down the whole village and all its 119 inhabitants with it. In the nearby museum one saw the relics of such barbarism, kept as a reminder of man's inhumanity to man: the charred remnants of coats, a burnt shoe, a belt buckle, a bent and blackened fork, bridle bits, a bible with a bullet hole. One was aghast at the ravages of fascism, preserved under glass in the little museum.

Over all this stood the very sad statue of a mourning Lithuanian woman called simply *Mother*, a masterpiece of sorrow, the inspired monument sculptured by the Lithuanian Gediminas Jokūbonis, who was awarded the Lenin Prize for this work. All over the Soviet Union stand the symbols of sadness over its lost children.

* * * * *

To die a little

We had our last drinks of ale in the underground drinking cellar in the old city, brought by a lad dressed like a medieval cellar man. We had visited the old Peter and Paul Cathedral with its intricate plasterwork and bas-reliefs in thousands of designs and patterns, while from the middle of the cupola of the ceiling God looked down at the marble chequered floor, and the altar shone all gold and silver. At the Young Communist League offices, I was received by young men and stunning girls, and one of the stunning girls was the second secretary or something Comrade Rudakova, who presented me with flowers and the recorded speech of LI Brezhnev to the Komsomol congress. I had visited the local newspaper *Tiesa* and met the editor Albertas Laurinčiukas, and they had published my Vietnamese short story 'Thang's Bicycle' in their Sunday edition. We had visited another old tavern where Prosper Merimée had drunk – that occasion would have come under literary adventures.

Vilnius is an old centre of book printing. As far back as the sixteenth century the first Lithuanian and Slavonic-Russian books had been printed there. The book has become an everyday requisite in Lithuania today. And among all the thousands of books printed (there are 7 000 libraries holding fifty million volumes) there must be some from other parts of the world. I browsed at a second-hand bookstall, and there was *Akmens Šalis* by Aleksis La Guma. It was *The Stone Country*, translated into Lithuanian. I have it now in my bookcase, a touching reminder of the last days of my Soviet journey, like the one wooden shoe presented to me in Vilnius – a custom which means you are invited to return to collect the other.

Edited version of Part 6 Harvest home by La Guma A in Lee CJ (ed.) (2024)
A Soviet journey: A critical annotated edition. Cape Town: Jacana Media

41

'I came here to sing': A tribute to Pablo Neruda

While the fascist tanks and guns blasted La Moneda Palace in Santiago de Chile on September 11, 1973, and President Salvador Allende died, the embattled Chilean people's greatest poet lay gravely ill in a nearby hospital. Perhaps he heard the rattle of gunfire and remembered another time when many of his people had given their lives in the struggle against tyranny.

> 'All along the ramparts of our fatherland,
> bright at the edge of the blank glass-glitter of snow,
> hidden behind the maze of the green-branched river,
> under the nitrate, under the fuse of bursting seed,
> I found thick-strewn the drops of my people's blood.
> And each drop burned like fire.' (The Dead in the Square)

Pablo Neruda died of cancer a short time after his friend and president passed at the hands of the military junta. 'Grave death, bird of harsh plumage' claimed the life of Chile's, and indeed all progressive mankind's, greatest poetic talents. Neruda is the most circulated poet in history, and in his own country the number of Chileans who do know his strongest poetry by heart, the number of Latin Americans who identify with him and to whom he gave heart, will outlast the tyranny of the junta.

Neruda was a poet of the twentieth century, one who was rich in the experience of our times. A great patriot, when he was awarded the Nobel Prize in 1971 the Chilean government of Salvador Allende declared a national holiday.

Born in 1904, the son of a railroad worker and a school teacher, Neruda produced his first book of verse, *Crepusculario*, when he was seventeen. After publishing several other volumes, including the neo-romantic *Twenty Love Poems and a Desperate Song*, which appeared when he was twenty, and which won him renown, Neruda was appointed Chilean consul in Rangoon. He remained in the Far East from 1927 to 1932, visiting China, India, Japan, Indonesia. During 1934 be served in a diplomatic post in Spain and when the fascists rose against the Republican Government he enlisted as a soldier, fighting side by side with the patriotic writers of Spain. A collection of his Spanish Civil War poems, *Spain in the Heart*, was published in Chile in 1938 and forcefully expressed his identification with the heroic anti-Franco struggle, in such lines as:

'Let them know, the ones who killed you,
that they will pay with blood.
Let them know, those who tortured you,
that they will face me one day.'
(For Miguel Hernandez, Murdered in the Prisons of Spain)

This period produced a great change in the poet who returned to his country resolved to serve the people as artist and as citizen.

He served as Chilean consul in Mexico in the early 1940s, during which period he visited the United States of America. Upon his return to Chile he threw himself into the political life of his country, was elected senator by the saltpetre miners and shortly afterwards joined the Communist Party. When the people's front government was betrayed Neruda took a leading role in the underground struggle to liberate Chile. He was also active in the world peace movement.

During those crowded years Neruda's evolution as a poet was significant. Addressing the Continental Congress for Peace in Mexico City in 1949, he said: 'We must give our American lands the strength, the joy and the youth they do not have. We shall not stand idly by while our treasures are shattered by the warmongers and while those philistines rob us of joy. We must overcome our sorrows and rise above destruction. We must teach the road and travel that road in the full view of our peoples. We must cleanse that road and make it resplendent so that tomorrow other human beings may travel over it.'

He had found much of his earlier work 'bore the marks of bitterness of a dead epoch ... So I renounced them.' His actual experience as a Chilean patriot and fighter in the world anti-fascist struggle impelled him to renounce the bourgeois aesthetic influences of his earlier period. He had begun as a brilliant innovator, somewhat given to pessimism and subjective fantasies. But his thought moved from almost exclusive concentration on form to a primary concern with social content; from a sort of detached contemplation to revolutionary partisanship.

In the fifties he started his *Elemental Odes*. These embodied a deliberate move to bring the language of poetry away from the exotic and closer to the ordinary.

Neruda was the true people's poet. In spite of the fascist terror at the time of his death, thousands of Chileans turned out for his funeral. The bourgeois aesthetes who had once been entranced with his earlier work had come to ignore Pablo Neruda who nevertheless grew immeasurably, and a worthier audience multiplied all over the world.

There is in his poetry such a depth of emotion, sincerity and truth that many who had regarded themselves deaf to the persuasion of poetry were kindled to a new understanding and enthusiasm. Whoever touches this poetry touches a man of vast sympathy, a heroic figure who was able to encompass the deepest striving of millions. He was above all the poet of the undefeated.

For Pablo Neruda humanity was living at the most inspiring hour.

The poetic testament of that inspiration is Neruda's immense *Canto General*, a work awesome in vision, begun in 1937 and published in Mexico City in 1950. This work embraced the life of his country and his continent in a variety of verse forms which set out to contain and celebrate the miraculous vastness of the Latin American continent historically, geographically, zoologically and politically. It is certain to remain the greatest poem of Latin America yet. Its spirit is expressed in Neruda'a usual simplicity: 'My people shall win. All people shall win.'

This is the heart of his poetry and the heart of our time.

The fascist followers of Chile's junta demonstrated the characteristic barbarism of their kind by sacking Neruda's house in Isla Negra, a little village on the Pacific coast. But for the Chilean people his words written years ago will remain a beacon:

> 'O fallen brothers, out of the silence
> your voices will rise in the mighty shout of freedom
> when the hope of the people flames into paeans
> of joy.' (The Dead in the Square)

This was the heart of a man whose greatness remains reflected in a simple ambition as stated in his 'Let the Rail Splitter Awake':

> 'I did not come to solve anything.
> I came here to sing
> and for you to sing with me.'

>> Alex La Guma personal scrapbook (n.d.) Typed draft of 'I came here to sing':
>> A tribute to Pablo Neruda, UWC-RIM Mayibuye Archives, Alex La Guma Collection,
>> MCH 118-2-1

42

Israel and South Africa: Where the vultures perch

This chapter prefigures by four decades the horror felt in South Africa and large parts of the world by the filmed genocide carried out by the Zionist state of Israel in Palestine from late 2023 onwards, which was enabled by the USA and other western allies who provided arms and impunity to the perpetrators. For years, South Africans, led by prominent moral figures like Nelson Mandela and Desmond Tutu, had opposed the repressive rule of Israel in the Occupied Territories, comparing it to the apartheid that had existed in this country before democracy. In December 2023, the South African government laid a charge of genocide against Israel before the International Court of Justice, which decided in favour of the complainant. This piece, written by Alex La Guma in the aftermath of Israel's invasion of Lebanon in 1982, highlights the long-standing support the Palestinian cause for self-determination and statehood has enjoyed from the ANC and sections of civil society in South Africa. It also makes clear how Israel and the apartheid regime actively cooperated during those years (supported then too by the USA and western countries) in order to derail anti-colonial struggles.

In the newspaper *Rand Daily Mail* it was reported on 10 July 1982 that 22 writers and academics protested to the Israeli ambassador to South Africa against Israeli military action in Lebanon. The group said in a letter that it considered Israel's invasion 'an act of genocide'. The signatories included Professor Ezekiel Mphahlele and Professor Chabani Manganyi from the University of the Witwatersrand, Mothobi Mutloatse, Stephen Gray, Mike Kirkwood and Jonathan Paton. Others who signed were Peter Wilhelm, Ahmed Essop, Jaki Seroke, Chris van Wyk, Farouk Asvat, Essop Patel, Shafa'at Ahmad Khan, Don Mattera, Cherry Clayton, Nape 'a Motana, Jean Marquard, Achmat Dangor, Sipho Sepamla, Gcina Mhlophe, Makhulu Ledwaba and Matsemela Manaka.

As the whole world voiced their indignation and anger at the Zionist butchery in Lebanon and Beirut, its capital, it was inevitable that voices from the confined, military- and police-dominated atmosphere of racist South Africa joined in protest in spite of the intimidating presence of the apartheid repressive machinery.

Ever since the racially discriminatory and Zionist entities were engineered by the fine hand of Lord Balfour in the early part of this century, racism and Zionism have gone hand in hand. Recognition of their interdependence forms the basis of relations between Zionism and apartheid today. Created as the twin outposts of imperialism – one guarding the eastern Mediterranean and the northern entry into Africa, the other guarding the economic and strategic interests of the imperialist powers in southern Africa, the Indian Ocean and the South Atlantic – they act as economic and military agents of their masters in their respective regions.

'I cannot stress sufficiently how we in Israel cherish relations with South Africa,' said Itzhak Unna, Israel's ambassador to South Africa in 1974–1975. 'South Africa has been consistent in her friendship towards us. South Africa must be seen as having special values for the free world ... It would be a disaster if South Africa were lost as a constructive and active member of the free community of nations.'

Israel and South Africa cooperate not only with imperialism but also with each other: strengthening racism, cooperating in their aggressive manoeuvres against their neighbours and providing mutual military and financial support to ensure the survival of their regimes.

The economic cooperation between apartheid South Africa and Israel is mutually beneficial. Israel provides a channel for exports into African and non-aligned countries, which operate a trade boycott of South African goods, and allows South African goods to enter the EEC [European Economic Community] under Israel's free trade agreement. In return, Israel benefits from the financial and other aid provided by South Africa.

On another level, South African Zionists have been sending larger per capita donations to Israel than any other group, not excluding the USA. There are regular fundraising drives in South Africa in which prominent Israeli political, military and commercial leaders participate. Despite its own foreign exchange shortages, the regime has permitted the regular transfer of these funds.

Israel obtains strategic goods and minerals from South Africa, including chrome, platinum, titanium and uranium, and there is growing collaboration in various fields of energy. Joint research projects have been set up, and there is a regular exchange of information and technology, including research into solar energy.

Military cooperation between Israel and South Africa, like their economic links, is comprehensive. There are exchanges of personnel, information and technical know-how at all levels. Israelis have served alongside apartheid forces, and South Africans have fought Israel's wars of aggression.

According to a retired South African officer, Brigadier Penn, more than 1 000 racist South Africans had served in the 1948 war that dispossessed the Palestinians.

The importance of the contribution of these was that they supplied the core of medical assistance, special developments such as artillery, and the Israeli Air Force [IAF] owes its birth to a former Western Desert pilot from Bothaville, Orange Free State Province, named Syd Cohen, who founded the IAF with some old German Me 109 fighters, which were later replaced by Spitfires.

South African Mirages were used in the 1967 war of aggression. In addition to the provision of Mirages and spares, racist South Africans served with the Israeli forces. The South African Zionist Federation launched a fund, which collected over R2.5 million. In all, over R21 million was transferred to Israel.

During the 1973 War, PW Botha was then Minister of Defence of South Africa and promised that South Africa would find ways and means of helping Israel without declaring war. 'There is a deep feeling on the part of thousands of South Africans for Israel in her battle against the forces supported by communistic militarism which also poses a threat to us,' Botha said.

Ninety-one doctors again flew to Israel; 1 500 South Africans served in the Israeli forces and 800 were among the troops that crossed the Suez Canal. At least one South African Mirage was shot down, and there were reports of a number of other South African planes being flown in the war.

A Canadian investigation, in November 1981, revealed that South Africa shipped 200 tanks to Israel by air to replace those Israel lost. This followed a promise by the US that it would help Israel replace those tanks after the war.

US nuclear technology has also reached South Africa directly and via Israel.

Israel has supplied technology, including information on its laser enrichment process, in exchange for uranium. Scientists of both countries have worked on the development of warheads and of the delivery system. The weapon that was tested in 1979 is generally considered to have been produced with Israeli assistance. Journalists who reported on the Israeli connection in this project had their permits to work in Israel withdrawn.

Israel is said to have cooperated with South Africa as well as Taiwan to build its nuclear capability. This [and other information is] contained in the book *Two Minutes Over Baghdad*, which purports to be the true story of the destruction by Israeli bombers of the Iraqi nuclear plant in 1981.

According to the American columnist Jack Anderson, Israel and South Africa have joined with Taiwan in further plans. In the framework of this triple-state cooperation, there are indications that a common effort is being made to develop a cruise missile with a 2 400-kilometre range. There are also signs that Israel and South Africa are managing to develop a neutron bomb and that they are working on the tactical arsenal no less than on the strategic one.

So the vultures of racism and Zionism perch at each end of the African continent waiting to devour the entrails of the freedom fighters of South Africa and the Middle East, Swapo, the African National Congress and the Palestine Liberation Organization; to ensure that the liberation movements in these regions will not help to prevent the reconquest of once-colonised peoples in the interests of imperialism and to liberate those still beleaguered by oppressive regimes.

The writers of South Africa acted in the spirit of the national liberation movement when they protested against the barbaric invasion of Lebanon. The African National Congress stated at that time:

> The timing of this aggression against the Palestinian people and Lebanon is remarkable in that it takes place just as world imperialism led by the United States of America is on the rampage, initiating and creating pockets of conflict all over the world. This is done in an attempt to reverse the progress attained by people in their revolutionary struggles for national independence, democracy and peace.

The ANC and the struggling people of South Africa express full support for the Palestine Liberation Organization, which is struggling against [the] odds, making heavy sacrifices for the right of the Palestinian people to self-determination. Israel plays the part played by the racists of South Africa in the imperialist global strategy. It is the cause of tension, destabilisation in the

Middle East and a threat to world peace like racist South Africa is in southern Africa and Africa as a whole.

We condemn the imperialist Zionist conspiracy against the Palestinian people. We call for the immediate unconditional withdrawal of the Zionist troops from Lebanon. We call for the international isolation of Israel.

La Guma A (1983) Israel and South Africa:
Where the vultures perch. *Lotus: Afro-Asian Writings* 1983.
As taken from pp. 199–203 in Lee CJ (ed.) (2024) *Alex La Guma: The exile years, 1966-1985*. Voices of Liberation series. Cape Town: HSRC Press

43

Alex La Guma's full body of work and his final assignment

Despite the fact that the responsibilities of Alex La Guma's ANC/SACP, international anti-apartheid and Soviet-aligned solidarity work increased as he settled into leadership roles in exile, he continued to write and to be published in the seventies.

In 1972, Heinemann brought out his fourth novel, *In the Fog of the Seasons' End*. In the same year, Lawrence and Wishart published his first edited volume of non-fiction titled *Apartheid: A Collection of Writings on South African Racism by South Africans*. His second non-fiction book, *A Soviet Journey*, 'one of the longest and most substantive first-hand accounts of the USSR by an African writer' (Lee 2024: 4), published in Moscow by Progress Publishers, followed in 1978. In 1979 Heinemann published La Guma's fifth and final novel, *Time of the Butcherbird*. Besides his books and official reports and work for the ANC,[1] he wrote regularly for a range of journals, including *Lotus: Afro-Asian Writings*, *Présence Africaine*, *Tricontinental* and the ANC and SACP's *Sechaba*, *Umsebenzi* and *African Communist*.

Meanwhile, scholars have been at work on La Guma too. Christopher J. Lee recently published 56 of La Guma's non-fiction pieces of his writing in exile in his contribution to the HSRC Press's Voices of Liberation series, *Alex La Guma: The Exile Years, 1966–1985*. This important study underlines the depth of La Guma's non-fiction in his second life outside South Africa and (like our book) points to the need for scholars to view his artistic expressions and the whole range of his writing, his novels and his published non-fiction, his early South African work and his exile writings, as a single body of work. This latest book on a period of La Guma's exile writings brings to five the published books containing substantial selections of La Guma's still relatively ignored non-fiction – and it ensures they neatly cover the full span of three decades in which he wrote: from the mid-1950s to the time of his death in 1985. This is, of course, the same number of books as his five novels published between 1962 and 1979.

Up until recently, despite their social realism dimensions, La Guma's novels have tended to be seen in isolation from his work in the non-fiction field. But, now, next to his well-discussed *A Walk in the Night*, *And a Threefold Cord*, *The Stone Country*, *In the Fog of the Seasons' End* and *Time of the Butcherbird*, there exists a complementary five-volumed body of his non-fiction. It consists of La Guma's *Apartheid* (1972); his *A Soviet Journey* (1978) with its 70 pieces; Cecil Abrahams' *Memories of Home: The writings of Alex La Guma* (1991); André Odendaal and Roger Field's first iteration of this work on his early writings (1993)[2] and, fifthly, Lee's *The Exile Years* (2024) mentioned above.

Christopher J. Lee recently further refined our understanding of La Guma's non-fiction offerings with his 'critically annotated' and republished *A Soviet Journey* (2017 and 2024). It contains a foreword by Ngũgĩ wa Thiong'o, a preface by Blanche La Guma and a valuable, conceptually fresh 60-page introduction by himself, titled 'Anti-Imperial Eyes'. This book, Blanche La Guma's autobiography (with Martin Klammer), *In the Dark with my Dress on Fire: My life in Cape Town, London, Havana and Home Again*, and Roger Field's *Alex La Guma: A Literary and Political Biography*, both published in 2010, neatly contextualise his life and writings and complement well the ten-book body of work containing Alex La Guma's novels and non-fiction. These works are part of a growing body of academic work and creative work analysing, debating and celebrating La Guma's life and oeuvre, and they are providing new analyses of and revealing new insights into La Guma's writings, which fall beyond the scope of our book.

Lee observes that La Guma, like many of his activist intellectual comrades in the liberation movement, 'inhabited an intercontinental political landscape' (Lee 2017: 5) from which emerged broad world views which have helped reshape and expand South African and African literary and political networks and ideas beyond conventional frameworks to encompass a broader global identity. As this author has pointed out, the freedom struggle from its earliest years acquired a distinct African universalism that drew strength from both deep-rooted African sensibilities and its internationalism, giving rise eventually to democratic South Africa's progressive transformative constitution with its built-in second and third generation rights (see for example Odendaal 2018). Lee contends further that *A Soviet Journey* and, by extension La Guma's other work, should be seen as building on and expanding the black radical tradition represented in trans-Atlantic writings in English by the likes of WEB Du Bois, George Padmore and CLR James, in its Francophone form by Aimé Césaire and Frantz Fanon, and in works that promote 'the gendering of black radicalism' by Suzanne Césaire, Jane Nardal and Paulette Nardal (Lee 2024: 5).

These peripheral Marxist insights from the Global South, sitting apart from the conventions of both western Marxism and the black radical tradition, therefore remain of value for current debates and offer opportunities for understanding and connecting more deeply with South Africa's intellectual history. This means looking not only at the still inadequately explored multiple intellectual influences of exile, but going back to the emergence of deep-rooted, inter-generational radical nationalist and class-based perspectives in South Africa from the 1920s, and before that the 19th century origins of concepts such as Pan-Africanism, Black Consciousness and Non-Racialism. (On this, see Odendaal 2012: 474–483 and Odendaal 2023).

Thus, as with the fresh perspectives brought home by Jimmy La Guma and Josiah Gumede 50 years earlier in their own boundary-crossing journeys, Alex La Guma opened up pioneering new networks and ideas of struggle, solidarity, thinking and identity creation. This irreverent critic of the ruling classes, the apartheid system and imperialism, who was silenced and made invisible by official decree in South Africa for several decades, has been truly unbanned and speaks to us in different ways today.

Alex's maps and internationalist dreams

As Alex La Guma traversed the world, he started to draw by hand with ink and ruler the routes he was taking on two maps. They are in his personal archive at the UWC-RIM Mayibuye Archive and convey in an intimate way the appreciation the once-caged writer had for the intellectual, writing and political opportunities his second life outside South Africa had brought him.

One can imagine Alex pouring over them at his desks in London and Havana, pencilling in the outlines of the history he was part of making, the identity he was busy building for himself as a global traveller and revolutionary internationalist. The first one is the British *Daily Mail*'s 'World Map', fifty years old by now. Three crow's nests of lines on it indicate his main centres of embarkation: London, Moscow and Havana. From there he travelled in his two decades in exile to every part of western and eastern Europe, from Helsinki and Oslo south. In Africa it was Addis Ababa (where the OAU had its headquarters), Tunis, Algiers, Alexandria and Bamako, and closer to home Brazzaville and the frontline states, in the cities of Dar es Salaam (where Alex taught briefly at the university made famous by Walter Rodney and other left thinkers), Maputo, Luanda and Lusaka. The ANC had its headquarters in a non-descript backyard building between Cairo and Chachacha roads in the city centre of Lusaka.

Blanche observed that 'For Alex and me, going to Moscow was like Muslims going to Mecca' (La Guma B 2010: 169). From Moscow, La Guma's main transport hub to new lands and the capital of his ideological beliefs, the pencilled transport lines shoot out west and south to the Soviet republics of the then-USSR and beyond that to the Middle East and independent Asia. The USSR was the largest country on earth, taking up nearly one-sixth of the Earth's landmass and covering an expanse of more than 22 million square kilometres. La Guma travelled across its vast swathes from the Finnish border to Leningrad (now St Petersburg), Byelorussia and Ukraine, and to many cities and republics including Tbilisi in Georgia, Baku in Azerbaijan, Ashgabat in Turkmenistan, Tashkent and Samarkand in Uzbekistan, Alma-Ata in Kazakhstan, and Nizhnevartovsk, Irkutsk and Lake Baikal deep in Siberia. Beyond that he went to Beirut, Damascus, Ulan Bator in Mongolia, Kabul, Kathmandu, Calcutta, Rangoon in Burma, Pyongyang in North Korea, Phnom Phen in Cambodia, Hanoi and Ho Chi Minh City (Saigon) in Vietnam, and Tokyo and Kyoto in Japan.

La Guma and his work were 'prohibited' at home. Yet he drew heavy pencil lines across four continents on his *Daily Mirror* map of the world as he crossed numerous boundaries globally, generating and picking up ideas in ferment, planning for freedom in dozens of places where, ironically, official South African passports were not valid because of growing, suffocating sanctions against apartheid.

The second map marked by Alex La Guma, in Spanish, is of *Centro America*. On this one he drew 20 distinctive blue or black ink dots on Caribbean island-nations and the cluster of mainly small countries stretching from lower North America to upper South America. They related to La Guma's second big post-Cape Town relocation, the second big front of activity that opened up for him in exile from late 1978 onwards.

'Chief Rep' in Cuba

After 12 years in London, in 1978 Alex La Guma was appointed as the ANC first chief representative for Cuba and the Caribbean based in Havana. 'It was the happiest time of my life – and Alex's', Blanche recalls in her biography (La Guma B 2010: 169). He went ahead to Havana in September 1978 and she followed three months later, becoming 'a sort of second-in-command'. They loved living in Havana and 'meeting the ordinary average Cuban person', she told Hilda Bernstein. Not to forget 'Fidel Castro himself and his solidarity committees and the Cuban Communist party'. 'Oh, I thoroughly enjoyed life in Cuba'. (Blanche La Guma interview n.d.)

The only room on the upper level of Alex and Blanche's new home in the Atabey suburb became the ANC's Havana office. The house had a 'large back garden, with mango, banana and paw-paw trees – all fruit bearing – and a large lawn' (La Guma B 2010: 164). It was in an area set aside for liberation movements, next to the official embassies, and because of their diplomatic status the La Gumas were given a car and were well catered for.

Alex continued with his travels and conferences with Blanche running the office when he was away. Meanwhile, their two boys had left London and were becoming settled in new places, too. Eugene La Guma had, via the movement, gone to Moscow to study Russian and then enrolled at Patrice Lumumba University (alma mater of many South African exiles), but he soon dropped out, married and found a job in Moscow as a bread delivery driver. His marriage to Elena 'Leni' Chelnikov, the daughter of a Russian army officer, was against ANC regulations. Blanche and Alex overrode the objections of comrades in London and, likewise, Leni's father, Sergei, resigned his position as a captain in the army after 25 years to make it possible for his daughter to marry a foreigner. The La Gumas were happy to become grandparents around the time they left for Cuba when James A La Guma junior came along (La Guma B 2010: chapter 23).

After Barto La Guma had finished his schooling in London, at age 19 he went to Leipzig in the German Democratic Republic to further his studies on a scholarship provided by the ANC. Having grown up 'always interested in painting and artistic kind of things and music as well', he first tried his hand as a trumpeter, painter and photographer before starting film studies in Potsdam. His parents were very supportive. 'Dad said, listen … photography is all very good and nice, but why don't you become more interested in making films, because … we'll need filmmakers for the future, to document the history of South Africa etc. etc.' (Barto La Guma interview n.d.) Having completed his studies, Barto did a stint in the ANC camps in Mazimbu and Dakawa in Tanzania and with the film unit in Lusaka before returning to live permanently in Germany.

As part of the ANC's forward momentum in exile, its external missions grew from 9 in the 1960s to 20 by 1980 and 41 in 1989. Being chosen by the ANC's National Executive Committee for the senior position in Fidel's Cuba was a plum posting for any anti-imperialist revolutionary of the 1970s. It was a time, post-Vietnam, when third world revolution was in the air. Mozambique and Angola were newly free. The Iranian revolution had just occurred. The Sandinistas led by a young Daniel Ortega would topple the vicious right-wing US-backed dictator Samoza in nearby Nicaragua only months after La Guma had taken up his position in

Havana, and back home Zimbabwe was heading for its independence in 1980, tightening the noose around apartheid South Africa. But, four years later, in October 1983, the shoe was on the other foot. In an event that echoed the dramatic assassination of Salvador Allende in Chile in 1970, the left-wing Prime Minister Maurice Bishop of Grenada and a number of his officials were executed by firing squad after a US-backed invasion. Right-wing 'banana republic' coups in an area the US regarded as its sphere of influence were common. La Guma found himself in a hemisphere where a lot was happening. Living in Cuba with its revolutionary symbolism, on Uncle Sam's very doorstep, and engaging with energetic Caribbean cultures and African diasporic thinking in literature, the arts and music at the time of reggae legend Bob Marley (died 1981) would have excited him. His musings on internationalism and anti-imperialism in *New Age* were mutating into living in times of actual revolution acted out on the most dramatic stages.

While activating anti-apartheid sympathies in a region of the Americas where countries were still struggling to establish stable post-colonial identities after the whiplashes of slavery, colonialism and outside interventions, the new 'chief rep' had to be fully cognisant, too, of the strategic geopolitical issues involved in the intensifying Cold War proxy battles close to South Africa's borders in Angola and Namibia. One of his main responsibilities was to manage the growing number of South Africans being sent to Cuba for education and military training in the wake of the Soweto uprisings. Several of the young recruits lived for a time with the La Gumas in their home.

The new Cuban phase of the struggle ambassador's travel and revolutionary activity lasted for seven years from 1978 to his death in 1985. Why did La Guma mark up by hand on the two already-mentioned maps so many Caribbean and South American countries? Blanche testified to his frequent travels in the region. It is feasible to assume it was his responsibility to engage with nearby nations from his office in *La Havana,* and that he most likely visited many of these countries. From Cuba, down the crescent-shaped two-stringed necklace of island-pearls of the Caribbean, the dots on the *Centro America* map travel to nearby Kingston, Jamaica (where he made one of his most important speeches); to Santa Domingo in the Dominican Republic (although there is no mark on Haiti, home of the legendary Toussaint Louverture and the dictator 'Baby Doc' Duvalier on the same land mass right next door); to St Martin; St Kitts; Guadeloupe; Dominica; St Lucia; St Vincente; Barbados and Grenada. Then, a last hop to Trinidad and Tobago and over to continental South America – now using his *Daily Express* map – he visited Caracas in Venezuela; Bogotá in Colombia; Lima in Peru; La Paz in Bolivia; and also Chile in the deep south, land of his heroes Allende and Neruda (see chapter 41). Then, switching back to the *Centro America* map, the dots go all the way back up to central America from Panama City to San Jose, Managua, Guatemala City and Belmopan in Belize. His pencilled flight paths show also that he went as far north as Montreal and Newfoundland and, surprisingly, when Mandela and many other ANC leaders were on a 'terrorist blacklist', La Guma also indicated Baltimore, Philadelphia, New York, Detroit, Los Angeles, San Francisco and Seattle on his map. Hardly any place in this hemisphere was left untouched by the ambassador's pen marks.

In May 1979, soon after taking up his post, La Guma outlined his agenda as the ANC's chief representative in the Caribbean at a session of the UN Special Committee Against Apartheid held in Kingston, Jamaica. Paying tribute to 'the governments and people of the Caribbean who are with us in our just struggle', he said 'we ask you to consider the following:

a) that the Caribbean countries continue and intensify all efforts to complete the isolation of the racist regimes of southern Africa. All efforts should be made to extend the arms embargo to include economic sanctions and the cessation of all forms of support for the Botha–Smith regimes;
b) that the campaigns for the release of political prisoners in southern Africa be intensified in the Caribbean region;
c) that the demand be pressed for the treatment of captured freedom fighters as prisoners of war in terms of the Geneva Conventions;
d) that Bantustan policies be isolated, and Bantustans be denied international recognition;
e) that support for the liberation movements in southern Africa, the ANC, Patriotic Front and Swapo [South West Africa People's Organisation] be increased;
f) that public opinion throughout the Caribbean be mobilised in support of these and similar initiatives. (Lee 2024: 177–178)'

Speaking alongside the likes of host Prime Minister Michael Manley, La Guma said, 'in the same spirit as the people of Nicaragua and Latin America face the dictatorships', the people of southern Africa from the Zambezi to the Cape of Good Hope were 'demonstrating finally, and emphatically … that they are no longer prepared to be ruled by the racists'. Continuing on this anti-imperialist theme he said, 'This apartheid system is not upheld by the South African racists alone. We have warned the Western powers that unless they discontinue the short-sighted political, economic and military support for the Botha–Smith clique, they will gain nothing but the enmity of the free people of the future' (Lee 2024: 175–178).

In the 19 years after his forced departure from Cape Town, Alex La Guma lived a life he could never have envisaged while growing up in District Six or during his confinement for years by a repressive state.

Notes

1. See for example La Guma A (1972) Apartheid and the coloured people of South Africa, United Nations Unit on Apartheid, Department of Political and Security Council Affairs, Notes and Documents, No. 18/72 (personal communication from ES Reddy, 13 June 1991).
2. See Odendaal A & Field R (eds) (1993) *Liberation Chabalala: The world of Alex La Guma*. Bellville: Mayibuye Press.

References

Lee CJ (ed.) (2024) *A Soviet journey: A critical annotated edition*, Johannesburg: Jacana Media

Odendaal A (2012) *The founders, The origins of the ANC and the struggle for democracy in South Africa*. Johannesburg: Jacana Media

Odendaal A (2018) Lived experience, active citizenry and South African intellectual history: Reflections on a colloquium on 'The intellectual heritage and inherited values of the Eastern Cape'. *Transformation: Critical Perspectives on Southern Africa* 97: 131–135

Odendaal A (2023) Providing the context for the debate on the 'human' imagined in the drafting of the ANC's Constitutional Guidelines in Lusaka, 1985–89. *Afrika Focus* 36: 11–40

Interviews

Blanche La Guma by Hilda Bernstein, n.d. [early 1990s], UWC-RIM Mayibuye Archives, Alex La Guma Collection, MCH 118-5-2-7

Barto La Guma by Hilda Bernstein, n.d. [early 1990s], UWC-RIM Mayibuye Archives, Alex La Guma Collection, MCH 118-5-2-9

44

Never mind, you will see Table Mountain again

Blanche cried often before going into exile. When she wondered whether or not they would ever see Table Mountain again, Alex replied, 'Never mind. We will work our way back. We will return home one day, and you will see Table Mountain again' (La Guma B 2010: 131). And Alex himself dreamt that he would one day sit on Signal Hill – 'Table Mountain is a bit high' – and 'I'll watch all of them scrambling for positions in Parliament' (La Guma B 2010: 192).

Alex's death in Havana in October 1985 meant this part of his dream would never materialise. It was his fourth heart attack. A devastated Blanche wondered whether she might have been responsible for his demise but realised that in the end it was something she could do little about. The ANC secretary general Alfred Nzo asked Blanche to take over Alex's chief representative position. But she was determined to return to her London home as soon as possible. The thought of staying on in the house without him was too much for her. She also felt she could not do the job without him there. It took a frustrating six months of waiting and Oliver Tambo's intervention before Blanche received permission to leave Cuba. She resumed her London life and work at *Soviet Weekly* in April 1986. She was offered a position at the ANC HQ in Lusaka but turned it down. After 31 years of struggle alongside Alex, Blanche was tired and felt it was time for 'very, very capable young people' to take over. Henceforth she would take a back seat politically (La Guma B 2010: 188, 194–200).

Blanche's decisions did not please some of her comrades in London and she felt ostracised. When Mandela was released:

> SACP members in London met at a member's house to commemorate the end of the Party's clandestine work. I wasn't invited to the celebration – I was not even told about it ... In view of the ostracism, I assumed I had been expelled from the Party, though I was never told. From that point on I was never asked to fulfil any more Party tasks, nor was I informed of Party activities. (La Guma B 2010: 201–202)

These reactions to Blanche were at least partly related to both petty party intolerance in London at the decisions the La Gumas had taken at the time Eugene and Elena married in Moscow, as well as the highly patriarchal nature of the SACP and ANC at the time. Policy positions proclaimed women as equal partners in the struggle, but the reality was that they faced 'traditional' attitudes on a daily basis and had generally been relegated to secondary roles in the organisation. However, the growing volume of women's voices from within, strengthened by deepening struggles for gender equality internationally and at 'home', were by now bringing about what would turn out to be concrete long-term changes. In 1988 and 1989, the ANC made major adaptations to its *Constitutional Guidelines for a Democratic South Africa*, which effectively became the template for the future constitution of democratic South Africa, putting gender equality and rights at the centre of its goals for the future (see Odendaal 2023: chapter 36). While Blanche has written her memoir and claimed her space in struggle narratives, she belonged to the decades when women's activists generally were classified as the 'wives of', and it was their men who occupied position or became 'famous'.

Louise Asmal's loved ones recently laid to rest her ashes in a hole dug to nourish a *Celtis Africana* or white stinkwood tree in the Kirstenbosch botanical gardens. They lie near those of her husband, the renowned human rights fighter Kader Asmal. In his tribute, Indra de Lanerolle (who knew the hard-working and impactful Louise from his childhood) reflected on the patriarchal attitudes of that period and how they need to be remembered and challenged:

> I think there was something particular about the elders in the lives of those of us who grew up as children of exiles. Many of us lived in found families or families constructed out of comradeship and common circumstances. We grew up away from the customs and heritages of our grandparents, in a culture that was sometimes made up 'on the go' by those young activists, much younger than we are now. And although they were radicals and free thinkers in many ways, they didn't really do much, certainly not enough, to change their own inheritances of gender roles, so that it was the women amongst our elders who were most responsible for shaping so many of the dimensions we grew up with. (De Lanerolle I 2025)

De Lanerolle noted that history has become silent about the significant roles played by many women in exile. 'There was little reward and in Louise's life, relatively little recognition, at least in comparison to Kader'. Instead, from his perspective:

> I saw Louise and Kader as members of a rock band (an unlikely image, I know, but stay with me). Kader is the front man, the singer. The lyrics have been co-written (with Louise sometimes credited and sometimes not). Louise plays the bass, and maybe guitar and drums as well. She has also organised the tour dates, kept the fan club informed and active, and found the artist to design the posters. And that image captures something about Louise for me. She did not demand attention but it was her band as much as his.

Such perceptive words. Even if this was not the whole story, or 'not even half of it', as this child of the struggle noted. Blanche and Alex La Guma's lives were lived differently, but the metaphor is just as applicable.

Alex could not have lived his large life and been the writer of ten books and the subject of an even bigger volume of newspaper and academic writings were it not for Blanche Herman. From the beginning of their 31 years of marriage she was the main breadwinner, and she was the one who was responsible for the practicalities of bringing up and looking after their boys. It has to be underlined, as we do in chapter 37, that Blanche was an activist in her own right, from their rock and roll and jitterbugging days, when Alex used to pull Blanche through his legs and flip her over his shoulder, to the day he died in Havana, and also that all the while they were a close and formidable 'team' (her word) in a political and personal sense.

There are many stories by and about women in the struggle like Blanche's, but where are they written? Much still has to be done by historians and story-tellers in different media to make up the deficit.

Alex and Blanche La Guma and the liberation movement activists of the 1960s to 1980s might have been part of something that may seem out of step, even anachronistic today, as Lee (2024) has observed. But they have left behind a priceless legacy of thinking, struggle, democratic aspirations and frameworks of questioning from which the world today could learn. At the core of bringing democratic South Africa into existence was an irrepressible universal impulse to see the 'human' recognised in those excluded and othered by society. They have left a huge legacy and also a way for people to look differently at the possibilities for a more just international world order in the time of big-tech juggernauts, AI, hyper-capitalism and filmed genocide in Palestine crassly masquerading as the West protecting human rights.

The musical 'Dance of the La Gumas: Revolution, Rumba and Romance', performed in 2022 at Artscape, Cape Town's main theatre, by playwright and producer Basil Appollis together with Sylvia Vollenhoven, as well as this book coming out to mark the centenary of Alex's birth, are indications of a legacy that lives on.

Alex's richly textured personal papers are safely lodged at UWC, the planned 'coloured juniversity' he mocked in 1962. It is sometimes still referred to as the University of the Working Class, which he would have appreciated.

Alex la Guma was posthumously awarded the Order of Ikhamanga in Gold by the South African President in 2003 for exceptional contributions to literature and the freedom struggle in South Africa, and he and Blanche's names are engraved and remembered in the walkways at Freedom Park, where an eternal flame burns.

You can find them at the bottom of a column listing, in a strangely random, dislocated way, some of the SACP heroes of the liberation struggle. The inscriptions 'La Guma, Alex' and 'Laguma Blanche' are signs of the numerous misspellings and sloppy technicalities you will find at this national site. But they confirm that the La Guma team is remembered and acknowledged again in their homeland sixty years after being silenced and stripped of their citizenship and sent into exile during dark days.

Blanche came back to settle permanently in Cape Town in 1995, when she stayed with family before buying her own flat close to Cavendish Square in Claremont. Back home she was treated with respect as one of the veterans of the struggle and socialised regularly with comrades from exile and her younger years. She died on 6 July 2023 aged 96, well cared for in her last days by staff at a care home in Wynberg. They were aware that the person who inhabited her emaciated body had been spirited and had stood up courageously when it mattered. A touching celebration of her life was held at the Homecoming Centre of the District Six Museum in the city centre, co-hosted by St George's Cathedral and the Friends of Cuba Society. It was well attended by a diminishing circle of left stalwarts and younger energetic social movement activists. The ubiquitous Pallo Jordan and Albie Sachs, present when Alex attended the historic 'council-of war' at Kabwe in Zambia months before his death in 1985, spoke with characteristic elegance about her, underlining the message that Blanche was a formidable fighter for freedom in her own right. She had stood resolute on the frontline during the toughest of times, when others shrank back. The totems of her communist allegiances were on display and the deep sounds of a trumpet, played by Darren English, who is making his way onto the international stage, ended the proceedings and made further words unnecessary.

At Blanche's request, her family scattered her ashes on Table Mountain. They chose a spot along the mountain drive, where one could sit and contemplate the beautiful view. The city and what remained of the District Six of Blanche and Alex's youth lay below. Somewhere there was St Monica's where she had trained as a midwife.

A gale blew on this wild stormy day. The twelve over-coated celebrants of her life had to huddle together beside a tree in order to hear Pallo, Albie and Barto's last words. They watched as Barto walked down to a green glen. He opened the urn, stretched up his arms. Blanche's remains were snatched by the wind, whirling in all directions. It was as if her spirit had been set free in one of Shakespeare's tempests.

Alex La Guma, the pioneering African novelist and someone whom JM Coetzee called 'plausibly … the most substantial writer the Western Cape has produced'[1], had walked these slopes in his youth and reassured Blanche as they faced their greatest tribulations that they would return one day to the mountain of their dreams. He did not make it, but it is tempting to imagine that on that day he was there in spirit watching from the position he promised to take on Signal Hill, while below, in Parliament, as he predicted, his old organisation and the tatty opposition fiddled.

Notes

1 Blanche La Guma quoted in proposal for the film 'Through my Eyes', n.d., UWC-RIM Mayibuye Archives, Alex La Guma Collection, MCH 118-5-2-12.

References

De Lanerolle I (2025) Louise Asmal memorial, 22 January 2025

Lee CJ (ed.) (2024) *Alex La Guma: The exile years, 1966–1985*. Voices of Liberation series. Cape Town: HSRC Press

Odendaal A (2023) Providing the context for the debate on the 'human' imagined in the drafting of the ANC's Constitutional Guidelines in Lusaka, 1985–89. *Afrika Focus* 36: 11–40

Acknowledgements

The idea for this book originated when I was researching the *New Age* newspaper on the politics of the 1950s and discovered that Alex La Guma had cut his teeth as a journalist on *New Age*. Struck by his distinct style and observations, his political incisiveness and the delightful, often irreverent way he celebrated the cross-cultural richness of South African life and language, I (grieving the loss of my father) temporarily put aside the work I was doing and buried myself in a search for the stories of the young La Guma, written before his debut as a pioneering African writer.

The bulk of the research was done in England in the late 1980s during a period of study leave from the University of the Western Cape granted by Rector Jakes Gerwel (who was also a mentor). Support from colleagues in the History Department and the Institute for Historical Research made this possible. The Centre for Research in Ethnic Relations at Warwick University and the Institute of Commonwealth Studies in London provided a temporary base in England. Liz Offen typed most of the manuscript and provided wholehearted encouragement. In London, Margie Castle, Sadie Forman, Eleanor Kasrils, Wolfie Kodesh and the other friends who visited in Golders Green gave advice and warm hospitality. Blanche La Guma was encouraging from the first time I met her at her home in London and we chatted over a meal she cooked for us. A respected friend until her passing in 2023, her farewell gift to me was a framed set of photographs of the Coloured Convention held in Malmesbury in 1961, which poignantly finds a place in the photo inserts. Meeting her son Eugene at his flat in Moscow and later back in Cape Town, I had a sense that I'd seen something of Alex. Many others helped in one way or another: Cecil Abrahams, Harbhajan Brar, Brian and Sonia Bunting, Pamela Cohen, Lisa Combrinck, Irwin Combrinck, John Daniel, Apollon Davidson, Bob Edgar, Dave Everatt, Eduardo (my 'guide' in Havana), Carmen Gonzalez, Bill and Penny Green, Mike Keith, Pallo Jordan, Ronnie Kasrils, Eliza Kentridge, Mike and Kate Kirkwood, Jeremy Krikler, Desiree Lewis, Wendy Manuel, Gordon Metz, Yvonne Muthien, Kumi Naidoo, Richard Nukuna, Bill and Kitty Offen, Essop, Meg and Aziz Pahad, Ronald Segal, Reg September, Syd Shall, Slava Tetioken, Tony Trew and David Maughan-Brown. My apologies to those whose names have been omitted.

The initial manuscript was first published as *Liberation Chabalala: The World of Alex La Guma* in 1993 in a small print run by Mayibuye Books based at the University of the Western Cape.

Roger Field came into the project as co-editor at a later stage, helping to lay the foundation for the introduction by bringing in essential literary insights. A Rhodes University Returning Exile Fellowship gave him the opportunity to complete his work. Although Roger was occupied with his work on Greek classical and modernist poets, we were able to work some essential fresh material into this book from his important *Alex La Guma: A Literary and Political Biography*, published in 2010, especially in chapter 17 and the select bibliography.

For this expanded edition with a new title, we have tidied up the text by adding the title of each of the numerous newspaper and magazine articles used and added a prologue, foreword, tribute, ten new chapters, a select bibliography and index, as well as fresh photographs and illustrations. We acknowledge and thank Christopher J. Lee, editor of *Alex La Guma: The Exile Years, 1966–1985* (2024) for the use of La Guma's 'Where the Vultures Perch' article from *Lotus: Afro-Asian Writings* that appeared in his book and which we use as chapter 42 in ours. I thank Professor Hein Willemse, a doyen of studies of black literature in Afrikaans, and Michael Weeder, poet and creative former Dean of St George's Cathedral, for their intimate Foreword and Tribute, which help us to understand La Guma better in his literary, political and cultural context. After we had scanned the original book into an electronic form, Russell Martin carefully edited the work, making sure there were no glitches. Barto La Guma was especially supportive, kindly giving permission for the use of Alex's material and family photographs, and scanning the best of these for us. At HSRC Press/BestRed, publishers of five of my books, the always supportive team of Jeremy Wightman, Mthunzi Nxawe, project manager Anthea Oosthuizen, copy editor Alison Paulin, indexer Hannalie Knoetze and Shouneez Khan rallied again to ensure a smooth path to publication. Jeremy retired as head of the press early in 2025. I treasure our friendship developed over ten productive years of working together.

Thanks also for their support to Andre Mohammed, Steve Gordon, Chante and Tye de la Cruz, Precious Bikitsha, Sanele ka Ntshingana, Wanga Gambushe, Athambile Masola, Bonita Bennett, Karin Cronje and those closest to us, first time around and now: Liz Offen, Moira Levy, Gemma Field, Zohra Ebrahim and Rehana, Adam and Nadia Odendaal.

Finally, my deep appreciation goes to Tony Tabatznik and the Bertha Foundation for their sustained, unqualified support for my writing, and to Professor Tyrone Pretorius, vice chancellor and rector of the University of the Western Cape, who honoured me by appointing me vice chancellor's writer in residence at the university. This career-capping opportunity allowed me to write full time while linked to an institution, which has had a profound impact on my life and learning. As a gesture of thanks, I dedicate this edition of the book to Jakes Gerwel, Tyrone (as he comes to the end of his ten-year term as head of UWC) and to my colleagues, students and friends at UWC over the years.

Way back in 1959, Alex La Guma wrote about how the apartheid designers were intending to turn Bellville South into a kind of capital for a new coloured 'Homeland', with the newly established Bush College there as 'our very own special kleurling juniversity'.[1] He scathingly imagined the marketing efforts behind this quixotically stupid apartheid planning in 1959: 'big bright posters showing the mayor of Athlone or Elsies River or Bellville South with his ball and chain of office against the picturesque background of the municipal housing schemes, and the Bush College'.[2] Indeed the college became UWC and the corruption called the Coloured Representative Council – apartheid's short-lived parliament for 'kleurlinge' – came to be built on campus. But UWC, embodying the irrepressible spirit of La Guma's writing and the communities he drew his inspiration from, liberated itself from those chains to become the declared 'intellectual home of the democratic left' and an outstanding place of learning. No surprise then that Ngũgĩ wa Thiong'o came in 1991 as a visitor to the campus, repeating his admiration for La Guma, and that Alex's personal papers came to be lodged for safekeeping in the UWC-RIM Mayibuye Archives, together with those of many of his comrades and contemporaries in the liberation struggle.

André Odendaal
23 September 2024

Notes

1. Up my alley, *New Age*, 30 July 1959.
2. Up my alley, *New Age*, 8 March 1962.

Alex La Guma's writings: A select bibliography

Personal archives
Alex La Guma personal scrapbook, UWC-RIM Mayibuye Archives, Alex La Guma Collection, MCH 118

La Guma's novels and long prose works
La Guma A (1962) *A Walk in the night and other stories*. Ibadan: Mbari

La Guma A (1964, 1988) *And a threefold cord*. Berlin: Seven Seas; and London: Kliptown

La Guma, A (1967) *A walk in the night and other stories*. London: Heinemann Books

La Guma A (1967) *The stone country*. London: Heinemann

La Guma A (1972) *In the fog of the seasons' end*. London: Heinemann

La Guma A (ed.) (1972) *Apartheid: A collection of writings on South African racism by South Africans*. London: Lawrence and Wishart

La Guma A (1978) *A Soviet journey*. Moscow: Progress Publishers

La Guma A (1979) *Time of the butcherbird*. London: Heinemann

Books on La Guma and his work
Abrahams C (ed.) (1991) *Memories of home: The writings of Alex La Guma*. Trenton: Africa World Press

Balasubramanyam C (1992) *A study in trans-ethnicity in modern South Africa: The writings of Alex La Guma, 1925–1985*. New York: Mellen Research University Press

Balutansky KM (1990) *The novels of Alex La Guma: The representation of a political conflict*. Washington: Three Continents Press

Cornwell G (2011) 'Style is the great betrayer': Socialist realism in Alex La Guma's *A walk in the night*. English Studies in Africa 54(1): 11–20

Field R (2010) *Alex La Guma: A literary and political biography*. Johannesburg: Jacana Media 2010

La Guma B with M Klammer (2010) *In the dark with my dress on fire: My life in Cape Town, London, Havana and home again*. Johannesburg: Jacana Media

Lee CJ (ed.) (2017) *A Soviet journey: A critical annotated edition*. Lanham MD: Lexington Books

Lee CJ (ed.) (2024) *Alex La Guma: The exile years, 1966–1985*. Voices of Liberation series. Cape Town: HSRC Press

Lee CJ (ed.) (2024) *A Soviet journey: A critical annotated edition*. Cape Town: Jacana Media

Odendaal A & Field R (eds.) (1993) *Liberation Chabalala: The world of Alex La Guma*. Bellville: Mayibuye Press

Articles and book chapters by La Guma

La Guma A, Etude, *New Age*, 23 January 1957

La Guma A, A child is born, *New Age*, 2 August 1956

La Guma A (1964) *Jimmy La Guma: A Biography*. Cape Town: Friends of the South African Library

La Guma A (1967) The time has come: New forms of struggle face the South African coloured community. *Sechaba* 1(3): 14

La Guma A (1967) The time has come: Part 2: SA coloured people's social and economic deterioration. *Sechaba* 1(4): 13–14

La Guma A (1967) The time has come: Third in the series by Alex La Guma on the struggle of the coloured people of South Africa. *Sechaba*, 1(6): 14–16

La Guma A (1974) I came here to sing: A tribute to Pablo Neruda', *Lotus: Afro-Asian Writings* 22: 143–147

La Guma A (1982 [1963]) A glass of wine. In R Rive (ed.) *Quartet: Four voices from South Africa*, pp. 91–96. London: Heinemann

La Guma A (1982 [1963]) Out of darkness. In R Rive (ed.) *Quartet: Four voices from South Africa*, pp. 33–38. London: Heinemann

La Guma A (1982 [1963]) Slipper satin. In R Rive (ed.) *Quartet: Four voices from South Africa*, pp. 67–73. London: Heinemann

La Guma A (1982) Why I joined the Communist Party, *The African Communist* (89): 49–52

La Guma A (1991) A wife's memory. In C Abrahams (ed.) *Memories of home: The writings of Alex La Guma*, pp. 7–14, Trenton NJ: Africa World Press

La Guma A (1991) On a wedding day. In C Abrahams (ed.) *Memories of home: The writings of Alex La Guma*, pp. 81-96. Trenton NJ: Africa World Press

Articles and book chapters on La Guma and his work

Field R (1999) Art and the man: Alex La Guma's comics and paintings. *Critical Survey* 11(2) Special issue. South African writing at the crossroads: 45–63

Fullerton I (1980) 'Politics and the South African novel in English'. In C Bold (ed.) *Cencrastus* 3: 22–23

Obituary (1986) *Rixaka* : 16–18

Silber I (ed.) (1970) Alex La Guma (South Africa) novelist. In *Voices of national liberation: The revolutionary ideology of the 'third world' as expressed by intellectuals and artists at the Cultural Congress of Havana, January 1968*, pp. 48–50. New York: Central Book Company

Radio interviews
Dennis Duerden Collection (DDC), Archives of Traditional Music, University of Indiana

Alex La Guma on Cyprian Ekwensi (1966) DDC: EC 10' 22

Alex La Guma on Dennis Brutus (1966) DDC: EC 10' 23

Alex La Guma on Ezekiel Mphahlele (1966) DDC: BC 10' 22

Alex La Guma on Amos Tutuola (1967) DDC: EC 10' 21

Radio plays
Dennis Duerden Collection (DDC), Archives of Traditional Music, University of Indiana

Here comes the bride (1967) DDC: EC 10' 71

High finance (1967) DDC: EC 10' 71

His Worship the Mayor (1967) DDC: EC 10' 70

Inside an African government (How an African Government works): Coup-Coup (1967) DDC: EC 10' 70

Nuts to you (1967) DDC: EC 10' 70

Situations vacant (1967) DDC: 10' 70

A Libyan night's entertainment (1968) DDC: BC 10' 80

A slight case of witchcraft (1968) DDC: EC 10' 79

A visit to the city (1968) DDC: BC 10' 79

Bon appetit (1968) DDC: EC 10' 78

Death line eight-thirty (1968) DDC: EC 10' 68

In memory of Mr Bambu (1968) DDC: BC 10' 78

Missing from home (1968) DDC: EC 10' 77

Nine thirty to Wamiru (1968) DDC: EC 10' 79

The hand of Kali (1968) DDC: BC 10' 77

The prisoner (1968) DDC; BC 10' 77

The rivals (1968) DDC: EC 10' 60

The Zondie series: A perfect crime (1968) DDC: EC 10' 77

Films
Blankenberg L (2003) *Through my eyes: Blanche La Guma*. Cape Town: Idol Pictures.

La Guma A (c. 1975) *USSR holiday*

Index

A

'A Matter of Honour'
   criticism   19
'A Threefold Cord'   **xxxiv**
   'A Walk in the Night'
   adapt for a musical   1
   African Writers Conference   1
   thematic analysis   21–23
Abdurrahman, Abdullah   xx–xxi, xxiii, 4
Achebe, Chinua   xxxv
African families
   forced removals   38–40
African nationalism   19, 106
African people   44
   apartheid   144–145
   oppressed   vi
   unity with coloured people   144–145
   urban culture   20
African Peoples Organisation (APO)   xx–xxi
African Writers Conference
   list of participants   1
Afrika Day   145
Afrikaans language   131
   Cape working-class speech   xii–xiii
Afrikaans writers   xiii
Afrikaner Nationalism   xviii, 8, 10, 138
State of Emergency   137
Afrikaners   15
   coloured people   124, 130, 131
   Immorality Act   188
   monopoly of political power   138
   Pampoen-onder-die-Bos stories   15, 201–210
   Voortrekker Monument   67
   Yuri Gagarin, description of   20, 165
Afro-Asian Writers   223
Afro-Asian Writers Association (AAWA)   xxxix, 2, 220, 221
   conference   **xxxviii**, 220
   Lotus Prize   220
All-in African Conference   11, 148
   open letter to coloured people   144–145
American popular culture   19
ANC   3, 216
   ambassador to the Caribbean and Latin America   xxxix
   Chief Representative in Cuba   vii, xxiii, 242–244
   CPSA alliance with   9
   Cuba   242
   external missions   242
   New Age   9
   spokesperson for   220
   writer's delegation   **xxxviii**
ANC/SAPC   219, 220, 239
   patriarchal nature   246, 247
Anderson, Joan   62
Anglo American company   74
Angola   128, 242, 243
   soldiers from Cuba   xxiii
Anti-CAD movement   4, 120
anti-imperialist   3, 14, 19, 221, 226, 242, 244
anti-pass campaigns   133–136
   see also pass laws
anti-shark nets   191–192
apartheid   xiv, 158-159, 173-178, 180-184, 187, 189, 195, 201-202, 215, 235-236, 239-241, 243-245, 251, 253
   absurdities   7, 12, 15, 175, 183
   African people   144–145
   conditions of life   x
   Immorality Act   189
   Indians   178
   philosophy in textbooks   113
   regulations   ix
   Sophiatown   82
   systemic repression   xiv
   trains   97, 98
Apollis, Basil   248
Arafat, Yasser   **xxxviii**
Asmal, Kader   247
Asmal, Louise   247

B

Bantu Education   113
Bantustans   125, 128, 178, 24
bar fights   51–53
Baragwanath Hospital   79
Beyleveld, Pieter   119, 120
   election manifesto   117
   elections   10, 116–118
black men   72, 73, 138
black writers   ix
   American popular culture   19
Bloomberg, Abe   10, 120, 121
B-movies   19, 21, 22
Botha, PW   132
boycotts   59
   Afrikaner nationalist firms   10
   buses   6–7, 9, 62, 73
   Coon Carnival   106
   potato   84
British passport   **xxxiv**

Bunting, Brian   1
buses   6
boycotts   6–7, 9, 62, 73
   segregation   6

C

Caledon Square police station
Cape Flats
   poor conditions   95, 98
Cape Malay Choir Board   108
Cape Times cartoon   **xxxi**
Cape Town
   culture   xi, xv, 13
   slums   166, 167
   popular culture   14, 104–109
   everyday life   13, 14, 94
Cape Town Nurses and Midwives Vigilance Association   215
Caribbean   xxiii, 242, 243
cartoon strip collection   xv, xxii, 86–92
Chevalier des Arts et des Lettres   221
Chief Representative   vii, xxiii, 242–244
Chile   224, 232, 233, 234, 243
China   130, 188
   communism   130
Chinatown   18, 75–76
Chinese people   72, 129, 188
Christian National Education   113–115, 175
Christians   65
Christmas   207
church services   182
'City of Gold' *see* Johannesburg
Cold War   20
colour-bar   95
   crime   xv, 44
   gangsters   75
   unemployment   37
Coloured Affairs Council (CAC)   125, 126, 127, 128, 129, 131
Coloured Affairs Department (CAD)   12, 107, 108, 130
   Coloured Education   113, 115
coloured children   185
Coloured Education   113–115
   disparities   114
   Coloured Affairs Department (CAD)   113, 115
Coloured National Convention   11, 146, 215
   called for a Bill of Rights   152
   Malmesbury meeting   151–152, **xxx–xxxi**
   Peake, George   148
   preparations for 7 July 1961   150
coloured people   11
   Afrikaners   124, 130, 131
   definitions of identity   23
   hardships   30
   identity problems   102
   liberation struggle   23

   national stayaway   11
   parable of two boxes   xix, 30
   unity with African people   144–145
Coloured People's Congress   6, 7, 112, 116, 117, 118
   mass demonstrations   146–147
   members detained   11
   role in liberation of non-white people   143
   statement   142–143
Coloured People's National Union (CPNU)   126, 127, 131
Coloured teachers   114
coloured voters   6
Colouredstans   125
Combrink, Irwin   **xxvi**
Commonwealth   176, 177
Communist Party of South Africa (CPSA)   3
   ANC alliance with   9
   La Guma, Blanche   212, 215
communists   155, 169
Congress Alliance   **xxix**, 6, 7, 20, 23, 145
Coon Carnival   17–18, 106–107
   boycotts   106
crime   xv
   colour-bar   xv, 44
   ghost squad   75
   Johannesburg   74–75
   youth   36
Cuba
   ANC   242
   harvest fruit in Domingo Rojo   **xxxix**
   identity   xxiii
   soldiers in Angola   xxiii
Curry, James   **xxxiii**
custody *see* remand yard

D

'Dance of the La Gumas, Revolution, Rumba and Romance'   **xl**, 248
dances   31
Darwish, Mahmoud   xxxv
De Klerk, WA   131
De Wet Nel, MDC   177, 178
dead-end kids   21, 36–37
death penalty   179
Defence Fund   55, 62, 63
Defiance Campaign   6, 64, 69, 192
Democratic Republic of Vietnam *see* Vietnam
Devil's Peak   102–103
Die Banier   130–131
District Six   5, 14
   BBC TV team   96
   family life   22
   'high' culture   5
   racially mixed area   18
   Roger Street   **xxvii**
Do Santos, Marcelino   xxxv

Dollie, Saleh   128, 129, 131
domestic workers   78, 184, 188
    church services   182
drive-in cinemas   183
Drum
    fiction characteristics   19
    'generation'   2, 20
    urban African culture   20
Du Plessis, ID   126, 127, 182

E

economic boycott   10, 122–123, 131
elections   116–120
    44 percent poll   119–120
    boycotts   9
    Beyleveld, Pieter   10, 116–118
Eoan Group   108, 125
exile   vi, ix
    challenges   219
    leaving South Africa   216–218
    non-fiction articles   15
    political ambassador   15
    Tambo, Oliver   219
    women   247, 248

F

Fairyland
    musicals   23
farm workers   xx, 172
    prisoners   44, 142
farmers   185
    coloured children   185
fascism   4, 6, 221, 230
February, Basil   xxxiv
Feinberg, Barry   **xxxviii**
Fietas   81
First, Ruth   8, 55, 220
fish and chips business   193
forced removals   38–40, 82–83, 110–112
    African families   38–40
    Newlands   110, 111
    Nyanga township   38–40
    Sea Point   95, 96, 110, 112
    statistics   83
    Tramway Road   110, 111
Fort   13, 57, 85, 94, 219
    see also prisons
    experiences in   58, 61
    Fish Keitsing   64, 65
    Glamorgan   141, 142
    Peter Nthite   62
Fort Hare University   180
Franchise Action Committee (FRAC)   6, 11, 146
Freedom Charter   7, 8
freedom fighters   57, 140, 237, 244

Hungary   57
Freedom Park   248
funerals   183

G

Gagarin, Yuri   20, 165, 228
Gamat language   xiii
Gandhi, Indira   **xxxv**
gangsters   22, 45, 74, 167
    casualties statistics   79
    colour-bar   75
    USA   75
gender equality   246, 247
ghost squad   60, 75, 94
gold mining   72
gold rush   72–73
Golding, George J   126, 127, 131, 148, 150
Gool, Cissie   xx, xxii, 4, 10, 121
griot   xxv
    meaning   xxvn3
Group Areas Act   82, 186
Guy Fawkes   61

H

Hanover Street   xxi, 13, 17, 23, 36, 94
Havana   vii, ix, xxiii
Heineman African writers   220
Hertzog, JBM   xviii
Hertzoggie   xviii
Higgs, Barry   **xxxviii**
Hitler   160, 168
homosexual rape   15
Hungary   57
Hutchinson, Alfred   1, 56, 215

I

Immorality Act   1, 109, 187, 188, 209
    apartheid   189
    convictions   192
    Kerkbode   13
    statistics   192
In the Fog of the Seasons' End manuscript   **xxxiv**
Indians   83, 145, 178
Industrial and Commercial Workers Union of Africa
    (ICU)   3
International Soccer Federation   202
Iran   242
Israel
    apartheid   235
    military action in Lebanon   235
    protest letter to ambassador in RSA   235
    South Africa, relationship with   236–238

J

Japanese people   129

jazz 36
job reservation 124, 172, 181
Johannesburg xv, 8, 14
    crime 74–75
    everyday life 73, 77–80
    gold rush 72–73
    poverty 74
    shebeens 73
    slums 73
    zoo 182
Jordan, Pallo 248, 249
journalism 5, 22
    American popular culture 19
    influence on short stories v, 15, 17
    training 19

K

Kaaps xiii, 14
    see also slang
    Afrikaans writers xiii
    Cape working-class speech xii–xiii
Kadalie, Clements 3
Keitseng, Fish 64–65
Kepe, Lungile 63
Kerkbode 13
    Immorality Act 13
Kliptown 7
Khrushchev, NS 161, 162
koesista xviii
Kunene, Mazisi
    writer's event in Tashkent xxxiv

L

La Guma, Alex xxvii, xxxi
    see also exile
    Afro-Asian Writers Conference xxxviii
    and Blanche on a visit to Moscow xxxix, 241
    arrested 10–11
    art classes 5
    assassination attempt 10
    birth 3
    body of work 239–240
    British passport xxxiv
    climb on Table Mountain xxvi
    criticism and scholarship 21–23
    Cuba 242–244
    death 246
    economic boycott 10
    funeral vii, ix, **xl**
    harvest fruit in Domingo Rojo xxxix
    in London xxxiii
    influence of father 5–7, 22
    Johannesburg 8
    language usage 14, 17
    marriage 214, **xxvi**
    meeting Yasser Arafat xxxviii
    non-fiction publications 239
    novels published 239
    parents xx, 3, 166
    political maturity 4
    school years 167
    signature xxxiv
    sketches of political education class in prison xxxii
    sketches of prison life xxxii
    talent for writing 5
    trade union involvement 6
    world travels xxxvi–xxxvii
    writer's event in Tashkent xxxiv
La Guma, Barto vi, **xxxi**, **xxxiii**, 1, 156, 212, 249
    ANC camps 242
    first names: Bartholomew Vanzettl 212
    in London xxxiii
    named after Italian-American 212
    study in Germany 242
La Guma, Blanche xxii, **xxxi**, 15
    see also exile
    and Alex on a visit to Moscow **xxxix**, 241
    ashes on Table Mountain 249
    autobiography xxii, xxiii, **xl**
    breadwinner 247
    Communist Party of South Africa (CPSA) 212, 215
    criticism from SACP 246
    Havana 242
    life celebration 248–249
    marriage xxvi
    midwife 6, 212, 214, 215, 249
    return to Cape Town 248
    return to South Africa 23
    Soviet Weekly 221, 246
La Guma, Eugene vi, **xxxi**, **xxxiii**, **xxxix**, 1, 212
    first names: Eugene Varlin
    named after hero of Paris Commune 212
    birth 7
    in London xxxiii
    study in Moscow 242
    marriage 242
La Guma, James xix–xx, **xxvii**, **xxviii**
    ANC meeting xxxii
    arrested 10–11
    career 3–4
    Congress Alliance 9
    death 12
    expelled from SA Communist Party xx
    role in Communist Party 3
La Guma, James A junior 242
Langa 38, 39, 40, 128, 143
    barracks 38
    night of terror 133–136
    Pan Africanist Congress (PAC) 133–136
    unrest 133–136

language usage   14, 17
language variety   xi, xiii
language
   see also Kaaps
League of African Rights (LAR)   xix–xx
leaving South Africa   216–218
Lenin Peace Prize   221, 230
Lenin, Vladimir   vii, 4, 70, 154, 155
   picture   4, 154–156
Lessing, Doris   xxxiii
liberation struggle   11
   coloured people   23
   heroes   248
   lessons from Vietnam   226
   newspapers   84
literary censorship   x
Little Libby   84–91
   cartoons   86–91
   popular culture   84, 85
Lollan, Stanley   55, 116
London   xxiii, 1, 219, 221
   Alex, Barto and Eugene at home   xxxiii
   World Youth Festival   64
   picture of Lenin   156
   arrival in   220
Lotus Prize for Literature   2, 220–221
   Alex and Blanche at awards ceremony   xxxv
   announcement in The Times of India   xxxv
   awarding   xxxv
Louw, Eric   178, 179
Luthuli, Albert   148, 215
   ANC meeting   xxxii

M

Magistrate's Court   33–35, 100–101
Makazana, Sobantu   63
Malmesbury meeting
   Coloured National Convention   xxx–xxxi, 151–152, 215
Mandela, Nelson   11, 148, 215, 235, 243
   released   246
   maps
   world travels   xxxvi–**xxxvii**, 241, 243
May Day   58
'Mayibuye iAfrika'   xix–xx
Middle East   160–161
mining industry   74, 172
Missing Men   140–142
mixed marriages   187, 188, 189, 191
Mkwayi, Wilton Zimasile   66
Moral Rearmament   126
Morolong, Joseph
   economic boycott   10
Mosaval, Johaar   108
Moscow
   award ceremony   xxxix

Alex, Eugene and Blanche   **xxxix**
movies   104, 108–109
   see also B-movies
   Mozambique   128, 242
Mpetha, Oscar
   ANC meeting   **xxxii**
municipal housing schemes   95–96
music   19, 31, 76
musicals   1, 248
   A Walk in the Night   1
   'Dance of the La Gumas, Revolution, Rumba and Romance'   **xl**, 248
   Fairyland   23
Muslims   147
   support mass demonstrations   147–148

N

Namibia   243
narrative strategies   16–17
National Liberation League (NLL)   xii
National party; Nats see Nationalists
Nationalists   xviii, 12, 13
   armed forces   139
   Bantu Education   113
   Coloured Education   114
   Die Banier   130–131
   misuse of constitutional devices   13
   propaganda about education   113
   threats against communists   169
Native Rebublic thesis   vi, 3
negro students   158
Neruda, Pablo
   Pablo   tribute to   232–234
Neto, Agostinho   xxxv
New Age   2
   ANC   9
   banned   9, 215
   formation   8–9
   importance   9
Newlands   110, 111
Nicaragua   242, 244
Nkosi, Lawrence   63
Nokwe, Duma   223
Non-European Unity Movement   4, 6, 143, 150
   criticism   10
non-white servants   180
Nthite, Peter   55, 62
Nyanga township   10
   forced removals   38–40
Nzo, Alfred   246

O

oil companies   160–161
Order of Friendship of the People   xxxix

P

Palestine Liberation Organisation 237
Pampoen-onder-die-Bos stories 7, 12, 85, 201–210
    Afrikaners 15
Pan Africanist Congress (PAC) 10
    Langa 133–136
pass laws 8, 185
    see also anti-pass campaigns
    police raids 60, 76
Patel, Archie 55, 56
patriarchal nature 246, 247
Peake, George 7, 9, 116, 148
    Coloured National Convention 148
petty crimes 18
police 60
    Afrikaans language xi
    ghost squad 60, 75, 94
    Langa unrest 133–136
    pass-raids 60, 76
    raids 100
    Security Branch 60, 122, 202
    Sergeant Arlow 99–100
political consciousness xiv, 22, 120
political identity xiv, xv, 23
political satire 20
poor white problem 181
popular culture 13, 22
    Cape Town 14
    Little Libby 84, 85
postal system 183
potato boycott 84
Press, Ronny 62
prisoners
    beatings 44
    deaths 101
    different treatment for Africans and Whites 44
    farm workers 44, 142
    homosexual rape 15
    medical treatment 45
    Missing Men 140–142
    unhealthy conditions 57–58
prisons 140,
    see also Fort; Roeland Street prison
    poor conditions 15, 16, 47–50, 57–58, 141
    sodomy 15, 16
    typhoid outbreak 57–58
prostitution 14, 18, 31
Putco buses 67, 81

R

race classification 187
race federation 124
racialism 73, 144, 235
    USA 159
    white supremacy 144
racketeers 197–198
remand yard 17, 41
privileges 43
Republic of South Africa *see* South Africa
Rive, Richard **xxxiii**
Roeland Street prison 15, 16, 140, 141
poor conditions 41–43, 44
Roger Street vi, xviii, xx, 3
    District Six **xxvii**
rugby 196, 202
Russia *see* Soviet Union

S

Sachs, Albert Louis (Albie) **xxxiii**, 7, 248, 249
    white people dissociate from apartheid 146
Sack, JB 62
Saratovskaya, Larissa **xxxviii**
sea 175–176
    water 194–195
    Sea Point 95, 96, 110, 112
Segal, Ronald
    economic boycott 10
Sembene, Ousmane xxxv
separate development 128, 174, 187
    Verwoerd, HF 174
Separate Representation of Voters Act 6, 116, 118, 119, 126
September, Reg xi, 7, 116
    banning order 12
    unity with African people 145
Sergeant Arlow 99–100
sexism 51–53
sexual politics 18–19
Shall, Syd 62
Sharpeville v, 2, 10, 128, 135, 143, 196, 202, 219
shebeens 8, 31
    Johannesburg 73
short stories 15
slang xiii, 14
    see also Kaaps
skollie xiii
    prison 17, 42, 45
slot machines 197
Slovo, Joe 56 61
slums 30, 31, 37
    Cape Town 166, 167
    Johannesburg 73
    New York 161
    USA 75
    Windermere 38, 39, 106
social justice xiv, 148
Sophiatown 8
    apartheid 82
    destruction 82–83
South Africa 236
    Israel, relationship with 236–238

Republic 1961   11
    referendum 1960   144
South African Coloured People's Organisation (SACPO)   vii, 4
    see also Coloured People's Congress
    contest elections   116–118
South African Communist Party (SACP)   220
    see also ANC/SACP
    Blanche La Guma   246
    liberation struggle   248
South African Panorama   96
South African writers   **xxxiii,** 85, 220
    dissident   ix
South West Africa   193, 244
Soviet Union   20, 161
    largest country   242
    Order of Friendship of the People   **xxxix**
    Sputnik   20, 163–165
    writer's event in Tashkent   **xxxiv**
    Vilnius, report of visit   228–231
Soviet Weekly   221, 246
Soyinka, Wole   v, 1, 85, 220
space race   20
Sputnik   20, 163–165
State of Emergency   vi, 4, 10, 11, 212
    Africans held without trial   140–142
    Afrikaner Nationalism   137
    detainees experiences   139–140
    Missing Men   140–142
    statistics   137
    suffering of detainees   137
Strijdom, JG   18, 96, 171, 176
    death   173
Suppression of Communism Act, 1950   ix, 4, 12, 64, 151

T

Table Mountain   vi, 41, 94, 110, 246
    Blanche La Guma ashes scattered   249
Tambo, Oliver   62, 219, 246
    exile challenges   219
Teachers League of South Africa   4, 122
textbooks
    apartheid philosophy   113
The Liberator   xxi, xxii, **xxviii,** 5, 85
The Times of India   **xxxv**
Thiong'o, Ngũgĩ   xxxv, 1, 220, 240
Thompson, DC   65
Tomlinson Commission   14
trade unions   vi, 6, 64, 154, 166, 168
trains
    apartheid   97, 98
Tramway Road   110, 111
Treason Trial   vi, xv, 7–8, 9, 14
    diary of events   67–70

Drill Hall   58, 61, 64
    friendships among accused   58–59
    judges   68
    South Africans of all races   55
    synagogue   67
    the 156 defendants   **xxix,** 55
    whodunit   56
Tshabalala, Henry (Chubby)   62
Tsukudu, Adelaide   62
Turok, Benny   63–64

U

uMkhonto we Sizwe   12, 208
UN Special Committee Against Apartheid   243–244
    appeals to   244
unemployment   32
    colour-bar   37
    youth   36–37
Union Council of Coloured Affairs *see* Coloured Affairs Cuncil
Union Festival 1960   107
Unity Movement   10, 130, 150
    criticism   10, 116, 118, 119
    insult voters   120
'Up My Alley' column   12, 14
    subjects   12–13
urban African culture   20
USA
    attacks in Vietnam   224–227
    coloureds   157
    gangsters   75
    negro students   158
    popular culture   19, 20
    racialism   159
    slums   75, 161
    way of life   158–159
USSR *see* Soviet Union

V

Van der Ross, Richard E   19, 106, 130, 131
Verwoerd, HF   11
    apartheid   174, 176
    assassination attempt   11, 13
    forced removals   83
    referendum 1960   144
    separate development   128, 174
Vietnam   223
    report of visit   224–227
    USA attacks   224–227
Vilnius
    report of visit   228–231
Volkspele   182
Voortrekker Monument   67, 129
Vrededorp   81

W

Walmer Estate 18
Weeder, Michael xxiv
   poem xxiii–xxiv
white supremacy 23, 37, 73, 74, 142, 196
   racialism 144
white workers xviii, 3
Whites 44
   culture xviii, 17
Windermere 38
   poor conditions 95, 98
   slums 38, 39, 106
women 40
   exile challenges 247, 248
   permits 39, 40
Woodstock beach 166
workers 58
   conditions in factories 168
   stay aways 135
   trade union involvement 64, 66
   wages 94

World Peace Council 221. 223, 224, 233, 238
world travels
   maps **xxxvi–xxxvii**, 241, 243
World War II 160
World Youth Festival 64

Y

Yengwa, MB 62
Young Communist League (YCL) 155, 169
   youth 36
   crime 36
   entertainment 104–105
   jazz 36
   unemployment 36–37

Z

Ziervogel, Chris xxii, 5
Zimbabwe 219, 242
Zionism 235